MEN AND
BOOKS

MEN & BOOKS

COLLECTED AND EDITED
BY

MALCOLM S. MacLEAN
Professor of English, University of Wisconsin
AND
ELISABETH K. HOLMES
University of Wisconsin

RICHARD R. SMITH, INC.
NEW YORK - - - - - - - - - - 1930

6V

PRINTED IN THE UNITED STATES OF AMERICA
The Branwell Press, New York

TABLE OF CONTENTS

THE PHILOSOPHER VIEWS LITERATURE

THE LITERARY MAN VIEWS HIS BRETHREN

TABLE OF CONTENTS

TABLE OF CONTENTS

TABLE OF CONTENTS

TABLE OF CONTENTS

THE LEGISLATORS VIEW LITERATURE

SCIENCE AND LITERATURE

MEDICAL AND PSYCHOLOGICAL VIEWS OF LITERATURE

THE HUMORIST PARODIES LITERATURE

TABLE OF CONTENTS

INTRODUCTION

> The advancing man discovers how deep a property he hath in all literature—in all fable as well as in all history. He finds that the poet was no odd creature who described strange and impossible situations, but that universal man wrote by his pen a confession true for one and true for all. His own secret biography he finds in lines wonderfully intelligible to him, yet dotted down before he was born.
>
> Emerson, *History*.

Our aims in compiling *Men and Books* are diverse. We wish to gather and present practically for students in college composition and literature courses and for the general book-lover material for study that will at the same time serve as a guide to wider reading, to reading in poetry, drama, biography, letters, essays and fiction. We feel that previous collections have not entirely satisfied this need. Their editors, spurred by recent developments in the shaping of Orientation courses, have compiled books of essays highly suitable for such courses. The essays they offer are, for the most part, tracts on the theory of education, sidelights on sociology, labor, economics, the machine age, the advancements in science and civilization. Important as these matters are, invaluable as Orientation may be, we feel that English courses are not quite the place to harbor them. Other compilers have collected essays on *style*, and, in so doing, have performed a service for English teachers and advanced students. But we find that the freshman and sophomore and the general reader without a rich background of literary and life experience, are bewildered by Stevenson, "obfuscated" by Dr. Johnson, lost in the first page of Pater.

We have, therefore, for some years past, adopted the policy in our classes of bringing to our students certain essays from various types of minds on men and books as additional testimony to the uses of reading. This collection is the result of winnowing many such. All but a few contained in this volume have been tested in class. We have found them, from the student point of view, lifting and illuminating; from the teacher's, finely teachable. The result has been happy. For the first time in their lives many young people discovered that reading was both pleasant and satisfying. They found men of all types from philosopher to politician taking a real interest in books and in the men who wrote books. They found the parodists laughing at some of the things they had had a guilty desire to laugh at but had not dared because they thought the printed word was sacred. They found, many of them, that literature contained, in Emerson's phrase, "lines wonderfully intelligible." Blatant young Philistines dropped their pose. The more difficult well-groomed young men and women who are ready to agree politely—nay even hastily—that "literature is good for them" but have no idea as to how or why, have shed their agreement and even their politeness in hot argument over whether books can be in themselves "good or bad," over romance *vs.* realism, over the critical ability of the co-ed and that of the student engineer or pre-business man, over Mr. Mencken and the late Professor Sherman, and even over the New Humanism and its opponents. They slough off their incredible and slightly unpalatable conception that books, especially those which have in many times and places appealed deeply to adults, might have any place in the life of ordinary undergraduates, particularly those of scientific leanings. They lose, we expect forever, their impression that literature is a collection of riddles to which only the initiate know the answers, answers which are to them only vaguely conceived morals.

We have chosen these essays also with a view to teaching composition by example as well as precept. Most of them are of literary importance in themselves. They present styles as widely variant as those of Stevenson, Dr. Johnson, and Mr. Mencken; of Henry Fielding and George Santayana; of Zona Gale and Robert Benchley. There is to be found in them a sustained attitude of cultivated good humor, which is not the least attribute to be set before those in process of education. There is skillful but not painful wit. There is stimulating attack and defense. And there are as many attitudes as there are men and women who write.

In this presentation of varying attitudes towards books, we believe one of the chief values of this volume to rest. It is undeniably the function of the teacher to knock vague, indecisive, silly or false notions out of undergraduate heads. It is another more important function to replace the notions knocked out with something substantial, logical, illuminating, satisfying. By *Men and Books* we have tried to achieve this desired result. Students are often afraid of their own opinions about books. They find Joyce dull when all the world seems to be declaring him "wonderful." They have a well-hidden dislike of the pyrotechnics of Mr. Mencken, but nurse it in silence because all their friends are enthusiastic about him. Such students find support for their thinking in the essays of the late Professor Sherman and Mr. Max Eastman. In fact, we believe there are few honest opinions about literature which do not find somewhere in this collection their justification no matter how contrary they may be one to another. We have found that the study of these essays has helped materially in brightening and strengthening not only class discussion of books but the sometimes burdensome sheaves of book reports and term papers on "outside" and inside reading.

Beside the stimulus given to intelligent reader thinking by these essays, we expect that other teachers and students will find, as we have found, that such good-humored, sometimes slightly satirical, always penetrating discourses on great books and writers produce interest enough so that readers will dip into the works, read the biographies of the men talked about, often with gratifying results. We find that the impulse to read given by these essays is more potent than that given by most other methods. The usual one in English departments is to issue to students mimeographed or printed book lists. Libraries prepare similar general and special lists for their patrons. There are books telling what is best to read. Pertinent and helpful as these things are, they often bewilder both by their magnitude and the scantiness of their description of individual volumes. A student really just beginning his reading quails before "the little done, the undone vast." His desire to read loses its glow in the formidable chill of columns of authors and titles. Not so, when he runs across a passionately appreciative paragraph on Fielding's *Journal of the Voyage to Lisbon* in an essay by a physician, nor when he is presented with a charming, whimsical glimpse of Steele and his pretty Prue through an essay on Steele's letters. We would challenge anyone to read Dr. Fosdick's *Blessed Be Biography* and come to the end without a desire to read at least half of the great "lives" he mentions. Book lists are here in plenty, but in solution, in a context of stimulating comment. And they are by no means limited to the classical, to the erudite, to the modern, or to any one field of writing. We have tried to choose without prohibition or favor, to limit only within the breadth of the title, *Men and Books*.

Perhaps some of our inclusions ask, nevertheless, for a word of explanation. First, the section on the humorist and his parody. It is a truism that only work of outstanding merit or demerit is capable of being parodied. Hence we have found that one of the surest ways to make students recognize the faults and virtues, the salient characteristics of the men they read is to offer them parody. The faults and valiant virtues of Browning are made immediately open and clear, in the most concrete, compact way, in Calverley's *The Cock and the Bull;* a critique of Henry James of many pages could say little more about his style than Squire has intimated in his prose parody. Arthur Guiterman has caught with laughter the sentimentality of the sad Irish poem and impaled it as skilfully as has Benchley the fulsome reviews of "books for Christmas" which plague us all in early December. We have been able to include in this section only a few of the most usable parodies. Many others are "good to teach."

We have, second, reprinted two articles on the detective novel because we believe that this branch of fiction has long been in reality and should now be admittedly taken out of the category of secret vices and brought into the legitimate family of literary offspring. Certainly at the hands of Dean Nicolson of Smith College and the anonymous writer of *The London Times*, it is cleared of its bar sinister, made welcome among the "classics." Sherlock Holmes, The Gray Seal, Dr. Thorndyke, take their places alongside The Red-Cross Knight, Sir Roger de Coverley, and Squire Western. We knew a visiting student from Germany on a chemistry scholarship who learned technical English with amazing rapidity because of the Dr. Thorndyke stories. His compositions in our English classes took on a striking tincture from the same source.

Third, the section on the medical, psychological, and psychiatric view of literature is necessarily scant as this field is just opening up in criticism. Dr. McLaurin pioneered in it. Charles A. Bennett's essay attacks from another and essential angle. Miss Jeannette Marks has recently written her *Genius and Disaster*, and there have been articles on *Shakespeare as Psychiatrist* and others like it. We will undoubtedly hear more from these sources directly. But for this book we have included only the two essays we found most representative.

These, then, are our aims in compiling *Men and Books*. We are convinced by our experience with these essays that they will serve to stimulate and enrich the many minds of many bents which are thrown together in English classrooms as in life; that they offer points of view to satisfy demands as different as those of the embryo engineer, sociologist, or divine; that they serve as amplified reading lists for those of diverse tastes; that they present models of many styles worthy of reading and of imitation by the young writer; that they do these things with intelligence and logic made supple by humor; and that they fulfill these purposes without, from the teacher's point of view, in any way departing from the idea that it is after all the function of English departments to teach English.

MALCOLM SHAW MACLEAN
ELISABETH K. HOLMES

Milwaukee, Wisconsin, September, 1930.

THE PHILOSOPHER VIEWS LITERATURE

BOOKS

(IN PART)

By RALPH WALDO EMERSON

IT IS easy to accuse books, and bad ones are easily found; and the best are but records, and not the things recorded; and certainly there is dilettanteism enough, and books that are merely neutral and do nothing for us. In Plato's *Gorgias,* Socrates says: "The shipmaster walks in a modest garb near the sea, after bringing his passengers from Ægina or from Pontus, not thinking he has done anything extraordinary, and certainly knowing that his passengers are the same, and in no respect better than when he took them on board." So it is with books, for the most part: they work no redemption in us. The bookseller might certainly know that his customers are in no respect better for the purchase and consumption of his wares. The volume is dear at a dollar; and, after reading to weariness the lettered backs, we leave the shop with a sigh, and learn, as I did without surprise, of a surly bank-director, that in bank-parlors they estimate all stocks of this kind as rubbish.

But it is not less true that there are books which are of that importance in a man's private experience, as to verify for him the fables of Cornelius Agrippa, of Michael Scott, or of the old Orpheus of Thrace,—books which take rank in our life with parents and lovers and passionate experiences, so medicinal, so stringent, so revolutionary, so authoritative,—books which are the work and the proof of faculties so comprehensive, so nearly equal to the world which they paint,

[1] Originally published in the *Atlantic Monthly,* January, 1858; later included in the volume *Society and Solitude*. Reprinted with the permission of Houghton Mifflin Company.

that, though one shuts them with meaner ones, he feels his exclusion from them to accuse his way of living.

Consider what you have in the smallest chosen library. A company of the wisest and wittiest men that could be picked out of all civil countries, in a thousand years, have set in best order the results of their learning and wisdom. The men themselves were hid and inaccessible, solitary, impatient of interruption, fenced by etiquette; but the thought which they did not uncover to their bosom friend is here written out in transparent words to us, the strangers of another age.

We owe to books those general benefits which come from high intellectual action. Thus, I think, we often owe to them the perception of immortality. They impart sympathetic activity to the moral power. Go with mean people, and you think life is mean. Then read Plutarch, and the world is a proud place, peopled with men of positive quality, with heroes and demigods standing around us, who will not let us sleep. Then they address the imagination: only poetry inspires poetry. They become the organic culture of the time. College education is the reading of certain books which the common sense of all scholars agrees will represent the science already accumulated. If you know that,—for instance, in geometry, if you have read Euclid and Laplace,—your opinion has some value; if you do not know these, you are not entitled to give any opinion on the subject. Whenever any sceptic or bigot claims to be heard on the questions of intellect and morals, we ask if he is familiar with the books of Plato, where all his pert objections have once for all been disposed of. If not, he has no right to our time. Let him go and find himself answered there.

Meantime the colleges, whilst they provide us with libraries, furnish no professor of books; and, I think, no chair is so much wanted. In a library we are surrounded by many hundreds of dear friends, but they are imprisoned by an enchanter in these paper and leathern boxes; and though they know us, and have been waiting two, ten, or twenty centuries for us—

some of them,—and are eager to give us a sign, and unbosom themselves, it is the law of their limbo that they must not speak until spoken to; and as the enchanter has dressed them, like battalions of infantry, in coat and jacket of one cut, by the thousand and ten thousand, your chance of hitting on the right one is to be computed by the arithmetical rule of Permutation and Combination,—not a choice out of three caskets, but out of half a million caskets all alike. But it happens, in our experience, that in this lottery there are at least fifty or a hundred blanks to a prize. It seems, then, as if some charitable soul, after losing a great deal of time among the false books, and alighting upon a few true ones which made him happy and wise, would do a right act in naming those which have been bridges or ships to carry him safely over dark morasses and barren oceans, into the heart of sacred cities, into palaces and temples. This would be best done by those great masters of books who from time to time appear,—the Fabricii, the Seldens, Magliabecchis, Scaligers, Mirandolas, Bayles, Johnsons, whose eyes sweep the whole horizon of learning. But private readers, reading purely for love of the book, would serve us by leaving each the shortest note of what he found.

There are books; and it is practicable to read them, because they are so few. We look over with a sigh the monumental libraries of Paris, of the Vatican, and the British Museum. In 1858, the number of printed books in the Imperial Library at Paris was estimated at eight hundred thousand volumes, with an annual increase of twelve thousand volumes; so that the number of printed books extant to-day may easily exceed a million. It is easy to count the number of pages which a diligent man can read in a day, and the number of years which human life in favorable circumstances allows to reading; and to demonstrate that, though he should read from dawn till dark, for sixty years, he must die in the first alcoves. But nothing can be more deceptive than this arithmetic, where none but a natural method is really pertinent. I visit occasionally the Cambridge Library, and I can seldom go there without renewing the conviction that the best of it all is already within the four walls of my study at home. The inspection of the catalogue brings me continually back to the few standard writers who are on every private shelf; and to these it can afford only the most slight and casual additions. The crowds and centuries of books are only commentary and elucidation, echoes and weakeners of these few great voices of Time.

The best rule of reading will be a method from Nature, and not a mechanical one of hours and pages. It holds each student to a pursuit of his native aim, instead of a desultory miscellany. Let him read what is proper to him, and not waste his memory on a crowd of mediocrities. As whole nations have derived their culture from a single book,—as the Bible has been the literature as well as the religion of large portions of Europe,—as Hafiz was the eminent genius of the Persians, Confucius of the Chinese, Cervantes of the Spaniards; so, perhaps, the human mind would be a gainer, if all the secondary writers were lost,—say, in England, all but Shakspeare, Milton, and Bacon,—through the profounder study so drawn to those wonderful minds. With this pilot of his own genius, let the student read one, or let him read many, he will read advantageously. Dr. Johnson said: "Whilst you stand deliberating which book your son shall read first, another boy has read both: read anything five hours a day, and you will soon be learned."

Nature is much our friend in this matter. Nature is always clarifying her water and her wine. No filtration can be so perfect. She does the same thing by books as by her gases and plants. There is always a selection in writers, and then a selection from the selection. In the first place, all books that get fairly into the vital air of the world were written by the successful class, by the affirming and advancing class, who utter what tens of thousands feel though they cannot say. There has already been a scrutiny and choice from many hundreds of young pens, before the pamphlet or political chapter which you read in a fugitive journal comes to your eye. All these are young adventurers, who produce their performance to the wise ear of Time, who sits and weighs, and, ten years hence, out of a million of pages reprints one. Again, it is judged, it is winnowed by all the winds of opinion, and what terrific selection has not passed on it before it can be reprinted after twenty years,—and reprinted after a century!—it is as if Minos and Rhadamanthus had indorsed the writing. 'Tis therefore an economy of time to read old and famed books. Nothing can be preserved which is not good; and I know beforehand that Pindar, Martial, Terence, Galen, Kepler, Galileo, Bacon, Erasmus, More, will be superior to the average intellect. In contemporaries, it is not so easy to distinguish betwixt notoriety and fame.

Be sure, then, to read no mean books. Shun the spawn of the press on the gossip of the hour. Do not read what you shall learn, without asking, in the street and the train. Dr. Johnson said, "he always went into stately shops;" and good travellers stop at the best hotels; for, though they cost more, they do not cost much more, and there is the good company and the best information. In like manner, the scholar knows that the famed books contain, first and last, the best thoughts and facts. Now and then, by rarest luck, in some foolish Grub Street is the gem we want. But in the best circles is the best information. If you should transfer the amount of your reading day by day from the newspaper to the standard authors—— But who dare speak of such a thing?

The three practical rules, then, which I have to offer, are—1. Never read any book that is not a year old. 2. Never read any but famed books. 3. Never read any but what you like; or, in Shakspeare's phrase—

> No profit goes where is no pleasure ta'en:
> In brief, sir, study what you most affect.

Montaigne says, "Books are a languid pleasure;" but I find

certain books vital and spermatic, not leaving the reader what he was: he shuts the book a richer man. I would never willingly read any others than such. And I will venture, at the risk of inditing a list of old primers and grammars, to count the few books which a superficial reader must thankfully use.

> Books without the knowledge of life are useless, for what should books teach but the art of living?
>
> DR. SAMUEL JOHNSON—*Remark as recorded by Mrs. Piozzi.*

BIOGRAPHY

By Dr. Samuel Johnson

The mischievous consequences of vice and folly, of irregular desires and predominant passions, are best discovered by those relations which are levelled with the general surface of life, which tell not how any man became great, but how he was made happy; not how he lost the favour of his prince, but how he became discontented with himself. Those relations are therefore commonly of most value in which the writer tells his own story. He that recounts the life of another commonly dwells most upon conspicuous events, lessens the familiarity of his tale to increase its dignity, shows his favourite at a distance, decorated and magnified like the ancient actors in their tragic dress, and endeavours to hide the man that he may produce a hero. *Idler*, No. 84.

* * *

If the biographer writes from personal knowledge and makes haste to gratify the public curiosity, there is danger lest his interest, his fear, his gratitude, or his tenderness, overpower his fidelity, and tempt him to conceal, if not to invent. There are many who think it an act of piety to hide the faults or failings of their friends, even when they can no longer suffer by their detection; we therefore see whole ranks of characters adorned with uniform panegyric, and not to be known from one another but by extrinsic and casual circumstances. 'Let me remember,' says Hale, 'when I find myself inclined to pity a criminal, that there is likewise a pity due to the country.' If we owe regard to the memory of the dead, there is yet more respect to be paid to knowledge, to virtue, and to truth. *Rambler*, No. 60.

* * *

The necessity of complying with times, and of sparing

persons, is the great impediment of biography. History may be formed from permanent monuments and records; but lives can only be written from personal knowledge, which is growing every day less, and in a short time is lost for ever. What is known can seldom be immediately told; and when it might be told, it is no longer known. The delicate features of the mind, the nice discriminations of character, and the minute peculiarities of conduct, are soon obliterated: and it is surely better that caprice, obstinacy, frolic, and folly, however they might delight in the description, should be silently forgotten, than that by wanton merriment and unseasonable detection, a pang should be given to a widow, a daughter, a brother, or a friend. As the process of these narratives is now bringing me among my contemporaries, I begin to feel myself 'walking upon ashes under which the fire is not extinguished,' and coming to the time of which it will be proper rather to say 'nothing that is false than all that is true.'

Works, vii. 444

* * *

I have often thought that there has rarely passed a life of which a judicious and faithful narrative would not be useful. For not only every man has, in the mighty mass of the world, great numbers in the same condition with himself to whom his mistakes and miscarriages, escapes and expedients, would be of immediate and apparent use; but there is such an uniformity in the state of man, considered apart from adventitious and separable decorations and disguises, that there is scarce any possibility of good or ill but is common to human kind.

Rambler, No. 60.

* * *

'Mr. Fowke once observed to Dr. Johnson that, in his opinion, the Doctor's literary strength lay in writing biography, in which he infinitely exceeded all his contemporaries. "Sir," said Johnson, "I believe that is true. The dogs don't know how to write trifles with dignity."'

Boswell's *Life of Johnson,* iv. 34 *n.* 5.

BLESSED BE BIOGRAPHY[1]

By Harry Emerson Fosdick

One of the most regrettable aspects of the modern book trade is the cost of biographies. To some of us there is no other reading that on the whole is so much worth while, but generally the Life and Letters of our heroes are sold at such outrageous prices that only nabobs can buy them. I am not accusing the publishers of profiteering; probably they are compelled to charge the prices that they do. But since for some of us biography long since ceased to be luxury and became intellectual and spiritual necessity, we lament the high costs which interfere with this most rewarding kind of reading.

Nevertheless I make my plea. There are libraries, and if enough people insist on it the lives of the "noble living and the noble Dead" will increasingly appear upon their shelves. Moreover, the publishers already have revealed their willingness to produce good biographies in comparatively inexpensive series if only the people want them. One suspects that we should have our satisfying fill of this most interesting, informing and refreshing sort of book if enough of us demanded it.

The first motive for reading biography is the sheer delight of it. Nothing on earth is so interesting as people. Whether they are wise or foolish, good or bad, rich or poor, high or low, to one who has seeing eyes folk are an unending source of curiosity and amazement. If anybody does not feel this, if the curmudgeon in him has beaten out his spirit of human fellowship, if this incredible drama of life with its mysteries, intrigues, plots and counterplots, its loves, temptations, sins,

[1] Reprinted by permission of the *Ladies' Home Journal*, Copyright, 1924, Curtis Publishing Company, and of the author.

joys, victories and deaths no longer fascinates him, then he will not enjoy biography. Nor anything else either!

If, however, one's interest is charmed by human life, biography can become one of his chief joys. It so eliminates all that is unpleasant in our living contacts with men, so retains all that is illuminating and refreshing, that one with a Puritan conscience might almost fear it as a sinfully selfish indulgence. For when folks are incarnate at our elbows, treading on our toes, competing with us in business and upsetting our hopes in politics, they can be decidedly unpleasant. Then we understand Keats' saying, "I admire Human Nature, but I do not like Men." In a biography, however, all possibility of friction has departed. The man will not undersell you, outbid you, or lead to victory a cause that you despise, and if you differ in opinion and argue lustily against his thoughts he will not answer back. Biography offers human contact in its most amiable form.

Billy Bray the drunkard, who, having been recovered from his habit, was so overjoyed that he said if they put him in a barrel he would shout "Glory" through the bunghole, might have been in visible presence an embarrassing table companion. But in his biography even he is not embarrassing at all. He is positively charming. You linger over his vivid, dramatic, catastrophic, and finally triumphant life, and are sorry when the book is done.

Even prophets, however notable in the world's reminiscence, are generally upsetting to their own generation and are not the kind of folk with whom one naturally wants to live. Savonarola is one of my heroes, but I am glad to meet him in Villari's biography rather than in the square at Florence burning popular books and vanities, or in the confessional, urging on my poor conscience the stern requirements of his code. And as for John Knox, another iron man of the Lord, I am glad that I know him as a preacher, "dinging the pulpit into blads" as he defied the queen in Edinburgh, or assuring her to her face that he would be "as well content to live under your grace as Paul under Nero," but I prefer the mediation of Cowan's life to the rigors of facing him in person.

Moreover, biography has this further advantage over life, that it not only eliminates contentious frictions, rivalries, and the unapproachableness of tremendous personalities, but it brings us into the presence of folk who most are worth our meeting. Had we lived in David Livingstone's time most of us would never have seen him, or, distantly seeing him, would have known the real man no better afterward than we did before. But now, for a dollar and a half in Blaikie's life of him we can live in intimate fellowship with that amazing character, from the day he left his spinning jenny and went down Greenock way to take ship for Africa to the day they carried his body into Westminster Abbey.

Think of being the familiar friend of Saint Francis of Assisi and Saint Francis Xavier, of Darwin and Huxley, of Gladstone and Disraeli, of Henry Drummond and Phillips Brooks! Yet any one of us can understand such men better now than most of their acquaintances could have done when they walked the earth.

When one thinks of the privilege that is waiting in the great biographies to know people whom to know living would have been worth a king's ransom, but could not have been bought at any price, to read their letters, to see their mistakes, to know their love affairs, to watch them deal with their handicaps, work out their philosophies of life, meet their sorrows, face their advancing age, and fall on death, one wonders why people who want nothing but entertainment read the trivial trash that the presses grind out while such a rich feast of human interest is awaiting them.

For sheer delight give me a biography. Shall we spend this evening with Thomas Huxley? Then he is waiting in his son's biography, with his determination "to smite all humbugs, however big; to give a nobler tone to science; to set an example of abstinence from petty personal controversies, and of toleration for everything but lying." Or shall we live for a while with Cardinal Newman and see how Catholicism looks through a proselyte's eyes? Then he is waiting in Ward's life of him, with his strange spiritual pilgrimage from the Oxford donship to the princedom of the Roman Church. Or shall we share with John Bright the thrill of launching social liberalism in England? Then in Trevelyan's life of him he awaits our fellowship, with his unconquerable faith in his cause: "If we can't win as fast as we wish, we know that our opponents can't in the long run win at all." Or shall we get behind the scenes of Dickens' long and prosperous experience and know the man who charmed our youth with David Copperfield? Then in Forster's life we may enjoy an intimacy denied to all but a very few of Dickens' closest friends while he was here. And as for autobiography, one has only to think of Augustine's Confessions or Pepys' Diary or Benjamin Franklin's incomparable story of his own life, to feel what endless interest is to be found in knowing people as they knew themselves.

One of the world's greatest needs is tolerance. But tolerance is no negative virtue to be won by not caring what people think, nor is it an easy virtue to be gotten by wishing it. It comes only from broad contacts, from sympathetic entrance into many points of view. It comes, as Voltaire said, from learning that there are thirty-two points to the compass. Was there ever such a teacher of tolerance, then, as a long list of great biographies? Henry Drummond, as George Adam Smith portrayed him, and Voltaire in Tallentyre's revealing biography; Walter Scott through Lockhart's eyes, and Charles Darwin through his son's; Mary Lyon by Gilchrist, and Queen Victoria by Strachey; Pasteur by Vallery-Radot, and Phillips Brooks by Allen; Saint Francis Xavier by Stewart, and Ruskin by Cook—what infinite diversity! Yet into the liberal education of wide outlooks, inclusive sympathies and generous appreciations biography introduces us by that most easy and irresistible of routes—delighted insight into the personal problems of worthwhile characters.

Another reason for reading biography is that it supplies a knowledge of history in most palatable form. Some folk can take history straight—its dates and dynasties, its political intrigues, wars and treaties; but to some of us a formal historical treatise is likely to be indigestible pabulum. Give us biographies, however, of the leading characters in whose stormy lives the conflict of some generation found expression, and we will live the period again with an interest vivid as a novel could create. After all, that is the only way to know history at its core—to see it from the viewpoints of its actors, to feel the play of their motives, the thrill of their success and the dull thud of their disillusionments.

I could not easily be hired to read a treatise on the unification of Italy, but the life of Cavour by Thayer will give most of the story set in terms of vivid and unforgettable experience. To be sure, one need consent to no exaggerated worship of the hero after the manner of Carlyle; one may recognize how truly the actor is himself more an expression of his generation's life than its creator; one may grant the measure of truth which lies in the economic interpretation of history, and may sometimes pity the man who seems to lead, but who like a marionette is simply dancing when economic forces pull the strings; but, for all that, men are the points of focus where a generation's experience comes into the light, and there is the place to see history in the making.

Bonapartism is a historic movement over which I can no longer be excited, but when Philip Guedalla writes The Second Empire, a fascinating biography of Napoleon III, he produces a work whose breathless interest is as engrossing as would be a newly discovered thriller by Dumas.

One reason for this ability of a good biography to mediate a vivid understanding of long-past events is that human nature is the most constant thing we know. Economic situations, philosophies, scientific systems, and practical circumstances shift and change in endless transmutation. But human nature changes little, if at all. We are living in an altogether different world from Tutenkhamun's, but we are not so very different from Tutenkhamun himself. Could we know his life, the motives that drove it, the aims that governed it, his loves, fears, sins, remorses, joys, handicaps and hopes, we should recognize a continuum of human nature between ourselves and him which all the changed circumstances could not conceal. When, therefore, we read history in the abstract we often feel far from home; but when we read history through biography we are as intimately introduced into the inwardness of events as though we had participated in them ourselves.

The Protestant Reformation is a long way back for most of us and deals with situations whose economic, political and intellectual factors long since have changed. But read McGiffert's life of Martin Luther, and one lives over again the thrill and agony of those revolutionary days.

To be sure, there are plenty of poor biographies—"too long and too idolatrous," as Leslie Stephen said, or too short, degenerating into mere catalogues of events. Not all can be immortal as Plutarch's Lives or incomparable as Boswell's Johnson. "Biography," wrote Sir Walter Scott, "the most interesting perhaps of every species of composition, loses all its interest with me when the shades and lights of the principal character are not accurately and faithfully detailed. . . . I can no more sympathize with a mere eulogist than I can with a ranting hero upon the stage." Nevertheless, there are good biographies beyond the power of most of us to exhaust, and while I will use special historical treatises when I must and *tours de force* of historical compilation, like H. G. Wells' Outline, when I can, for the vivid visualizing of the past I will turn to biographies.

If the biographical approach to history is vivifying when one is thinking of ancient events, how much more so when one is thinking of ancient ideas and systems of philosophy. It is weary plodding for most of us to wade through the ordered, abstract statements of some old system of ethics or metaphysics long since as dead as Nebuchadnezzar. Even a book like Arnold's Roman Stoicism, which does the business about as well as it can be done, is not easy reading. But Henry Dwight Sedgwick's life of Marcus Aurelius, the Stoic emperor, is something to sit up nights over and to stay home from the theatre to get another bite of. A Christian who knows well that Marcus Aurelius persecuted Christians lays down the book feeling that, even so, the latchets of his sandals most of us are unworthy to unloose. He was Stoicism incarnate and at its best, and, as Gladstone said, one example is worth a thousand arguments.

Of course one could exaggerate this point. Once in a while the reader had better get a thoroughly scientific treatment of the era of history or system of thought which he is studying, and so check up his impressions, balance his picture, allow for the personal equation of the biographers, and see the matter steadily and whole. But that is not for me the fun of history. The fun of history is living it all over again in the lives of the men who made it.

A third motive for enjoying biography is that it will give to the average reader an intelligible introduction to the world's great music, literature and art. This statement is likely to be criticized at first and perhaps derided. A poem is beautiful in itself—so runs the purist's argument—and, no matter who wrote it or when it was written, should be appreciated for itself. But you cannot pick up poems as you would pick up apples and eat them, if they are good, without regard to the special tree they came from. Poems are the quintessential expression of life, and you never fully understand them until you know the man from whom they came, his problems, developments, conflicts, ideals, handicaps and ultimate philosophy.

The proof of this lies in the trying of it. Some of Wordsworth's poems, like Lines Above Tintern Abbey or ode on Intimations of Immortality, at once make their appeal to those with souls tuned in. But one cannot blame the average reader for his evident reluctance to read Wordsworth's poetry, his endeavors to enjoy it, his sporadic dives into it and swift emergences, his final frank confession that he cannot make much out of it. One reason is plain—the average reader does not understand Wordsworth himself. We must get at the man before we will get at his work. Read Harper's life of Wordsworth and intersperse the reading of the poems as they were written out of the moods and insights which developed with the author's changing circumstances and thought, and see if reading poetry through biography is not an open door into a new and rewarding realm.

Of course, one would love a poem like Keat's Ode on a Grecian Urn even if he saw it printed for the first time in a daily newspaper. But if a man will take Colvin's life of Keats and Keats' poems together on a holiday and read the writings as they come, each in its proper place in the author's life, he will find beauties made doubly luminous, difficulties made easy, and darkness made light.

Just such a service William Lyon Phelps has been doing in the columns of the Home Journal in his series on Makers of American Literature. He is one of the most popular of teachers, in part because he has habitually seen the author's life behind his writings until the stiff, formal analysis of literary works has in his hands given way to a vivid discovery of human nature gloriously revealed, and the desperate driving of student minds to "get a lesson" has been replaced by fascinated interest in men who lived deeply, thought nobly and spoke splendidly. Read his brief summary of Cooper's life and see if even The Last of the Mohicans does not gain in interest.

I urge this with some persistency because I am weary of hearing folks say lightly that they do not like poetry, or essays, or great books in general, when I know well that they are denying themselves what they would love and profit by if only they knew how to get at it. It is a great day for a man when he makes up his mind that the best belongs to him and that he can have it if he will. Let him then read the life of

Henry Wadsworth Longfellow by his brother Samuel and read the poems along with it if he wishes an easy start. If Emerson's prose and poems are reluctantly absorbed, let him get Firkins' study of the sage's life. Why should Americans content themselves with merely knowing a few of Whittier's hymns when Carpenter's life can be purchased for what a detective story would cost? And in general there is a whole series of English Men of Letters, edited by John Morley, purchasable for a song and waiting to put biographical setting behind the poems, novels, essays, dramas, that are the glory of our Anglo-Saxon speech.

The greatest religious poem of our generation is Francis Thompson's The Hound of Heaven, but no man can plumb the depth of this magnificent description of God's pursuit of the human soul unless he knows Thompson's life. Let him get Everard Maynell's story of this man whom the Hound of Heaven pursued when he was so far away from heavenly precincts that he even held horses' heads on London streets to make a few pence for opiates to give him sleep and forgetfulness. The poem is simply the autobiographical transcription of a tremendous experience.

The application of this biographical approach to music and to painting may not be so obvious, but it is there. Even the symphony programs recognize this and tell the audience something of the composers which adds human interest to the evening's music. I presume that Beethoven's symphonies are no better because he was stone deaf at middle age. But from the day I learned how Beethoven, walking with a friend, failed to hear the piping of a shepherd who was pointed out to him, and realizing his deafness for the first time, faced up to his terrific handicap, saying, "I will grapple with fate; it shall never drag me down," I have heard overtones in his music that I never heard before.

So, too, in painting. Munkácsy's Christ Before Pilate is the first great picture that I ever saw. Into its presence in a quiet tent, with the tinsel and turmoil of a county fair left outside,

I stepped, a little boy, to stand abashed and hushed before the Master silent at the Roman judgment seat. But one who knows Munkácsy's life—his father dying after release from prison, his early poverty so severe, his toil so unremitting that he scarcely survived the strain, his long and patient struggle for opportunity and his resounding triumph at the end, will see even in so great a picture not less but more.

Who does not love Millet's canvases, in particular The Gleaners and The Angelus? But read Julia Cartwright's life of him and you will love them better. A wealth of human tenderness was in that Normandy peasant home from which he came, a mingled dignity and gentleness in his father uncovering before a sunset and saying, "It is God," and in his mother a depth of piety which followed the painter all his life. One hardly sees Millet's paintings truly who does not see them with the eyes of the painter himself, who had come from the coasts of Normandy and who, unspoiled by the sophistications of Paris, ended in the woods of Barbizon.

Here at our hands is a kind of book that millions of people never touch, and yet to those who know the secret talisman a way is opened by this neglected road into a new world where even unpoetical souls find interest in poetry, and musical ignoramuses are helped to enjoy music, and eyes artistically dull find fresh significance in art.

Perhaps the innermost service which reading of biography does for a man consists in giving him a wide perspective around his own life's problems. A man who has read many biographies has lived vicariously through many lives. He may be only forty-five himself, but he has gone through the journey to the end with many men whom he has known and loved; he has watched their youth pass into manhood and manhood into age; he has seen the death of loved ones break up their family circles and has read their letters when health gave way or success turned into defeat or property was lost or friends proved false. Biography makes a man feel at home with anything that can happen to him. It keeps him from being too much surprised by any problem or calamity that fate may present him with. It familiarizes him with the mysterious, amiable and sometimes tragic face of life in all her changing moods.

Nor is this disheartening; it is challenging and tonic. One discovers that many a man whose achievement has seemed so spontaneous that we envied him his ease and fluency of output was in fact a handicapped man making good in a hard place. We gain a new interest in Watt when we think of him, not simply as a great inventor but as a man sickly of body, starving on eight shillings a week and saying, "Of all things in life there is nothing more foolish than inventing."

We may never have read Kant's philosophy, but we are almost tempted to try when we see him working in constant bodily pain and saying, "I have become master of its influence on my thoughts and actions by turning my attention away from this feeling altogether, just as if it did not at all concern me." We may be glad that Herbert Spencer's point of view has been over-passed in a more comprehensive outlook on the universe, but we are interested in the man himself when we recall him doing his tremendous work on such short reserves of strength that he used to intersperse half hours of work with half hours of pitching quoits.

It is this unknown side to notable lives that makes the reading of biography so valuable a voyage of discovery. We know Whittier the Quaker poet, whose gentle hymns we sing, but do we know Whittier the vehement young reformer, disguised in a wig and a big white overcoat, trying to save his effects from a mob sacking the Abolitionists' headquarters in Philadelphia? We know Francis Parkman the historian, whose stories of the California and Oregon Trail are unsurpassable, but do we know Francis Parkman, almost blind, running his pencil along the wire screen that covered his manuscripts in order that he might write legibly? We know Phillips Brooks the preacher, but do we know Phillips Brooks who failed as a teacher, and who all his life so wanted to teach that in his maturity he came white as a sheet from

President Eliot's office at Harvard, where he had turned down what he thought would be his last opportunity?

It is not alone the endless human interest of thus knowing men which makes biography so much the most worthwhile reading that there is; it is the steadying power which all this contributes to a man's own life. Nothing can take him wholly unawares if he knows wide ranges of biography. Life's successes are less likely to turn his head and life's failures less likely to oppress his heart.

He has seen life work out its issues too often to overestimate prosperity or to overemphasize failure. When men attack him he finds himself in good company; when health is troublesome he feels himself in a notable succession of handicapped men who have made good; when temptations come to unworthy living he is likely to recall the lesson of all biography that no sin is without its Nemesis; and when old age comes he can lift with understanding heart the ancient prayer: "Let me die the death of the righteous, and let my last end be like his."

> An author may influence the fortunes of the world to as great an extent as a statesman or a warrior. A book may be as great a thing as a battle.
>
> BENJAMIN DISRAELI.

DICKENS[1]

By George Santayana

If Christendom should lose everything that is now in the melting-pot, human life would still remain amiable and quite adequately human. I draw this comforting assurance from the pages of Dickens. Who could not be happy in his world? Yet there is nothing essential to it which the most destructive revolution would be able to destroy. People would still be as different, as absurd, and as charming as are his characters; the springs of kindness and folly in their lives would not be dried up. Indeed, there is much in Dickens which communism, if it came, would only emphasize and render universal. Those schools, those poorhouses, those prisons, with those surviving shreds of family life in them, show us what in the coming age (with some sanitary improvements) would be the nursery and home of everybody. Everybody would be a waif, like Oliver Twist, like Smike, like Pip, and like David Copperfield, and amongst the agents and underlings of social government, to whom all these waifs would be entrusted, there would surely be a goodly sprinkling of Pecksniffs, Squeers's, and Fangs; whilst the Fagins would be everywhere commissioners of the people. Nor would there fail to be, in high places and in low, the occasional sparkle of some Pickwick or Cheeryble Brothers or Sam Weller or Mark Tapley; and the voluble Flora Finchings would be everywhere in evidence, and the strong-minded Betsey Trotwoods in office. There would also be, among the inefficient, many a Dora and Agnes and Little Emily—with her charm but without her tragedy, since this is one of the things which the promised social reform would happily render impossible; I mean, by removing all the

[1] Reprinted by permission of Chas. Scribner's Sons.

disgrace of it. The only element in the world of Dickens which would become obsolete would be the setting, the atmosphere of material instrumentalities and arrangements, as traveling by coach is obsolete; but traveling by rail, by motor, or by airship will emotionally be much the same thing. It is worth noting how such instrumentalities, which absorb modern life, are admired and enjoyed by Dickens, as they were by Homer. The poets ought not to be afraid of them; they exercise the mind congenially, and can be played with joyfully. Consider the black ships and the chariots of Homer, the coaches and river-boats of Dickens, and the aeroplanes of to-day; to what would an unspoiled young mind turn with more interest? Dickens tells us little of English sports, but he shares the sporting nature of the Englishman, to whom the whole material world is a playing-field, the scene giving ample scope to his love of action, legality, and pleasant achievement. His art is to sport according to the rules of the game, and to do things for the sake of doing them, rather than for any ulterior motive.

It is remarkable, in spite of his ardent simplicity and openness of heart, how insensible Dickens was to the greater themes of the human imagination—religion, science, politics, art. He was a waif himself, and utterly disinherited. For example, the terrible heritage of contentious religions which fills the world seems not to exist for him. In this matter he was like a sensitive child, with a most religious disposition, but no religious ideas. Perhaps, properly speaking, he had no *ideas* on any subject; what he had was a vast sympathetic participation in the daily life of mankind; and what he saw of ancient institutions made him hate them, as needless sources of oppression, misery, selfishness, and rancor. His one political passion was philanthropy, genuine but felt only on its negative, reforming side; of positive utopias or enthusiasms we hear nothing. The political background of Christendom is only, so to speak, an old faded back-drop for his stage; a castle, a frigate, a gallows, and a large female angel with white wings standing above an orphan by an open grave—a decoration which has to serve for all the melodramas in his theater, intellectually so provincial and poor. Common life as it is lived was varied and lovable enough for Dickens, if only the pests and cruelties could be removed from it. Suffering wounded him, but not vulgarity; whatever pleased his senses and whatever shocked them filled his mind alike with romantic wonder, with the endless delight of observation. Vulgarity—and what can we relish, if we recoil at vulgarity?—was innocent and amusing; in fact, for the humorist, it was the spice of life. There was more piety in being human than in being pious. In reviving Christmas, Dickens transformed it from the celebration of a metaphysical mystery into a feast of overflowing simple kindness and good cheer; the church bells were still there—in the orchestra; and the angels of Bethlehem were still there—painted on the back-curtain. Churches, in his novels, are vague, desolate places where one has ghastly experiences, and where only the pew-opener is human; and such religious and political conflicts as he depicts in *Barnaby Rudge* and in *A Tale of Two Cities* are street brawls and prison scenes and conspiracies in taverns, without any indication of the contrasts in mind or interests between the opposed parties. Nor had Dickens any lively sense for fine art, classical tradition, science, or even the manners and feelings of the upper classes in his own time and country: in his novels we may almost say there is no army, no navy, no church, no sport, no distant travel, no daring adventure, no feeling for the watery wastes and the motley nations of the planet, and—luckily, with his notion of them—no lords and ladies. Even love of the traditional sort is hardly in Dickens's sphere—I mean the soldierly passion in which a rather rakish gallantry was sobered by devotion, and loyalty rested on pride. In Dickens love is sentimental or benevolent or merry or sneaking or canine; in his last book he was going to describe a love that was passionate and criminal; but love for him was never chivalrous, never poetical. What he paints most tragically is a quasipaternal devotion in the old to the young, the love of Mr. Peggotty for Little Emily, or of Solomon Gills for Walter Gay. A series of shabby little adventures, such as might absorb the interest of an average youth, were romantic enough for Dickens.

I say he was disinherited, but he inherited the most terrible negations. Religion lay on him like the weight of the atmosphere, sixteen pounds to the square inch, yet never noticed nor mentioned. He lived and wrote in the shadow of the most awful prohibitions. Hearts petrified by legality and falsified by worldliness offered, indeed, a good subject for a novelist, and Dickens availed himself of it to the extent of always contrasting natural goodness and happiness with whatever is morose; but his morose people were wicked, not virtuous in their own way; so that the protest of his temperament against his environment never took a radical form nor went back to first principles. He needed to feel, in his writing, that he was carrying the sympathies of every man with him. In him conscience was single, and he could not conceive how it could ever be divided in other men. He denounced scandals without exposing shams, and conformed willingly and scrupulously to the proprieties. Lady Dedlock's secret, for instance, he treats as if it were the sin of Adam, remote, mysterious, inexpiable. Mrs. Dombey is not allowed to deceive her husband except by pretending to deceive him. The seduction of Little Emily is left out altogether, with the whole character of Steerforth, the development of which would have been so important in the moral experience of David Copperfield himself. But it is not public prejudice alone that plays the censor over Dickens's art; his own kindness and even weakness of heart act sometimes as marplots. The character of Miss Mowcher, for example, so brilliantly introduced, was evidently intended to be shady, and to play a very important part in the story; but its original in real life, which was recognized, had to be conciliated, and the sequel was omitted and patched up with an apology—itself admirable—for the poor dwarf. Such a sacrifice does honor to Dickens's heart; but artists should meditate on their works in time, and it is easy to remove any too great likeness in a portrait by a few touches making it more consistent than real people are apt to be; and in this case, if the little creature had been really guilty, how much more subtle and tragic her apology for herself might have been, like that of the bastard Edmund in *King Lear!* So, too, in *Dombey and Son*, Dickens could not bear to let Walter Gay turn out badly, as he had been meant to do, and to break his uncle's heart as well as the heroine's; he was accordingly transformed into a stage hero miraculously saved from shipwreck, and Florence was not allowed to reward the admirable Toots, as she should have done, with her trembling hand. But Dickens was no free artist; he had more genius than taste, a warm fancy not aided by a thorough understanding of complex characters. He worked under pressure, for money and applause, and often had to cheapen in execution what his inspiration had so vividly conceived.

What, then, is there left, if Dickens has all these limitations? In our romantic disgust we might be tempted to say, Nothing. But in fact almost everything is left, almost everything that counts in the daily life of mankind, or that by its presence or absence can determine whether life shall be worth living or not; because a simple good life is worth living, and an elaborate bad life is not. There remains in the first place eating and drinking; relished not bestially, but humanly, jovially, as the sane and exhilarating basis for everything else. This is a sound English beginning; but the immediate sequel, as the England of that day presented it to Dickens, is no less delightful. There is the ruddy glow of the hearth; the sparkle of glasses and brasses and well-scrubbed pewter; the savory fumes of the hot punch, after the tingle of the wintry air; the coaching-scenes, the motley figures and absurd incidents of travel; the changing sights and joys of the road. And then, to balance this, the traffic of ports and cities, the hubbub of crowded streets, the luxury of shop-windows and of palaces not to be entered; the procession of the passers-by, shabby or ludicrously genteel; the dingy look and musty smell of their lodgings; the labyrinth of back-alleys, courts, and mews, with their crying children, and scolding old women, and listless, half-drunken loiterers. These sights, like fables, have a sort of moral in them to which Dickens was very sensitive; the important airs of nobodies on great occasions, the sadness and preoccupation of the great as they hasten by in their mourning or on their pressing affairs; the sadly comic characters of the tavern; the diligence of shopkeepers, like squirrels turning in their cages; the children peeping out everywhere like grass in an untrodden street; the charm of humble things, the nobleness of humble people, the horror of crime, the ghastliness of vice, the deft hand and shining face of virtue passing through the midst of it all; and finally a fresh wind of indifference and change blowing across our troubles and clearing the most lurid sky.

I do not know whether it was Christian charity or naturalistic insight, or a mixture of both (for they are closely akin) that attracted Dickens particularly to the deformed, the half-witted, the abandoned, or those impeded or misunderstood by virtue of some singular inner consecration. The visible moral of these things, when brutal prejudice does not blind us to it, comes very near to true philosophy; one turn of the screw, one flash of reflection, and we have understood nature and human morality and the relation between them.

In his love of roads and wayfarers, of river-ports and wharves and the idle or sinister figures that lounge about them, Dickens was like Walt Whitman; and I think a second Dickens may any day appear in America, when it is possible in that land of hurry to reach the same degree of saturation, the same unquestioning pleasure in the familiar facts. The spirit of Dickens would be better able to do justice to America than was that of Walt Whitman; because America, although it may seem nothing but a noisy nebula to the impressionist, is not a nebula but a concourse of very distinct individual bodies, natural and social, each with its definite interests and story. Walt Whitman had a sort of transcendental philosophy which swallowed the universe whole, supposing there was a universal spirit in things identical with the absolute spirit that observed them; but Dickens was innocent of any such claptrap, and remained a true spirit in his own person. Kindly and clear-sighted, but self-identical and unequivocally human, he glided through the slums like one of his own little heroes, uncontaminated by their squalor and confusion, courageous and firm in his clear allegiances amid the flux of things, a pale angel at the Carnival, his heart aflame, his voice always flute-like in its tenderness and warning. This is the true relation of spirit to existence, not the other which confuses them; for this earth (I cannot speak for the universe at large) has no spirit of its own, but brings forth spirits only at certain points, in the hearts and brains of frail living creatures, who like insects flit through it, buzzing and gathering what sweets they can; and it is the spaces they traverse in this career, charged with their own moral burden, that they can report on or describe, not things rolling on to infinity in their vain tides. To be hypnotized by that flood would be a heathen idolatry. Accordingly Walt Whitman, in his comprehensive democratic vistas, could never see the trees for the wood, and remained incapable, for all his diffuse love of the human herd, of ever painting a character or telling a story; the very things in which Dickens was a master. It is this life of the individual, as it may be lived in a given nation, that determines the whole value of that nation to the poet, to the moralist, and to the judicious historian. But for the excellence of the typical single life, no nation deserves to be remembered more than the sands of the sea; and America will not be a success, if every American is a failure.

Dickens entered the theater of this world by the stage door; the shabby little adventures of the actors in their private capacity replace for him the mock tragedies which they enact before a dreaming public. Mediocrity of circumstances and mediocrity of soul for ever return to the center of his stage; a more wretched or a grander existence is sometimes broached, but the pendulum soon swings back, and we return, with the relief with which we put on our slippers after the most romantic excursion, to a golden mediocrity—to mutton and beer, and to love and babies in a suburban villa with one frowsy maid. Dickens is the poet of those acres of yellow brick streets which the traveler sees from the railway viaducts as he approaches London; they need a poet, and they deserve one, since a complete human life may very well be lived there. Their little excitements and sorrows, their hopes and humors are like those of the Wooden Midshipman in *Dombey and Son;* but the sea is not far off, and the sky—Dickens never forgets it—is above all those brief troubles. He had a sentiment in the presence of this vast flatness of human fates, in spite of their individual pungency, which I think might well be the dominant sentiment of mankind in the future; a sense of happy freedom in littleness, an open-eyed reverence and religion without words. This universal human anonymity is like a sea, an infinitive democratic desert, chock-full and yet the very image of emptiness, with nothing in it for the mind, except, as the Moslems say, the presence of Allah. Awe is the counterpart of humility—and this is perhaps religion enough. The atom in the universal vortex ought to be humble; he ought to see that, materially, he doesn't much matter, and that morally his loves are merely his own, without authority over the universe. He can admit without obloquy that he is what he is; and he can rejoice in his own being, and in that of all other things in so far as he can share it sympathetically. The apportionment of existence and of fortune is in Other Hands; his own portion is contentment, vision, love, and laughter.

Having humility, that most liberating of sentiments, having a true vision of human existence and joy in that vision, Dickens had in a superlative degree the gift of humor, of mimicry, of unrestrained farce. He was the perfect comedian. When people say Dickens exaggerates, it seems to me they can have no eyes and no ears. They probably have only *notions* of what things and people are; they accept them conventionally, at their diplomatic value. Their minds run on in the region of discourse, where there are masks only and no faces, ideas and no facts; they have little sense for those living grimaces that play from moment to moment upon the countenance of the world. The world is a perpetual caricature of itself; at every moment it is the mockery and the contradiction of what it is pretending to be. But as it nevertheless intends all the time to be something different and highly dignified, at the next moment it corrects and checks and tries to cover up the absurd thing it was; so that a conventional world, a world of masks, is superimposed on the reality, and passes in every sphere of human interest for the reality itself. Humor is the perception of this illusion, the fact allowed to pierce here and there through the convention, whilst the convention continues to be maintained, as if we had not observed its absurdity. Pure comedy is more radical, cruder, in a certain sense less human; because comedy throws the convention over altogether, revels for a moment in the fact, and brutally says to the notions of mankind, as if it slapped them in the face, There, take that! That's what you really are! At this the polite world pretends to laugh, not tolerantly as it does at humor, but a little angrily. It does not like to see itself by chance in the glass, without having had time to compose its features for demure self-contemplation. "What a bad mirror," it exclaims; "it must be concave or convex; for surely I never looked like that. Mere caricature, farce, and horse play. Dickens exaggerates; *I* never was so sentimental as that; *I* never saw anything so dreadful; *I* don't believe there were ever any people like Quilp, or Squeers, or Serjeant Buzfuz." But the polite world is lying; there *are* such people; we are such people ourselves in our true moments, in our veritable impulses; but we are careful to stifle and to hide those moments from ourselves and from the world; to purse and pucker ourselves into the mask of our conventional personality; and so simpering, we profess that it is very coarse and inartistic of Dickens to undo our life's work for us in an instant, and remind us of what we are. And as to other people, though we may allow that considered superficially they are often absurd, we do not wish to dwell on their eccentricities, nor to mimic them. On the contrary, it is good manners to look away quickly, to suppress a smile, and to say to ourselves that the ludicrous figure in the street is not at all comic, but a dull ordinary Christian, and that it is foolish to give any importance to the fact that its hat has blown off, that it has slipped on an orange-peel and unintentionally sat on the pavement, that it has a pimple on its nose, that its one tooth projects over its lower lip, that it is angry with things in general, and that it is looking everywhere for the penny which it holds tightly in its hand. That may fairly represent the moral condition of most of us at most times; but we do not want to think of it; we do not want to see; we gloss the fact over; we console ourselves before we are grieved, and reassert our composure before we have laughed. We are afraid, ashamed, anxious to be spared. What displeases us in Dickens is that he does not spare us; he mimics things to the full; he dilates and exhausts and repeats; he wallows. He is too intent on the passing experience to look over his shoulder, and consider whether we have not already understood, and had enough. He is not thinking of us; he is obeying the impulse of the passion, the person, or the story he is enacting. This faculty, which renders him a consummate comedian, is just what alienated from him a later generation in which people of taste were esthetes and virtuous people were higher snobs; they wanted a mincing art, and he gave them copious improvisation, they wanted analysis and development, and he gave them absolute comedy. I must confess, though the fault is mine and not his, that sometimes his absoluteness is too much for me. When I come to the death of Little Nell, or to What the Waves were always Saying, or even to the incorrigible perversities of the pretty Dora, I skip. I can't take my liquor neat in such draughts, and my inner man says to Dickens, Please don't.

But then I am a coward in so many ways! There are so many things in this world that I skip, as I skip the undiluted Dickens! When I reach Dover on a rough day, I wait there until the Channel is smoother; am I not traveling for pleasure? But my prudence does not blind me to the admirable virtue of the sailors that cross in all weathers, nor even to the automatic determination of the sea-sick ladies, who might so easily have followed my example, if they were not the slaves of their railway tickets and of their labeled luggage. They are loyal to their tour, and I to my philosophy. Yet as wrapped in my great-coat and sure of a good dinner, I pace the windy pier and soliloquize, I feel the superiority of the bluff tar, glad of breeze, stretching a firm arm to the unsteady passenger, and watching with a masterful thrill of emotion the home cliffs receding and the foreign coasts ahead. It is only courage (which Dickens had without knowing it) and universal kindness (which he knew he had) that are requisite to nerve us for a true vision of this world. And as some of us are cowards about crossing the Channel, and others about "crossing the bar," so almost everybody is a coward about his own humanity. We do not consent to be absurd, though absurd we are. We have no fundamental humility. We do not wish the moments of our lives to be caught by a quick eye in their grotesque initiative, and to be pilloried in this way before our own eyes. For that reason we don't like Dickens, and don't like comedy, and don't like the truth. Dickens could don the comic mask with innocent courage; he could wear it with a grace, ease, and irresistible vivacity seldom given to men. We must go back for anything like it to the very greatest comic poets, to Shakespeare or to Aristophanes. Who else, for instance, could have penned this:

"It was all Mrs. Bumble. She *would* do it," urged Mr. Bumble; first looking round to ascertain that his partner had left the room.

"That is no excuse," replied Mr. Brownlow. "You were present on the occasion of the destruction of these trinkets, and indeed are the more guilty of the two, in the eye of the law; for the law supposes that your wife acts under your direction."

"If the law supposes that," said Mr. Bumble, squeezing his hat emphatically in both hands, "the law is a ass, a idiot. If that's the eye of the law, the law is a bachelor; and the worst I wish the law is, that his eye may be opened by experience—by experience."

Laying great stress on the repetition of these two words, Mr. Bumble fixed his hat on very tight, and putting his hands in his pockets, followed his helpmate downstairs.

This is high comedy; the irresistible, absurd, intense dream of the old fool, personifying the law in order to convince and to punish it. I can understand that this sort of thing should not be common in English literature, nor much relished; because pure comedy is scornful, merciless, devastating, holding no door open to anything beyond. Cultivated English feeling winces at this brutality, although the common people love it in clowns and in puppet shows; and I think they are right. Dickens, who surely was tender enough, had so irresistible a comic genius that it carried him beyond the gentle humor which most Englishmen possess to the absolute grotesque reality. Squeers, for instance, when he sips the wretched dilution which he has prepared for his starved and shivering little pupils, smacks his lips and cries: "Here's richness!" It is savage comedy; humor would come in if we understood (what Dickens does not tell us) that the little creatures were duly impressed and thought the thin liquid truly delicious. I suspect that English sensibility prefers the humor and wit of Hamlet to the pure comedy of Falstaff; and that even in Aristophanes it seeks consolation in the lyrical poetry for the flaying of human life in the comedy itself. Tastes are free; but we should not deny that in merciless and rollicking comedy life is caught in the act. The most grotesque creatures of Dickens are not exaggerations or mockeries of something other than themselves; they arise because nature generates them, like toadstools; they exist because they can't help it, as we all do. The fact that these perfectly self-justified beings are absurd appears only by comparison, and from outside; circumstances, or the expectations of other people, make them ridiculous and force them to contradict themselves; but in nature it is no crime to be exceptional. Often, but for the savagery of the average man, it would not even be a misfortune. The sleepy fat boy in *Pickwick* looks foolish; but in himself he is no more foolish, nor less solidly self-justified, than a pumpkin lying on the ground. Toots seems ridiculous; and we laugh heartily at his incoherence, his beautiful waistcoats, and his extreme modesty; but when did anybody more obviously grow into what he is because he couldn't grow otherwise? So with Mr. Pickwick, and Sam Weller, and Mrs. Gamp, and Micawber, and all the rest of this wonderful gallery; they are ridiculous only by accident, and in a context in which they never intended to appear. If Œdipus and Lear and Cleopatra do not seem ridiculous, it is only because tragic reflection has taken them out of the context in which, in real life, they would have figured. If we saw them as facts, and not as emanations of a poet's dream, we should laugh at them till doomsday; what grotesque presumption, what silly whims, what mad contradiction of the simplest realities! Yet we should not laugh at them without feeling how real their griefs were; as real and terrible as the griefs of children and of dreams. But facts, however serious inwardly, are always absurd outwardly; and the just critic of life sees both truths at once, as Cervantes did in *Don Quixote*. A pompous idealist who does not see the ridiculous in *all* things is the dupe of his sympathy and abstraction; and a clown, who does not see that these ridiculous creatures are living quite in earnest, is the dupe of his egotism. Dickens saw the absurdity, and understood the life; I think he was a good philosopher.

It is usual to compare Dickens with Thackeray, which is like comparing the grape with the gooseberry; there are obvious points of resemblance, and the gooseberry has some superior qualities of its own; but you can't make red wine of it. The wine of Dickens is of the richest, the purest, the sweetest, the most fortifying to the blood; there is distilled in it, with the perfection of comedy, the perfection of morals. I do not mean, of course, that Dickens appreciated all the values that human life has or might have; that is beyond any man. Even the greatest philosophers, such as Aristotle, have not always much imagination to conceive forms of happiness or folly other than those which their age or their temperament reveals to them; their insight runs only to discovering the *principle* of happiness, that it is spontaneous life of any sort harmonized with circumstances. The sympathies and imagination of Dickens, vivid in their sphere, were no less limited in range; and of course it was not his business to find philosophic formulas; nevertheless I call his the perfection of morals for two reasons: that he put the distinction between good and evil in the right place, and that he felt this distinction intensely. A moralist might have excellent judgment, he might see what sort of life is spontaneous in a given being and how far it may be harmonized with circumstances, yet his heart might remain cold, he might not suffer nor rejoice with the suffering or joy he foresaw. Humanitarians like Bentham and Mill, who talked about the greatest happiness of the greatest number, might conceivably be moral prigs in their own persons, and they might have been chilled to the bone in their theoretic love of mankind, if they had had the wit to imagine in what, as a matter of fact, the majority would place their happiness. Even if their theory had been correct (which I think it was in intention, though not in statement) they would then not have been perfect moralists, because their maxims would not have expressed their hearts. In expressing their hearts, they ought to have embraced one of those forms of "idealism" by which men fortify themselves in their bitter passions or in their helpless commitments; for they do not wish mankind to be happy in its own way, but in theirs. Dickens was not one of those moralists who summon every man to do himself the greatest violence so that he may not offend them, nor defeat their ideals. Love of the good of others is something that shines in every page of Dickens with a truly celestial splendor. How entirely limpid is his sympathy with life—a sympathy uncontaminated by dogma or pedantry or snobbery or bias of any kind! How generous is this keen, light spirit, how pure this open heart! And yet, in spite of this extreme sensibility, not the least wobbling; no deviation from a just severity of judgment, from an uncompromising distinction between white and black. And this happens as it ought to happen; sympathy is not checked by a flatly contrary prejudice or commandment, by some categorical imperative irrelevant to human nature; the check, like the cheer, comes by tracing the course of spontaneous impulse and circumstances that inexorably lead it to success or to failure. There is a bed to this stream, freely as the water may flow; when it comes to this precipice it must leap, when it runs over these pebbles it must sing, and when it spreads into that marsh it must become livid and malarial. The very sympathy with human impulse quickens in Dickens the sense of danger; his very joy in joy makes him stern to what kills it. How admirably drawn are his surly villains! No rhetorical vilification of them, as in a sermon; no exaggeration of their qualms or fears; rather a sense of how obvious and human all their courses seem from their own point of view; and yet no sentimental apology for them, no romantic worship of rebels in their madness or crime. The pity of it, the waste of it all, are seen not by a second vision but by the same original vision which revealed the lure and the drift of the passion. Vice is a monster here of such sorry mien, that the longer we see it the more we deplore it; that other sort of vice which Pope found so seductive was perhaps only some innocent impulse artificially suppressed, and called a vice because it broke out inconveniently and displeased the company. True vice is human nature strangled by the suicide of attempting the impossible. Those so self-justified villains of Dickens never elude their fates. Bill Sikes is not let off, neither is

Nancy; the oddly benevolent Magwitch does not escape from the net, nor does the unfortunate young Richard Carstone, victim of the Circumlocution Office. The horror and ugliness of their fall are rendered with the hand of a master; we see here, as in the world, that in spite of the romanticists it is not virtue to rush enthusiastically along any road. I think Dickens is one of the best friends mankind has ever had. He has held the mirror up to nature, and of its reflected fragments has composed a fresh world, where the men and women differ from real people only in that they live in a literary medium, so that all ages and places may know them. And they are worth knowing, just as one's neighbors are, for their picturesque characters and their pathetic fates. Their names should be in every child's mouth; they ought to be adopted members of every household. Their stories cause the merriest and the sweetest chimes to ring in the fancy, without confusing our moral judgment or alienating our interest from the motley commonplaces of daily life. In every English-speaking home, in the four quarters of the globe, parents and children will do well to read Dickens aloud of a winter's evening; they will love winter, and one another, and God the better for it. What a wreath that will be of ever-fresh holly, thick with bright berries, to hang to this poet's memory—the very crown he would have chosen!

Books are men of higher stature.

E. B. Browning—*Lady Geraldine's Courtship.*

THE LITERARY MAN VIEWS HIS BRETHREN

ON MALTREATING WORDS[1]

By G. K. Chesterton

I read a phrase in a newspaper the other day, printed in very large letters at the top of a column, which ran as follows: "Crusade to Reform Auction Bridge." And I mused, in a slightly melancholy mood, upon the destiny and the decline of human words; and how clearly the fate of words illustrates the fall of man.

Surely anyone will see something a little strange in that remarkable combination of terms and topics; anyone at least who knows what has been for mankind the meaning of the Crusade, not to speak of the meaning of the Cross. Indeed it is quite equally incongruous whether our sympathies are with the Cross or the Crescent. A Moslem of any historical imagination might well be annoyed at such treatment of the tremendous and heroic trial, through which his own creed and culture passed. And when we consider what the Crusade meant to the men of our own race, the fathers and founders of us all, it will indeed seem a steep and staggering disproportion; when we call up all the imagery which was familiar for so long in all European history and poetry and all the stages of that marvelous story; the first vast movement, anonymous and almost anarchical, moving by mere popular impulse across the world, the mightiest mob in history. For no revolutionary movement of republicans or communists was ever so popular, for it is said that in all that wild democracy there were only nine knights. Then their destruction in the desert and the revenge or recovery, when the despair and darkness opened before the

[1] Reprinted by permission of Dodd, Mead and Company, Inc. Copyright, 1929.

glory of Godfrey's ride; when the toppling battle-towers swayed and sank in flames around the city as Godfrey leapt upon the wall; the high place where he refused the crown of gold under the shadow of the crown of thorns; the return of a deeper darkness, and the last stand under the Horns of Hattin, where the knights died around the True Cross; the rush of the rescuer upon Acre and that vain victory after which Lion Heart threw his lance to earth and turned his back on Jerusalem, that he might not see what he must not save; the strange and gloomy story of the Fourth Crusade and old Simon de Montfort riding away alone because he would not draw the sword against Christian men; the way in which that golden or crimson thread was woven into the tapestries of every land; whether they showed Douglas hurling the heart of Bruce before him in battle with the Saracens, or old Barbarossa sunken under the river but still waiting with his hand on his barbaric sword, or a light that shone in the desert where St. Louis lay like one dying and mingling the Crucifixion with the Crusade. If we have any sense of the historic influence of these images among men, of how Godfrey blazed among the Nine Worthies or what it was that lingered on the lyre of Tasso, we shall perhaps repeat to ourselves in a curious and meditative voice those simple words, "Crusade to Reform Auction Bridge."

Of course this loss of verbal values comes gradually; and at the beginning may even be a tribute of the lesser thing to the greater. Somebody talks naturally enough about a crusade for liberty or a crusade for knowledge; then the hunt is up and everybody who honestly believes in anything uses the term as a cliché; and we are all made familiar with the rush and hustle of a crusade for vaccination or against vivisection. In fact, the word "crusade" begins by meaning "movement" and ends with meaning merely "proposal," when it does not mean merely "fuss." We receive leaflets that are decidedly waste paper. We receive visitors with a crusade against muzzling dogs: visitors whom we ardently desire to muzzle. Crusades for painting lamp-posts green or putting the costermongers into livery follow each other with unabated enthusiasm; and we have already a crusade to reform auction bridge, and shall doubtless have another to improve ping-pong. *Dieu le Veult.*

Of course there are a great many other examples in everyday English, which may be represented as every bit as bad. We talk about a man being a martyr to indigestion, without being haunted or shamed by the burning shades of St. Lawrence or St. Sebastian. We say that Pebbleswick-on-Sea is a God-forsaken place, without committing ourselves to the highly heretical dogma that it is really forsaken of God. For it is heresy to suggest that even a successful watering place can really be an exception, either to the divine omnipresence or to the divine charity and forgiveness. But that single phrase "God-forsaken," in itself so tragic, is also in itself a tragedy. I mean it is a marked example of this tragedy of the gradual weakening of words. For it is in itself a very powerful and even appalling phrase. It is not a piece of sound theology, but it is a piece of vigorous and vivid literature. It reminds us of some great phrase in "Paradise Lost," giving a glimpse of a sort of lurid negation and ruinous quiet; not light, but rather darkness visible. Yet, strange to say, a human being can say this awful thing about Pebbleswick without shuddering. Doubtless there are any number of other examples, which I could think of if I stopped to think. Perhaps there is some touch of such levity even in saying a thing is "crucial" or in declaring that it is the crux of the question. Perhaps there is a grim reminder of it in the fact that "a Resurrectionist" generally means a body-snatcher and not a believer in the Resurrection.

But my wandering thoughts have strayed rather backwards to the origins of these things than outwards to the numberless examples of them. I think it obvious that the tendency is a general one, apart from extreme examples; though I would still lift a faint and feeble protest against the reformer of auction bridge being literally elevated to the position of Pontifex Maximus. But though we may reasonably remonstrate with some very abrupt accelerations of the process, it may be that it generally goes on as a slow process; and especially as a sleepy process. Most thoroughly bad processes are slow and sleepy; which is why I have sometimes been found wanting in a full and fanatical faith in evolution. And it seems to me that the moral of all these things is the very opposite of that which is offered to us by many evolutionists. There are indeed many of them so clear-headed as not to confuse strictly scientific evolution with a vague notion of ethical exaltation or expansion. But others do ask us to accept a sort of general upward tendency; and it seems to me that in these things there is a general downward tendency. In the matter of language, which is the main matter of literature, it is clear that words are perpetually falling below themselves. They are ceasing to say what they mean or to mean something that is not only quite different, but much less definite and strong. And, in this fall of man's chosen symbols, there may well be a symbol of his own fall. He has a difficulty in ruling his tongue; not only in the sense of the talking organ, but in the sense of the language that he talks. Almost when he is not looking, it is always running wild; or, worse still, running weak.

Now this distinction directly concerns all the talk about new art or experiments in literature. It does not make me believe in these things as progress; but it does in a sense make me believe in them as a change. I am at once more tolerant of them and less trustful of them. I can see that people must be allowed to play about with human language to a certain extent; because unless it is kept stirring it goes stale. But I do not think a thing is necessarily great because we feel it as fresh; or necessarily small because we feel it as stale. All we are doing, when we pick our words or try our experiments, is resisting the general trend of all style towards staleness. Some traditionalists do go a little too stale. Many get a great deal too fresh, as the landladies were supposed to say. But their mistake is merely in supposing that they have any claim to progress or claim to pride. What they are doing, at the best, is to resist retrogression that simply goes with repetition. In other words, all artists are dedicated to an eternal struggle against the downward tendency of their own method and medium. For this reason they must sometimes be fresh; but there is no reason why they should not also be modest. There is nothing to brag about, in the mere fact that your only mode of expression is perpetually going to the dogs. The dignity of the artist lies in his duty of keeping awake the sense of wonder in the world. In this long vigil he often has to vary his methods of stimulation; but in this long vigil he is also himself striving against a continual tendency to sleep. There are some to whom this may even seem a sombre version of human existence; but not to me; for I have long believed that the only really happy and hopeful faith is a faith in the Fall of Man.

> The best books are those which every reader feels that he might have written; the natural, which alone is good, the familiar and common.
>
> PASCAL—*Pensées.*

A CHAPTER ON LOVE

From THE HISTORY OF TOM JONES

By Henry Fielding

In our last book we have been obliged to deal pretty much with the passion of love; and in our succeeding book shall be forced to handle this subject still more largely. It may not therefore in this place be improper to apply ourselves to the examination of that modern doctrine, by which certain philosophers, among many other wonderful discoveries, pretend to have found out, that there is no such passion in the human breast.

Whether these philosophers be the same with that surprising sect, who are honourably mentioned by the late Dr. Swift, as having, by the mere force of genius alone, without the least assistance of any kind of learning, or even reading, discovered that profound and invaluable secret that there is no God; or whether they are not rather the same with those who some years since very much alarmed the world, by showing that there were no such things as virtue or goodness really existing in human nature, and who deduced our best actions from pride, I will not here presume to determine. In reality, I am inclined to suspect, that all these several finders of truth, are the very identical men who are by others called the finders of gold. The method used in both these searches after truth and after gold, being indeed one and the same, viz., the searching, rummaging, and examining into a nasty place; indeed, in the former instances, into the nastiest of all places, A BAD MIND.

But though in this particular, and perhaps in their success, the truth-finder and the gold-finder may very properly be compared together; yet in modesty, surely, there can be no comparison between the two; for who ever heard of a gold-finder that had the impudence or folly to assert, from the ill success of his search, that there was no such thing as gold in the world? whereas the truth-finder, having raked out that jakes, his own mind, and being there capable of tracing no ray of divinity, nor anything virtuous or good, or lovely, or loving, very fairly, honestly, and logically concludes that no such things exist in the whole creation.

To avoid, however, all contention, if possible, with these philosophers, if they will be called so; and to show our own disposition to accommodate matters peaceably between us, we shall here make them some concessions, which may possibly put an end to the dispute.

First, we will grant that many minds, and perhaps those of the philosophers, are entirely free from the least traces of such a passion.

Secondly, that what is commonly called love, namely, the desire of satisfying a voracious appetite with a certain quantity of delicate white human flesh, is by no means that passion for which I here contend. This is indeed more properly hunger; and as no glutton is ashamed to apply the word love to his appetite, and to say he LOVES such and such dishes; so may the lover of this kind, with equal propriety, say, he HUNGERS after such and such women.

Thirdly, I will grant, which I believe will be a most acceptable concession, that this love for which I am an advocate, though it satisfies itself in a much more delicate manner, doth nevertheless seek its own satisfaction as much as the grossest of all our appetites.

And, lastly, that this love, when it operates towards one of a different sex, is very apt, towards its complete gratification, to call in the aid of that hunger which I have mentioned above; and which it is so far from abating, that it heightens all its delights to a degree scarce imaginable by those who have never been susceptible of any other emotions than what have proceeded from appetite alone.

In return to all these concessions, I desire of the philosophers to grant, that there is in some (I believe in many) human breasts a kind and benevolent disposition, which is gratified by contributing to the happiness of others. That in this gratification alone, as in friendship, in parental and filial affection, as indeed in general philanthropy, there is a great and exquisite delight. That if we will not call such disposition love, we have no name for it. That though the pleasures arising from such pure love may be heightened and sweetened by the assistance of amorous desires, yet the former can subsist alone, nor are they destroyed by the intervention of the latter. Lastly, that esteem and gratitude are the proper motives to love, as youth and beauty are to desire, and, therefore, though such desire may naturally cease, when age or sickness overtakes its object; yet these can have no effect on love, nor ever shake or remove, from a good mind, that sensation or passion which hath gratitude and esteem for its basis.

To deny the existence of a passion of which we often see manifest instances, seems to be very strange and absurd; and can indeed proceed only from that self-admonition which we have mentioned above: but how unfair is this! Doth the man who recognizes in his own heart no traces of avarice or ambition, conclude, therefore, that there are no such passions in human nature? Why will we not modestly observe the same rule in judging of the good, as well as the evil of others? Or why, in any case, will we, as Shakespeare phrases it, "put the world in our own person?"

Predominant vanity is, I am afraid, too much concerned here. This is one instance of that adulation which we bestow on our own minds, and this almost universally. For there is scarce any man, how much soever he may despise the character of a flatterer, but will condescend in the meanest manner to flatter himself.

To those therefore I apply for the truth of the above observations, whose own minds can bear testimony to what I have advanced.

Examine your heart, my good reader, and resolve whether you do believe these matters with me. If you do, you may now proceed to their exemplification in the following pages: if you do not, you have, I assure you, already read more than you have understood; and it would be wiser to pursue your business, or your pleasures (such as they are), than to throw away any more of your time in reading what you can neither taste nor comprehend. To treat of the effects of love to you, must be as absurd as to discourse on colours to a man born blind; since possibly your idea of love may be as absurd as that which we are told such blind man once entertained of the colour scarlet; that colour seemed to him to be very much like the sound of a trumpet: and love probably may, in your opinion, very greatly resemble a dish of soup, or a sirloin of roast-beef.

And choose an author as you choose a friend.

EARL OF ROSCOMMON—*Essay on Translated Verse.*

THE REWARD OF VIRTUE

From THE HISTORY OF TOM JONES

By Henry Fielding

There are a set of religious, or rather moral writers, who teach that virtue is the certain road to happiness, and vice to misery, in this world. A very wholesome and comfortable doctrine, and to which we have but one objection, namely, that it is not true.

Indeed, if by virtue these writers mean the exercise of those cardinal virtues, which like good housewives stay at home, and mind only the business of their own family, I shall very readily concede the point; for so surely do all these contribute and lead to happiness, that I could almost wish, in violation of all the antient and modern sages, to call them rather by the name of wisdom, than by that of virtue; for, with regard to this life, no system, I conceive, was ever wiser than that of the antient Epicureans, who held this wisdom to constitute the chief good; nor foolisher than that of their opposites, those modern epicures, who place all felicity in the abundant gratification of every sensual appetite.

But if by virtue is meant (as I almost think it ought) a certain relative quality, which is always busying itself without-doors, and seems as much interested in pursuing the good of others as its own; I cannot so easily agree that this is the surest way to human happiness; because I am afraid we must then include poverty and contempt, with all the mischiefs which backbiting, envy, and ingratitude, can bring on mankind, in our idea of happiness; nay, sometimes perhaps we shall be obliged to wait upon the said happiness to a jail; since many by the above virtue have brought themselves thither.

I have not now leisure to enter upon so large a field of speculation, as here seems opening upon me; my design was to wipe off a doctrine that lay in my way; since, while Mr. Jones was acting the most virtuous part imaginable in labouring to preserve his fellow-creatures from destruction, the devil, or some other evil spirit, one perhaps cloathed in human flesh, was hard at work to make him completely miserable in the ruin of his Sophia.

This therefore would seem an exception to the above rule, if indeed it was a rule; but as we have in our voyage through life seen so many other exceptions to it, we chuse to dispute the doctrine on which it is founded, which we don't apprehend to be Christian, which we are convinced is not true, and which is indeed destructive of one of the noblest arguments that reason alone can furnish for the belief of immortality.

But as the reader's curiosity (if he hath any) must be now awake, and hungry, we shall provide to feed it as fast as we can.

Books cannot always please, however good; minds are not ever craving for their food.

George Crabbe—*Schools.*

ON WORDSWORTH

(IN PART)

By WILLIAM HAZLITT

MR. WORDSWORTH is at the head of that which has been denominated the Lake school of poetry; a school which, with all my respect for it, I do not think sacred from criticism or exempt from faults, of some of which faults I shall speak with becoming frankness; for I do not see that the liberty of the press ought to be shackled, or freedom of speech curtailed, to screen either its revolutionary or renegade extravagances. This school of poetry had its origin in the French revolution, or rather in those sentiments and opinions which produced that revolution; and which sentiments and opinions were directly imported into this country in translations from the German about that period. Our poetical literature had, towards the close of the last century, degenerated into the most trite, insipid, and mechanical of all things, in the hands of the followers of Pope and the old French school of poetry. It wanted something to stir it up, and it found that something in the principles and events of the French revolution. From the impulse it thus received, it rose at once from the most servile imitation and tamest commonplace, to the utmost pitch of singularity and paradox. The change in the belles-lettres was as complete, and to many persons as startling, as the change in politics, with which it went hand in hand. There was a mighty ferment in the heads of statesmen and poets, kings and people. According to the prevailing notions, all was to be natural and new. Nothing that was established was to be tolerated. All the commonplace figures of poetry, tropes, allegories, personifications, with the whole heathen mythology, were instantly discarded; a classical allusion was considered as a piece of antiquated foppery; capital letters were no more allowed in print than letters-patent of nobility were permitted in real life; kings and queens were dethroned from their rank and station in legitimate tragedy or epic poetry, as they were decapitated elsewhere: rhyme was looked upon as a relic of the feudal system, and regular metre was abolished along with regular government. Authority and fashion, elegance or arrangement, were hooted out of countenance as pedantry and prejudice. Every one did that which was good in his own eyes. The object was to reduce all things to an absolute level; and a singularly affected and outrageous simplicity prevailed in dress and manners, in style and sentiment. A striking effect produced where it was least expected, something new and original, no matter whether good, bad, or indifferent, whether mean or lofty, extravagant or childish, was all that was aimed at, or considered as compatible with sound philosophy and an age of reason. The licentiousness grew extreme: Coryate's Crudities were nothing to it. The world was to be turned topsy-turvy; and poetry, by the good will of Adam-wits, was to share its fate and begin *de novo*. It was a time of promise, a renewal of the world and of letters; and the Deucalions, who were paid to perform this feat of regeneration, were the present poet-laureate and the two authors of the Lyrical Ballads. The Germans, who made heroes of robbers, and honest women of castoff mistresses, had already exhausted the extravagant and marvelous in sentiment and situation; our native writers adopted a wonderful simplicity of style and matter. The paradox they set out with was, that all things are by nature equally fit subjects for poetry; or that if there is any preference to be given, those that are the meanest and most unpromising are the best, as they leave the greatest scope for the unbounded stores of thought and fancy in the writer's own mind. Poetry had with them "neither buttress nor coigne of vantage to make its pendant bed and procreant cradle." It was not "born so high: its aiery buildeth in the cedar's top, and dallies with the wind, and scorns the sun." It grew like a mushroom out of the ground, or was hidden in it like a truffle, which it required a particular sagacity and industry to find out and dig up. They founded the new school on a principle of sheer humanity, on pure nature void of art. It could not be said of these sweeping reformers and dictators in the republic of letters, that "in their train walked crowns and crownets; that realms and islands, like plates, dropt from their pockets": but they were surrounded, in company with the Muses, by a mixed rabble of idle apprentices and Botany Bay convicts, female vagrants, gypsies, meek daughters in the family of Christ, of idiot boys and mad mothers, and after them "owls and night-ravens flew." They scorned "degrees, priority, and place, insisture, course, proportion, season, form, office, and custom in all line of order:" the distinctions of birth, the vicissitudes of fortune, did not enter into their abstracted, lofty, and levelling calculation of human nature. He who was more than man, with them was none. They claimed kindred only with the commonest of the people: peasants, pedlars, and village barbers were their oracles and bosom friends. Their poetry, in the extreme to which it professedly tended and was in effect carried, levels all distinctions of nature and society; has "no figures nor no fantasies" which the prejudices of superstition or the customs of the world draw in the brains of men; "no trivial fond records" of all that has existed in the history of past ages; it has no adventitious pride, pomp, or circumstances, to set it off: "the marshal's truncheon, nor the judge's robe:" neither tradition, reverence, nor ceremony "that to great ones 'longs:" it breaks in pieces the golden images of poetry, and defaces its armorial bearings, to melt them down in the mould of common humanity or of its own upstart self-sufficiency. They took the same method in their new-fangled "metre ballad-mongering" scheme which Rousseau did in his prose paradoxes, of exciting attention by reversing the established standards of opinion and estimation in the world. They were for bringing poetry back to its primitive simplicity and state of nature, as he was for bringing society back to the savage state: so that the only thing remarkable left in the world by this change would be the persons who had produced it. A thorough adept in this school of poetry and philanthropy is jealous of all excellence but his own. He does not even like to share his reputation with his subject; for he would have it all proceed from his own power and originality of mind. Such a one is slow to admire anything that is admirable, feels no interest in what is most interesting to others, no grandeur in anything grand, no beauty in anything beautiful. He tolerates only what he himself creates; he sympathizes only with what can enter into no competition with him, with "the bare trees and mountains bare, and grass in the green field." He sees nothing but himself and the universe. He hates all greatness and all pretensions to it, whether well or ill founded. His egotism is in some respects a madness; for he scorns even the admiration of himself, thinking it a presumption in any one to suppose that he has taste or sense enough to understand him. He hates all science and all art; he hates chemistry; he hates conchology; he hates Voltaire; he hates Sir Isaac Newton; he hates wisdom; he hates wit; he hates metaphysics, which he says are unintelligible, and yet he would be thought to understand them; he hates prose; he hates all poetry but his own; he hates the dialogues in Shakespeare; he hates music, dancing, and painting; he hates Rubens; he hates Rembrandt; he hates Raphael; he hates Titian; he hates Vandyke; he hates the antique; he hates the Apollo Belvidere; he hates the Venus of Medici. This is the reason that so few people take an interest in nothing that others do! The effect has been perceived as something odd; but the cause or principle has never been distinctly traced to its source before, as far as I know.

MEN OF LETTERS

(IN PART)

By ALEXANDER SMITH

MR. HAZLITT has written many pleasant essays, but none pleasanter than that entitled 'My First Acquaintance with Poets,' which, in the edition by his son, opens the *Winterslow* series. It relates almost entirely to Coleridge; containing sketches of his personal appearance, fragments of his conversation, and is filled with a young man's generous enthusiasm, belief, admiration, as with sunrise. He had met Coleridge, walked with him, talked with him, and the high intellectual experience not only made him better acquainted with his own spirit and its folded powers, but—as is ever the case with such spiritual encounters—it touched and illuminated the dead outer world. The road between Wem and Shrewsbury was familiar enough to Hazlitt, but as the twain passed along it on the winter day, it became etherialised, poetic—wonderful, as if leading across the Delectable Mountains to the Golden City, whose gleam is discernible on the horizon. The milestones were mute with attention, the pines upon the hill had ears for the stranger as he passed. Eloquence made the red leaves rustle on the oak; made the depth of heaven seem as if swept by a breath of spring; and when the evening star appeared, Hazlitt saw it as Adam did while in Paradise and but one day old. 'As we passed along,' writes the essayist, 'between Wem and Shrewsbury, and I eyed the blue hill tops seen through the wintry branches, or the red, rustling leaves of the sturdy oak-trees by the wayside, a sound was in my ears as of a syren's song. I was stunned, startled with it as from deep sleep; but I had no notion that should ever be able to express my admiration to others in motley imagery or quaint allusion, till the light of his genius shone into my soul, like the sun's rays glittering in the puddles of the road. I was at that time dumb, inarticulate, helpless, like a worm by the wayside, crushed, bleeding, lifeless; but now, bursting from the deadly bands that bound them, my ideas float on winged words, and as they expand their plumes, catch the golden light of other years. My soul has indeed remained in its original bondage, dark, obscure, with longings infinite and unsatisfied; my heart, shut up in the prison-house of this rude clay, has never found, nor will it ever find, a heart to speak to; but that my understanding also did not remain dumb and brutish, or at length found a language to express itself, I owe to Coleridge.' Time and sorrow, personal ambition thwarted and fruitlessly driven back on itself, hopes for the world defeated and unrealised, changed the enthusiastic youth into a petulant, unsocial man; yet ever as he remembered that meeting and his wintry walk from Wem to Shrewsbury the early glow came back, and again a 'sound was in his ears as of a syren's song.'

We are not all hero-worshippers like Hazlitt, but most of us are so to a large extent. A large proportion of mankind feel a quite peculiar interest in famous writers. They like to read about them, to know what they said on this or the other occasion, what sort of house they inhabited, what fashion of dress they wore, if they liked any particular dish for dinner, what kind of women they fell in love with, and whether their domestic atmosphere was stormy or the reverse. Concerning such men no bit of information is too trifling; everything helps to make out the mental image we have dimly formed for ourselves. And this kind of interest is heightened by the artistic way in which time occasionally groups them. The race is gregarious; they are visible to us in clumps like primroses; they are brought into neighborhood and flash light on each other like gems in a diadem. We think of the wild geniuses who came up from the universities to London in the dawn of the English drama.

Greene, Nash, Marlowe—our first professional men of letters —how they cracked their satirical whips, how they brawled in taverns, how pinched they were at times, how, when they possessed money, they flung it from them as if it were poison, with what fierce speed they wrote, how they shook the stage. Then we think of the 'Mermaid' in session, with Shakspeare's bland, oval face, the light of a smile spread over it, and Ben Jonson's truculent visage, and Beaumont and Fletcher sitting together in their beautiful friendship, and fancy as best we can the drollery, the repartee, the sage sentences, the lightening gleams of wit, the thunder-peals of laughter.

> What things have we seen
> Done at the Mermaid! Heard words that have been
> So nimble, and so full of subtle flame,
> As if that every one from whence they came
> Had meant to put his whole soul in a jest,
> And had resolved to live a fool the rest
> Of his dull life.

Then there is the 'Literary Club', with Johnson, and Garrick, and Burke, and Reynolds, and Goldsmith sitting in perpetuity in Boswell. The Doctor has been talking there for a hundred years, and there will he talk for many a hundred more. And we of another generation, and with other things to think about, can enter any night we please, and hear what is going on. Then we have the swarthy ploughman from Ayrshire sitting at Lord Monboddo's with Dr. Blair, Dugald Stewart, Henry Mackenzie, and the rest. These went into the presence of the wonderful rustic thoughtlessly enough, and now they cannot return even if they would. They are defrauded of oblivion. Not yet have they tasted forgetfulness and the grave. The day may come when Burns shall be forgotten, but till that day arrives—and the eastern sky as yet gives no token of its approach—*him* they must attend as satellites the sun, as courtiers their king. Then there are the

Lakers—Wordsworth, Coleridge, Southey, De Quincey burdened with his tremendous dream, Wilson in his splendid youth. What talk, what argument, what readings of lyrical and other ballads, what contempt of critics, what a hail of fine things! Then there is Charles Lamb's room in Inner Temple Lane, the hush of a whist table in one corner, the host stuttering puns as he deals the cards; and sitting round about, Hunt, whose every sentence is flavoured with the hawthorn and the primrose, and Hazlitt maddened by Waterloo and St. Helena, and Godwin with his wild theories, and Kemble with his Roman look. And before the morning comes, and Lamb stutters yet more thickly—for there is a slight flavour of punch in the apartment—what talk there has been of Hogarth's prints, of Izaak Walton, of the old dramatists, of Sir Thomas Browne's 'Urn Burial', with Elia's quaint humour breaking through every interstice, and flowering in every fissure and cranny of the conversation! One likes to think of these social gatherings of wits and geniuses; they are more interesting than conclaves of kings or convocations of bishops. One would like to have been the waiter at the 'Mermaid', and to have stood behind Shakspeare's chair. What was that functionary's opinion of his guests? Did he listen and become witty by infection? or did he, when his task was over, retire unconcernedly to chalk up the tavern score? One envies somewhat the damsel who brought Lamb the spirit-case and the hot water. I think of these meetings, and, in lack of companionship, frame for myself imaginary conversations—not so brilliant, of course, as Mr. Landor's, but yet sufficient to make pleasant for me the twilight hour while the lamp is yet unlit, and my solitary room is filled with the ruddy lights and shadows of the fire.

Of human notabilities men of letters are the most interesting, and this arises mainly from their outspokenness as a class. The writer makes himself known in a way that no other man makes himself known. The distinguished engineer may be as great a man as the distinguished writer, but as a rule we know little about him. We see him invent a locomotive, or bridge a strait, but there our knowledge stops; we look at the engine, we walk across the bridge, we admire the ingenuity of the one, we are grateful for the conveniency of the other, but to our apprehensions the engineer is undeciphered all the while. Doubtless he reveals himself in his work as the poet reveals himself in his song, but then this revelation is made in a tongue unknown to the majority. After all, we do not feel that we get nearer him. The man of letters, on the other hand, is outspoken, he takes you into his confidence, he keeps no secret from you. Be you beggar, be you king, you are welcome. He is no respecter of persons. He gives without reserve his fancies, his wit, his wisdom; he makes you a present of all that the painful or the happy years have brought him. The writer makes his reader heir in full. Men of letters are a peculiar class. They are never commonplace or prosaic—at least those of them that mankind care for. They are airy, wise, gloomy, melodious spirits. They give us the language we speak, they furnish the subjects of our best talk. They are full of generous impulses and sentiments, and keep the world young. They have said fine things on every phase of human experience. The air is full of their voices. Their books are the world's holiday and playground, and into these neither care, nor the dun, nor despondency can follow the enfranchised man. Men of letters forerun science as the morning star the dawn. Nothing has been invented, nothing has been achieved, but has gleamed a bright-coloured Utopia in the eyes of one or the other of these men. Several centuries before the Great Exhibition of 1851 rose in Hyde Park, a wondrous hall of glass stood, radiant in the sunlight, in the verse of Chaucer. The electric telegraph is not so swift as the flight of Puck. We have not yet realised the hippogriff of Ariosto. Just consider what a world this would be if ruled by the best thoughts of men of letters! Ignorance would die at once, war would cease, taxation would be lightened, not only every Frenchman, but every man in the world, would have his hen in the pot. May would not marry January. The race of lawyers and physicians would be extinct. Fancy a world, the affairs of which are directed by Goethe's wisdom and Goldsmith's heart! In such a case methinks the millennium were already come. Books are a finer world within the world. With books are connected all my desires and aspirations. When I go to my long sleep, on a book will my head be pillowed. I care for no other fashion of greatness. I'd as lief not be remembered at all as remembered in connexion with anything else. I would rather be Charles Lamb than Charles XII. I would rather be remembered by a song than by a victory. I would rather build a fine sonnet than have built St. Paul's. I would rather be the discoverer of a new image than the discoverer of a new planet. Fine phrases I value more than bank-notes. I have ear for no other harmony than the harmony of words. To be occasionally quoted is the only fame I care for.

But what of the literary life? How fares it with the men whose days and nights are devoted to the writing of books? We know the famous men of letters, we give them the highest place in our regards; we crown them with laurels so thickly that we hide the furrows on their foreheads. Yet we must remember that there are men of letters who have been equally sanguine, equally ardent, who have pursued perfection equally unselfishly, but who have failed to make themselves famous. We know the ships that come with streaming pennons into the immortal ports; we know but little of the ships that have gone on fire on the way thither—that have gone down at sea. Even with successful men we cannot know precisely how matters have gone. We read the fine raptures of the poet, but we do not know into what kind of being he relapses when the inspiration is over, any more than, seeing and hearing the lark shrilling at the gate of heaven, we know with what effort it has climbed thither, or into what kind of nest it must descend. The lark is not always singing; no more is the poet. The lark is only interesting *while* singing, at other times it is but a plain brown bird. We may not be able to recognise the poet when he doffs his singing robes; he may then sink to the level of his admirers. We laugh at the fancies of the humorist, but he may have written his brilliant things in a dismal enough mood. The writer is not continually dwelling amongst the roses and lilies of life, he is not continually uttering generous sentiments, and saying fine things. On him, as on his brethren, the world presses with its prosaic needs. He has to make love and marry, and run the usual matrimonial risks. The income-tax collector visits him as well as the others. Around his head at Christmas-times drives a snowstorm of bills. He must keep the wolf from the door, and he has only his goose-quills to confront it with. And here it is, having to deal with alien powers, that his special temperament comes into play, and may work him evil. Wit is not worldly wisdom. A man gazing on the stars is proverbially at the mercy of the puddles on the road. A man may be able to disentangle intricate problems, be able to recall the past, and yet be cozened by an ordinary knave. The finest expression will not liquidate a butcher's account. If Apollo puts his name to a bill, he must meet it when it becomes due, or go into the Gazette. Armies are not always cheering on the heights which they have won; there are forced marches, occasional shortness of provisions, bivouacs on muddy plains, driving in of pickets, and the like, although these inglorious items are forgotten when we read the roll of victories inscribed on their banners. The books of the great writer are only portions of the great writer. His life acts on his writings; his writings react on his life. Apollo's

> Branch that might have grown full straight,

may have the worm of a vulgar misery gnawing at its roots. The heat of inspiration may be subtracted from the household fire; and those who sit by it may be colder in consequence. A man may put all his good things in his books, and leave none for his life, just as a man may expend his fortune on a splendid dress, and carry a pang of hunger beneath it.

There are few less exhilarating books than the biographies of men of letters, and of artists generally; and this arises from the pictures of comparative defeat which, in almost every instance, such books contain. In these books we see failure more or less—seldom clear, victorious effort. If the art is exquisite, the marble is flawed; if the marble is pure, there is a defect in art. There is always something lacking in the poem; there is always irremediable defect in the picture. In the biography we see persistent, passionate effort, and almost constant repulse. If, on the whole, victory is gained, one wing of the army has been thrown into confusion. In the life of a successful farmer, for instance, one feels nothing of this kind; his year flows on harmoniously, fortunately: through ploughing, seed-time, growth of grain, the yellowing of it beneath meek autumn suns and big autumn moons, the cutting of it down, riotous harvest-home, final sale, and large balance at the banker's. From the point of view of almost unvarying success the farmer's life becomes beautiful, poetic. Everything is an aid and help to him. Nature puts her shoulder to his wheel. He takes the winds, the clouds, the sunbeams, the rolling stars into partnership, and, asking no dividend, they let him retain the entire profits. As a rule the lives of men of letters do not flow on in the successful way. In their case there is always either defect in the soil or defect in the husbandry. Like the Old Guard at Waterloo, they are fighting bravely on a lost field. In literary biography there is always an element of tragedy, and the love we bear the dead is mingled with pity. Of course the life of a man of letters is more perilous than the life of a farmer; more perilous than almost any other kind of life which it is given a human being to conduct. It is more difficult to obtain the mastery over spiritual ways and means than over material ones, and he must command *both*. Properly to conduct his life he must not only take large crops off his fields, he must also leave in his fields the capacity of producing large crops. It is easy to drive in your chariot two horses of one breed; not so easy when the one is of terrestrial stock, the other of celestial; in every respect different—in color, temper, and pace.

At the outset of his career, the man of letters is confronted by the fact that he must live. The obtaining of a livelihood is preliminary to everything else. Poets and cobblers are placed on the same level so far. If the writer can barter MSS. for sufficient coin, he may proceed to develop himself; if he cannot so barter it, there is a speedy end of himself, and of his development also. Literature has become a profession; but it is in several respects different from the professions by which other human beings earn their bread. The man of letters, unlike the clergyman, the physician, or the lawyer, has to undergo no special preliminary training for his work, and while engaged in it, unlike the professional persons named, he has no accredited status. Of course, to earn any success, he must start with as much special knowledge, with as much dexterity in his craft, as your ordinary physician; but then he is not recognised till once he is successful. When a man takes a physician's degree, he has done something; when a man betakes himself to literary pursuits, he has done nothing—till once he is lucky enough to make his mark. There is no special preliminary training for men of letters, and, as a consequence, their ranks are recruited from the vagrant talent of the world. Men that break loose from the professions, who stray from the beaten tracks of life, take refuge in literature. In it are to be found doctors, lawyers, clergymen, and the motley nation of Bohemians. Any one possessed of a nimble brain, a quire of paper, a steel pen, and ink-bottle, can start business. Any one who chooses may enter the lists, and no questions are asked concerning his antecedents. The battle is won by sheer strength of brain. From all this it comes that the man of letters has usually a history of his own; his individuality is more pronounced than the individuality of other men; he has been knocked about by passion and circumstance. All his life he has had a dislike for iron rules and commonplace maxims. There is something of the gypsy in his nature. He is to some extent eccentric, and he indulges his eccentricity. And the misfortunes of men of letters—the vulgar and patent misfortunes, I mean—arise mainly from the want of harmony between their impulsiveness and volatility, and the staid unmercurial world with which they are brought into conflict. They are unconventional in a world of conventions; they are fanciful, and are constantly misunderstood in prosaic relations. They are wise enough in their books, for there they are sovereigns, and can shape everything to their own likings; out of their books, they are not unfrequently extremely foolish, for they exist then in the territory of an alien power, and are constantly knocking their heads against existing orders of things. Men of letters take prosaic men out of themselves; but they are weak where the prosaic men are strong. They have their own way in the world of ideas, prosaic men in the world of facts. From his practical errors the writer learns something, if not always humility and amendment. A memorial flower grows on every spot where he has come to grief; and the chasm he cannot over-leap he bridges with a rainbow.

FALSTAFF AND HIS CIRCLE[1]

By J. B. Priestley

The Falstaff of the above title is, of course, the famous fat knight of *Henry IV.*, parts 1 and 2, and has nothing to do with the impostor, the up-river bully, the provincial dupe, of the *Merry Wives of Windsor*. If there is any one who, at this late date, thinks the two are the same, who imagines that our Sir John, companion of Prince Hal, could be successfully gulled by wives of Windsor or any other place, then this essay is not for him: let him read elsewhere, particularly in the works of Maurice Morgann, Hazlitt, and Mr. A. C. Bradley. Our concern, then, is with the two parts of *Henry IV.* and, as a kind of melancholy epilogue, *Henry V.* With the exception of Hamlet, no character in literature has been more discussed than this Falstaff, who is, like Hamlet, a genius, fastening immediately upon the reader's imagination, living richly in his memory, and inviting comment and interpretation that varies with the personality and point of view of every new reader. So splendid is the progress of this great figure in the earlier part of the drama, when he bestrides all Cockaigne like a colossus, so strange and puzzling is his rejection by the new king, so melancholy his end, with a heart "fracted and corroborate," that he engages all our attention and interest, dwarfing everybody with whom he comes into contact. For this reason, the comic grotesques who form his circle and are his foils, Pistol, Bardolph, Hostess Quickly, Doll Tearsheet, Justice Shallow and his cousin, Silence, have hardly been noticed, although most of the comedy in the second part of *Henry IV.* is of

[1] Reprinted by permission of Dodd, Mead and Company, Inc. Copyright, 1929.

their making. But though we would rather bask in the warmth and light of this great sun of humour, the fantastic little planets that revolve about it deserve some attention. We will leave Sir John in peace for a while, nodding over his tankard, and creep away to the anteroom where his friends and followers are assembled.

I

Bardolph, attendant to Sir John and corporal in his service, is not witty in himself, but he is certainly the cause that wit is in other men. His face is his fortune, for at sight of it the comic fancy takes wing. His famous nose, that everlasting bonfire which Falstaff says has saved him a thousand marks in links and torches, is for ever igniting gunpowder trails of comic metaphor. Such a nose is not cheaply burnished, and Falstaff contends that the sack Bardolph has drunk would have bought lights as cheap at the dearest chandler's in Europe; but Bardolph's nose, that salamander consuming the fire of sack, has not been an unprofitable investment. This is proved by the fact that Bardolph has been with his master two and thirty years, after first being hired or "bought" in St. Paul's churchyard, where masterless servants, usually bad ones, were to be had at that time. That he has served his master very faithfully there can be no doubt: it is he who supplies us with one of the most striking tributes to Falstaff's ascendancy over his companions and to his power of winning affection, for after his master's death it is he who cries: "Would I were with him, wheresome'er he is, either in Heaven or in Hell!"—a genuine cry this, for ever thrown in the blank face of the universe by bereaved humanity. But his real value lies in his nose, warming to life innumerable jests. With such a face near at hand, Falstaff need never be at a loss—though it is only fair to say that there are never any signs that he is at any time at a loss, for his wit gushes out of a perennial spring. It is only right that a comic philosopher should be followed by such a gorgeous caricature of a nose. Bardolph is his admiral, bearing the lantern in the poop; he is the Knight of the Burning Lamp; Falstaff never sees his face but what he thinks upon hell-fire and Dives that lived in purple; and he tells the Hostess, when she says that Bardolph is poor and therefore cannot pay the knight's bill, to "look upon his face; what call you rich? let them coin his nose, let them coin his cheeks." Even the diminutive page finds matter for his newly fledged wit in Bardolph's face. Does he not tell the Prince that Bardolph called to him through a red lattice— "and I could discern no part of his face from the window: at last I spied his eyes; and methought he had made two holes in the alewife's new petticoat, and so peeped through." This is indeed to be, in Gadshill's phrase, "a purple-hued malt-worm." During their long association the number of jokes that Falstaff must have made at the expense of Bardolph's face must be beyond computation; the imagination boggles at the very thought; and we may say that Falstaff has indeed coined his man's nose and cheeks. What could be better, as an example of Falstaffian humour, than his offering Bardolph as security to Master Dombledon for two and twenty yards of satin for a short coat and slops? He would not be without Bardolph for the world, and neither would we. We are sorry he comes to such a bad end.

But if Bardolph is good, his superior officer, Ancient Pistol, is even better. His character is that of the common tavern bully of the period, a fellow who tries to make up for his want of courage and ability by his boldness of address, a mad moustachio'd, loud-voiced craven, whose scars are the marks of pots hurled in tavern brawls and of public beatings. This is a character that brags and swaggers his way throughout Elizabethan comedy, as much a formula as the roaring retired Indian Army major ("By gad, sir") in modern farce. But Pistol differs from the other fellows of his class in the fact that he has a mode of speech all his own. Indeed, he is actually one of those comic characters that hardly pretend to real existence at all and are obviously nothing but grotesque shadows, figures from a comic day-dream. Pistol's type was common enough, but the Ancient himself is not of this world. He is a walking parody of dramatic highfalutin. How many of his speeches are actual quotations from old plays and ballads we do not know, and probably never shall know, however the commentators may busy themselves tracking down his wild phrases, but it obviously does not matter; nearly everything he says sounds like a quotation from some bombastic drama; and all of it has a note of its own, the real Pistol ring. Most of the phrases he uses, strained and high-flown as they are, would be a trifle ridiculous even in their context, even though they express overwhelming emotion and refer to matters of great moment, the massacre of a family or the ruin of great empires, but brought in as they are by a ragged, drunken rascal to heighten a tavern quarrel or to silence a rustic, they are ludicrous in the extreme. So much can be said by way of explanation, but no more, for the fact is that it is the actual choice of phrases that matters, the individual flavour of the words, with which only our appreciation of the ridiculous can cope. The comic *idea* in Pistol is very slight and is amply covered by what has been said above; it is his actual speeches themselves, which we could not possibly invent for him, that make him so funny; and for this reason there are many admirable persons, lacking the ability to taste, as it were, the absurdity of a phrase, who cannot enjoy Pistol. Thus an intelligent foreigner, who knew his Shakespeare, would perceive that Pistol is a loud-mouthed, swaggering, cowardly bully, of a type familiar in the literature of the time, and leave it at that. He would miss the glorious absurdity, just as many insensitive or over-serious English readers do. For all his passion for quotations, Pistol really has a style of his own, particularly when roused and in Ercles' vein. We can recognise it at once. "Hold hook and line, say I"; "Have we not Hiren here?"; "Die men like dogs! give crowns like pins!"; "What! we have seen the seven stars"; "Shall we have incision? shall we imbrue?"; "Base is the slave that pays"; "Let gallows gape for dog; let man go free"; so many of his pithy and weighty phrases leap to the mind that we feel that we could easily compile a Pistol calendar. He is funny enough when he is driven out of the tavern, breathing bad blank verse, but he is even funnier when he bursts into Shallow's orchard with the great news. It is his ability to reach the tragic height on the smallest provocation that makes him so ludicrous. When he tells Falstaff that he is now one of the greatest men in the realm, and Silence, emboldened by his wine, calls attention to goodman Puff of Barson, some dim rural idol of his, what could be more ludicrous than Pistol's tremendous "Puff! Puff in thy teeth, most recreant coward base!" or his retort upon a further interruption, this time in song, by Silence?—

> Shall dunghill curs confront the Helicons?
> And shall good news be baffled?
> Then, Pistol, lay thy head in Furies' lap.

Nothing less than blank verse, and blank verse at its wildest, will satisfy Pistol in a moment of excitement. How he raves of "golden times, and happy news of price," of "Africa and golden joys"; and as he stands there under the apple trees raving, a whole school of drama is being parodied by this ragged grotesque. There is one common type of romantic literature that is summed up to perfection in the single question he addresses to Shallow: "Under which king, Besonian? speak or die." After the great collapse, Pistol marries Hostess Quickly (and we would give much to hear the phrases he used to assault that battered heart), goes to the French wars, there to steal and run away, and, like Bardolph, comes at last to a bad end. He is not a caricature of something in life, but of something in literature; his flesh is paper, and his blood ink. He has not been without his influence, for more than once when the tragic dramatist or the high-falutin writer of romances has lost his head, some echo of Pistol has reached us and there has flitted across the scene this grotesque shadow, this strutting parody, out of Shakespeare's comic fancy, and we have been back again in the Boar's Head Tavern or in Shallow's orchard, our tragedy or romance crumpled to nothing, dissolved once more in laughter.

In his somewhat ruthless dispersal and final hunting down of all Falstaff's old associates, so that no shadow should fall on the new and rather easy glory of his hero, Shakespeare was unnecessarily cruel to Dame Quickly, hostess of the Boar's Head Tavern, who is killed off "i' the spital." It may well be, however, that with Falstaff gone, and with him all the old days and roaring nights, she grew careless at the end. Nor can we deny, however friendly we may be towards the dame and her companion, Doll Tearsheet, that both these ladies were in a fair way to encounter that malady from which they succumbed. Nevertheless, the Hostess Quickly of the greater part of *Henry IV.*, though no better than she should be, is at least something better than a ruffianly old trull, and we cannot help feeling that she was deliberately smirched when the blow had to fall upon Falstaff and all his friends. She is the mother of a great line of comic Cockney landladies, charwomen, and the like, in her wandering but vehement speech, her absurd mispronunciations, her oscillation between a native delight in mirth and easy living and an equally innate desire for respectability and a good name in the parish. The type changes very little. Both she and Doll, and particularly Doll, who has forfeited all title to it, are lovers of respectability. Nothing could be truer to nature than Doll's shrill abuse of Pistol, the mere ensign, where his captain is present and willing. The whole scene, with the gross raillery of Falstaff and Doll (and Hostess Quickly's sentimental delight in it—"By my troth, this is the old fashion; you two never meet but you fall to some discord");

the pretended delicacy of the easy dames, with their mutual encouragement, two women among men; Doll's delight in Falstaff as a man of war; his lordly "What stuff wilt have a kirtle of"—the secretly delighted male; the whole scene of broad comedy through which there flickers, as a glance of firelight, a touch of natural unforced sentiment (Doll's "Come, I'll be friends with thee, Jack: thou art going to the wars; and whether I shall ever see thee again or no, there is nobody cares" is masterly), is a creation of sheer genius, and lifts Shakespeare as high above his fellows as does any of his great tragic scenes, for they tried in play after play to make such scenes come to life and yet did nothing like this, seemingly thrown out carelessly.

But there is not a moment when the Hostess is not alive, not a sentence of her speech that does not ring with truth to nature. How admirable is her oscillation between anger at Falstaff's debts and continued borrowings and lies and her pride in his patronage and delight in his company. He has her under a spell, and after abusing her heartily is able not only to escape his present debt to her, but to borrow money from her and then exclaim, with a wave of the hand, "Hostess, I forgive thee: go, make ready breakfast; love thy husband, look to thy servants, cherish thy guests; thou shalt find me tractable to any honest reason; thou see'st I am pacified." She has all her sex's delight in a plausible and ingratiating rascal, particularly when he bends, like Jove, from a superior social station. Nothing could better illustrate the characters of both persons concerned than her account of how Falstaff swore to marry her "sitting in my Dolphin-chamber, at the round table, by a sea-coal fire, upon Wednesday in Wheeson week, when the Prince broke thy head for liking his father to a singing-man of Windsor," and how, after goodwife Keech, the butcher's wife, had come in to borrow vinegar for a dish of prawns and Sir John had asked for some prawns, he had told her—delicious flattery—not to be so familiar with such poor people, and had ended by borrowing thirty shillings. One might almost imagine that the dame worked herself up into these rages, excusable as they are, merely in order that Falstaff might cajole her out of them again, as he always does. When she says that she will have to pawn her plate and the tapestry of her dining-chambers to provide him with more money, it is with characteristic impudence that he consoles her by saying that there is nothing like plain glassware and cheap water-colour hangings. And when the poor soul hesitates, the astute old sponger immediately stands upon his dignity and waves the whole matter aside, at which she capitulates and would pawn her very gown that he might have the money. But the "poor soul" slipped into the last sentence without permission and has no right to be there, for though she was scandalously plucked, she received as much as she gave; she had the company of the famous Sir John Falstaff, and though it is an excellent thing to have one's bills paid, to keep one's plate and tapestries from the pawnshop, to be accounted respectable and stand well with Master Tisick, the deputy, and Master Dumb, the minister, it is even better to have the company, in his hours of glorious ease, of Sir John Falstaff. That this is not merely our opinion, born of hero-worship and a safe distance that keeps plate and tapestry intact, but her opinion too, is proved by her own testimony: "Well, fare thee well: I have known thee these twenty-nine years, come peascod time; but an honester and truer-hearted man, —well, fare thee well." Falstaff is neither honest nor true-hearted, as she has known to her cost, but he has her admiration and affection, and so she uses the words of praise that come most easily to her tongue. It is she, of course, who rings down the curtain upon this companion of princes, this erstwhile emperor of Cockaigne, in a speech that is famous, and well deserves to be, for it has all the tragi-comedy of this life blended together, with exquisite art, in its seemingly natural artless progress: "'A made a fine end, and went away, an it had been any christom child: 'a parted even just between twelve and one, even at the turning o' the tide: for after I saw him fumble with the sheets, and play with flowers, and smile upon his fingers' ends, I knew there was but one way; for his nose was as sharp as a pen, and 'a babbled of green fields."

All these figures about Falstaff, comic as they are in themselves, chiefly serve as foils to him; they are the grotesque landscape lit up by the summer lightning of his wit and humour. Not one is a better foil than Justice Shallow. Except in years, he is everything that Falstaff is not. When they made Sir John, the gods dipped their hands deep in the stuff of creation, so that he overflows with everything that a man could have, short of virtue; he is a liberal helping of humanity; immense in body, "larding the lean earth" as he goes his way upon it; brimmed with energy, in spite of his years and bulk; crammed with experience and master of almost every occasion that comes his way; overflowing with wit and humour; bursting with good spirits and laughter; he is an alderman's feast of a man. Shallow, his contemporary, is the shadow of a lenten breakfast, who, even in his youth, was "like a man made after supper of a cheese-paring," a forked radish, with a head fantastically carved upon it with a knife, and now that his wisp of a carcase and his wisp of a mind have entered into their winter, there is hardly anything left of him but a few bones, a mouthful of silly phrases, and an idea or two, kept together only by his notion of his own importance. He has little to say, being as feeble in mind as in body, but being the greatest man in the district, and feeling that he ought to be saying something all the time, he repeats himself over and over again, without paying much attention to the person to whom he is talking, in a manner peculiar to half-witted self-important old men. This fussy empty mode of speech has never been caught so well as it is in Shallow: "Come on, come on, come on, sir; give me your hand, sir; give me your hand, sir; an early stirrer, by the Rood." These accents may be overheard any day in the smoking room of almost any club. After hearing Shallow talk, Falstaff, the clear-sighted old rascal, exclaims: "Lord, Lord, how subject we old men are to this vice of lying." That wild youth of his, to which Shallow so often refers, to the admiration of Silence, is entirely imaginary; Falstaff remembers him and tells us how " 'a came ever in the rearward of the fashion; and sung those tunes to the overscutch'd huswives that he heard the carmen whistle, and sware they were his Fancies or his Good-nights," and you could have thrust him and all his apparel into an eel-skin, the case of a treble hautboy was a mansion to him. We can see him, pinched and rural and for ever behind the fashion, palely trembling on the edge of debauchery. And now fifty years have ripened these shadowy adventures into a kind of reality, and as he drags his old bones along by the side of Falstaff's heaving mountain of flesh, and hears his "We have heard the chimes at midnight, Master Shallow," he warms into reminiscence, and spectral wine and women and cudgel-play and all the wild nights of youth come to life. And Master Silence, for the thousandth time, hears the tale again (he knows it well—"That's fifty-five years ago," he prompts), and fixes his bucolic gaze, in which awe, envy, fear, and admiration are mingled, upon this rollicking head of the family. Even that unknown idol, goodman Puff of Barson, probably could not show such a past.

Silence is one of those characters (Slender and Sir Andrew Aguecheek are two others) that only Shakespeare could bring on the stage and leave us convinced of their reality. As Hazlitt has remarked: "In point of understanding and attainments, Shallow sinks low enough; and yet his cousin Silence is a foil to him; he is the shadow of a shade, glimmers on the very edge of downright imbecility, and totters on the brink of nothing." Revolving round the great roaring sun of Falstaff, we discover, in the far outer spaces, this dim fantastic planet of a Shallow, and yet this poor cinder in the darkness has its satellite, Silence, its faint little moon.

So slight is Silence's demand upon life that he can bask even in the meagre bleak sunshine of his cousin, the Justice, and hear things even in this orchard that add colour to his dreams. Nay, when there has been an unusually liberal allowance of sack at supper, in honour of the great Sir John's presence, he can not only sit in the garden with the rest but can break into song without encouragement, lifting his faint voice like some roistering sparrow, some care-free sprawling field-mouse. Should Falstaff, with ironic appraisement, declare that he had not thought Master Silence had been a man of such mettle, he can reply "Who, I? I have been merry twice and once ere now," and thus flash a light upon his Sahara of an existence through which has trickled a tiny wasted brook of sack and song. Poor Silence!—we leave him, drowned by the last bumper, stunned by the fiery rhetoric of Pistol, asleep under the apple trees. He is not carried to the triumph in London, and so, at least, is saved a night in the Fleet. Shallow kept that adventure to himself, and perhaps it was worth all the thousand pounds he lost to Sir John when he returned to amaze Cousin Silence again over the pippins and caraways in Glostershire.

Into these grotesques, these dim rural shades, Shakespeare has breathed the life that he could spare for all his creatures. No one but he could have written that dialogue between Shallow and Silence when we first meet them, that dialogue which Hazlitt and others have so rightly singled out for praise, a passage of talk so ludicrous and yet so commonplace, so characteristic of the speakers and yet so touched with universality. The fussy, vain, trivial, prattling Justice, determined to talk and yet not able to keep to one point for two sentences together, never forgetting, whatever he is saying, his own importance, the figure he cuts in the eyes of his companion; and Silence, so proud of being where he is and of talking so familiarly to his great relative, so foolish and simple; and both of them, in their vanity and simplicity, so very human that their silly talk lights up, for a moment, the whole strange business of this life:

SHALLOW. Certain, 'tis certain; very sure, very sure: death, as the Psalmist saith, is certain to all; all shall die. How a good yoke of bullocks at Stamford fair?

SILENCE. Truly, cousin, I was not there.

SHALLOW. Death is certain. Is old Double of your town living yet?

SILENCE. Dead, sir.

SHALLOW. Jesu, Jesu, dead!—'a drew a good bow; and dead!—'a shot a fine shoot: John o' Gaunt loved him well, and betted much money on his head. Dead!—'a would have clapped i' the clout at twelve score; and carried you a forehand shaft a fourteen and fourteen and a half, that it would have done a man's heart good to see. How a score of ewes now?

SILENCE. Thereafter as they be: a score of good ewes may be worth ten pounds.

SHALLOW. And is old Double dead?

Let us leave the two old men, nodding and talking, creasing their wintry faces in the sunshine. They have said everything, foolish as they are. Even old Double, who shot a fine shoot and was loved by John o' Gaunt, is dead, and a score of good ewes may be worth ten pounds, and death is certain. This is the world's news, and this is the world's history, and all the philosophers have told us little more.

MR. CREEVEY [1]

By LYTTON STRACHEY

CLIO is one of the most glorious of the Muses; but, as every one knows, she (like her sister Melpomene) suffers from a sad defect: she is apt to be pompous. With her buskins, her robes, and her airs of importance she is at times, indeed, almost intolerable. But fortunately the Fates have provided a corrective. They have decreed that in her stately advances she should be accompanied by certain apish, impish creatures, who run round her tittering, pulling long noses, threatening to trip the good lady up, and even sometimes whisking to one side the corner of her drapery, and revealing her undergarment in a most indecorous manner. They are the diarists and letter-writers, the gossips and journalists of the past, the Pepyses and Horace Walpoles and Saint-Simons, whose function it is to reveal to us the littleness underlying great events and to remind us that history itself was once real life. Among them is Mr. Creevey. The Fates decided that Mr. Creevey should accompany Clio, with appropriate gestures, during that part of her progress which is measured by the thirty years preceding the accession of Victoria; and the little wretch did his job very well.

It might almost be said that Thomas Creevey was "born about three of the clock in the afternoon, with a white head and something of a round belly." At any rate, we know nothing of his youth, save that he was educated at Cambridge, and he presents himself to us in the early years of the nineteenth century as a middle-aged man, with a character and a habit of mind already fixed and an established position in the world. In 1803 we find him what he was to be for the rest of his life—

[1] From *Books and Characters* by Lytton Strachey, copyright, 1922, by Harcourt, Brace and Company, Inc.

a member of Parliament, a familiar figure in high society, an insatiable gossip with a rattling tongue. That he should have reached and held the place he did is a proof of his talents, for he was a very poor man; for the greater part of his life his income was less than £200 a year. But those were the days of patrons and jobs, pocket-boroughs and sinecures; they were the days, too, of vigorous, bold living, torrential talk, and splendid hospitality; and it was only natural that Mr. Creevey, penniless and immensely entertaining, should have been put into Parliament by a Duke, and welcomed in every great Whig House in the country with open arms. It was also only natural that, spending his whole political life as an advanced Whig, bent upon the destruction of abuses, he should have begun that life as a member for a pocket-borough and ended it as the holder of a sinecure. For a time his poverty was relieved by his marriage with a widow who had means of her own; but Mrs. Creevey died, her money went to her daughters by her previous husband, and Mr. Creevey reverted to a possessionless existence—without a house, without servants, without property of any sort—wandering from country mansion to country mansion, from dinner-party to dinner-party, until at last in his old age, on the triumph of the Whigs, he was rewarded with a pleasant little post which brought him in about £600 a year. Apart from these small ups and downs of fortune, Mr. Creevey's life was static—static spiritually, that is to say; for physically he was always on the move. His adventures were those of an observer, not of an actor; but he was an observer so very near the centre of things that he was by no means dispassionate; the rush of great events would whirl him round into the vortex, like a leaf in an eddy of wind; he would rave, he would gesticulate, with the fury of a complete partisan; and then, when the wind dropped, he would be found, like the leaf, very much where he was before. Luckily, too, he was not merely an agitated observer, but an observer who delighted in passing on his agitations, first with his tongue, and then—for so the Fates had decided—with his pen. He wrote easily, spicily, and persistently; he had a favourite step-daughter, with whom he corresponded for years; and so it happens that we have preserved to us, side by side with the majestic march of Clio (who, of course, paid not the slightest attention to him), Mr. Creevey's exhilarating *pas de chat.*

Certainly he was not over-given to the praise of famous men. There are no great names in his vocabulary—only nick-names: George III. is "Old Nobs," the Regent "Prinney," Wellington "the Beau," Lord John Russell "Pie and Thimble," Brougham, with whom he was on very friendly terms, is sometimes "Bruffam," sometimes "Beelzebub," and sometimes "Old Wickedshifts;" and Lord Durham, who once remarked that one could "jog along on £40,000 a year," is "King Jog." The latter was one of the great Whig potentates, and it was characteristic of Creevey that his scurrility should have been poured out with a special gusto over his own leaders. The Tories were villains of course—Canning was all perfidy and "infinite meanness," Huskisson a mass of "intellectual con-fusion and mental dirt," Castlereagh. . . . But all that was obvious and hardly worth mentioning; what was really too exacerbating to be borne was the folly and vileness of the Whigs. "King Jog," the "Bogey," "Mother Cole," and the rest of them—they were either knaves or imbeciles. Lord Grey, besides passing the Reform Bill, presented Mr. Creevey with the Treasurership of the Ordinance, and in fact was al-together a most worthy man.

Another exception was the Duke of Wellington, whom, somehow or other, it was impossible not to admire. Creevey, throughout his life, had a trick of being "in at the death" of every important occasion; in the House, at Brooks's, at the Pavillion, he invariably propped up at the critical moment; and so one is not surprised to find him at Brussels during Water-loo. More than that, he was the first English civilian to see the Duke after the battle, and his report of the conversation is admirable; one can almost hear the "It has been a damned serious business. Blücher and I have lost 30,000 men. It has been a damned nice thing—the nearest run thing you ever saw in your life," and the "By God! I don't think it would have done if I had not been there." On this occasion the Beau spoke, as was fitting, "with the greatest gravity all the time, and without the least approach to anything like triumph or joy." But at other times he was jocular, especially when "Prinney" was the subject. "By God! you never saw such a figure in your life as he is. Then he speaks and swears so like old Falstaff, that damn me if I was not ashamed to walk into the room with him."

When, a few years later, the trial of Queen Caroline came on, it was inevitable that Creevey should be there. He had an excellent seat in the front row, and his descriptions of "Mrs. P.," as he preferred to call her Majesty, are characteristic:

Two folding doors within a few feet of me were suddenly thrown open, and in entered her Majesty. To describe to you her appearance and manner is far beyond my powers. I had been taught to believe she was as much improved in looks as in dignity of manners; it is therefore with much pain I am obliged to observe that the nearest resemblance I can recollect to this much injured Princess is a toy which you used to call Fanny Royds (a Dutch doll). There is another toy of a rabbit or a cat, whose tail you squeeze under its body, and then out it jumps in half a minute off the ground into the air. The first of these toys you must suppose to represent the person of the Queen; the latter the manner by which she popped all at once into the House, made a *duck* at the throne, another to the Peers, and a concluding jump into the chair which was placed for her. Her dress was black figured gauze, with a good deal trimming, lace, &c., her sleeves white, and perfectly episcopal; a handsome white veil, so thick as to make it very difficult to me, who was as near to her as anyone, to see her face; such a back for variety and in equality of ground as you never beheld; with a few straggling ringlets on her neck, which I flatter myself from their appearance were not her Majesty's own property.

Mr. Creevey, it is obvious, was not the man to be abashed by the presence of Royality.

But such public episodes were necessarily rare, and the main stream of life flowed rapidly, gaily, and unobtrusively through the fat pastures of high society. Everywhere and always he enjoyed himself extremely, but his spirits and his happiness were at their highest during his long summer sojourns at those splendid country houses whose hospitality he chronicles with indefatigable *verve*. "This house," he says at Raby, "is itself *by far* the most magnificent and unique in several ways that I have ever seen. . . . As long as I have heard anything, I have heard of being driven into the hall of this house in one's carriage, and being set down by the fire. You can have no idea of the magnificent perfection with which this is accomplished." At Knowsley "the new dining room is opened; it is 53 feet by 37, and such a height that it destroys the effect of all the other apartments. . . . There are two fireplaces; and the day we dined there, there were 36 wax candles over the table, 14 on it, and ten great lamps on tall pedestals about the room." At Thorp Perrow "all the living rooms are on the ground floor, one a very handsome one about 50 feet long, with a great bow furnished with rose-coloured satin, and the whole furniture of which cost £4,000." At Goodwood the rooms were done up in "brightest yellow satin," and at Holkham the walls were covered with Genoa velvet, and there was gilding worth a fortune on "the roofs of all the rooms and the doors." The fare was as sumptuous as the furniture. Life passes amid a succession of juicy chops, gigantic sirloins, plump fowls, pheasants stuffed with pâté de foie gras, gorgeous Madeiras, ancient Ports. Wine had a double advantage: it made you drunk; it also made you sober it was its own cure. On one occasion, when Sheridan, after days of riotous living, showed signs of exhaustion, Mr. and Mrs. Creevey pressed upon him "five or six glasses of light French wine" with excellent effect. Then, at midnight, when the talk began to flag and the spirits grew a little weary, what could be more rejuvenating than to ring the bell for a broiled bone? And one never rang in vain—except, to be sure, at King Jog's. There, while the host was gozzling, the guests starved. This was too much for Mr. Creevey, who, finding he could get nothing for breakfast, while King Jog was "eating his own fish as comfortably as could be," fairly lost his temper.

> My blood beginning to boil, I said: "Lambton, I wish you could tell me what quarter I am to apply to for some fish." To which he replied in the most impertinent manner: "The servant, I suppose." I turned to Mills and said pretty loud: "Now, if it was not for the fuss and jaw of the thing, I would leave the room and the house this instant"; and dwelt on the damned outrage. Mills said: "He hears every word you say": to which I said: "I hope he does." It was a regular scene.

A few days later, however, Mr. Creevey was consoled by finding himself in a very different establishment, where "everything is of a piece—excellent and plentiful dinners, a fat service of plate, a fat butler, a table with a barrel of oysters and a hot pheasant, &c., wheeled into the drawingroom every night at half-past ten."

It is difficult to remember that this was the England of the Six Acts, of Peterloo, and of the Industrial Revolution. Mr. Creevey, indeed, could hardly be expected to remember it, for he was utterly unconscious of the existence—of the possibility—of any mode of living other than his own. For him, dining-rooms 50 feet long, bottles of Madeira, broiled bones, and the brightest yellow satin were as necessary and obvious a part of the constitution of the universe as the light of the sun and the law of gravity. Only once in his life was he seriously ruffled; only once did a public question present itself to him as something alarming, something portentous, something more than a personal affair. The occasion is significant. On March 16, 1825, he writes:

I have come to the conclusion that our Ferguson is *insane.* He quite foamed at the mouth with rage in our Railway Committee in support of this infernal nuisance—the loco-motive Monster, carrying *eighty tons* of goods, and navigated by a tail of smoke and sulphur, coming thro' every man's grounds between Manchester and Liverpool.

His perturbation grew. He attended the committee assiduously, but in spite of his efforts it seemed that the railway Bill would pass. The loco-motive was more than a joke. He sat every day from 12 to 4; he led the opposition with long speeches. "This railway," he exclaims on May 31, "is the devil's own." Next day, he is in triumph: he had killed the Monster.

Well—this devil of a railway is strangled at last. . . . To-day we had a clear majority in committee in our favour, and the promotors of the Bill withdrew it, and took their leave of us.

With a sigh of relief he whisked off to Ascot, for the festivities of which he was delighted to note that "Prinney" had prepared "by having 12 oz. of blood taken from him by cupping."

Old age hardly troubled Mr. Creevey. He grew a trifle deaf, and he discovered that it was possible to wear woollen stockings under his silk ones; but his activity, his high spirits, his popularity, only seemed to increase. At the end of a party ladies would crowd around him. "Oh, Mr. Creevey, how agreeable you have been!" "Oh, thank you, Mr. Creevey! how useful you have been!" "Dear Mr. Creevey, I laughed out loud last night in bed at one of your stories." One would like to add (rather late in the day, perhaps) one's own praises. One feels almost affectionate; a certain sincerity, a certain immediacy in his response to stimuli, are endearing qualities; one quite understands that it was natural, on the pretext of changing house, to send him a dozen of wine. Above all, one wants him to go on. Why should he stop? Why should he not continue indefinitely telling us about "Old Salisbury" and "Old Madagascar"? But it could not be.

> Le temps s'en va, le temps s'en va, Madame;
> Las! Le temps non, mais nous, nous, en allons.

It was fitting that, after fulfilling his seventy years, he should catch a glimpse of "little Vic" as Queen of England, laughing, eating, and showing her gums too much at the Pavillion. But that was enough: the piece was over; the curtain had gone down; and on the new stage that was preparing for very different characters, and with a very different style of decoration, there would be no place for Mr. Creevey.

> Dreams, books, are each a world; and books, we know,
> Are a substantial world, both pure and good.
> Round these, with tendrils strong as flesh and blood,
> Our pastime and our happiness will grow.
>
> WILLIAM WORDSWORTH—*Personal Talk.*

BOOKS[1]

SPEECH DELIVERED AT THE DINNER OF THE ENGLISH ASSOCIATION, 28TH OCTOBER 1927

By STANLEY BALDWIN

MY FIRST duty to-night, as President of this Association, is to apologise to it—though it failed in an apology to me—for not having written for it the customary address of the President. I don't think that any Association ought to ask the Prime Minister to write any address. I am quite clear that no Prime Minister ought to accept the invitation. I did it, and I have failed you. I do not think I need waste any time in explaining to you the impossibility in these days of anyone holding my office being able to give the time that is necessary to write such an address as would be worthy of presentation before such a body. I had hoped to have attempted it this summer when I returned from Canada after nearly two years' work with no holiday—for I cannot count the short time I was away from London last year as a holiday. I was too tired to sit down to do the necessary thinking for such a piece of work. It would have been quite easy to have produced something; I felt that was not treating you with the respect that was due to you from your President, and I must content myself, having made my apology, by offering such observations to-night as occur to me.

It is no easy task to stand up before a gathering of this kind, so representative and knowing so much more than I do, but there is one bond between us. We are all lovers of our own tongue and our own literature, or we should not

[1] Reprinted from *Our Inheritance* by permission of the author and of the publishers, Hodder and Stoughton.

be here. However humble the lover may be, surely that bond is sufficient to bind you to him who speaks to you at the moment, and to unite us in that common love.

Now it struck me in the presence of so many who are much younger than I, that I might make an apology for us older people, like Lord Ernle and myself, and many another, and ask you to remember that, after all, we have not been able to share many of the advantages which have fallen to you. If we throw our minds back to our childhood—that most impressionable time—and we ask ourselves what it was then that moved us and how we first began to forge those links that have gone on being strengthened throughout our lives, you must remember that we had not the advantage of reading one single word of any author who is alive to-day.

I can look back through the ages to a small boy. I can see him far away in Worcestershire, reading all day in that most comfortable attitude, lying on his stomach on the hearthrug in front of the fire. He was brought up with none of our modern conveniences, and none of what, on the *lucus a non lucendo* principle, we call labour-saving appliances. I merely mention that in passing, because as Prime Minister I recognise there is not a single labour-saving appliance that has not doubled, trebled and quadrupled the work of a public man.

Now when I look back on those far distant years I think I can recognise my own good fortune, which may have been shared by many here. I was left to myself to find my own provender in the library. If you do that with a child, he will always take the nourishment that is suitable to him, just as when you look over a meadow over which cattle are grazed you will find certain grasses are taken and certain are rejected. You may depend on it that the cow knows what is suitable to her own health. It is the same with the child. You may leave the child with perfect safety in any library you like, and if that child has a natural turn for books he will take the right sustenance and thrive on it.

The first sustenance I had was Scott. I was left alone in the country sometimes for long periods with an aunt who was fond of being read aloud to; and I read aloud to her, by the time I was nine years of age, the whole of *Guy Mannering, Ivanhoe, Red Gauntlet, Rob Roy, The Pirate,* and *Old Mortality*. I owed to Scott my first introduction to poetry. I was not a great reader of poetry as a small boy. That came later; but I lived for a time in those early days on "The Lay" and on "Marmion," and I can see myself now striding along the country lanes and reciting long passages, and I remember a line that seemed so to strike my youthful imagination that I used to repeat it over and over again, and it was "William of Deloraine, good at need." It is an extraordinary thing that, to any child that has been brought up amongst books for years, the people you live with and know in books are far more real than the phantasmagoria of the world and, as life goes on, the words, the phrases, the sentences, come back to you in the most unexpected places and illuminate the darkest portions of your path.

My first introduction to history was *The Tales of a Grandfather*, and that only confirmed me in what I said in a speech some time ago, that I am convinced that the best and most readable history is that written with the strongest bias. Mark you, there is nothing old-fashioned in that.

My mother used to try to introduce me to poetry by reading to me pieces, which I wrote down at her dictation. Her selection was admirable, but she put me for years against Wordsworth because there came a line which my youthful critical mind felt was not poetry. It was this—and I submit it as a devout disciple of that great man—"The street that from Oxford hath borrowed its name." I remember now the look of wonder I turned upon her as she read that out and expected me to put it down on paper as poetry. She was more successful in introducing me to Blake, and I do not think I ever go to the Zoo and look at the tiger but those words, which I see you all know, come back to me.

Well now, besides Scott there was an Englishman—a common or garden Englishman—that I loved more than most, and that was Bunyan. I have heard people say *The Pilgrim's Progress* is rather boring, because of its theological discussions, but there I say again that a child may be trusted to know everything that is good for it. I knew every part of *The Pilgrim's Progress* that I thought was good for me, and I never touched the theological discussions. The book itself I knew by heart. That was my first introduction to the work that the unlettered Englishman can do. It is a subject on which I have often felt that an interesting paper could be written by some person capable of doing it. Whence comes that gift of writing our language perfectly on the part of a man who has had no education, and why is it that so often education takes from him that gift of simple expression? You may see that gift throughout the story of Abraham Lincoln, though of course there must be many instances which go to the other extreme. Another book I browsed in a great deal was Malory's *Morte d'Arthur*. I have a copy I remember taking with me when nine years old on a voyage to Madeira, and I am always affected on seeing one of the dirtiest little thumb marks on that book that I have ever seen on any book. I keep that privately in my library. No thumb marks should be allowed to get loose in these days. I think perhaps all unconsciously there one laid the foundations of a love for the wonderful English that was written at that time, which perhaps was enhanced by sundry excursions into Berners's Froissart. I cannot say that I read much of him as a child, but there was a glorious volume which belonged to William Morris and was given to my mother as a girl of twelve. It was a volume of illuminations from Froissart, and from them I learned a great deal not only of mediæval history, but of the appearance of the mediæval world. Being familiar with those pictures I remember with what pleasure I read some observations of Mr. Belloc many years ago, in a delightful book he wrote on the City of Paris; he was pointing out that one of the things that would surprise us most, if we could drop back into the Middle Ages, would be to see the newness of all the buildings, all the cathedrals and castles that are so old and grey, and many in ruins, bright and shining white. These Froissart pictures showed the buildings of many a castle and church with the masons at work on them; and towns, around which the armies sat in siege, were not then old and grey, like the castles we see, but white and shining—and so different from anything I have noticed being built!

Then, to come to another field, I remember *Grimm's Fairy Tales,* which I still think the finest collection ever made. I knew them every one, and my world was peopled with witches, maidens, and dwarfs from them. I don't know whether it was the sure instincts of childhood, but I always felt they were the real thing, and I think what the grown-ups used to say is true, that Hans Anderson winked at the grown-ups over the heads of the children. Grimm seemed to me to be not only something that had happened, but something that might easily be happening at that moment—at any moment—in the world—even in Worcestershire. Then I think I learnt a good deal from a book I was very fond of reading when I went down to dessert with my parents at dinner—I was an only child, and I might have been indulged in that—I used to pull down the two volumes of Hone's *Every Day Book*. I don't suppose anyone has ever looked at that? I like to hear those cries of "yes." My word, I am really beginning to enjoy myself! I was merely going to observe that anyone who is not familiar with those works has never heard of the Storm at Bungay, or realised what happened in the interview between St. Dunstan and the Devil.

There are some people who can claim that, by the time they were ten, they had read the whole of Shakespeare. I hadn't. I approached Shakespeare in a very simple manner through Lamb's *Tales* and Lamb's *Tales* I used to read with immense enjoyment. Shakespeare I only got in fragments, but I think of all the debts we owe to the Lambs there is none greater than that for their paving the way for children to get into the heart of Shakespeare.

My first touch with the classics was through Kingsley's *Heroes,* a book I think I have not seen since I was a boy. My only recollection is that it was extraordinarily good. By the way, I am only giving my own views, and do not commit the Government in any way.

I remember someone lending me a book called *Tanglewood Tales.* I don't know how or why, but I felt Kingsley had the stuff in him, and that Hawthorne hadn't. That is just the thought of a child. Now, my apprenticeship to Dickens—I reverence Dickens as in some ways the greatest genius this country ever produced—my introduction to Dickens was slow. Of *Pickwick* one heard a good deal being read aloud by the grownups, and there were certain bits one used to read and, even in those days, appreciate fully. When I used to ride a little pony I appreciated to the full, "'What makes him go sideways?' said Mr. Snodgras in the bin, to Mr. Winkle in the saddle," and every year I live I ask that question with more wonder. That again would bear a disgression of some minutes. The first book of his, oddly enough, which I read in those early days—although that was not till I got to a private school—was *The Tale of Two Cities,* which thrilled me to the marrow. But as I am only dwelling on the recollections of a very early date my acquaintance with Dickens must stop there; and I turn from him to another book of a very different kind, a book bound in very soft green leather, bearing for its frontispiece the immortal work of Dürer "Death and the Knight," and that book was *Sintram,* which I must say caught hold of my youthful imagination and held it for a long time. And from *Sintram* I think we might well fly to the Antipodes to a man who gave immense joy to my generation, and that was Captain Marryat. I think by the time I was nine I knew *Peter Simple* and *Midshipman Easy* by heart. I was talking a minute ago to Lord Ernle about children's books. Of course, nothing varies more from generation to generation, and I think in the early and middle seventies, although we had the great joy of being introduced to *Alice,* who was then very young, plus Tenniel, we had for the most part books one's parents had known—*Sandford and Merton,* with the inevitable Mr. Barlow; *Holiday House, Harry and Lucy, Rosamund, Rosamund and Her Terrible Charge.* I often think Cabinet Ministers are very much like Rosamund. There was another great work which came out in my childhood besides *Alice,* and I think in some ways it was the best book that came from across the Atlantic for young people. It struck a new note. It was natural and there was nothing forced in it, as always seemed to me was the case with the later works of the great man who wrote it, and that was *Tom Sawyer. Huckleberry Finn* followed a little later. I read it during one of my regular visits to London with a cousin of mine, and we enjoyed it enormously. It opened up a new world to us—a world we should very much like to have joined. Then I remember dabbling in a very different kind of book, introducing me to a subject I have always been interested in, and this was comprised in two admirable volumes by Miss Byrne and Miss Jackson on Shropshire folklore and Shropshire words; and much of the folklore was folklore which was still alive to some extent in my own neighbourhood. It is dead now, but it was alive then—I came in just at the end of it—and I don't think anyone ought to forget the books one got after consultation with one's nurse and the cook. Then I come to one or two books Lord Ernle was fond of. I was reminded of these by an article he wrote. From the cook and my nurse I heard of *The Children of the Abbey* and *The Romance of the Forest,* but when I saw that Lord Ernle had put his *imprimatur* on them as books of the times, I felt I had not lived in vain. Then there were two books of poetry. I have forgotten whom they were by. One was about a young lady who went for a walk in Cavendish Square—a name I have the greatest difficulty in pronouncing. In the other I remember one verse:

The monkey's cheek is very bald;
The goat is fond of play;
The dog will come when he is called;
The cat will run away.

I know these lines were written by a woman, but I cannot remember the name, and if anyone can remember it I shall be very grateful for it before the evening is over. I have never known more literal and graphic truth than is contained in that stanza. I should just like to mention one more book a little bit outside that period, but which I got when I was about thirteen, because it was a book, I suppose, that no one ever reads now. I don't know whether it was purely a matter of temperament or partly a matter of the period that caused it to impress itself on my young mind so much, but the book was *John Inglesant.* I think whatever fault you may find in the writing of that book—and I admit critics may find many faults—yet there are two passages in it which will live. There is about half a page describing the appearance of the ghost of Strafford to King Charles, which, I think, is about as fine as anything in our language, and the whole of the passage of the ride down to Minton of John and his brother, Eustace, when Eustace is murdered by the Italian in the end. There is an atmosphere there which is unmistakable, and you have that kind of atmosphere in *The Beleaguered City,* in Jonas Chuzzlewit's drive to Salisbury, in—to take a very different type of book—*Uncle Silas,* and in many other books. In *John Inglesant* you have it in concentrated essence, and I seldom go to bed in my room at Chequers, where there is a Tudor fireplace with the fire flickering on the ceiling, without seeing Eustace Inglesant's body lying on the hearthrug with the knife of the Italian in him. Now all these things are woven into one's very being. There are yet two more things I want to put before you which I think must have played their part in the lives of many children who were brought up at that time, and who have preserved into their mature years a great love of their own tongue and a desire, so far as they can, to use that tongue in a worthy manner. Fifty years ago all children went to church, and they often went reluctantly, but I am convinced, looking back, that the hearing—sometimes almost unconsciously—of the superb rhythm of the English Prayer Book Sunday after Sunday, and the language of the English Bible leaves its mark on you for life. Though you may be all unable to speak with these tongues, yet they do make you immune from rubbish in a way that nothing else does, and they enable you naturally and automatically to sort out the best from the second best and the third best; and the other great advantage to us who lived in the country in those days was that we were brought up among the country people, and we moved in and out on terms of perfect equality among the old country people of England. No one who has not done that can realize what the power of expression and speech is amongst those people, whom—and now I am going to use a beastly word—the *intelligentsia* would call illiterate. If we in our part of the world, the lineal descendants of Shakespeare, could have spoken our tongue to him, he would have understood it, and he would have heard more power of concentrated discussion among our folk than, I think, is represented in ninety-five per cent of the books written by educated and intellectual people. I do not think that anything in my education, using the word in its widest sense, has stood me in better stead in after life than that close heart-to-heart knowledge that I had of our own common people. And perhaps one or two more words and I have finished. One got much, I think, from the talk of the grown-ups when one was fortunate enough to live with grown-ups who lived with books. Through that talk one was introduced, without knowing it, to all the best people in the best sense of the word. It seemed perfectly natural to look on as friends and to take on the friends of one's parents, and in that way one came on naturally and gradually into "Bozzie" and into Lamb, of whom my mother and her sisters never spoke unless as "Dear Lamb" with a sort of wistful look as of a friend they had buried only four or five years ago. I did not then associate the name of *Elia* on the back of a book with a book of Lamb. I took him on as a friend of my mother's, and it was the same with Thackeray, Trollope, Jane Austen—God bless her! And it was the same with Borrow, whom then I could not read, but in whose names I revelled—the name of Petulengro—what a name! We had the real Romanies on the common near us, and I remember going with John Kipling into a Romanies' camp when he was anxious to find out whether his Hindustani would carry him far with the Romany. And there was another friend that I gained in this way, whom my dear friend Mackail mentions in *Morris' Life,* where he refers to Jorrocks. I came to him later, but again, like Dickens, I am always meeting his friends. It is always a pleasure to me to meet him. I am never asked out to dinner when I go to the country without writing: "Where I dines I sleeps." I walk every morning in the park, and when I wander at the beginning of winter up to the Victoria Gate and see that the dahlias have caught the frost, I say: "Blister my kidneys, I see the dahlias has fruz." What I feel in the life I lead is this: I think of those words, "I have sought for peace and I have never found it save in a nook with a book." And back to the nook some time I go. I do not know whether physical conditions will allow me to enjoy my reading as a child; whether I can balance myself on the hearthrug as I did when a child, time alone will show. But that I hope to do before I die, and then I have no higher ambition than that of my cousin, Rudyard Kipling. If the first people to greet me in the next world should be good Sir Walter and Jane—and may I just add a little Schubert music?—who so happy as I, provided always that afterwards I may be allowed to sit in a corner for a real good talk with Mrs. Gamp?

> Pope's talent lay remarkably in what one may naturally enough term the condensation of thoughts. I think, no other English poet ever brought so much sense into the same number of lines with equal smoothness, ease, and poetical beauty. Let him who doubts of this peruse his Essay on Man with attention. Perhaps, this was a talent from which he could not easily have swerved; perhaps, he could not have sufficiently rarefied his thoughts to produce that flimsiness which is required in a ballad or love-song. . . . I durst not have censured Mr. Pope's writings in his life-time, you say. True. A writer surrounded with all his fame, engaging with another that is hardly known, is a man in armour attacking another in his night-gown and slippers.
>
> WILLIAM SHENSTONE, *Essays on Men and Manners.*

THE MISSION OF HUMOUR[1]

By Agnes Repplier

> "Laughter is my object: 'tis a property
> In Man, essential to his reason."
> *Thomas Randolph, The Muses' Looking-Glass.*

American humour is the pride of American hearts. It is held to be our splendid national characteristic, which we flaunt in the faces of other nations, conceiving them to have been less favoured by Providence. Just as the most effective way to disparage an author or an acquaintance—and we have often occasion to disparage both—is to say that he lacks a sense of humour, so the most effective criticism we can pass upon a nation is to deny it this valuable quality. American critics have written the most charming things about the keenness of American speech, the breadth and insight of American drollery, the electric current in American veins, and we, reading these pleasant felicitations, are wont to thank God with greater fervour than the occasion demands that we are more merry and wise than our neighbours. Mr. Brander Matthews, for example, has told us that there are newspaper writers in New York who have cultivated a wit, "not unlike Voltaire's." He mistrusts this wit because he finds it "corroding and disintegrating"; but he makes the comparison with that casual assurance which is a feature of American criticism.

Indeed, our delight in our own humour has tempted us to overrate both its literary value and its corrective qualities. We are never so apt to lose our sense of proportion as when we consider those beloved writers whom we hold to be humourists because they have made us laugh. It may be conceded

[1] Reprinted by permission of, and by arrangement with Houghton Mufflin Company.

that, as a people, we have an abiding and somewhat disquieting sense of fun. We are nimble of speech, we are more prone to levity than to seriousness, we are able to recognize a vital truth when it is presented to us under the familiar aspect of a jest, and we habitually allow ourselves certain forms of exaggeration, accepting, perhaps unconsciously, Hazlitt's verdict: "Lying is a species of wit, and shows spirit and invention." It is true also that no adequate provision is made in this country for the defective but valuable class without humour, which in England is exceedingly well cared for. American letters, American journalism, and American speech are so coloured by pleasantries, so accentuated by ridicule, that the silent and stodgy men, who are apt to represent a nation's real strength, hardly know where to turn for a little saving dulness. A deep vein of irony runs through every grade of society, making it possible for us to laugh at our own bitter discomfiture, and to scoff with startling distinctness at the evils which we passively permit. Just as the French monarchy under Louis the Fourteenth was wittily defined as despotism tempered by epigram, so the United States have been described as a free republic fettered by jokes, and the taunt conveys a half-truth which it is worth our while to consider.

Now there are many who affirm that the humourist's point of view is, on the whole, the fairest from which the world can be judged. It is equally remote from the misleading side-lights of the pessimist and from the wilful blindness of the optimist. It sees things with uncompromising clearness, but it judges of them with tolerance and good temper. Moreover, a sense of the ridiculous is a sound preservative of social virtues. It places a proper emphasis on the judgments of our associates, it saves us from pitfalls of vanity and self-assurance, it lays the basis of that propriety and decorum of conduct upon which is founded the charm of intercourse among equals. And what it does for us individually, it does for us collectively. Our national apprehension of a jest fosters whatever grace of modesty we have to show. We dare not inflate ourselves as superbly as we should like to do, because our genial countrymen stand ever ready to prick us into sudden collapse. "It is the laugh we enjoy at our own expense which betrays us to the rest of the world."

Perhaps we laugh too readily. Perhaps we are sometimes amused when we ought to be angry. Perhaps we jest when it is our plain duty to reform. Here lies the danger of our national light-mindedness,—for it is seldom light-heartedness; we are no whit more light-hearted than our neighbours. A carping English critic has declared that American humour consists in speaking of hideous things with levity; and while so harsh a charge is necessarily unjust, it makes clear one abiding difference between the nations. An Englishman never laughs—except officially in "Punch"—over any form of political degradation. He is not in the least amused by jobbery, by bad service, by broken pledges. The seamy side of civilized life is not to him a subject for sympathetic mirth. He can pity the stupidity which does not perceive that it is cheated and betrayed; but penetration allied to indifference awakens his mocking contempt. "If you think it amusing to be imposed on," an Englishwoman once said to me, "you need never be at a loss for a joke."

In good truth, we know what a man is like by the things he finds laughable, we gauge both his understanding and his culture by his sense of the becoming and of the absurd. If the capacity for laughter be one of the things which separates men from brutes, the quality of laughter draws a sharp dividing-line between the trained intelligence and the vacant mind. The humour of a race interprets the character of a race, and the mental condition of which laughter is the expression is something which it behooves the student of human nature and the student of national traits to understand very clearly.

Now our American humour is, on the whole, good-tempered and decent. It is scandalously irreverent (reverence is a quality which seems to have been left out of our composition); but it has neither the pitilessness of the Latin, nor the grossness of the Teuton jest. As Mr. Gilbert said of Sir Beerbohm Tree's "Hamlet," it is funny without being coarse. We have at our best the art of being amusing in an agreeable, almost an amiable, fashion; but then we have also the rare good fortune to be very easily amused. Think of the current jokes provided for our entertainment week by week, and day by day. Think of the comic supplement of our Sunday newspapers, designed for the refreshment of the feebleminded, and calculated to blight the spirits of any ordinarily intelligent household. Think of the debilitated jests and stories which a time-honoured custom inserts at the back of some of our magazines. It seems to be the custom of happy American parents to report to editors the infantile prattle of their engaging little children, and the editors print it for the benefit of those who escape the infliction first-hand. There is a story, pleasant but piteous, of Voltaire's listening with what patience he could muster to a comedy which was being interpreted by its author. At a certain point the dramatist read, "At this the Chevalier laughed"; whereupon Voltaire murmured enviously, "How fortunate the Chevalier was!" I think of that story whenever I am struck afresh by the ease with which we are moved to mirth.

A painstaking German student, who has traced the history of humour back to its earliest foundations, is of the opinion that there are eleven original jokes known to the world, or rather that there are eleven original and basic situations which have given birth to the world's jokes; and that all the pleasantries with which we are daily entertained are variations of these eleven originals, traceable directly or indirectly to the same sources. There are times when we are disposed to think eleven too generous a computation, and there are less weary moments in which the inexhaustible supply of situations still suggests fresh possibilities of laughter. Granted that the ever fertile mother-in-law jest and the one about the talkative barber were venerable in the days of Plutarch; there are others more securely and more deservedly rooted in public esteem which are, by comparison, new. Christianity, for example, must be held responsible for the missionary and cannibal joke, of which we have grown weary unto death; but which nevertheless possesses astonishing vitality, and exhibits remarkable breadth of treatment. Sydney Smith did not disdain to honour it with a joyous and unclerical quatrain; and the agreeable author of "Rab and his Friends" has told us the story of his fragile little schoolmate whose mother had destined him for a missionary, "though goodness knows there wasn't enough of him to go around among many heathen."

To Christianity is due also the somewhat ribald mirth which has clung for centuries about Saint Peter as gate-keeper of Heaven. We can trace this mirth back to the rude jests of the earliest miracle plays. We see these jests repeated over and over again in the folklore of Latin and Germanic nations. And if we open a comic journal to-day, there is more than a chance that we shall find Saint Peter, key in hand, uttering his time-honoured witticisms. This well-worn situation depends, as a rule, upon that common element of fun-making, the incongruous. Saint Peter invaded by air-ships. Saint Peter outwitting a squad of banner-flying suffragettes. Saint Peter losing his saintly temper over the expansive philanthropy of millionaires. Now and then a bit of true satire, like Mr. Kipling's "Tomlinson," conveys its deeper lesson to humanity. A recently told French story describes a lady of good reputation, family, and estate, presenting herself fearlessly at the gates of Heaven. Saint Peter receives her politely, and leads her through a street filled with lofty and beautiful mansions, any one of which she thinks will satisfy her requirements; but, to her amazement, they pass them by. Next they come to more modest but still charming houses with which she feels she could be reasonably content; but again they pass them by. Finally they reach a

small and mean dwelling in a small and
fare. "This," says Saint Peter, "is your hab
cries the indignant lady; "I could not pos
place so shabby and inadequate." "I am
replies the saint urbanely; "but we have d
could with the materials you furnished us."

There are no bounds to the loyalty with
clings to a well-established jest, there is
number of times a tale will bear retelling.
give it a fresh setting, adorn it with fresh
present it as new-born to the world; but thi
indication of our affectionate tenacity. I
caustic gibe of Queen Elizabeth's anent the
the bishop's wife (the Tudors had a bit
own) retold at the expense of an excellent
a living American bishop; and the story
professing religion, gave her ear-rings to
she knew they were taking *her* to Hell,—a
from the early Wesleyan revivals in Engla
located in Philadelphia, and assigned to on
evangelistic services. We still resort, as in the
to our memories for our jokes, and to our
our facts.

Moreover, we Americans have jests of
things for the most part, but our own.
from the Atlantic to the Pacific, they a
mendable regularity in our newspapers an
and they have become endeared to us by a lif
The salient characteristics of our great ci
traditions of our mining-camps, the contr
and West, the still more familiar cont
torpor of Philadelphia and Brooklyn ("In
says Mr. Oliver Herford, "we are—in Br
uneasy speed of New York,—these things
material for everyday American humou
example, the encounter between the Bos

small and mean dwelling in a small and mean thoroughfare. "This," says Saint Peter, "is your habitation." "This!" cries the indignant lady; "I could not possibly live in any place so shabby and inadequate." "I am sorry, madame," replies the saint urbanely; "but we have done the best we could with the materials you furnished us."

There are no bounds to the loyalty with which mankind clings to a well-established jest, there is no limit to the number of times a tale will bear retelling. Occasionally we give it a fresh setting, adorn it with fresh accessories, and present it as new-born to the world; but this is only another indication of our affectionate tenacity. I have heard that caustic gibe of Queen Elizabeth's anent the bishop's lady and the bishop's wife (the Tudors had a biting wit of their own) retold at the expense of an excellent lady, the wife of a living American bishop; and the story of the girl who, professing religion, gave her ear-rings to a sister, because she knew they were taking *her* to Hell,—a story which dates from the early Wesleyan revivals in England,—I have heard located in Philadelphia, and assigned to one of Mr. Torrey's evangelistic services. We still resort, as in the days of Sheridan, to our memories for our jokes, and to our imaginations for our facts.

Moreover, we Americans have jests of our own,—poor things for the most part, but our own. They are current from the Atlantic to the Pacific, they appear with commendable regularity in our newspapers and comic journals, and they have become endeared to us by a lifetime of intimacy. The salient characteristics of our great cities, the accepted traditions of our mining-camps, the contrast between East and West, the still more familiar contrast between the torpor of Philadelphia and Brooklyn ("In the midst of life," says Mr. Oliver Herford, "we are—in Brooklyn") and the uneasy speed of New York,—these things furnish abundant material for everyday American humour. There is, for example, the encounter between the Boston girl and the

Chicago girl, who, in real life, might often be taken for each other; but who, in the American joke, are as sharply differentiated as the Esquimo and the Hottentot. And there is the little Boston boy who always wears spectacles, who is always named Waldo, and who makes some innocent remark about "Literary Ethics," or the "Conduct of Life." We have known this little boy too long to bear a parting from him. Indeed, the mere suggestion that all Bostonians are forever immersed in Emerson is one which gives unfailing delight to the receptive American mind. It is a poor community which cannot furnish its archaic jest for the diversion of its neighbours.

The finest example of our bulldog resoluteness in holding on to a comic situation, or what we conceive to be a comic situation, may be seen every year when the twenty-second of February draws near, and the shops of our great and grateful Republic break out into an irruption of little hatchets, by which curious insignia we have chosen to commemorate our first President. These toys, occasionally combined with sprigs of artificial cherries, are hailed with unflagging delight, and purchased with what appears to be patriotic fervour. I have seen letter-carriers and post-office clerks wearing little hatchets in their button-holes, as though they were party buttons, or temperance badges. It is our great national joke, which I presume gains point from the dignified and reticent character of General Washington, and from the fact that he would have been sincerely unhappy could he have foreseen the senile character of a jest, destined, through our love of absurdity, our careful cultivation of the inappropriate, to be linked forever with his name.

The easy exaggeration which is a distinctive feature of American humour, and about which so much has been said and written, has its counterpart in sober and truth-telling England, though we are always amazed when we find it there, and fall to wondering, as we never wonder at home, in what spirit it was received. There are two kinds of exaggeration; exaggeration of statement, which is a somewhat primitive form of humour, and exaggeration of phrase, which implies a dexterous misuse of language, a skilful juggling with words. Sir John Robinson gives, as an admirable instance of exaggeration of statement, the remark of an American in London that his dining-room ceiling was so low that he could not have anything for dinner but soles. Sir John thought this could have been said only by an American, only by one accustomed to have a joke swiftly catalogued as a joke, and suffered to pass. An English jester must always take into account the mental attitude which finds "Gulliver's Travels" "incredible." When Mr. Edward FitzGerald said that the church at Woodbridge was so damp that fungi grew about the communion rail, Woodbridge ladies offered an indignant denial. When Dr. Thompson, the witty master of Trinity, observed of an undergraduate that "all the time he could spare from the neglect of his duties he gave to the adornment of his person," the sarcasm made its slow way into print; whereupon an intelligent British reader wrote to the periodical which had printed it, and explained painstakingly that, inasmuch as it was not possible to spare time from the neglect of anything, the criticism was inaccurate.

Exaggeration of phrase, as well as the studied understatement which is an even more effective form of ridicule, seem natural products of American humour. They sound, whereever we hear them, familiar to our ears. It is hard to believe that an English barrister, and not a Texas ranchman, described Boston as a town where respectability stalked unchecked. Mazarin's plaintive reflection, "Nothing is so disagreeable as to be obscurely hanged," carries with it an echo of Wyoming or Arizona. Mr. Gilbert's analysis of Hamlet's mental disorder,—

"Hamlet is idiotically sane,
With lucid intervals of lunacy,"—

has the pure flavour of American wit,—a wit which finds its most audacious expression in burlesquing bitter things, and which misfits its words with diabolic ingenuity. To match these alien jests, which sound so like our own, we have the whispered warning of an American usher (also quoted by Sir John Robinson) who opened the door to a late comer at one of Mr. Matthew Arnold's lectures: "Will you please make as little noise as you can, sir. The audience is asleep;" and the comprehensive remark of a New England scholar and wit that he never wanted to do anything in his life, that he did not find it was expensive, unwholesome, or immoral. This last observation embraces the wisdom of the centuries. Solomon would have endorsed it, and it is supremely quotable as expressing a common experience with very uncommon felicity.

When we leave the open field of exaggeration, that broad area which is our chosen territory, and seek for subtler qualities in American humour, we find here and there a witticism which, while admittedly our own, has in it an Old-World quality. The epigrammatic remark of a Boston woman that men get and forget, and women give and forgive, shows the fine, sharp finish of Sydney Smith or Sheridan. A Philadelphia woman's observation, that she knew there could be no marriages in Heaven, because—"Well, women were there no doubt in plenty, and some men; but not a man whom any woman would have," is strikingly French. The word of a New York broker, when Mr. Roosevelt sailed for Africa, "Wall Street expects every lion to do its duty!" equals in brevity and malice the keen-edged satire of Italy. No sharper thrust was ever made at prince or potentate.

The truth is that our love of a jest knows no limit and respects no law. The incongruities of an unequal civilization (we live in the land of contrasts) have accustomed us to absurdities, and reconciled us to ridicule. We rather like being satirized by our own countrymen. We are very kind and a little cruel to our humourists. We crown them with praise, we hold them to our hearts, we pay them any price they ask for their wares; but we insist upon their being funny all the time. Once a humourist, always a humourist, is our way of thinking; and we resent even a saving lapse into seriousness on the part of those who have had the good or the ill fortune to make us laugh.

England is equally obdurate in this regard. Her love of laughter has been consecrated by Oxford,—Oxford, the dignified refuge of English scholarship, which passed by a score of American scholars to bestow her honours on our great American joker. And because of this love of laughter, so desperate in a serious nation, English jesters have enjoyed the uneasy privileges of a court fool. Look at poor Hood. What he really loved was to wallow in the pathetic,—to write such harrowing verses as the "Bridge of Sighs," and the "Song of the Shirt" (which achieved the rare distinction of being printed—like the "Beggar's Petition"—on cotton handkerchiefs), and the "Lady's Dream." Every time he broke from his traces, he plunged into these morasses of melancholy; but he was always pulled out again, and reharnessed to his jokes. He would have liked to be funny occasionally and spontaneously, but it was the will of his master, the public, that he should be funny all the time, or starve. Lord Chesterfield wisely said that a man should live within his wit as well as within his income; but if Hood had lived within his wit—which might then have possessed a vital and lasting quality—he would have had no income. His rôle in life was like that of a dancing bear, which is held to commit a solecism every time it settles wearily down on the four legs nature gave it.

The same tyrannous demand hounded Mr. Eugene Field along his joke-strewn path. Chicago, struggling with vast and difficult problems, felt the need of laughter, and required of Mr. Field that he should make her laugh. He accepted the responsibility, and, as a reward, his memory is hallowed in the city he loved and derided. New York echoes this sentiment (New York echoes more than she proclaims; she confirms rather than initiates); and when Mr. Francis Wilson wrote some years ago a charming and enthusiastic paper for the "Century Magazine," he claimed that Mr. Field was so great a humourist as to be—what all great humourists are,—a moralist as well. But he had little to quote which could be received as evidence in a court of criticism; and many of the paragraphs which he deemed it worth while to reprint were melancholy instances of that jaded wit, that exhausted vitality, which in no wise represented Mr. Field's mirth-loving spirit, but only the things which were ground out of him when he was not in a mirthful mood.

The truth is that humour as a lucrative profession is a purely modern device, and one which is much to be deplored. The older humourists knew the value of light and shade. Their fun was precious in proportion to its parsimony. The essence of humour is that it should be unexpected, that it should embody an element of surprise, that it should startle us out of that reasonable gravity which, after all, must be our habitual frame of mind. But the professional humourist cannot afford to be unexpected. The exigencies of his vocation compel him to be relentlessly droll from his first page to his last, and this accumulated drollery weighs like lead. Compared to it, sermons are as thistle-down, and political economy is gay.

It is hard to estimate the value of humour as a national trait. Life has its appropriate levities, its comedy side. We cannot "see it clearly and see it whole," without recognizing a great many absurdities which ought to be laughed at, a great deal of nonsense which is a fair target for ridicule. The heaviest charge brought against American humour is that it never keeps its target well in view. We laugh, but we are not purged by laughter of our follies; we jest, but our jests are apt to have a kitten's sportive irresponsibility. The lawyer offers a witticism in place of an argument, the diner-out tells an amusing story in lieu of conversation. Even the clergyman does not disdain a joke, heedless of Dr. Johnson's warning which would save him from that pitfall. Smartness furnishes sufficient excuse for the impertinence of children, and with purposeless satire the daily papers deride the highest dignitaries of the land.

Yet while always to be reckoned with in life and letters, American humour is not a powerful and consistent factor either for destruction or for reform. It lacks, for the most part, a logical basis, and the dignity of a supreme aim. Moliere's humour amounted to a philosophy of life. He was wont to say that it was a difficult task to make gentlefolk laugh; but he succeeded in making them laugh at that which was laughable in themselves. He aimed his shafts at the fallacies and the duplicities which his countrymen ardently cherished, and he scorned the cheaper wit which contents itself with mocking at idols already discredited. As a result, he purged society, not of the follies that consumed it, but of the illusion that these follies were noble, graceful, and wise. "We do not plough or sow for fools," says a Russian proverb, "they grow of themselves"; but humour has accomplished a mighty work if it helps us to see that a fool is a fool, and not a prophet in the market-place. And if the man in the market-place chances to be a prophet, his message is safe from assault. No laughter can silence him, nor ridicule weaken his words.

Carlyle's grim humour was also drilled into efficacy. He used it in orderly fashion; he gave it force by a stern principle of repression. He had (what wise man has not?) an honest respect for dulness, knowing that a strong and free people argues best—as Mr. Bagehot puts it—"in platoons." He had some measure of mercy for folly. But against the whole complicated business of pretence, against the pious, and respectable, and patriotic hypocrisies of a successful civilization, he hurled his taunts with such true aim that it is not too much to say there has been less real comfort and safety in lying ever since.

These are victories worth recording, and there is a big battlefield for American humour when it finds itself ready for the fray, when it leaves off firing squibs, and settles down to a compelling cannonade, when it aims less at the superficial incongruities of life, and more at the deep-rooted delusions which rob us of fair fame. It has done its best work in the field of political satire, where the "Biglow Papers" hit hard in their day, where Nast's cartoons helped to overthrow the Tweed dynasty, and where the indolent and luminous genius of Mr. Dooley has widened our mental horizon. Mr. Dooley is a philosopher, but his is the philosophy of the looker-on, of that genuine unconcern which finds Saint George and the dragon to be both a trifle ridiculous. He is always undisturbed, always illuminating, and not infrequently amusing; but he anticipates the smiling indifference with which those who come after us will look back upon our enthusiasms and absurdities. Humour, as he sees it, is that thrice blessed quality which enables us to laugh, when otherwise we should be in danger of weeping. "We are ridiculous animals," observes Horace Walpole unsympathetically, "and if angels have any fun in their hearts, how we must divert them."

It is this clear-sighted, non-combative humour which Americans love and prize, and the absence of which they reckon a heavy loss. Nor do they always ask, "a loss to whom?" Charles Lamb said it was no misfortune for a man to have a sulky temper. It was his friends who were unfortunate. And so with the man who has no sense of humour. He gets along very well without it. He is not aware that anything is lacking. He is not mourning his lot. What loss there is, his friends and neighbours bear. A man destitute of humour is apt to be a formidable person, not subject to sudden deviations from his chosen path, and incapable of frittering away his elementary forces by pottering over both sides of a question. He is often to be respected, sometimes to be feared, and always—if possible—to be avoided. His are the qualities which distance enables us to recognize and value at their worth. He fills his place in the scheme of creation; but it is for us to see that his place is not next to ours at table, where his unresponsiveness narrows the conversational area, and dulls the contagious ardour of speech. He may add to the wisdom of the ages, but he lessens the gayety of life.

> He (Pliny the Elder) read no books without making extracts; and he used to say that "no book was so bad but some good might be got out of it."
>
> PLINY the Younger—*Book III Letter v. 10.*

THAT HISTORY SHOULD BE READABLE[1]

By Samuel M. Crothers

That was a clever device which a writer of "mere literature" hit upon when he boldly dedicated his book to a man of prodigious learning. "Who so guarded," he says, "can suspect his safety even when he travels through the Enemy's Country, for such is the vast field of Learning, where the Learned (though not numerous enough to be an Army) lie in small Parties, maliciously in Ambush, to destroy all New Men who look into their Quarters."

It is doubtful, however, whether in these days a lover of Ignorance—or, if you prefer, an ignorant lover of good things—could be safe in the enemy's country, even under the protection of such a Mr. Greatheart. It is no longer true that the Learned are not numerous enough to be an army and are content with guerrilla warfare; on the contrary, they have increased to multitudes, and their well-disciplined forces hold all the strategic points. As for those who love to read and consider, rather than to enter into minute researches, it is as in the days of Shamgar, the son of Anoth, when "the highways were unoccupied and the people walked through by-ways."

There is one field, however, that the Gentle Reader will not give up without a struggle—it is that of history. He claims that it belongs to Literature as much as to Science. History and Story are variations of the same word, and the historian who is master of his art must be a story-teller. Clio was not a school-mistress, but a Muse, and the papyrus roll in her hand does not contain mere dates and statistics, it is filled with the record of heroic adventures. The primi-

[1] Reprinted by permission of, and by arrangement with Houghton Mifflin Company.

tive form of history was verbal tradition, as one generation told the story of the past to the generation that followed.

"There was a great advantage in that method," says the Gentle Reader, "the irrelevant details dropped out. It is only the memorable things that can be remembered. What a pleasant invitation that was in the eighty-first psalm to the study of Hebrew History, in order to learn what had happened when Israel went out through the land of Egypt:—

'Take up the psalm and bring hither the timbrel,
The pleasant harp with the psaltery,
Blow up the trumpet in the new moon,
And the full moon on our solemn feast days.'

"The Jews had a way of setting their history to music, and bringing in the great events as a glorious refrain, which they never feared repeating too often; perhaps that is one reason why their history has lasted so long."

The Gentle Reader's liking for histories that might be read to the accompaniment of the "pleasant harp and psaltery," and which now and then stir him as with the sound of a trumpet, brings upon him many a severe rebuke. He is told that his favorite writers are frequently inaccurate and one-sided. The true historian, he is informed, is a prodigy of impartiality, who has divested himself of all human passions, in order that he may set down in exact sequence the course of events. The Gentle Reader turns to these highly praised volumes and finds himself adrift, without human companionship, on a bottomless sea of erudition,—writings, writings everywhere and not a page to read! Returning from this perilous excursion, he ever after adheres to his original predilection for histories that are readable.

He is of the opinion that a history must be essentially a work of the imagination. This does not mean that it must not be true, but it means that the important truth about any former generation can only be reproduced through the imagination. The important thing is that these people were once alive. No critical study of their meagre memorials can make us enter into their joys, their griefs, and their fears. The memorials only suggest to the historic imagination what the reality must have been.

Peter Bell could recognize a fact when he saw it:—

"A primrose on the river's brim
A yellow primrose was to him,
And it was nothing more."

As long as the primrose was there, he could be trusted to describe it accurately enough. But set Peter Bell the task of describing last year's primrose. "There aren't any last year's primroses on the river's brim," says Peter, "so you must be content with a description of the one in my herbarium. Last year's primroses, you will observe, are very much flattened out." To Mr. Peter Bell, after he has spent many years in the universities, a document is a document, and it is nothing more. When he has compared a great many documents, and put them together in a mechanical way, he calls his work a history. That's where he differs from the Gentle Reader who calls it only the crude material out of which a man of genius may possibly make a history.

To the Gentle Reader it is a profoundly interesting reflection that since this planet has been inhabited people have been fighting, and working, and loving, and hating, with an intensity born of the conviction that, if they went at it hard enough, they could finish the whole business in one generation. He likes to get back into any one of these generations just "to get the feel of it." He does not care so much for the final summing up of the process, as to see it in the making. Any one who can give him that experience is his friend.

He is interested in the stirring times of the English Revolution, and goes to the historical expert to find what it was all about. The historical expert starts with the Magna Charta and makes a preliminary survey. Then he begins his march down the centuries, intrenching every position lest he be caught unawares by the critics. His intellectual forces lack mobility, as they must wait for their baggage trains. At last he comes to the time of the Stuarts, and there is much talk of the royal prerogative, and ship money, and attainders, and acts of Parliament. There are exhaustive arguments, now on the one side and now on the other, which exactly balance one another. There are references to bulky volumes, where at the foot of every page the notes run along, like little angry dogs barking at the text.

The Gentle Reader calls out: "I have had enough of this. What I want to know is what it's all about, and which side, on the whole, has the right of it. Which side are you on? Are you a Roundhead or a Cavalier? Are your sympathies with the Whigs or the Tories?"

"Sympathies!" says the expert. "Who ever heard of a historian allowing himself to sympathize? I have no opinions of my own to present. My great aim is not to prejudice the mind of the student."

"Nonsense," says the Gentle Reader; "I am not a student, nor is this a school-room. It's all in confidence; speak out as one gentleman to another under a friendly roof! What do you think about it? No matter if you make a mistake or two, I'll forget most that you say, anyway. All that I care for is to get the gist of the matter. As for your fear of warping my mind, there's not the least danger in the world. My mind is like a tough bit of hickory; it will fly back into its original shape the moment you let go. I have a hundred prejudices of my own,—one more won't hurt me. I want to know what it was that set the people by the ears. Why did they cut off the head of Charles I., and why did they drive out James II.? I can't help thinking that there must have been something more exciting than those discussions of yours about constitutional theories. Do you know, I sometimes doubt whether most of the people who went to the wars knew that there was such a thing as the English Constitution; the subject hadn't been written up then. I suspect that something happened that was not set down in your book; something that made those people fighting mad."

Then the Gentle Reader turns to his old and much criticised friend Macaulay, and asks,—

"What do you think about it?"

"Think about it!" says Macaulay. "I'll tell you what I think about it. To begin with, that Charles I., though good enough as a family man, was a consummate liar."

"That's the first light I've had on the subject," says the Gentle Reader. "Charles lied, and that made the people mad?"

"Precisely! I perceive that you have the historic sense. We English can't abide a liar; so at last when we could not trust the king's word we chopped off his head. Mind you, I'm not defending the regicides, but between ourselves I don't mind saying that I think it served him right. At any rate our blood was up, and there was no stopping us. I wish I had time to tell you all about Hampden, and Pym, and Cromwell, but I must go on to the glorious year 1688, and tell you how it all came about, and how we sent that despicable dotard, James, flying across the Channel, and how we brought in the good and wise King William, and how the great line of Whig statesmen began. I take for granted—as you appear to be a sensible man—that you are a Whig?"

"I'm open to conviction," says the Gentle Reader.

In a little while he is in the very thick of it. He is an Englishman of the seventeenth century. He has taken sides and means to fight it out. He knows how to vote on every important question that comes before Parliament. No Jacobite sophistry can beguile him. When William lands he throws up his hat, and after that he stands by him, thick or thin. When you tell him that he ought to be more dispassionate in his historical judgments, he answers: "That would be all very well if we were not dealing with living issues,—but with Ireland in an uproar and the Papists ready to swarm over from France, there is a call for decision. A man must know his own mind. You may stand off and criticise William's policy; but the question is, What policy do you propose? You say that I have not exhausted the subject, and that there are other points of view. Very likely. Show me another point of view, only make it as clear to me as Macaulay makes his. Let it be a real view, and not a smudge. Some other day I may look at it, but I must take one thing at a time. What I object to is the historian who takes both sides in the same paragraph. That is what I call offensive bi-partisanship."

The Gentle Reader is interested not only in what great men actually were, but in the way they appeared to those who loved or hated them. He is of the opinion that the legend is often more significant than the colorless annals. When a legend has become universally accepted and has lived a thousand years, he feels that it should be protected in its rights of possession by some statute of limitation. It has come to have an independent life of its own. He has, therefore, no sympathy with Gibbon in his identification of St. George of England with George of Cappadocia, a dishonest army contractor who supplied the troops of the Emperor Julian with bacon. Says Gibbon: "His employment was mean; he rendered it infamous. He accumulated wealth by the basest arts of fraud and corruption; but his malversations were so notorious that George was compelled to escape from the pursuit of his enemies. . . . This odious stranger, disguising every circumstance of time and place, assumed the mask of a martyr, a saint, and a Christian hero; and the infamous George of Cappadocia has been transformed into the renowned St. George of England, the patron of arms, of chivalry, and of the garter."

"That is a serious indictment," says the Gentle Reader. "I have no plea to make for the Cappadocian; I can readily believe that his bacon was bad. But why not let bygones be bygones? If he managed to transform himself into a saint, and for many centuries avoid all suspicion, I believe that it was a thorough reformation. St. George of England has long been esteemed as a valiant gentleman,—and, at any rate, that affair with the dragon was greatly to his credit."

Sometimes the Gentle Reader is disturbed by finding that different lines of tradition have been mixed, and his mind becomes the battleground whereon old blood feuds are fought out. Thus it happens that as a child he was brought up on the tales of the Covenanters and imbibed their stern resentment against their persecutors. He learned to hate the very name of Graham of Claverhouse who brought desolation upon so many innocent homes. On the other hand, his heart beats high when he hears the martial strains of Bonnie Dundee. "There was a man for you!"

"Dundee he is mounted, he rides up the street,
The bells are rung backward, the drums they are beat.

. . . .

'Away to the hills, to the caves, to the rocks—
Ere I own as usurper, I'll couch with the fox!
And tremble, false Whigs, in the midst of your glee,
You have not seen the last of my bonnet and me!'

. . . .

He waved his proud hand, and the trumpets were blown,
The kettle-drums clashed, and the horsemen rode on,
Till on Ravelston's cliffs and on Clermeston's lee
Died away the wild war notes of Bonnie Dundee."

"When I see him wave his proud hand," says the Gentle Reader, "I am his clansman, and I'm ready to be off with him."

"I thought you were a Whig," says the student of history.

"I thought so too,—but what's politics where the affections are enlisted? Don't you hear those wild war notes?"

"But are you aware that the Bonnie Dundee is the same

man whom you have just been denouncing under the name of Graham of Claverhouse?"

"Are you sure they are the same?" sighs the Gentle Reader. "I cannot make them seem the same. To me there are two of them: Graham of Claverhouse, whom I hate, and the Bonnie Dundee, whom I love. If it's all the same to you, I think I shall keep them separate and go on loving and hating as aforetime."

But though the Gentle Reader has the defects of his qualities and is sometimes led astray by his sympathies, do not think that he is altogether lacking in solidity of judgment. He has a genuine love of truth and finds it more interesting than fiction—when it is well written. If he objects to the elimination of myth and fable it is because he is profoundly interested in the history of human feeling. The story that is the embodiment of an emotion is itself of the greatest significance. In Shelley's Prometheus Unbound, before Jupiter himself is revealed, the Phantasm of Jupiter appears and speaks. Prometheus addresses him:

> "Tremendous Image, as thou art must be
> He whom thou shadowest forth."

On the stage of history each great personage has a phantasmal counterpart; sometimes there are many of them. Each phantasm becomes a centre of love and hate.

The cold-blooded historian gives us what he calls the real Napoleon. He is, he asserts, neither the Corsican Ogre of the British imagination nor the Heroic Emperor for whom myriads of Frenchmen gladly died. Perhaps not; but when the Napoleonic legend has been banished, what about the Napoleonic wars? The Phantasms of Napoleon appear on every battlefield. The men of that day saw them, and were nerved to the conflict. The reader must, now and then, see them, or he can have no conception of what was going on. He misses "the moving why they did it." And as for the real Napoleon, what was the magic by which he was able to call such phantasms from the vasty deep?

The careful historian who would trace the history of Europe in the centuries that followed the barbarian invasion is sorely troubled by the intrusion of legendary elements. After purging his work of all that savors of romance, he has a very neat and connected narrative.

"But is it true?" asks the Gentle Reader. "I for one do not believe it. The course of true history never did run so smooth. Here is a worthy person who undertakes to furnish me with an idea of the Dark Ages, and he forgets the principal fact, which is that it was dark. His picture has all the sharp outlines of a noonday street scene. I don't believe he ever spent a night alone in a haunted house. If he had he would have known that if you don't see ghosts you see shapes that look like them. At midnight mysterious forms loom large. The historian must have a genius for depicting Chaos. He must make me dimly perceive 'the fragments of forgotten peoples,' with their superstitions, their formless fears, their vague desires. They were all fighting them in the dark.

" 'For friend and foe were shadows in the mist,
And friend slew friend not knowing whom he slew;
And some had visions out of golden youth,
And some beheld the faces of old ghosts
Look in upon the battle; and in the mist
Was many a noble deed, and many a base
And chance and craft and strength in single fights,
And ever and anon with host to host
Shocks, and the splintering spear, the hard mail hewn,
Shield-breakings, and the clash of brands, the crash
Of battle axes on shattered helms, and shrieks
After the Christ, of those who falling down
Looked up for heaven and only saw the mist.' "

"But, Gentle Reader," says the Historian, "that is poetry, not history."

"Perhaps it is, but it's what really happened."

He is of the opinion that many histories owe their quality of unreadableness to the virtues of their authors. The kind-hearted historians overload their works through their desire to rescue as many events and persons as possible from oblivion. When their better judgment tells them that they should be off, they remain to drag in one more. Alas, their good intention defeats itself; their frail craft cannot bear the added burden, and all hands go to the bottom. There is no surer oblivion than that which awaits one whose name is recorded in a book that undertakes to tell all.

The trouble with facts is that there are so many of them. Here are millions of happenings every day. Each one has its infinite series of antecedents and consequents; and each takes longer in the telling than in the doing. Evidently there must be some principle of selection. Naturalists with a taste for mathematics tell us of the appalling catastrophe which would impend if every codfish were to reach maturity. It would be equaled by the state of things which would exist were every incident duly chronicled. A foretaste of this calamity has been given in our recent war,—and yet there were some of our military men who did not write reminiscences.

What the principle of selection shall be depends upon the predominant interest of the writer. But there must be a clear sequence; one can relate only what is related to the chosen theme. The historian must reverse the order of natural evolution and proceed from the heterogeneous to the homogeneous. Alas for the ill-fated pundit who, forgetting his aim, flounders in the bottomless morass of heterogeneity. The moment he begins to tell how things are he remembers some incongruous incident which proves that they were quite otherwise. The genius for narrative consists in the ability to pick out the facts which belong together and which help each other along. The company must keep step, and the stragglers must be mercilessly cut off. One cannot say of any fact that it is important in itself. The important thing is that which has a direct bearing on the subject. The definition of dirt as matter in the wrong place is suggestive. All the details that throw light on the main action are of value. Those that obscure it are but petty dust. It is no sufficient plea that the dust is very real and that it took a great deal of trouble to collect it.

As vivid a bit of history as one may read is the Journal of Sally Wister, a Quaker girl who lived near Philadelphia during the period of the American Revolution. She gives a narrative of the things which happened to her during those fateful years. In October, 1777, she says, "Here, my dear, passes an interval of several weeks in which nothing happened worth the time and paper it would take to write it."

The editor is troubled at this remark, because during that very week the Battle of Germantown had been fought not far away. But Sally Wister had the true historical genius. The Battle of Germantown was an event, and so was the coming of a number of gay young officers to the hospitable country house; and this latter event was much more important to Sally Wister. So omitting all irrelevant incidents, she gives a circumstantial account of what was happening on the centre of the stage.

"Cousin Prissa and myself were sitting at the door; I in my green skirt, dark gown, etc. Two genteel men of the military order rode up to the door. 'Your servant, ladies,' etc. Asked if they could have quarters for General Smallwood."

"I can see just how they did it," says the Gentle Reader, "and what a commotion the visit made. Now when a person who is just as much absorbed in the progress of the Revolutionary War as Sally Wister was in those young officers writes about it I will read his history gladly."

Some otherwise excellent histories fall into the abyss of unreadableness because of the author's unnecessary pains to justify his heroes to the critical intelligence of the reader. He is continually making apologies when he should be telling a story. He is comparing the deeds of one age with the ethical standards of another; and the result is a series of moral anachronisms. There is a running fire of more or less irrelevant comment.

What a delightful plan that was, which the author of the Book of Judges hit upon to avoid this difficulty! He had a hard task. His worthies were not persons of settled habits, and they did many things that might appear shocking to later generations. They were called upon to do rough work and they did it in their own way. If the author had undertaken to justify their conduct by any conventional standard he would have made sorry work of it. What he did was much better than that. Whenever he came to a point where there was danger of the mind of the reader becoming turbid with moral reflections that belonged to a later age, he threw in the clarifying suggestion, "And there was no King in Israel, and every man did what was right in his own eyes." This precipitated all the disturbing elements, and the story ran on swift and clear. It was as if when the reader was about to protest the author anticipated him with, "What would you do, reader, if the Philistines were upon you and there were no King in Israel?" Undoubtedly under such circumstances it would be a great relief to catch sight of Gideon or Samson. It would not be a time for fastidiousness about their shortcomings; they would be hailed as strong deliverers.

"That is just the point of it," cries the Gentle Reader. "They were on our side. The important thing is to recognize our friends. To teach us who our friends are is the purpose of history. Here is a conflict that has been going on for ages. The men who have done valiant service are not all smooth-spoken gentlemen in black coats—but what of it? They have done what they could. We can't say that each act was absolutely right, but they were moving in the right direction. When a choice was offered they took the better part. The historian should not only know what they did, but what was the alternative offered them. There was the Prophet Samuel. Some persons will have no further respect for him after they learn that he hewed Agag in pieces before the Lord.

They think he ought to have stood up for Free Religion. They take for granted that the alternative offered him was religious toleration as we understand it. It was nothing of the sort. The question for a man of that age was, Shall Samuel hew Agag in pieces, or shall Agag hew Samuel in pieces, and my sympathies are with Samuel."

Having once made allowance for the differences of time and place, he follows with eager interest the fortunes of the men who have made the world what it is. What if they do have their faults? He does not care for what he calls New England Primer style of History:

> "Young Obadias, David, Josias
> All were pious."

Such monotony of excellence wearies him, and the garment of praise is accompanied by a spirit of heaviness.

"I like saints best in the state of nature," he says; "the process of canonization does not seem good for them. When too many of them are placed together in a book their virtues kill one another, and at a little distance all halos look very much alike."

There are certain histories which he finds readable, not because he cares very much for their ostensible subject, but because of the light they throw on the author's personality. He, good man, thinks he is telling the story of the Carlovingian Dynasty, or the rise of the Phoenician sea power, while in reality he is giving an intimate account of his own state of mind. The author is like a bee which wanders far afield and visits many flowers, but always brings back the spoil to one hollow tree. The Gentle Reader, like a practiced bee hunter, is careless of the outward journeys, but watches closely the direction of the return flight.

"If you would know a person's limitations," he says, "induce him to write on some large subject like the History of Civilization, or the History of the Origin and Growth of the Moral

Sentiment. You will find his particular hobby writ large."

He takes up a History of the Semites. "What a pertinacious fellow he is," alluding not to any ancient Semite but to the Author, "how closely he sticks to his point! He has discovered a new fact about the Amalekites,—I wonder what he will do with it. Just as I expected! there he is back with it to that controversy he is having with his Presbytery. I notice that he calls the children of Israel the Beni-Israel. He knows that that sort of thing irritates the conservative party. It suggests that he is following Renan, and yet it may only prove that he thinks in Hebrew."

> O have for my friends books, friends extremely agreeable, of all ages, of every land; of easy access, for they are always at my service; I admit them to my company, and dismiss them from it, whenever I please. They are never troublesome, but immediately answer every question I ask them.
>
> PETRARCH.

THE LANTERN-BEARERS[1]

By Robert Louis Stevenson

I

These boys congregated every autumn about a certain easterly fisher-village, where they tasted in a high degree the glory of existence. The place was created seemingly on purpose for the diversion of young gentlemen. A street or two of houses, mostly red and many of them tiled; a number of fine trees clustered about the manse and the kirkyard, and turning the chief street into a shady alley; many little gardens more than usually bright with flowers; nets a-drying, and fisher-wives scolding in the backward parts; a smell of fish, a genial smell of seaweed; whiffs of blowing sand at the street-corners; shops with golf-balls and bottled lollipops; another shop with penny pickwicks (that remarkable cigar) and the *London Journal*, dear to me for its startling pictures, and a few novels, dear for their suggestive names: such, as well as memory serves me, were the ingredients of the town. These, you are to conceive posted on a spit between two sandy bays, and sparsely flanked with villas—enough for the boys to lodge in with their subsidiary parents, not enough (not yet enough) to cocknify the scene; a haven in the rocks in front: in front of that, a file of gray islets: to the left, endless links and sand wreaths, a wilderness of hiding-holes, alive with popping rabbits and soaring gulls: to the right, a range of seaward crags, one rugged brow beyond another; the ruins of a mighty and ancient fortress on the brink of one; coves between—now charmed into sunshine quiet, now whistling

[1] From *Across the Plains.* Reprinted with the kind permission of Charles Scribner's Sons.

with wind and clamorous with bursting surges; the dens and sheltered hollows redolent of thyme and southernwood, the air at the cliff's edge brisk and clean and pungent of the sea—in front of all, the Bass Rock, tilted seaward like a doubtful bather, the surf ringing it with white, the solan-geese hanging round its summit like a great and glittering smoke. This choice piece of seaboard was sacred, besides, to the wrecker; and the Bass, in the eye of fancy, still flew the colours of King James; and in the ear of fancy the arches of Tantallon still rang with horseshoe iron, and echoed to the commands of Bell-the-Cat.

There was nothing to mar your days, if you were a boy summering in that part, but the embarrassment of pleasure. You might golf if you wanted; but I seem to have been better employed. You might secrete yourself in the Lady's Walk, a certain sunless dingle of elders, all mossed over by the damp as green as grass, and dotted here and there by the streamside with roofless walls, the cold homes of anchorites. To fit themselves for life, and with a special eye to acquire the art of smoking, it was even common for the boys to harbour there; and you might have seen a single penny pickwick, honestly shared in lengths with a blunt knife, bestrew the glen with these apprentices. Again, you might join our fishing parties, where we sat perched as thick as solan-geese, a covey of little anglers, boy and girl, angling over each other's heads, to the much entanglement of lines and loss of podleys and consequent shrill recrimination—shrill as the geese themselves. Indeed, had that been all, you might have done this often; but though fishing be a fine pastime, the podley is scarce to be regarded as a dainty for the table; and it was a point of honour that a boy should eat all that he had taken. Or again, you might climb the Law, where the whale's jawbone stood landmark in the buzzing wind, and behold the face of many counties, and the smoke and spires of many towns, and the sails of distant ships. You might bathe, now in the flaws of fine weather, that we pathetically call our summer, now in a gale of wind, with the sand scourging your bare hide, your clothes thrashing abroad from underneath their guardian stone, the froth of the great breakers casting you headlong ere it had drowned your knees. Or you might explore the tidal rocks, above all in the ebb of springs, when the very roots of the hills were for the nonce discovered; following my leader from one group to another, groping in slippery tangle for the wreck of ships, wading in pools after the abominable creatures of the sea, and ever with an eye cast backward on the march of the tide and the menaced line of your retreat. And then you might go Crusoeing, a word that covers all extempore eating in the open air: digging perhaps a house under the margin of the links, kindling a fire of the seaware, and cooking apples there—if they were truly apples, for I sometimes suppose the merchant must have played us off with some inferior and quite local fruit, capable of resolving, in the neighbourhood of fire, into mere sand and smoke and iodine; or perhaps pushing to Tantallon, you might lunch on sandwiches and visions in the grassy court, while the wind hummed in the crumbling turrets; or clambering along the coast, eat geans (the worst, I must suppose, in Christendom) from an adventurous gean tree that had taken root under a cliff, where it was shaken with an ague of east wind, and silvered after gales with salt, and grew so foreign among its bleak surroundings that to eat of its produce was an adventure in itself.

There are mingled some dismal memories with so many that were joyous. Of the fisher-wife, for instance, who had cut her throat at Canty Bay; and of how I ran with the other children to the top of the Quadrant, and beheld a posse of silent people escorting a cart, and on the cart, bound in a chair, her throat bandaged, and the bandage all bloody—horror!—the fisher-wife herself, who continued thenceforth to hag-ride my thoughts, and even to-day (as I recall the scene) darkens daylight. She was lodged in the little old jail in the chief street; but whether or no she died there, with a wise terror of the worst, I never inquired. She had been tippling; it was but a dingy tragedy; and it seems strange and hard that, after all these years, the poor crazy sinner should be still pilloried on her cart in the scrap-book of my memory. Nor shall I readily forget a certain house in the Quadrant where a visitor died, and a dark old woman continued to dwell alone with the dead body; nor how this old woman conceived a hatred to myself and one of my cousins, and in the dread hour of the dusk, as we were clambering on the garden-walls, opened a window in that house of mortality and cursed us in a shrill voice and with a marrowy choice of language. It was a pair of very colourless urchins that fled down the lane from this remarkable experience! But I recall with a more doubtful sentiment, compounded out of fear and exultation, the coil of equinoctial tempests; trumpeting squalls, scouring flaws of rain; the boats with their reefed lugsails scudding for the harbour mouth, where danger lay, for it was hard to make when the wind had any east in it; the wives clustered with blowing shawls at the pier-head, where (if fate was against them) they might see boat and husband and sons—their whole wealth and their whole family—engulfed under their eyes; and (what I saw but once) a troop of neighbours forcing such an unfortunate homeward, and she squalling and battling in their midst, a figure scarcely human, a tragic Maenad.

These are things that I recall with interest; but what my memory dwells upon the most, I have been all this while withholding. It was a sport peculiar to the place and indeed to a week or so of our two months' holiday there. Maybe it still flourishes in its native spot; for boys and their pastimes are swayed by periodic forces inscrutable to man; so that tops and marbles reappear in their due season, regular like the sun and moon; and the harmless art of knucklebones has seen the fall of the Roman empire and the rise of the United States. It may still flourish in its native spot, but nowhere else, I am persuaded; for I tried myself to introduce it on Tweedside, and was defeated lamentably; its charm being quite local, like a country wine that cannot be exported.

The idle manner of it was this:—

Toward the end of September, when school-time was drawing near and the nights were already black, we would begin to sally from our respective villas, each equipped with a tin bull's-eye lantern. The thing was so well known that it had worn a rut in the commerce of Great Britain; and the grocers, about the due time, began to garnish their windows with our particular brand of luminary. We wore them buckled to the waist upon a cricket belt, and over them, such was the rigour of the game, a buttoned top-coat. They smelled noisomely of glistered tin; they never burned aright, though they would always burn our fingers; their use was naught; the pleasure of them merely fanciful; and yet a boy with a bull's-eye under his top-coat asked for nothing more. The fishermen used lanterns about their boats, and it was from them, I suppose, that we had got the hint; but theirs were not bull's eyes, nor did we ever play at being fishermen. The police carried them at their belts, and we had plainly copied them in that; yet we did not pretend to be policemen. Burglars, indeed, we may have had some haunting thoughts of; and we had certainly an eye to past ages when lanterns were more common, and to certain story-books in which we had found them to figure very largely. But take it for all in all, the pleasure of the thing was substantive; and to be a boy with a bull's-eye under his top-coat was good enough for us.

When two of these asses met, there would be an anxious "Have you got your lantern?" and a gratified "Yes!" That was the shibboleth, and very needful too; for, as it was the rule to keep our glory contained, none could recognize a lantern-bearer, unless (like the pole-cat) by the smell. Four or five would sometimes climb into the belly of a ten-man lugger, with nothing but the thwarts above them—for the cabin was usually locked, or choose out some hollow of the links where the wind might whistle overhead. There the coats would be unbuttoned and the bull's-eye discovered; and in the chequering glimmer under the huge windy hall of the night, and cheered by a rich steam of toasting tinware, these fortunate young gentlemen would crouch together in the cold sand of the links or on the scaly bilges of the fishing-boat, and delight themselves with inappropriate talk. Woe is me that I may not give some specimens—some of their foresights of life, or deep inquiries into the rudiments of man and nature, these were so fiery and so innocent, they were so richly silly, so romantically young. But the talk, at any rate, was but a condiment; and these gatherings themselves only accidents in the career of the lantern-bearer. The essence of this bliss was to walk by yourself in the black night; the slide shut, the top-coat buttoned; not a ray escaping, whether to conduct your footsteps or to make your glory public: a mere pillar of darkness in the dark; and all the while, deep down in the privacy of your fool's heart, to know you had a bull's-eye at your belt, and to exult and sing over the knowledge.

II

It is said that a poet has died young in the breast of the most stolid. It may be contended, rather, that this (somewhat minor) bard in almost every case survives, and is the spice of life to his possessor. Justice is not done to the versatility and unplumbed childishness of man's imagination. His life from without may seem but a rude mound of mud; there will be some golden chamber at the heart of it, in which he dwells delighted; and for as dark as his pathway seems to the observer, he will have some kind of a bull's-eye at his belt.

It would be hard to pick out a career more cheerless than that of Dancer, the miser, as he figures in the *Old Bailey Reports*, a prey to the most sordid persecutions, the butt of his neighbourhood, betrayed by his hired man, his house beleaguered by the impish school-boy, and he himself grinding and fuming and impotently fleeing to the law against these pin-pricks. You marvel at first that any one should willingly prolong a life so destitute of charm and dignity; and then you call to memory that had he chosen, had he ceased to be a miser, he could have been freed at once from these trials, and might have built himself a castle and gone escorted by a squadron. For the love of more recondite joys, which we cannot estimate, which, it may be, we should envy, the man had willingly foregone both comfort and consideration. "His mind to him a kingdom was"; and sure enough, digging into that mind, which seems at first a dust-heap, we unearth some priceless jewels. For Dancer must have had the love of power and the disdain of using it, a noble character in itself; disdain of many pleasures, a chief part of what is commonly called wisdom; disdain of the inevitable end, that finest trait of mankind; scorn of men's opinions, another element of virtue; and at the back of all, a conscience just like yours and mine, whining like a cur, swindling like a thimble-rigger, but still pointing (there or thereabout) to some conventional standard. Here were a cabinet portrait to which Hawthorne perhaps had done justice; and yet not Hawthorne either, for he was mildly minded, and it lay not in him to create for us that throb of the miser's pulse, his fretful energy of gusto, his vast arms of ambition clutching in he knows not what: insatiable, insane, a god with a muck-rake. Thus, at least, looking in the bosom of the miser, consideration detects the poet in the full tide of life, with more, indeed, of the poetic fire than usually goes to epics; and tracing that mean man about his cold hearth, and to and fro in his discomfortable house, spies within him a blazing bonfire of delight. And so with others, who do not live by bread alone, but by some cherished and perhaps fantastic pleasure; who are meat salesmen to the external eye, and possibly to themselves are Shakespeares, Napoleons, or Beethovens; who have not one virtue to rub against another in the field of active life, and yet perhaps, in the life of contemplation, sit with the saints. We see them on the street, and we can count their buttons;

but heaven knows in what they pride themselves! heaven knows where they have set their treasure!

There is one fable that touches very near the quick of life: the fable of the monk who passed into the woods, heard a bird break into song, hearkened for a trill or two, and found himself on his return a stranger at his convent gates; for he had been absent fifty years, and of all his comrades there survived but one to recognise him. It is not only in the woods that this enchanter carols, though perhaps he is native there. He sings in the most doleful places. The miser hears him and chuckles, and the days are moments. With no more apparatus than an ill--smelling lantern I have evoked him on the naked links. All life that is not merely mechanical is spun out of two strands: seeking for that bird and hearing him. And it is just this that makes life so hard to value, and the delight of each so incommunicable. And just a knowledge of this, and a remembrance of those fortunate hours in which the bird has sung to us, that fills us with such wonder when we turn the pages of the realist. There, to be sure, we find a picture of life in so far as it consists of mud and of old iron, cheap desires and cheap fears, that which we are ashamed to remember and that which we are careless whether we forget; but of the note of that time-devouring nightingale we hear no news.

The case of these writers of romance is most obscure. They have been boys and youths; they have lingered outside the window of the beloved, who was then most probably writing to some one else; they have sat before a sheet of paper, and felt themselves mere continents of congested poetry, not one line of which would flow; they have walked alone in the woods, they have walked in cities under the countless lamps; they have been to sea, they have hated, they have feared, they have longed to knife a man, and maybe done it; the wild taste of life has stung their palate. Or, if you deny them all the rest, one pleasure at least they have tasted to the full—their books are there to prove it—the keen pleasure of successful literary composition. And yet they fill the globe with volumes, whose cleverness inspires me with despairing admiration, and whose consistent falsity to all I care to call existence, with despairing wrath. If I had no better hope than to continue to revolve among the dreary and petty businesses, and to be moved by the paltry hopes and fears with which they surround and animate their heroes, I declare I would die now. But there has never been an hour of mine gone quite so dully yet; if it were spent waiting at a railway junction, I would have some scattering thoughts, I could count some grains of memory, compared to which the whole of one of these romances seems but dross.

These writers would retort (if I take them properly) that this was very true; that it was the same with themselves and other persons of (what they call) the artistic temperament; that in this we were exceptional, and should apparently be ashamed of ourselves; but that our works must deal exclusively with (what they call) the average man, who was a prodigious dull fellow, and quite dead to all but the paltriest considerations. I accept the issue. We can only know others by ourselves. The artistic temperament (a plague on the expression!) does not make us different from our fellow-men, or it would make us incapable of writing novels; and the average man (a murrain on the word!) is just like you and me, or he would not be average. It was Whitman who stamped a kind of Birmingham sacredness upon the latter phrase; but Whitman knew very well, and showed very nobly, that the average man was full of joys and full of a poetry of his own. And this harping on life's dulness and man's meanness is a loud profession of incompetence; it is one of two things: the cry of the blind eye, *I cannot see*, or the complaint of the dumb tongue, *I cannot utter*. To draw a life without delights is to prove I have not realized it. To picture a man without some sort of poetry—well, it goes near to prove my case, for it shows an author may have little enough. To see Dancer only as a dirty, old, small-minded, impotently fuming man, in a dirty house, besieged by Harrow boys, and probably beset by small attorneys, is to show myself as keen an observer as . . . the Harrow boys. But these young gentlemen (with a more becoming modesty) were content to pluck Dancer by the coat-tails; they did not suppose they had surprised his secret or could put him living in a book: and it is there my error would have lain. Or say that in the same romance—I continue to call these books romances, in the hope of giving pain—say that in the same romance, which now begins really to take shape, I should leave to speak of Dancer, and follow instead the Harrow boys; and say that I came on some such business as that of my lantern-bearers on the links; and described the boys as very cold, spat upon by flurries of rain, and drearily surrounded, all of which they were; and their talk as silly and indecent, which it certainly was. I might upon these lines, and had I Zola's genius, turn out, in a page or so, a gem of literary art, render the lantern-light with the touches of a master, and lay on the indecency with the ungrudging hand of love; and when all was done, what a triumph would my picture be of shallowness and dulness! how it would have missed the point; how it would have belied the boys! To the ear of the stenographer, the talk is merely silly and indecent; but ask the boys themselves, and they are discussing (as it is highly proper they should) the possibilities of existence. To the eye of the observer they are wet and cold and drearily surrounded; but ask themselves, and they are in the heaven of a recondite pleasure, the ground of which is an ill-smelling lantern.

III

For, to repeat, the ground of a man's joy is often hard to hit. It may hinge at times upon a mere accessory, like the lantern; it may reside, like Dancer's, in the mysterious inwards of psychology. It may consist with perpetual failure, and find exercise in the continued chase. It has so little bond with externals (such as the observer scribbles in his note-book) that it may even touch them not; and the man's true life, for which he consents to live, lies altogether in the field of fancy. The clergyman, in his spare hours, may be winning battles, the farmer sailing ships, the banker reaping triumph in the arts: all leading another life, plying another trade from that they chose; like the poet's house-builder, who, after all is cased in stone,

> By his fireside, as impotent fancy prompts,
> Rebuilds it to his liking.

In such a case the poetry runs underground. The observer (poor soul, with his documents!) is all abroad. For to look at the man is but to court deception. We shall see the trunk from which he draws his nourishment; but he himself is above and abroad in the green dome of foliage, hummed through by winds and nested in by nightingales. And the true realism were that of the poets, to climb up after him like a squirrel, and catch some glimpse of the heaven for which he lives. And the true realism, always and everywhere, is that of the poets: to find out where joy resides and give it a voice far beyond singing.

For to miss the joy is to miss all. In the joy of the actors lies the sense of any action. That is the explanation, that the excuse. To one who has not the secret of the lanterns, the scene upon the links is meaningless. And hence the haunting and truly spectral unreality of realistic books. Hence, when we read the English realists, the incredulous wonder with which we observe the hero's constancy under the submerging tide of dulness, and how he bears up with his jibbing sweetheart, and endures the chatter of idiot girls, and stands by his whole unfeatured wilderness of an existence, instead of seeking relief in drink or foreign travel. Hence, in the French, in that meat-market of middle-aged sensuality, the disgusted surprise with which we see the hero drift sidelong, and practically quite untempted, into every description of misconduct and dishonour. In each, we miss the personal poetry, the enchanted atmosphere, that rainbow work of fancy that clothes what is naked and seems to ennoble what is base; in each, life falls dead like dough, instead of soaring away like a balloon into the colours of the sunset; each is true, each inconceivable; for no man lives in the external truth, among salts and acids, but in the warm, phantasmagoric chamber of his brain, with the painted windows and the storied walls.

Of this falsity we have had a recent example from a man who knows far better—Tolstoi's *Powers of Darkness.* Here is a piece full of force and truth, yet quite untrue. For before Mikita was led into so dire a situation he was tempted, and temptations are beautiful at least in part; and a work which dwells on the ugliness of crime and gives no hint of any loveliness in the temptation, sins against the modesty of life, and even when a Tolstoi writes it, sinks to melodrama. The peasants are not understood; they saw their life in fairer colours; even the deaf girl was clothed in poetry for Mikita, or he had never fallen. And so, once again, even an Old Bailey melodrama, without some brightness of poetry and lustre of existence, falls into the inconceivable and ranks with fairy tales.

IV

In nobler books we are moved with something like the emotions of life; and this emotion is very variously provoked. We are so moved when Levine labours in the field, when André sinks beyond emotion, when Richard Feverel and Lucy Desborough meet beside the river, when Antony, "not cowardly, puts off his helmet," when Kent has infinite pity on the dying Lear, when, in Dostoieffsky's *Despised and Rejected,* the uncomplaining hero drains his cup of suffering and virtue. These are notes that please the great heart of man. Not only love, and the fields, and the bright face of danger, but sacrifice and death and unmerited suffering humbly supported, touch in us the vein of the poetic. We love to think of them, we long to try them, we are humbly hopeful that we may prove heroes also.

We have heard, perhaps, too much of lesser matters. Here is the door, here is the open air. *Itur in antiquam silvam.*

> As good almost kill a man as kill a good book: who kills a man kills a reasonable creature, God's image; but he who destroys a good book kills reason itself.
>
> JOHN MILTON—*Areopagitica.*

THE CO-EDS: GOD BLESS THEM![1]

WITH SOME REFLECTIONS UPON HER MALE CLASSMATES

By Bernard DeVoto

I

Not long ago a man with whom I had roomed at college came to visit me and during his stay expressed a desire to observe me perform as a teacher. The motive that prompted him was no doubt malicious, but it was quite forgotten before he had sat through his first class. For he and I had gone to one of those monastic Eastern colleges where few women ever get past the visitors' gallery at the commons, and now for the first time he was seeing co-education. I expected him to say something appropriate about the lecture I delivered, for I had talked about Coleridge, and Professor Lowes's book was hot from the press; but he seemed to have forgotten that I had been any part of the hour's diversion. As we strolled across the campus he tried vigorously to reduce to order the confusion that his experience had brought him.

The first coherent idea that he voiced was, "Good Lord! I was expecting a college, not a sample room. That front row! It looked like the hosiery window at a spring opening or the finale of a Vanities first act. What do you teach 'em, dancing?"

A moment later, "Educational patter from the little ash-blonde: 'Does a poet know what he is writing or does he just tap the subconscious?' That's what happens when you expose a predestinate chocolate-dipper to Psych A."

And then, "How can a man teach with a roomful of beau-

[1] Reprinted by kind permission of the author.

tiful girls listening to him? Do you expect the men to keep their minds on Coleridge? And you can't be ass enough to want girls who look like that to handicap themselves with an education."

Later still he settled matters to his satisfaction. "Don't tell me you even try to teach 'em anything. You've got a living to make, and you merely elect to make it talking about Coleridge to a chorus of ravishing girls who all their life long will continue to associate Coleridge with henna and *Narcisse Noir*, and who merely use your classroom as a convenient place to pry luncheon-dates out of susceptible males. It's an old delusion that you can educate women. You're not fool enough to think that even one of that ballet has any idea that Coleridge wrote poetry, or what poetry is, or gives a damn, anyway. Sure! I saw 'em putting down pages of notes. You'll give them A when they come back to you on the final."

It was all very amusing. It reminded me forcibly of the day, some five years before, when I faced my first co-educational class. The offer of the position had reached me on a desert ranch, where I was working for my board and where even the pittance the Dean offered me seemed munificent. I traveled two thousand miles and bolted from the train-shed directly to a room containing thirty-five freshmen who were waiting to be told what to do for their first college assignment. I was on the rostrum before I fully realized that Atlantis was, after all, a co-educational university; and the sight of "that front row," crammed with new fall creations and shiny with French-nude stockings, appalled me. For the moment I wished myself back in the Idaho desert, untempted by an instructor's salary fully half as large as a milkman's, eating mutton three times a day, and rejoicing in the only beard I have ever owned. I was not long from that Eastern college, you see, and I knew all about the higher education of women. I knew that Middle-Western universities were contemptible from the point of view of scholarship (the knowledge had been confirmed by my being hired to teach at one).

I knew that girls went to such places primarily to find husbands who didn't live in the old home town. I knew furthermore that women didn't belong to the class of *educabilia*, which included in fact only a distressingly small percentage of males. And I knew, finally, that most women didn't pretend to take education seriously and that the few who did were not only æsthetic atrocities but also the most saddening numbskulls to be encountered anywhere by a vigorous mind.

To be sure, several of the graduate schools of my own university admitted women; and there was a regulation whereby students of a neighbouring women's college might very occasionally enter an undergraduate course. That I had been in a philosophy course which one of these rare specimens attended probably contributed to my idea of her sex's mentality. She was so homely that we called her "The Pure Reason," and she was eternally interrupting the professor's lecture, no matter what it concerned, with the stern question, "Is that reconcilable with Kant?" She was miserable whenever his language descended to intelligibility, and her distress at his mild, unworldly witticisms so saddened him that he gave them up altogether.

I could not see, after a desperate glance, anything corresponding to The Pure Reason in my first class. Quite the contrary. There were fully as many men as women in that class, but I was not aware of them. I could see only women, and they were all staggeringly beautiful. It could not be possible that such stunning girls would even pretend to take an interest in intellectual matters. They were undoubtedly a frivolous and giddy crew who would ogle me out of passing grades and coax me into letting them go free of assignments, and chatter and make up their faces during my most solemn flights. The room seemed oppressive with femininity, and I was quite sure that such an atmosphere, however favorable it might be to nature's designs for the perpetuation of the race, was frost and blight and mildew to that orderly discipline of the mind which I considered education.

Well, one learns, and I wonder now that in the moment of shock I did not recall the empirical fact that nine-tenths of the truly wise people I had known were women. Even if I had, at that stage I should doubtless have contended that wisdom was something apart from education, some derivative from the nebulous function which is called intuition.

Before long, however, I began to realize that not all my pupils were beautiful, and with that first discrimination began a series of readjustments which quite reversed most of my preconceptions. The whole point of this article, which is a recantation, is my discovery that the greater part of the education which the modern college manages to achieve, in the intervals between endowment campaigns, football championships, and psychological surveys, is appropriated by the very sex who presumably do not belong to the *educabilia* at all.

The women, these scatterbrained co-eds, are better material for education than the men and readier at acquiring it, and are also the chief hope for the preservation of the values which were long declared to be the ideals of liberal education.

II

Here I must make one or two stipulations. It must be understood that I speak entirely in generalizations, having no space to take account of exceptions, and that I generalize about the average student, not the exceptional one. To judge the colleges on the basis of the superior student—two per cent of the enrollment—would be foolish, and to attempt a differentiation between superior men and superior women would be more foolish still. Above a certain level of intelligence there seems to be little fundamental difference between the sexes, so far as their work in college is concerned. The tendencies with which I am now concerned are those of the mass, the undistinguished young folk who are the backbone of the colleges; and I am speaking of the tendency, not of any given individual who may oppose it. It must also be understood that I am generalizing from my own experience. I have checked it so far as possible by the experience of others, but without much finality on either side. A publicly expressed opinion on this subject is rare, since it exposes one to the headlines and editorials of the press, the recriminations of a dean who is harassed by officious associations, and an avalanche of letters from the nation's cranks. It is easier to get a privately expressed opinion, but it is also more likely to be conditioned by the accidents of the week. The Kappa Alpha weeper may have cried Professor Smith out of a passing mark for a sister half an hour before he defies the whole University Club to find him one co-ed who ever did a lick of work. Or Professor Smith may have married his brightest senior and so wedded an idea that the co-eds, as a sex, comprise the upper three-fourths of the intellectual scale, to the complete exclusion of the men.

The first observation is that the old debate is over, and the old problem of what aim a college education should have, if not solved, is at least settled forevermore. Even ten years ago the battle between the humanists on the one hand and the vocationalists on the other was still vigorous. Its outcome though unmistakable was not yet achieved, and the dwindling but vigorous defenders of liberal education showed no signs of panic. To-day, after ten years that have telescoped a century of evolution and have left the American colleges completely bewildered, hardly even the tradition survives. Not eight colleges in the country even pretend to champion the old ideals or to adapt them to post-war problems; and of those that do pretend, the loudest-voiced has done more to injure the cause than any dozen of its most Rotarian rivals.

By and large, the American college is now a training-school. It is engaged in preparing its students for their vocations. It is a feeder for the professional schools, on the one hand, and for business, on the other. Primarily it provides training for salesmanship. In the mass, young men come to college to learn how to sell. In the mass, they are not interested in the kind of education that is generally called liberal—or humanistic or cultural or intellectual. The man who comes to college to-day is not there to grow in wisdom, or to invite the truth to make him free, to realize his fullest intellectual possibilities, to learn the best that has been said and thought, or to fit himself to any other of the mottoes carved above his college gates. He is there to get through the prerequisites of a professional school or of business. In either case he is righteously intolerant of all flapdoodle whatsoever that does not contribute directly to the foreseen end. Anything which undertakes to make him more efficient he will embrace with as much enthusiasm as he has left over from "activities" which are the organized *hokum* of college life. Anything else—be it anthropology or zoölogy or any elective in between—he will resent and actively condemn. He'll be damned if he's got time to waste on wisdom—or knowledge—or truth and beauty—or cultural development—or individuality—or any of the other matters with which the colleges used to be concerned.

One who speaks to the college man of a different kind of education meets not the derision his opponents might have cast on him before the War, but an incomprehension, a complete failure to understand his language that is a thousand times more conclusive. Such an outcome was inevitable from the moment that the higher education became democratic, and its original momentum dates from the establishment of State-supported universities. But whereas, in spite of its democratic power, the really powerful authorities were opposed to the development as late as 1917, those same authorities have been since then its most enthusiastic leaders. Where the ideals of liberal education still survive they are cherished by aging and solitary men who can never head an educational body or sit on a president's throne. The administrations have gone over wholly to the popular cause. Recently the President of one of our largest universities said flatly to his faculty, "The students are our customers and we must give them what they want." His language was more forthright than that of most of his peers, who adopt the terminology of Service, but unquestionably he expressed the philosophy of most of them. With this policy in the throne-room the faculties in general whoop up the process. Ask any college teacher which departments have their budgets ratified without a murmur of complaint. Ask any department-head what courses he must stress to the trustees who guard the purse-strings. Ask anyone what the dominant ideas of his campus are and what professors are picked for the key-positions in the faculty committees. The colleges have gone out to give the student what he wants. And what he wants may be defined as courses that are thought to provide training in efficient salesmanship.

This is, however, education from the point of view of men. The women—those lovely co-eds whose stockings so disturbed my friend—are another matter. In the mass, they see no need to prepare themselves for law or dentistry and feel no call to become expert at selling. Their lives still have room for the qualities that education once dealt with. They have time for wisdom—and knowledge—and truth and beauty—and cultural development—and individuality. That is why they are so significant for the future if society has any use for liberal education and expects the colleges to have anything to do with it.

III

The canons of liberal education—if I correctly interpret its champions—may be summarized as receptiveness to new ideas, freedom from prejudice or other emotional bias, insistence on factual or logical demonstration of everything presented as truth, ability to distinguish between appearance and reality developed somewhat beyond the naïve faith of the uneducated, refusal to accept authority or tradition as final, and skepticism of the fads, propagandas, and panaceas that may be called the patent medicines of the mind. To abbreviate some centuries of definition still farther, the liberally educated man is supposed to possess an intelligently discriminating mind. The avenues by which this desirable possession may be acquired need not be scrutinized here. It suffices to remember what attributes have been considered the desiderata of liberal education and to estimate their relative distribution between the sexes in the colleges of to-day.

According to ancient theory, women's judgment is swayed by emotional considerations to a far greater extent than that of men. The daily routine in the colleges quite controverts the theory. It is the men, for instance, who die for dear old Rutgers. Here at Atlantis we have just emerged from a period of athletic failure which has given me an excellent chance to observe the passions in their natural state. I have seen many men in tears because the football employees of Utopia, that university of poltroons, had walloped our own; but I have never seen a co-ed leaving the stadium other than dry-eyed. The bales of themes that have rolled in upon me demanding a sterner athletic policy, bigger salaries for bigger fullbacks, in order to vindicate Atlantis as the best college in the world, have been without exception the work of men. The idea that the worth of a college is to be judged by the success of its football team is a man's idea. So is the idea that Atlantis is the best college in the world. A man is not satisfied, it seems, unless he can assure himself and the world at large that the college he attends is clearly superior to all others: a co-ed does not bother her mind with such infantile rationalizations.

As with football and world-leadership, so with the other functions of the college. Some years ago a newspaper, during a dearth of excitement, discovered the foul taproot of Bolshevism and the dead hand of Lenin (its own phrases) in an Epworth League at Atlantis. The organization that promptly had itself photographed kissing the Stars and Stripes, to prove Atlantis free of that moral plague, was a fraternity, not a sorority. The parade of patriotic youth carrying posters that damned all Bolshevists to the American Legion was entirely male. Male, too, were the petitions praying the President to redeem Atlantis before the world by expelling the Epworth League—they originated and circulated among the fraternities. So jingoism widens out: the co-eds think, the men throb. It is not enough that Atlantis is the world's-champion university with the loveliest campus and the most modern gadgets from the school of education. America, as the nation that is graced by Atlantis, must necessarily be immaculate, inimitable, and in all ways supreme.

Every year passionate organizations in the colleges pass hundreds of resolutions condemning the un-American conduct of some hapless professor who has suggested that the English plan of government is better than the American plan, that the Germans have a better civic policy, that the French eat better cooking, that a Japanese has thus far done the best research in this or that, that a Portuguese preceded a native Bostonian in sailing round Africa, or that the Mona Lisa is clearly superior to a fire-insurance calendar. Everyone who knows the colleges will recognize the phenomenon as one of the weariest bores of campus life. How many of these resolutions come from co-ed organizations? I have yet to observe one. It was a man, I remember, who refused to find any literary value in the Old Testament—obviously there couldn't be, he said, for it was written by a bunch of kikes.

In my survey of contemporary literature I deal perforce with much fiction and poetry of the day that, in method, is Freudian, and with much that is behavioristic. In general, the men are antagonistic to it. They object to both Freud and the behaviorists, partly on the ground that they are new, but mostly on the ground that they are unpleasant. The young male is affronted by the public discussion of sex-motives though he is a whale at discussing them in private, and he is much more deeply affronted by behaviorism. Consequently, he does not consider whether they are true, but merely loathes them. Now this is proverbially a feminine response, and it exhibits with admirable clarity one of the crucial functions of intelligence. The person who says, for instance, "I'd hate to think that Freud is right" betrays an essentially ignorant attitude of mind; the seeker after truth has nothing to do with liking or hating and the only intelligent question is, Is Freud right? But this ignorant, or proverbially feminine, response in my advanced class is confined to the men. The dispassionate point of view is invariably that of the co-eds. They do not unthinkingly accept the new literature. They welcome it as an interesting phenomenon, something to be analyzed and appraised without preconceptions. That, I submit, is the intelligent, the educated attitude.

Perhaps a few examples are relevant. It was a man who rejected *Elmer Gantry* because it must be bad art since Sinclair Lewis could not possibly be sincere in such a biased and contemptible book. The tangle of fallacies displayed by this earnest senior was the kind traditionally ascribed to the feminine mind which cannot think impersonally; yet it was a co-ed who in class informed him that a man who differed from him was not necessarily insincere, asked him what an author's sincerity had to do with his art, and criticized *Elmer Gantry* from an intelligent point of view. It was another man who in amazement and disgust pronounced Mr. Anderson's *Winesburg, Ohio* an utterly untrue book, the phantasm of a diseased mind. It was a co-ed who checked off on her fingers the analogues of Anderson's characters whom she had observed in her own home town and named a number of Russian and French novelists who, though respectable in her opponent's eyes, used precisely the same method. It was a man who called Katherine Mansfield "nasty-minded" and found no moral teaching in her work: it was a co-ed who put him in his place. Finally, after we had read *Ulysses* it was the men who pretended to understand it and, without pretense, condemned it utterly—but the co-eds who admitted that they could not understand it but found occasional passages of magnificent prose and tentatively accepted the method as valid.

This, however, is all literary criticism. I am, perhaps, betrayed by the limitations of my subject? Not if I correctly observe the adventures of my colleagues. Is the campus stirred by a protest against the atheistical teachings of the zoölogy department? Then the howl is sure to be traced to some embryo revivalist from the Red-Flannels Belt—someone whose sister is not in the least appalled. Does the Dean have to listen for some hours to complaints against Mr. Dash of the history department, who has suggested that economic considerations somewhat influenced the wisdom of the Fathers in 1787, and so is patently subsidized from Leningrad? Then the complainant is Bill Juicy, the pride of Sigma Sigma, who would die the death rather than hear Hamilton traduced. At that very moment Alice Apple, with whom Bill has a heavy date to-night, is writing a report for Mr. Dash's class and adding in a postscript that Mr. Dash must be wrong about Jefferson, for Alice cannot believe that even Jefferson could be so consistently high minded as Mr. Dash maintains. Or the large class files out of University Hall where Mr. Circle has been lecturing on Watson's theory of conditioned response. Bill Juicy lights a cigarette and ponders the lecture briefly. It's all a bunch of hooey, for if Watson is right then Bill can't think for himself. And that, in the face of Sigma Sigma's united stand for compulsory military training, is absurd. Bill dismisses Watson—whom he will thereafter associate with a brand of shock-absorbers—and goes to the fraternity house to find out whom to vote for in the class elections. But Alice, who also lights a cigarette as soon as she is screened from the Dean of Women, is also pondering. If Watson can establish his thesis; if those experiments Circle talks about are exhaustive, then—well, it's going to chase Mr. Dot of the Ethics course and Mr. Starr of the Social Progress course into a corner they'll never escape from. H'm—it rather knocks old Dot's idea of the Moral Will into a cocked hat.

IV

In various courses I have taught the wide expanse of English literature from Chaucer to James Joyce, but, apart from the tittering bromides of Polonius, I have found only one sentiment that appealed irresistibly to the male students in the class. That is the declaration in which Pope plumbed the depths of Bolingbroke and dredged up the assurance that whatever is, is right. It is the hoariest and most awesome conviction of the Babbitt mind, and its acceptance by the college youth of to-day is a broadly farcical commentary on our times. Here, I realize, I run counter to the shibboleths of the newspapers, which intermittently grow hydrophobic over a rebellious generation. It would be delightful and encouraging if the newspapers were right, but they are not. The wave of revolution that Mr. Coolidge discerned from afar when Vice-President never broke among our classic halls. How should salesmen-to-be revolt against anything? If whatever is, isn't right to the last electron, then the future is unsure and efficiency is imperilled. It must be right, and the bozo that says it isn't must be extinguished with the full police power of undergraduate taboos. There need be no apprehension about college men among those shadowy personages who are assumed to be interested in the preservation of the established order, for college men are sound to the core. Beside the conservatism of a fraternity, a Directors' meeting of United States Steel would have a pronounced Bolshevistic tinge. A caucus of the Republican Old Guard is distinctly radical in comparison with the men of a normal American college. They are not only instinctively reactionary, but even consciously so—and with an unctuousness that would appall the editor of the *Wall Street Journal*.

I have just said that this condition is farcical, and to my low, pedagogical mind, which studies the American scene without rancor, it is precisely that. But from another point of view it is pitiful and, indeed, tragic. For youth is the gallant season when the milk bill is of less consequence than certain spears and the glory of dashing oneself against them. Youth satisfied with anything is youth curdled with the hope of selling bonds. There is a time for the slaying of dragons and the pursuit of Utopias. I must maintain, even, that a fair share of revolutionary thought is essential for the full development of intelligence; for soil is made fruitful by plowing, and dynamite in deep-blast charges is acknowledged to be the best means of breaking up the clods and setting free the chemistry of creation. Ideally, college should give young minds four years of splendid intoxication. Made drunk with the freedom of ideas, college students should charge destructively against all the institutions of a faulty world and all the conventions of a silly one. I need not say that they do not.

My courses in advanced composition are an outlet for the ideas of the students who take them. In five years I have had a number of dissenters. I have had themes that inveighed against war and against marriage, themes that advocated an immediate proletarian revolution in the United States, themes that spoke highly of free-love or anarchy or communism, compulsory education in birth-control or the unionization of the farmers, military despotism or the creation of American soviets. One might focus on these themes—the work of some fifteen or twenty persons—and feel gratefully sure that all was well with the colleges, that such bright if momentary enthusiasms were evidence that college youth remained generous and undiscouraged. I might not dissent from such a judgment, but I must add that of the fifteen or twenty only one was a man.

I do not mean to suggest that the co-eds as a group are radical, but only that the college radical is more apt to appear among them. And I do insist that, as a group, they are more liberal than the men, less terrified by the prospect of social or intellectual change, and less suspicious of novelty. They seem to take for granted that in whatever is there must be, *ipso facto*, a great deal of nonsense. They are willing to examine what is proposed in place of it. The men merely set up a yell for the police or what, intellectually, corresponds to the police.

Above all, they are interested. The college man lives up to the type that has been created for him by the humorous magazines in that he seems perpetually bored. His is not the boredom of cynicism, not even of the callow cynicism of the cartoons, but the boredom that is usually called Philistine. Show him that the principles of Mr. Blank's course in "Business Psychology" will enable him hereafter to close a sale, and he will cast off his lethargy and dig; but through courses in the Greek thought of the Fourth Century or the social institutions of Medieval Spain he wanders somnolent and pathetic, a weary, grumbling low-brow who has been cruelly betrayed into registering for what rumor held to be a snap course. The excitements and the ecstasies of the intellectual life are not for him. He has no hunger for those impractical, breathless, dizzying wisdoms that add stature to the soul. But the co-eds, whether self-consciously or not, are really interested in living by the higher centers of the brain. Education retains, for them, something of its old adventurousness; and, for them, there is still some delight to be had in the pursuit of intellectual ends which can never, by any conceivable means, be turned into commissions. The sex is proverbially curious—and curiosity is no poor synonym for intelligence. And no doubt another proverbial attribute, stubbornness, is responsible for the other virtue that remains to be dealt with. Skepticism seems to be indispensable for education, but the college man neither possesses it nor respects its possession in others. He relies on the commercial honesty of the institution that accepts his tuition: surely no professor would accept money for saying something that was not true. A text-book cannot lie, and a professor will not. Logic, evidence, experimentation, and verification are all very well, no doubt, but an uneconomic waste of time. In a pinch, I would undertake to convince a class of men of nearly anything, merely by repeating many times that it was so because I said it was so. One does not teach women in that way. One painstakingly examines all the facts, goes over the evidence, caulks the seams of one's logic, and in every way prepares oneself for intelligent opposition. It may be the devilish obstinacy of the sex.

No doubt it is, but also, whatever its place in the ultimate synthesis of wisdom, it is the beginning of knowledge.

All this narrows down to one very simple thing. Democracy has swamped the colleges and, under its impetus, college men tend more and more to reverse evolution and to develop from heterogeneity to homogeneity. They tend to become a type, and, our civilization providing the mold, the type is that of the salesman. The attributes that distinguish it are shrewdness, craftiness, alertness, high-pressure affability and, above all, efficiency. There seems to me little reason to believe that the tendency will change in any way. I have not, indeed, any reason to believe that for the Republic any change is desirable. The mass-production of salesmen, we may be sure, will not and cannot stop. But, at least, there is one force that moves counter to this one. The co-eds, in general, develop into individuals; and, in general, they oppose and dissent from the trend of college education. I do not pretend to say whether their opposition is conscious or merely instinctive, nor can I hazard any prophecy about its possible influence on our national life. But if, hereafter, our colleges are to preserve any of the spirit that was lovely and admirable in their past, I am disposed to believe that the co-eds, those irresponsible and over-dressed young nitwits, will save it unassisted.

> Learning hath gained most by those books of which the printers have lost.
>
> THOMAS FULLER—*Of Books.*

NOVELS

By DR. SAMUEL JOHNSON

IT IS not a sufficient vindication of a character, that it is drawn as it appears; for many characters ought never to be drawn: nor of a narrative, that the train of events is agreeable to observation and experience; for that observation which is called knowledge of the world will be found much more frequently to make men cunning than good. . . . Many writers, for the sake of following nature, so mingle good and bad qualities in their principal personages that they are both equally conspicuous; and as we accompany them through their adventures with delight, and are led by degrees to interest ourselves in their favour, we lose the abhorrence of their faults because they do not hinder our pleasure, or, perhaps, regard them with some kindness for being united with so much merit. . . . Vice, for vice is necessary to be shown, should always disgust; nor should the graces of gaiety or the dignity of courage be so united with it, as to reconcile it to the mind. Wherever it appears, it should raise hatred by the malignity of its practices and contempt by the meanness of its stratagems: for while it is supported by either parts or spirit, it will be seldom heartily abhorred. The Roman tyrant was content to be hated if he was but feared; and there are thousands of the readers of romances willing to be thought wicked if they may be allowed to be wits. It is therefore to be steadily inculcated, that virtue is the highest proof of understanding and the only solid basis of greatness, and that vice is the natural consequence of narrow thoughts; that it begins in mistake and ends in ignominy. *Rambler*, No. 4.

APOLLYON VERSUS POLLYANNA[1]

By Samuel Hopkins Adams

The scope of fiction? Why "scope?" The word implies breadth of choice and treatment, and that in an art already dangerously subversive of the present age's vitalizing principle of conduct, benevolent censorship. That way peril lies.

Let us endeavor to approach this subject from the viewpoint of that admirable organization, so representative of our best and most decorous minds, the League for the Promotion of Prudery. As the League points out in its introductory enunciation of principles, the error and sin of modernist literature is that it tends to portray life as it is. All respectable persons realize that life in many of its phases is wholly unfit for the consideration of the pure. Take, for example, the regrettable matter of birth and all that precedes it. If our novelists, playwrights, and publicists would unanimously agree to refrain from any mention of natal or pre-natal processes, is it too much to hope that we could presently raise up a generation which should retain its unsullied mental innocency until, let us say, the legal age of twenty-one, or even conceivably later? Leave these undesirable matters to the biologists. Nobody reads biology anyway.

It is gratifying to note that the great and virtuous commonwealth of Pennsylvania has already initiated the good work by barring from its motion picture theatres any indication of how population is maintained. A young couple, though they be pasted over with marriage certificates as thick as hotel labels on a bargain sale trunk, may not be shown in the provocative act of purchasing a perambulator for a prospective baby. Even

[1] Reprinted by permission of the author and *The New Republic*.

that gallinaceous makeshift, the stork, is banished from the screen. Ohio is not far behind. A publisher who ventured to invade its unsullied borders with an edition of Rabelais has been apprehended. In this propitious soil the League for the Promotion of Prudery is quietly working to have the Bible expurgated and the Talmud revised. Shakespeare must go.

Eventually as public support accrues to the League and after it has cleansed and disinfected fiction, poetry, and the drama, it purposes to direct its attention to art and journalism.

It must not be inferred that all imaginative creation, per se, is interdicted. Writers may still hold the mirror up to nature, provided nature is suitably clad. Modern fashions are regarded as impermissible.

While the growing strength of censorship is a profound satisfaction and encouragement to the truly upright, it is evident that this method can never go far enough. A complete Index Expurgatorius is the eventual aim, or, better still, an Index Prohibitus. Thus far there has been devised only a broadly modelled White List herewith presented for consideration. Stories, plays, and poems are to be regarded as allowable in the following classes:

(a) Political and business stories wherein honesty triumphs.

(b) Sunday school stories.

(c) Children and farm stories.

(d) Love stories; object, matrimony.

(e) Nature stories, though it must be remembered that some animals are coarse in their habits. It is the League's plan to license only such authors as subscribe to the restrictions above. Others will be forbidden publication. Can any genuinely artistic heart fail to thrill at the prospect of a brighter, cleaner, purer world, wherein all the books will be of the school of Harold Bell Wright or Gene Stratton-Porter; wherein Apollyon and all his legions of darkness will flee before Pollyanna with her forces of sweetness and light?

THE DIFFERENCE BETWEEN LIFE AND FICTION [1]

By Floyd Dell

It seems to me that fiction, in whatever stage of development, still retains the purpose of the fairy-tale. But the fairy-tale, contrary to what many people suppose, has a very serious purpose. We come into the world equipped with a capacity of varied emotional response to our environment. That environment, even in its simplest terms, the home and family, presents itself to our childish intelligence as a mysterious chaos of facts; and the greater world outside this little world seems, as we come in contact with it, more chaotic and mysterious still. In the task of growing up, it is necessary for our emotional responses to this chaotic world to be co-ordinated; we must deal with this huge world quite as if we understood what it was really like. So that from the first a process of education goes on which undertakes to tell us—not so much what the world is really like, for that would only be to make confusion worse confounded—but a notion of it which will arrange our impulses toward it into some kind of order. What is required—for we have as children a wealth of emotions and little experience—is an *emotionally intelligible* interpretation of the world. The most preposterous fairy-tale, if it is a good fairy-tale—if it is in any sense a work of art, and arranges the emotions with which it so fantastically deals into some kind of rhythmic pattern—tells us more about friendship, love, ambition, folly and heroism, and their significance to ourselves,—than we knew before. So that it is, essentially, a kind of simple pragmatic truth that is aimed at in the fairy-tale. We cannot

[1] Reprinted by the kind permission of the author and *The New Republic.*

learn life by living it—we must have some kind of notion about it to enable us to digest our experiences as we get them. And of all kinds of teachings, that which comes to us through our emotional perceptions is the most fundamental, precisely because it is the most effective.

But the pragmatic truth of these simple works of art if different from plain factual truth, and in a sense an opposite of it, in so far as factual truth remains, for all our efforts to understand and arrange it, chaotic. Underneath all the picturesque disorder of the fairy-tale, there are the outlines of a very simple and orderly world.

And the same, I think, is true of the adult novel. Our experience has by this time been enlarged, so that we delight in a picture of life, let us say, in terms of jobs, wages, politics, and erotic misadventures, rather than in one in terms of quests, treasures, talking bushes and dragons. But underneath these recognizable incidents of our chaotic daily lives there must be the outlines of a simple and orderly world—a world more simple and orderly than the unfathomable nature of life's mysteries—but emotionally we require the satisfaction which only simple certainties can bring. For we still, as adults, read novels for the same unconscious and serious purpose with which we read fairy-tales as children. We want to know more about our relation to the world. But we emphatically do not want the raw material of life; we want life made emotionally intelligible—and that can only be effected by a process of simplification and arrangement which a hostile observer, indifferent to these purposes, might call suppression, or censorship, or lying.

Even so, the fable serves the purpose which the mere facts fail to serve. I have read in my life only one book which was, in my opinion, measurably true to the more common facts which constitute ordinary life. That book—and I recommend it to the curious reader as a perfect illustration of the difference between artistic truth and truth to facts—is One Man, by Robert Steele. Since I have mentioned it, I suppose I should add that its truth to the facts of ordinary life does not consist in the specific nature of the crimes, misdemeanors and follies there related—but rather in the irrelevance to each other of the emotional states which it records. There are in this book episodes—dozens of them—which would have served Dostoievsky for a climax. But, as here presented, they have no emotional validity whatever, because they have no relation to what comes before or after. Judged as a work of art, the book is preposterous and trivial. Its sole significance is as a document showing what human life, before it has been subjected to the processes of art, is like. Ordinary people are not as "bad" as the hero of this book; but they are, I think, quite as absurd and contradictory. The true-to-facts story of anyone I know would make a document equally inchoate and meaningless with this, if perhaps a little less sensational. And it is because human life in the raw is like this, that human beings need and desire those simplifications, those interpretations, which by suppressing, altering, rearranging the facts, permit what is left to have some emotional meaning.

No one, I think, who has a very acute sense of the variety and jumbled irrelevance of the facts of life as they present themselves to us in ordinary human experience would either imagine that the literal record of these facts constituted a story, or be so ambitious as to attempt to frame them *all* into an intelligible emotional sequence. Yet this—either or both—is what the writers of "realistic" fiction are currently and disapprovingly said to be doing by many American critics. There is supposed to be a "school" of writers whose theory of fiction is to put down everything "just as it happens in real life." There are gloomy forebodings of the death of the art of fiction under the assaults of the "literal chroniclers of life." These fears are quite unnecessary, and the lovers of romance can take heart. Not Theodore Dreiser in his most zealous realistic mood ever undertook to set down more than the limited and particular selection of facts which he deemed necessary to convey the quality of his emotion.

There is, I think, no quarrel between romance and realism. The selection of facts is more rigorous and more conventional in romantic fiction, more generous and more adventurous in realistic fiction. I cannot even assert, as a writer of fiction that has been very flatteringly called realistic, that realism aims more ardently than romance at truth. It does seem to me to have the merit, whatever that may count for, of being more intimately recognizable as a vehicle of truth by those whose experiences afford them the opportunity of testing in their own minds the literalness of the accounts by which that truth is sought to be conveyed. The literal truthfulness of Sinclair Lewis's account of a day-coach in the Middle West may not imply an imaginative insight into the souls of its passengers; but there is no doubt that it puts many of us into a receptive frame of mind toward emotional conclusions about middle-western souls which we might otherwise be disposed to reject as too painful. The function of literalness in factual detail would seem, in fiction, to be much the same as it is in the court-room—to make it harder to escape the obligation of feeling "unpleasant" emotions. The author's motive is plain: he has these emotions, and he wishes to lessen the burden of them by sharing them with others. And the reason why realism is so often of this "unpleasant" character, is simply that happy emotions need no such elaborate reinforcement. We do not need to have it proved that the hero and heroine lived happily ever after; the assertion suffices. It is when they did not live happily ever after that many painful—and intimately recognizable—details are needed to persuade us to believe that so it happened. But if we read these realistic accounts of our human misadventures, it is not because the manner of the telling has a virtue of its own, but because we desire to enlarge our conception of our lives so as to bring these difficult and painful facts also to some emotionally intelligible relationship with the rest of our experience.

And if any of the new kinds of scientific knowledge, such for example as psycho-analysis, are to be of use to the novelist, it must be, I think, not by virtue of any magic of "truth" which they contain, and certainly not by bringing new facts within the scope of the novelist's interest, but rather because they may possibly simplify his task of selection and arrangement—because they give him certain conceptions of life as emotionally intelligible and possibly as fundamentally appealing as the oldest fairy-tale.

In science, read, by preference the newest works; in literature, the oldest. The classics are always modern.

EDWARD BULWER LYTTON,
Caxtoniana: Hints on Mental Culture.

THE NOVEL OF TOMORROW[1]

By Zona Gale

Already we have mosaics of beauty in the American novel. But it lacks organic beauty.

In the modern novels of England the high example of organic beauty seems to be the work of Hudson. No one knows what he does; but his touch unseals an essence.

In the American novel we have nothing approaching this essence. One is grateful, in these days of the triumphant discovery of the commonplace, for mere beautiful mosaics. But these have little to do with the basic beauty, the organic beauty which a novel must breathe before it can approximate its potential scope and function.

Now organic beauty in any art must be compact of beauty not already familiar to us. Familiar beauty can give us the mosaics. But it is strangeness in beauty which alone can weave the spell and bear the perfume. This is not to say unreality; but on the contrary a deeper reality than we are accustomed to divine. The reality of literal levels of perception to which we do not ordinarily penetrate or of which, rather, we are not often conscious as they penetrate our own plane. Professor Eucken's claim that the spiritual world is "an independent reality, waiting to be apprehended, waiting to be incorporated into our universe" is enormously served by art whose functioning is so largely in extensions of the ordinary faculties. Between the naturalistic novel, which is a record, and the romantic novel, which is the product of human imagining, lies this other novel, the novel of tomorrow, concerned with imminent yet almost undivined

[1] Reprinted from *Portage, Wisconsin*, by Zona Gale, by and with permission of, and special arrangement with Alfred A. Knopf, Inc., authorized publishers.

reality of human conduct, human dream, perceived "for their own sakes, with the eyes of disinterested love."

Our failure may lie in the fact that such beauty as our novels have is chiefly concerned with moral idealism and romantic love, as we know them now. Our moral idealism is still intent on the exoteric with—shall we say?—either simple standards which ought long ago to have been taken for granted or conventionalized standards having no correspondence with the mystery of conduct. Therefore our novels devote themselves to, say, one emerging from a crude upbringing to the point of being hounded by her "furies" to escape tawdriness. Or even with those records of Henry James, that —Conrad calls him—that "historian of the individual conscience, of adventure in which only choice souls are involved" —crucial instances, always suffused with a certain beauty, but always the beauty of the individual conscience in areas. Moral beauty rather than esoteric beauty. And as for the treatment in novels of romantic love, that is always a matter of bright feathers, of the pas de seul before the cave door, our only advance from that cave door courting being that there are antiphonal feathers and dancing instead of masculine antics alone. In spite of the fact that there is, both in idealism and in love, something not ourselves which is the glory of the experience, still the novel continues to treat only of measurable reactions, rarely calling down the utter sunlit areas where every human soul does sometime enter. Now these sunlit areas are a part of life, of reality. If they can be experienced, they can be incarnated in the novel. And it is these sunlit spaces of discernible reality which alone can give to the novel a basis of beauty.

Moreover these reaches are not merely extensions of moral idealism or of romantic love. Neither the one nor the other may be of dominating concern there, save in some form so heightened that it has passed into pure beauty. Nor are these areas remote; it is their power that they interpenetrate the homeliest lives and the most ordinary surroundings. This is a point which the worshipper of mosaics of beauty will not readily admit and perhaps he is right about his mosaics. But organic beauty is everywhere at home.

The function of the novel is not to treat of life as it appears to the ordinary eye; or even to treat life in its ordinary aspect if that were ascertainable. It is not even to treat of life as it should be, if *that* were ascertainable. Its function is not primarily to report the familiar at all. The function of the novel is to reflect the familiar as permeated by the unfamiliar; to reflect the unknown in its daily office of permeating the known.

Thus the novelist is to go not only "joying in his visible universe" but in that universe by which his own is interpenetrated. That universe invisible save as music or color or the word or some other high manifestation causes it to flower in human experience.

It is this high manifestation of the word which Hudson makes. He causes unfamiliar verities to enter our ken as verities. For the poetic mind, the mind then of the novelist at his best, is the perceiver of the real curve of life, the knower of something at least of its inner ecstasy.

. . . How shall this interpretation best be made? This accomplishment concerns the form of the novel.

However extreme has been the modern novel in stressing the commonplace, it has developed a form suitable for the expression of reality. Any reality, commonplace or not. This form is direct, unreflective, highly selective. It is in immediate contact with its material. It is uncompromising, tactless, unashamed. And its style is as bare and clear as a plain.

It may be that the whole flair for the commonplace will be found to have contributed chiefly to the formation of a new purity of form. The treatment of the commonplace calls for stark precision and the novel has learned something of stark precision through treating the commonplace. If the novel had continued to treat of "the good, the true and the beautiful" it might be, with the redundance of that phrase itself, laboring on in a fringed and silken fashion, tasseled, plumed, melancholy.

When the novel can take that form—that naked and lovely instrument—and that stark style, and cause them to function in the expression of nameless beauty, such as Hudson summons, it will have sounded the new note, the note of the novel of tomorrow. And this will be a note of romanticism, but not of romanticism as we have ever known it.

Ten years ago a wise man said: Free verse is all well enough. It is now a vehicle for many who otherwise would have nô vehicle. But wait until the poets begin to use it. *Then!*

So it is of the terse, the staccato, the compact, the shorn form and style of the modern American novel. Heighten its compactness, take from it certain affectations such as deliberate sordidness, saturate it with all that divination can capture of communicable beauty. *"Then!"*

To use his divination to clarify the interpenetrating beauty of common life and to draw down still other beauty; not to manufacture it from unreality but to discern it in Reality and to reflect it; and then to pour this beauty through the clear crystal of a form as honest as a milk bottle—there lies the novelist's lovely, his imperative task.

But this he will never do if he is working with his mind alone. Only when he knows that his divination of beauty, of all life is "an independent growth which he himself tends and watches" will he incarnate in the novel the vast and lovely proportion of the days.

SPLITTING FICTION THREE WAYS[1]

By William Allen White

Any attempt to place the novel inside of definitions, setting its meets and bounds brings us up sharply against the insistent question asked of old and never answered "What is art?" And for himself, and his cosmos, one man's guess at the answer is as good as another's, probably rather better. For every man has his own scheme of creation. Every man is set down alone under the stars and on the more or less solid earth, to build out of his conscious experience the fabric of the dream in which he walks. If he sets down some account of his dream, some definition of his universe in terms of love or fear or hate or joy or any emotional medium in which his conviction comes to him about life, what he makes, for him is art. But it is of necessity not art for any one else. It may be an obscure picture on the sand, drawn with a shell or stick. It may be a Poem of Ecstasy or it may be a cathedral or a large fat Mrs. Rubens in oil, or a patient Madame X. leisurely waiting for the laundry wagon to bring her first aid in the matter of clothes! Whatever it may be, to some man the thing means a conviction about the meaning of life. To its creator, if to no other soul on earth, the thing created in joy or pain or fear or love or whatever rise of pulse beat, means art. Others, of course, need not accept it as art; being in ribald spirits they may laugh at it, or otherwise, being mean and supercilious they may try to suppress and censor the man's expression, which may seem to others ugly or indecent, or stupid or wicked beyond tears. But whether they censor it in laughter or in rage, they must not forget that for the man who made it the thing was art.

[1] Reprinted by the kind permission of the author and *The New Republic.*

He has a right to issue his challenge to the world and stand or fall by it.

So any man's novel has its rights. Its rights are limited. We don't have to read it, thank Heavens! We don't have to approve it, having read it. We have the royal privilege of declaring that the author is a fool; that no such world as he has tried to depict ever did or could or should exist; which being translated only means that the novelist does not see our world. But, as fellow travelers in a number of different universes, and varying stages of cosmic environment, we have no right as potential artists to deny him the right to print and peddle the poor thing that is his own.

Now, here we come to the doctrine of a democratic theory in criticism. And we must come to it when we admit a variety of different worlds surrounding the consciousness of human beings. Now, this democratic theory of criticism like all democratic theories and doctrines is based upon a principle of tolerance, of mutual respect, of neighborly kinship in the cosmos. And if we follow a democratic theory of criticism art must not develop a snobbery, in its lower levels, in, say, the level of criticism. To set up rigid standards, to make inexorable rules, to apply static tests, to accept or reject any man's account of the world in which he lives as false and foolish is dangerous. Also democratically it is unfair. A number of critics affect to giggle at the novels of Mr. Harold Bell Wright. Their fathers sniffed at Bertha M. Clay. To some of us Mr. Wright does seem to walk among chromos as one who lives in a vast forest of Sunday supplements. And there are those who feel that Mr. Theodore Dreiser's world is afflicted with misanthropy and worms. As between a world of "Simply to Thy Cross I Cling" done in gaudy colors and a world painted from the mud of a pig pen many an average man or woman shrinks from choice. It is not a question of art. There is no more art in Sister Carrie for instance than in Pollyanna.. It is largely a question of the world in which the authors move, of the philosophy of life which inspires the writer. And Sister Carrie may well be as false as Pollyanna in its philosophy. Life is doubtless highly carrieful—to coin a word—for Mr. Dreiser, and for Mrs. Porter it is surely pollyaneous; but for a lot of us it is neither. We trek along on the middle plane out of the heights where Pollyanna walks in trailing clouds of glory, and above the depths where Sister Carrie sloshes in the mud and muck. Possibly these middle averages toddle about with Alice Adams.

So let us for the sake of illustration say that broadly there abide these three views of modern American life personified by these three estimable young women, Sister Carrie, Pollyanna and Alice Adams. They personify rather distinctive groups in our novel reading public. Possibly the groups represent stratifications in the matter of viewpoint of life found in our book buying public. Why has not each crowd the right to its own opinion, and why should the exponents of either group stick up their noses at the others? If it pleases the Freeman as the exponent of soured and pickled brains and hearts and genital intestines to purvey that kind of wares—say literary tripes and caviar—well and good. The soured soul market is a trifle slow; but it is steady and seems to be growing. Then why try to stimulate it by affecting that those who deal in spiritual marshmallows under the Wright and Porter brand are ignorant venders of adulterated goods? And why insist that those who make and sell common cooking food—say Roast Beef Medium, for example—are base vulgarians. There is no particular virtue either of craftsmanship, in the making, or in the salesmanship in the selling as between those who handle gamey tripe, or marshmallows, or baker's bread. And the snobbery of the tripe makers is as unjustifiable as the unction of King's Daughters at the marshmallow counter. And as for the disdain of the prune and potato peddler, the workers in the other two departments of spiritual refreshment, it is positively wicked; if the tripe department will permit the use even in rhetoric of a word implying the existence of the right and wrong.

"DREAMING TRUE"[1]

By Edith Franklin Wyatt

I

From time to time dialogues between enterprising reporters and authors visiting this country gladden the pages of the daily press. Among these I remember reading some years ago an opinion on novels which has always interested me.

The reporter mentioned to the visiting author a novel presenting a brilliant delineation of a newspaper-writer who becomes a drug-fiend.

"The book is greatly over-rated," the visiting author replied. "Why this newspaper-writer—the hero—is only a second-rate man! I should not care to ask him to my home to lunch."

Think of the "noted names of fiction" who could not survive this simple test. Consider the imaginary figures that you cannot picture as enjoying lunch with your relatives, and with whom your relatives could not enjoy lunching. "I should not care to ask him (her) to my home to lunch." Goneril—or Regan either—Bill Sikes, Gilbert Osmond, Medea, Werther, Bradley Headstone, any of the people in Wuthering Heights—

Without indulging myself further in regarding this or other aspects of this quick test of the value of fiction I will hasten to say that the chief reason why it seems so dismal an absurdity is perhaps because it could only serve to cut off the visiting author from the most profoundly entertaining experience fiction offers. This is, for me at least, the experience of "dreaming true," the experience of being someone else, of being a hundred, a thousand other people.

[1] Reprinted by permission of the author and *The New Republic.*

II

This interest in becoming somebody else has never seemed to me to arise from seeking novels as an "escape" from real life or from one's own life. One enjoys the power of identification with the million-peopled cosmos of novels not for the negative reason of seeing an escape but because the exercise of this power is a positive pleasure in itself, comparable to the pleasure of looking at well-composed colors, or of hearing sound beautifully ordered.

If one cannot ask everyone to lunch, if one cannot meet, converse with, live with, identify oneself with every kind of human life in the pages of a novel, then there is no place in the world where one can ask everyone to lunch, meet everyone, converse with, live with, identify oneself with every form of human life.

This is in my belief the chief distinctive contribution that the art of the novel makes to the life of the mind. In the other arts of letters the readers is more or less a listener, and part of the audience. In the art of the novel he is a participant.

Yet, besides this there are of course many elements of existence—too many to mention—which are the peculiar province of the novel; many kinds of truth that no other form of letters is so well fitted to express.

A way of life over a long space of time; the change of community opinion; the contrast of social groups; the several aspects of one man's or woman's nature; a correction of vision and gradual revelation; the development of human resources; above all the free and fecund power of life, its variety, its improvisational force in virtue of which one situation grows out of another in many-colored, creative continuance—these are some of the many truths that the novel tells best.

After he has been left by his thin-hearted wife, Lavretzky in Turgenev's Liza returns to live on and manage his father's estate:

"There under the window climbs the large-leaved burdock from the thick grass. . . . Farther away in the field shines the rye, and the oats are already in ear, and every leaf or tree, every blade of grass on its stalk stretches itself out to its fullest extent. 'On a woman's love my best years have been wasted,' Lavretzky proceeded to think. 'Well, then, let the dullness here sober me and calm me down; let it educate me into being able to work like others without hurrying.' And he again betook himself to listening to the silence without expecting anything, and yet, at the same time, as if expecting something. The stillness embraced him on all sides; the sun went down quietly in a calm, blue sky. . . . In other parts of the world at that very moment life was seething noisily bestirring itself. Here the same life flowed silently along, like water over meadow-grass. It was late in the evening before Lavretzky could tear himself away from the contemplation of this life so quietly welling forth—so tranquilly flowing past. Sorrow for the past melted in his mind as the snow melts in spring; but strange to say, never had the love of home exercised so strong or so profound an influence upon him."

This has for me the singular magic of the novel's faculty for quietly welling forth, the profound charm of a work in which each part of the tale develops and enhances what has gone before, and is the moving prelude of what is to come.

Many instances occur to one of the genius of novelists in employing the unique opportunity the form affords for spacious original design. One thinks of the magnificent river-journey at the close of Tono-Bungay where one rides and rides past the high-piled tokens of changing civilization out and out to the open sea from which one looks back with emotion at the lives of George and of Edward Ponderevo as seen from afar now, through a veil of reflection on the greater ways of mortal dream and destiny.

One thinks of the tremendous scene of the wild populace at the guillotining at Auxerre in The Old Wives Tale, as contrasted with the staid persons and streets of the Five

Towns whence Sophia Baines has come to stand at her hotel-window and look forth in disgust and fascination.

One thinks of the wide, bright tide of world-letters and word-criticism bearing Wilhelm Meister through his Lehr- und Wanderjahre; and of Daudet's Sappho with the painter Corot touched in among the guests at that brilliant ball in one of the opening chapters. Vista, panorama, multitude, spontaneous succession—all these the novel tells us supremely.

III

The changing world of novels is full of surprises. One will have thought that, in general, literary fashions are rather unrewarding and tend to cheap standardizations of material. Then suddenly a literary fashion will be productive of admirable results. Or perhaps it would be more precise to say that often some new theme chances to be excellently expressed at about the same time by many novelists.

Thus the past season has been especially rich in the criticism of husbands and fathers. Inspired exposures have occurred on all sides—the exposure of Herbert Dwight Deacon, the exposure of Mr. Weemys in Vera and the exposure of Mr. Waddington. Among these Herbert Dwight Deacon is the most liberally treated by the author. This is to the good, as liberality is seriously needed by the male characters of fiction where they are too often disfranchised and appear purely in a vicarious relation as sons, fathers or lovers.

This vicarious discriminatory manner of regarding men in fiction is especially noticeable in the character of Tito Melema. Seen solely from the standpoint of his exceedingly feeble abilities as a lover, Tito, though physical beauty is almost too richly lavished upon him by his creator, has never the slightest chance as a human being. Always in a miserable subordinate state as a mere adjunct of Romola he is never for an instant permitted to come forward except on the depressing grounds of love and beauty and as a sort of male houri. His position is far more discouraging than that of Nora in A Doll's House. And one need only compare Ninian Deacon's treatment as a bigamist by his creator to Tito's treatment as a bigamist by his creator to appreciate the increase of enfranchisement for males in fiction.

Perhaps it is because of the recent overshadowing appreciation of Miss Lulu Bett that one has not heard much of an extremely beautiful and original novel of Miss Zona Gale's entitled Birth.

It is a story of a "superfluous man" in a Wisconsin town, the story of a whole town of men and women, a place most individually perceived. Yet its outline has some of the national angles of the town that imprisoned Thoreau, and where Stephen Crane saw the tragedy of The Monster. Years flow by and the changes of years. Death is here and love and pain, all touched with swift ironic humor. Each soul is imagined by this humor, and in the wisdom of truth intimate and profound. The neighbors walk past in the evening —the wise, the silly, the generous, the small. The band plays. The trains thunder overland. And you walk in sun and rain where

> Burage numbers her trees by thousands. In the morning the sun comes in strong gold, lavished upon the grass, save where the leaves lay their bright veils. All the narrow strips outside the walks turn bright.
>
> In rain the town, like any other, lying folded in a visible medium, becomes an enclosure cut off from something. Rooms become more intimate. Something ceases, and something is present instead.

You too walk under the thousand-numbered trees over the November pavements. The possibilities of your fast-flying life hurry past you unrealized; and at their passage you despair and laugh at yourself and hope again. Your heart burns at the mean injustice of existence, its petty cruelty and hardness to those who are forgotten upon earth. Sometimes

I have thought every splendid novel is about justice and injustice. This novel has the presence of genius. When you read it something ceases; and something is present instead.

It has the power of social imagination, the light which beyond any other illumines the art of the novel; and makes us hope ever to dream more truly of all the mortal ſortunes in our world.

What a sense of security in an old book which Time has criticised for us!

James Russell Lowell, *Library of Old Author.*

THE CRITIC VIEWS THE WORK OF OTHERS

STEELE'S LETTERS[1]

By Austin Dobson

On the 19th of May, 1708, Her Majesty Queen Anne being then upon the throne of Great Britain and Ireland, a coach with two horses, gaudy rather than neat in its appointments, drew up at the door of my Lord Sunderland's Office in Whitehall. It contained a lady about thirty, of considerable personal attractions, and dressed richly in cinnamon satin. She was a brunette, with a rather high forehead, the height of which was ingeniously broken by two short locks upon the temples. Moreover, she had distinctly fine eyes, and a mouth which, in its normal state, must have been arch and pretty, but was now drawn down at the corners under the influence of some temporary irritation. As the coach stopped, a provincial-looking servant promptly alighted, pulled out from the box-seat a large case of the kind used for preserving the voluminous periwigs of the period, and subsequently extracted from the same receptacle a pair of shining new shoes with square toes and silver buckles. These, with the case, he carried carefully into the house, returning shortly afterwards. Then ensued what, upon the stage, would be called 'an interval,' during which time the high forehead of the lady began to cloud visibly with impatience, and the corners of her mouth to grow more ominous. At length, about twenty minutes later, came a sound of laughter and noisy voices; and by-and-by bustled out of the Cockpit portal a square-shouldered, square-faced man in a rich dress, which, like the coach, was a little showy. He wore a huge black full-bottomed periwig. Speaking with a marked Irish accent, he made profuse apol-

[1] Reprinted by permission of the Oxford University Press and Mr. Alban Dobson, acting for the executors.

ogies to the occupant of the carriage—apologies which, as might be expected, were not well received. An expression of vexation came over his good-tempered face as he took his seat at the lady's side, and he lapsed for a few minutes into a moody silence. But before they had gone many yards, his dark, deep-set eyes began to twinkle once more as he looked about him. When they passed the Tilt-Yard, a detachment of the Second Troop of Life Guards, magnificent in their laced red coats, jack boots, and white feathers, came pacing out on their black horses. They took their way towards Charing Cross, and for a short distance followed the same route as the chariot. The lady was loftily indifferent to their presence; and she was, besides, on the farther side of the vehicle. But her companion manifestly recognized some old acquaintances among them, and was highly gratified at being recognized in his turn, although at the same time it was evident he was also a little apprehensive lest the 'Gentlemen of the Guard,' as they were called, should be needlessly demonstrative in their acknowledgment of his existence. After this, nothing more of moment occurred. Slowly mounting St. James's Street, the coach turned down Piccadilly, and, passing between the groups of lounging lackeys at the gate, entered Hyde Park. Here, by the time it had once made the circuit of the Ring, the lady's equanimity was completely restored, and the gentleman was radiant. He was, in truth, to use his own words, 'no undelightful Companion.' He possessed an infinite fund of wit and humour; and his manner to women had a sincerity of deference which was not the prevailing characteristic of his age.

There is but slender invention in this little picture. The gentleman was Captain Steele, late of the Life Guards, the Coldstreams, and Lucas's regiment of foot, now Gazetteer, and Gentleman Waiter to Queen Anne's consort, Prince George of Denmark, and not yet 'Mr. Isaac Bickerstaff' of the immortal 'Tatler.' The lady was Mrs. Steele, *née* Miss Mary Scurlock, his 'Ruler' and 'absolute Governesse' (as he called her), to whom he had been married some eight months before. If you ask at the British Museum for the Steele manuscripts (Add. MSS. 5,145, A, B, and C), the courteous attendant will bring you, with its faded ink, dusky paper, and hasty scrawl, the very letter making arrangements for this meeting ('best Periwigg' and 'new Shoes' included), at the end of which the writer assures his 'dear Prue' (another pet name) that she is 'Vitall Life to Y^{r} Oblig'd Affectionate Husband & Humble Ser^{nt} Rich^{a} Steele.' There are many such in the *quarto* volume of which this forms part, written from all places, at all times, in all kinds of hands. They take all tones; they are passionate, tender, expostulatory, playful, dignified, lyric, didactic. It must be confessed that from a perusal of them one's feeling for the lady of the chariot is not entirely unsympathetic. It can scarcely have been an ideal household, that 'third door right hand turning out of Jermyn Street,' to which so many of them are addressed; and Mrs. Steele must frequently have had to complain to her *confidante,* Mrs. (or Miss) Binns (a lady whom Steele is obviously anxious to propitiate), of the extraordinary irregularity of her restless lord and master. Now a friend from Barbados has stopped him on his way home, and he will come (he writes) 'within a Pint of Wine;' now it is Lord Sunderland who is keeping him indefinitely at the Council; now the siege of Lille and the proofs of the 'Gazette' will detain him until ten at night. Sometimes his vague 'West Indian business' (that is, his first wife's property) hurries him suddenly into the City; sometimes he is borne off to the Gentlemen Ushers' table at St. James's. Sometimes, even, he stays out all night, as he had done not many days before the date of the above meeting, when he had written to beg that his dressing-gown, his slippers, and 'clean Linnen' might be sent to him at 'one Legg's,' a barber 'over against the Devill Tavern at Charing Crosse,' where he proposes to lie that night, chiefly, it has been conjectured from the context, in order to escape certain watchful 'shoulder-dabbers' who were hanging obstinately about his own mansion in St. James's. For—to tell the truth—he was generally hopelessly embarrassed, and scarcely ever without a lawsuit on his hands. He was not a bad man; he was not necessarily vicious or dissolute. But his habits were incurably generous, profuse, and improvident; and his sanguine Irish nature led him continually to mistake his expectations for his income. Naturally, perhaps, his 'absolute Governesse' complained of an absolutism so strangely limited. If her affection for him was scarcely as ardent as his passion for her, it was still a genuine emotion. But to a coquette of some years' standing, and 'a cried-up beauty' (as Mrs. Manley calls her), the realities of her married life must have been a cruel disappointment; and she was not the woman to conceal it. 'I wish,' says her husband in one of his letters, 'I knew how to Court you into Good Humour, for Two or Three Quarrells more will dispatch me quite.' Of her replies we have no knowledge; but from scattered specimens of her style when angry, they must often have been exceptionally scornful and unconciliatory. On one occasion, where he addresses her as 'Madam,' and returns her note to her in order that she may see, upon second thoughts, the disrespectful manner in which she treats him, he is evidently deeply wounded. She has said that their dispute is far from being a trouble to her, and he rejoins that to him any disturbance between them is the greatest affliction imaginable. And then he goes on to expostulate, with more dignity than usual, against her unreasonable use of her prerogative. 'I Love you,' he says, 'better than the light of my Eyes, or the life-blood in my Heart but when I have lett you know that, you are also to understand that neither my sight shall be so far inchanted, or my affection so much master of me as to make me forgett our common Interest. To attend my businesse as I ought and improve my fortune it is necessary that my time and my Will should be under no direction but my own. Clearly his bosom's queen had been inquiring too closely into his goings and comings. It is a strange thing, he says, in another letter, that, because she is handsome, he must be always giving her an account of every trifle, and minute of his time. And again—'Dear Prue, do not send after me, for I shall be ridiculous!' It had happened to him, no doubt. 'He is governed by his wife most abominably, as bad as Marlborough,' says another contemporary letter-writer. And we may fancy the blue eyes of Dr. Swift flashing unutterable scorn as he scribbles off this piece of intelligence to Stella and Mrs. Dingley.

In the letters which follow Steele's above quoted expostulation, the embers of misunderstanding flame and fade, to flame and fade again. A word or two of kindness makes him rapturous; a harsh expression sinks him to despair. As time goes on, the letters grow fewer, and the writers grow more used to each other's ways. But to the last Steele's affectionate nature takes fire upon the least encouragement. Once, years afterwards, when Prue is in the country and he is in London, and she calls him 'Good Dick,' it throws him into such a transport that he declares he could forget his gout, and walk down to her at Wales. 'My dear little peevish, beautiful, wise Governess, God bless you,' the letter ends. In another he assures her that, lying in her place and on her pillow, he fell into tears from thinking that his 'charming little insolent might be then awake and in pain' with headache. She wants flattery, she says, and he flatters her. 'Her son,' he declares, 'is extremely pretty, and has his face sweetened with something of the Venus his mother, which is no small delight to the Vulcan who begot him.' He assures her that, though she talks of the children, they are dear to him more because they are hers than because they are his own.[1] And this reminds us that some of the best of his later letters are about his family. Once, at this time of their mother's absence in Wales, he says that he has invited his eldest daughter to dinner with one of her teachers, because she had represented to him 'in

[1] A few sentences in this paper are borrowed from the writer's "Life of Steele," 1886.

her pretty language that she seemed helpless and friendless, without anybody's taking notice of her at Christmas, when all the children but she and two more were with their relations.' So now they are in the room where he is writing. 'I told Betty,' he adds, 'I had writ to you; and she made me open the letter again, and give her humble duty to her mother, and desire to know when she shall have the honour to see her in town.' No doubt this was in strict accordance with the proprieties as practised at Mrs. Nazereau's polite academy in Chelsea; but somehow one suspects that 'Madam Betty' would scarcely have addressed the writer of the letter with the same boarding-school formality. Elsewhere the talk is all of Eugene, the eldest boy. 'Your son, at the present writing, is mighty well employed in tumbling on the floor of the room and sweeping the sand with a feather. He grows a most delightful child, and very full of play and spirit. He is also a very great scholar: he can read his Primer; and I have brought down my Virgil. He makes most shrewd remarks upon the pictures. We are very intimate friends and play-fellows.' Yes: decidedly Steele's children must have loved their clever, faulty, kindly father.

A home without books is like a house without windows; no man has the right to bring up children without books to surround them.

H. W. Beecher.

THE PROGRESS OF POETRY [1]

By F. L. Lucas

In the tom-tom lying, silent now, in some museum-gallery the dreaming imagination may discern the cradle of Shakespeare. When some hairy object in a wilderness first found that making a regular series of noises somehow gave vent to something he felt, and, further, that it mysteriously infected with a similar excitement all his fellows who heard it, one of the greatest of all human discoveries had begun. Rhythm had become conscious. The mother of music came now into the voice of man as she had come, even then, thousands of centuries before, into the cry of the cuckoo amid the woods of a yet unhuman world. We can still dimly imagine the strange noises from apelike throats that the quiet stars somewhere heard, while the ice froze thick above the London clay and slow glaciers crept where now whirls the traffic by the Place de l'Opéra. To this day poetry remembers sometimes in our nurseries her own; as when in that sad, delightful book *Mary Olivier,* 'Dumpling hid her face and sang—

> Aw, dinny, dinny dy-Doomplin',
> Dy-Doomplin', dy-Doomplin',
> Dinny, dinny dy-Doomplin',
> Dy-Doomplin' daay.'

Thus it must have happened in the beginning, that among meaningless noises meaning began to appear, so that chant and thought were wedded and poetry was born. It must have become at once a thing of sorcery. There was no meta-

[1] Reprinted from *Authors Dead and Living* by courtesy of The Macmillan Company.

phor at first about the 'magic' of verse; and the mediæval Dominican whose fanaticism wished to impeach all poets as professors of the Black Art, was only a few thousand years behind his time. These rough voices that chanted their exultation over the harvested fruits of the earth or heads of enemies, chanted likewise, in incantation, when they hungered to harvest more; just as the artist painted the buffalo he desired magically to multiply, on his sunless cavern-walls. Art, born of play, seems always to have fallen thus at once under the purposeful tutelage of Magic and Religion, till it was of an age to stand alone. But now came the day when Poetry sold herself to Time for immortality. She had expressed the feeling of the moment at the moment for the moment; but soon men found that words set in recurrent rhythm were not only intoxicating, but as easy to remember as drunkenness is to forget. And since what was in metre they could remember, what they wished to remember they began to put in metre. So that now Poetry turned to embrace not the present only, but past and future as well: an artistic tradition became possible—the very life of literature in its early growth, though hereafter to be sometimes its death. Verse had at first been improvised—like those hoarse raven-croaks of sudden song uttered by the men of the Icelandic sagas when their steel has bitten to their foeman's brain, or their foeman's steel to their own. But now, as metre grew associated with remembrance and the Muses revealed themselves the daughters of Mnemosyne, poetry not only itself gained permanence and the strength and sanctity of age, but it flowered into new forms that could record more lastingly than stone or bronze the long-done deeds of the warrior and the ancient wisdom of the wise. And so beside chants like that worn monument from the well head of our civilisation, the *Carmen Saliare* with its Latin too obscure for even a Roman of Horace's day to understand, a mingled prayer and dance for the blessing of the fields of Rome, there grew up also such lays telling of men's deeds as

Homer makes Achilles sing before Troy fell, such versifications of peasant wisdom as lie embedded in Hesiod's *Works and Days;* or, in our own literature, narratives like the ballads, adages like the vividly terse

Wikked tunge breketh bone
Though the tunges self hath none.

And all this while the style of poetry has been becoming ever more thoughtful, more full of association and analogy, of ideas first supposed true, then found false, and yet, for their beauty's sake, dreamed truthful still. It dons conscious ornament and becomes an art, learning to tell not only what is actual or actually felt, but beautiful lies of what might be. There was once a man who, watching how the sun mounted up from the earth to the height of heaven and then sank westward to earth again, thought to himself: 'The sun is like a chariot driving up and down a hill—the sun *is* a chariot driven up and down the hill of heaven.' He died and his name perished and, long after, his belief died also; already to Homer his vision had more than half become a dream, but a dream more beautiful than the drier beliefs that replaced it and therefore by the poets still feigned true. So man's wisdom, like the wise serpent, casts off dead skin after skin; and the artist's imagination adorns itself with the empty speckled case. It was never so precious until it became useless—

The gods are forgotten in Morven of the glens,
  The sun shines clearly and gentle is the day.
Like snow from summer corries, like mist upon the bens,
  The lovely gods of darkness are vanished away——

but not from poetry. For swift the answer comes—

Paganisme immortel, es-tu mort? On le dit.
Mais Pan tout bas s'en moque, et la Sirène en rit.

And the same transition from the need of the intellect to the indulgence of the imagination for its own sake has meanwhile been at work also with simile and metaphor, those arts of saying or implying 'this is like that,' which a moment's analysis will reveal to be, still and always, the strangely simple basis of much of the most complicated poetry. At first the struggling circumlocutions of a language that in its simplicity has not enough single words for all it wants to say, as the vocabulary widens, these devices become unnecessary and so the poet's prize; and to-day, poor as Midas among the abstract riches of our dictionaries, our writers are driven back to the English of the past or the English that still lingers among the peasantry of Wessex or Connaught, to find a language which has not lost itself in the clouds, but still nests close to the earth amid the rough reality of concrete things.

Up to a point, then, this growth of poetry from its first beginnings has been almost pure gain. With ever new forms, new devices, new ideas it becomes able to give utterance (there is no prose as yet) to all that men think and feel and do. It has acquired the gift of immortality and of giving immortality,

> Where breath most breathes, even in the mouths of men.

But already there has been some slight price to pay. With the conscious art that composes to be remembered, there cannot be quite the old spontaneity; and with the art that succeeds in being remembered, comes artistic tradition. The dead singers of the past begin to rise from their graves to sit by the living poet's side, dimming his glory, daunting his courage, tempting him to imitate or to be different instead of being himself. And from now on poetry has much more serious losses than these to set against her still continued gains. Prose appears in literature, and gradually annexes all that part of human experience which has unceasingly widened with the growth of the critical intellect. And with prose appears the prosaic. Homer could make into poetry the poleaxing of an ox and his cutting up and cooking; but who after him? And in our own tongue never again since Chaucer could the Wife of Bath have ambled in metre so naturally as she does in his company along the Pilgrims' Way. As the human intelligence partly transforms, partly weakens, the naked human emotions, as 'the passionate heart' yields to 'the quiet eye,' poetry does still share some of the new conquests, becoming more complex and metaphysical and following the gropings of philosophy into the outer darkness of human destiny, or sitting down to grow carefully descriptive, so that as her infancy was cradled with music, her latter age draws closer to painting. Poetry has never been greater indeed than when, as in Æschylus and Lucretius and Shakespeare, the vitality of a ruder age has survived to give its energy to the mind's new subtlety, while the subtlety sobers, but does not sicken as yet, the old vitality. But as time goes on and men think more and act and feel less violently, some of the old giant vigour dies away, and some of the main branches of the tree begin to wither. The verse drama becomes a sapless thing; epic gives place to prose romance; and as the exuberance which produced and enjoyed poems that numbered their lines by thousands, begins to disappear, the voice of a Callimachus or a Poe makes itself heard, proclaiming the very idea of the long poem a mistake. The logical evolution of poetry here traced has not, needless to say, gone on as obviously or as uniformly as this century after century. Continually new shoots break out where all seemed dead; yet slowly the year sets on towards autumn. There may come a real St. Martin's summer, like the Alexandrian Age of Greece and our own nineteenth century, when the older forms of the springtime of poetry revive and the world's great age seems to begin anew, as beautiful as ever—Argo sails once more for Colchis through the pages of Morris and Apollonius, nature reveals her utmost loveliness before the eyes of Theocritus and Keats—and yet on their woodland beauty the touch of September lies. Twice all this has happened in the memory of man, in the Græco-Roman world and in the modern; with the winter-rest of the Dark Ages in between. Of course our world has now reached a vastness and complexity where analogy cannot be pressed into prediction; yet there is surely a vivid interest in the resemblance that has already come to be. We have seen poetry begin in momentary lyrics by nameless men; it becomes remembered; the growth of a tradition aids it, the growth of thought makes it deeper; it branches bravely out into forms that embrace all life. Prose appears as its rival, less beautiful, but strong in its swift utility, more versatile to keep pace with the progress of the intellect. Poetry triumphs indeed over growing difficulties and rivalries more splendidly than ever before; but the difficulties grow. It remains to trace further the working of the forces that have made those difficulties acute to-day—tradition, that once helped, turning more and more to hinder; thought, without which poetry could never have gained its highest, changing both our life and our poetry more and more to prose.

There is nothing obscure about the influence of the first of these. Thrice in all, Poetry has come to terms with Time—when verse began to be remembered instead of extemporised; when it began to be written; when books grew common and it began to be widely read. And the more it has thus secured the future, the more it has become subject to the past. At first, as has been said, the resulting growth of a tradition was essential to the growth of poetry itself; without the singers before Homer, no Homer. But at the stage in literature when a Theocritus or a Dryden appears, the past is growing a burden. 'Homer suffices all men,' sighs the one; and the other—

> Then fame was cheap and the first-comers sped,
> And they have kept it since by being dead.

So the fatal attempt begins to make literature out of literature instead of life. A few of the greatest have succeeded. There is no magic more potent than the necromancy with which Virgil and Milton raise to the reader's mind by their allusions ghost after ghost of poets dead before them. Yet the ivy that adds so venerable a beauty ends by strangling the tree; and poetry in its youth escaped that cancer of literatures in their later age, like Greek in the time of 'Longinus,' like our own to-day, the obsession with the need for novelty.

If this is one of our maladies, the other is likewise middle-aged—disillusion. It is no mere literary phenomenon, but the reflection of changes in human nature itself. For even human nature does change. Heracles gives place to Plato, Hardrada to Hamlet. More and more, as civilisations mature, men feel about their feelings, think about their thoughts. It is no new process—it began with the eating of the apple in Eden; but it is modern to feel it acutely. The Berserk saw nothing beyond the moment of his own red rage; it was his limitation yet his strength. 'C'est une grande force de ne pas comprendre.' But when the ballad passes from the wild, unrecking swiftness of the cry—

> Is there ony room at your head, Saunders?
> Is there ony room at your feet?
> Is there ony room at your side, Saunders,
> Where fain, fain, I wad sleep?——

to the wistful reflectiveness of the not less lovely

> O waly, waly but love be bonnie
> A little time while it is new,
> But when it's auld, it waxeth cauld
> And fadeth awa' like the morning dew.

then the day of the ballad itself is almost done. It is lost, for it has stopped to think. And yet that process is only beginning and it is a far cry still to the complexity of Hamlet, the first of modern men who feel that they have grown, somehow, too intelligent—

> Which is a proud and yet a wretched thing.

'I am always insincere, as always knowing that there are other moods'—in that avowal of Emerson's lies the essence of our time. More and more the past and the future force themselves before us, crushing the unhappy present like upper and nether millstones between them. It is this vivid sense of other moods beside those at the moment felt, that makes so true to its title Meredith's *Modern Love*. It is his anguished memory of all that Time has taken, his anguished foreseeing of all it yet will take, that give to the poetry of Hardy that almost morbid intensity which makes it so dominating, so final, so desolate, as though the eye looked on a great precipice where the ends of all the earth sank suddenly sheer to the sea. And meanwhile the critical, scientific part of the human mind, all that was anathema to Blake, has grown like the genie of an Arabian tale. Amid the veering perplexities of our age Science alone sweeps on with its strange, purposeful blindness, it knows not whither, except that it is assuredly to fresh conquests; and childish scientists perfect for our childish society with childish indiscrimination toys to amuse it, or to murder. We are enabled to hear voices saying across the Atlantic things not worth hearing across a room; to buzz round the globe like flies round a chandelier, without knowing any better what on earth to do when we arrive, than the jaded Roman noble who had flogged his horses in a whirl of dust across the Campagna from Rome to Tibur, and from Tibur back to Rome. Indeed our society may be likened to that quaint American who spent years constructing a machine which first chloroformed, then decapitated him. And yet Science is at least alive, while Philosophy mopes and Religion mutters. This in itself need not so much matter to Poetry; but it does matter to Poetry, to all our creative literature, that the thinking section of society has largely lost its scale of values and is thence in danger of ceasing to have any values at all. It has come to see through so many things. It is astray in a Sahara of wind-blown, whirling dust into which the rocks of ages have disintegrated at last. The war was in the intellectual world only one of a series of explosions—an unusually spectacular, but no isolated, one. When the advanced minds of the last century threw off Christianity and 'Hebrew old clothes,' they were almost ludicrously insistent in repeating that their moral beliefs, so far from being shaken, were merely intensified thereby. Naturally the orthodox disputed this; but in fact never prophets preached more devotedly than Carlyle and Ruskin and Arnold; and the lives of Mill and George Eliot might have done credit in their altruism to the austerest creed. Yet slowly the leaven worked. There came the sure reaction from Victorian morality, the questioning of Victorian values. From behind the broken chancel with a broken cross whence Arthur had passed, never to return, came ever more insistently as the century wore to its end, the older, more enduring chant of the Lotus-eaters—

> Death is the end of life; ah, why
> Should life all labour be?

Even the present writer can remember a disgusted birthday in childhood, celebrated by the gift of Smiles' *Self-Help,* with its complacent immortalising of men who by lives of unremitting toil rose from five shillings to fifty thousand pounds, and died and went to heaven; and now to look round at the intelligent undergraduate of to-day is to realise how dead that ideal (if it deserve the name) has become in the eyes of youth, that wants to find Life rather than a living. Is it strange? The new generation is disillusioned about professional success and about politics and about philosophy and indeed about most things. And in some ways it is none the worse for that. For who can read without a cold disgust some of those Victorian lives of people who never lied to any one except, always, to themselves; who lived in a sort of moral Crystal Palace, and stood in queues to fling the first stone at the woman taken in adultery? There is indeed much truth in the remark of some defender of our time—'We are a great deal less moral than you were, but a great deal decenter.'

And yet what a mass of real literature that century produced! Partly because its great men shared its illusions and believed in progress, and felt that many things were worth while; but still more because they did not share its superstitions, and so felt their lives well and nobly filled in fighting against these dragons of their time. And now we sit, a little bleakly, on that battlefield whence the Arnolds and Huxleys and Swinburnes have vanished. Those forts of folly have fallen, those once massive objects of belief been shaken and overthrown—God's Englishmen and the original virtue of the middle classes, and the value of work for work's sake, and freedom for freedom's sake, and chastity for chastity's sake. And the war and the peace were merely a culmination of this process of cynicising a race which still believed that its governments were honest, and its clergy Christian. Here too there were redeeming things. While bishops defended the leaving of Zeppelin crews to drown in the North Sea, the kindly cynicism of the British soldier was pressing cigarettes on his captured enemies; and whatever came of the oaths of politicians, Wilfred Owen could still write in words that might well have bewildered a Victorian—

> I have perceived much beauty
> In the hoarse oaths that kept our courage straight.

And then the Peace. . . . And now the critical reason having devoured so much, has been turning more and more to rend itself; it becomes 'intelligent' to disbelieve in the intellect, and to imagine that literature can become young again by learning to have no sense.

Doch jetzt ist alles wie verschoben,
  Das ist ein Drängen, eine Not!
Gestorben ist der Herrgott oben,
  Und unten ist der Teufel tot.

Und alles schaut so grämlich trübe,
  So krausverwirrt und morsch und kalt,
Und wäre nicht das bisschen *Liebe,*
  So gäb es nirgends einen Halt.

And so in fact our creative literature has reduced itself to novels, to lyrics, and to plays, which deal almost exclusively with this one surviving passion. The two things that still inspire us are love and disillusion—the disillusion of the poetry of Hardy and Housman, Miss Millay and Mr. Eliot, of novels like *Antic Hay,* of plays like *The Vortex.* No one has better uttered than Miss Iris Tree this blank greyness of our world—

Grey house and grey house and after that grey house,
Another house as grey and steep and still:
An old cat tired of playing with a mouse,
A sick child tired of chasing down the hill.

Shuffle and hurry, idle feet and slow,
Grim face, and merry face, so ugly all!
Why do you hurry? Where is there to go?
Why are you shouting? Who is there to call?

We have jettisoned the old iron that was the Victorian ballast; we have torn up the old charts by which they sailed so hopefully towards the port of El Dorado; and in consequence we roll sickly, without steerage-way, in the trough of an empty sea. And because everything in life matters as much as anything else, provided it is novel enough to distract our *ennui,* there has arisen among us an ingenious type of fiction which, with many individual differences, has this in common—that it sees existence through a microscope. Some of these works have great qualities; they have revealed us things no eye had seen before; their microscopes are marvels of ingenuity and their observation a miracle of skill and patience. With others of these writers one would think that 'trivial' was a word they were incapable of understanding, and sense a thing of which they had never heard. And, when all is said, this art of magnifying the minutiæ of life and feeling finds scant room for greater matters; and it makes the observer short-sighted. 'Tout montrer c'est ne rien faire voir.' Often amused, often fascinated, I grow weary of this day of small things, of these acute and highly polished writers lost in their myriad details like sharp little needles in haystacks, of these incoherent characters who derive emotions of equal interest and intensity from the look of a woman and a tea-leaf, or feel that they have found Reality and all's right with the world, because they caught the eye of a narcissus that morning, walking through the park. Life may be futile; but such a fiddling as this? We do not ask, or want, 'one increasing purpose.' Life is worth while, if it is, for its own sake alone. But this sort of life? This class of fiction is obsessed, to adapt the current jargon, with an in*ter*iority complex. Its figures have so much psychology that they have no room for character. It has worked up the weakness of Hamlet and forgotten the fineness; it has travestied the nobility of the *Odyssey* into that dreary *reductio ad absurdum* of itself, *Ulysses.*

Like such fiction, much of our would-be advanced poetry suffers from the same lust for novelty, the same loss of values, the same lack of sanity. If it is less microscopic, it is equally indiscriminating, and even more anti-rational. The reaction which raves in the novels of Mr. D. H. Lawrence not merely against the abuse, but the use, of the intellect, has found easier expression in whole volumes of metrical incoherence. A single example will more than suffice, from a type of verse much discussed, and sometimes read, in 'intellectual' society—

> When
> Don
> Pasquito arrived at the seaside
> Where the donkey's hide tide brayed, he
> Saw the banditto Jo in a black cape
> Whose slack shape waved like the sea——
> Thetis wrote a treatise noting wheat is silver like the sea; the lovely cheat is sweet as foam; Erotis notices that she
> Will
> Steal
> The
> Wheat-king's luggage, like Babel
> Before the League of Nations grew——
> So Jo put the luggage and the label
> In the pocket of Flo the Kangaroo.

It will surely seem very revealing to the future social historian that in the England of our time it should have been worth a publisher's while, even with all the resources of advertisement, to put this sort of verse in print. It may serve, if for nothing else, as a post-war memorial of a period when a section of society was so obsessed by the weight of established tradition, that it was prepared to go on four legs for the sole reason that its fathers had walked on two; yet intellectually so exhausted that it could only snatch at vulgarity as the best substitute for vitality, whimsicality as the nearest thing to wit. This is an extreme case; but even the work of writers not to be named in the same breath suffers from a not dissimilar lack of simple good taste and simple good sense. These things do not need exemplifying; it is extraordinary that they should need saying. A poet may well feel the need to utter his repulsion at certain sides of life; only, inventorying dustbins does not happen to be the way to do it. It is the true poet's secret to be able to touch even pitch without becoming foul; but to touch, not to wallow. Dante's *Inferno* bubbles with slime that might easily have grown disgusting; but no fleck stains that haughty, bitter face as it passes through the smother and the stench of Hell. And were Dante writing of the modern counterpart, do we suppose that he could not or would not make us feel the squalid horror that lives in our cities, without versified exhibitions of typists' combinations drying out of tenement windows? Are such distinctions arbitrary? Of course they are. These things are, in either sense, a matter of taste. They cannot be argued. It is even possible to do in one language what is impossible in another, to say with dignity in Latin or with grace in French what cannot be said without meanness in English. There is no test but the result; and the critic speaks only for himself. But it seems to me a pity that a good deal of modern talent should waste itself because, in the passion for something new, it forgets that in certain directions it cannot go further without faring worse. For there are things that do not really follow fashions nor admit of innovation. In those words of the Delphic Apollo that became a proverb of Greek wisdom—

Seek not to move Camarina; for unmoved it had best remain.

Again, even granting that civilised conceptions of what is vulgar may vary over long periods, to cultivate incoherence by way of a change from connected thinking is really an experiment not worth the making. We have developed a veritable somnambulance corps of poets who reel and wander through page on page of dream and trance, with a contempt for the human reason that in some instances they would do better to reserve for their own. In one case out of ten it may be that unintelligible writers are honestly trying to say clearly what is fundamentally obscure; in the other nine they are trying to put obscurely what, put clearly, would as clearly be nonsense or platitude. We have too many authors who, like cuttlefish, use ink as camouflage.

But it is not merely that the reaction against tradition makes such modern fiction and poetry sometimes squalid, or that the reaction against reason makes it often muddle-headed and occasionally bedlamite; it is more serious that, helped by both these tendencies, it seems so frequently to have lost the sense that after all some things do matter more than others in human life, some things are finer than others in human nature. The essential thrill that comes in common from the literature of a hundred differing ages, I cannot get from work which seems too indifferent to lucidity and good sense to be good art, too blind to human greatness to be great. Great poetry may be written though a man drab and cheat and rob hen-roosts all his days, if he has yet Villon's sense of the desolate magnificence of the pageant of man's life, of the queenliness of its beauty that fades so swiftly away. It may be written though its writer cry to the deaf heavens that 'all is filth,' if he has yet Leopardi's sense, in that very utterance, of pride in his own clearness of vision and fortitude of soul. Poetry may leave us saddened, yet not unsatisfied, though it search with unflinching fingers the miserable cesspools of our society, provided it gives, like Crabbe's, the impression of a personality behind, that holds with a Roman strength to its sense of form and order, of unexpected beauty and sudden pity, of certain values and certain standards, mistaken it may be, but genuine, amid the chaos of the world. Whatever else such men have disbelieved in, they have believed in the value of the intellect, of courage, of pity, even if they half denied it to themselves. These things are fine, not fashions; and without some touch of them great literature is not written. Whatever else reason may have undermined, it is not reason that has blunted or can blunt our instinctive sense of what is magnificent and what is mean, any more than botany can touch our sense of the beauty of the rose. These things reach on across space and time, while moralities change from frontier to frontier and from generation to generation. Whatever the gulf between West and East, something in us rises at once in answer to the proud spirit of the Japanese saying, 'It is better to be a crystal and be broken than to be perfect like a tile upon the housetop.' And the things that Homer felt splendid move us still. There is a story (a favourite with Sainte-Beuve) how, when after the sack of Corinth the consul was reviewing the captives destined to be slaves in Rome, he was struck by the look of a boy among them and calling him forward, to test his education, bade him write something in the dust at their feet. In silence the boy traced the lines of Homer where Odysseus, in the bitterness of death at sea, cries aloud his longing to have fallen fighting instead on the plains of Ilios—

> Τρισμάκαρες Δαναοὶ καὶ τετράκις, οἵ τότ' ὄλοντο
> Τροίῃ ἐυ εὐρείῃ, χάριν 'Ατρείδῃσι Φέροντες.

> Ah, thrice and four times blest those Greeks that fell
> In Troy's wide land for the sons of Atreus' sake!

Mummius was a Roman, and a plebeian Roman, and is a byword still for his greedy inappreciation of Greek works of art. Yet he realised the boy's mingled pride in his fallen country's poetry and bitterness at not having found, himself, a better end before the disgrace of Greece; and in pity and admiration gave him his liberty. And we to-day in our distant land and time and civilisation can still feel a sudden sympathy with that touch of greatness in both the Roman conqueror and the Corinthian boy, called forth in its turn by the eternal greatness of Homer. These things that wake the deepest and finest echoes in men's hearts are not the things that change; they are stronger than custom and creed; and they are still the only foundation on which men can build themselves a living poetry, and not too prosaic lives.

For these two cannot be wholly separated; and if much modern writing seems not to respond, not to have eyes for this beauty where life and poetry join hands, that is partly, I suspect, because it is written by men of letters who are nothing more. The division of labour has torn our lives in two. While our workers drudge, our intellectuals become mere intellectuals; the hand forgets the brain and the brain the hand. George Scudéry is a ridiculous figure enough in literature; yet literature might have gained much and escaped a great deal, if only more of those who have practised it had been able to echo or even to appreciate his boast: 'I have passed more days in the camp than in the library. I have used more matches to light my musket than my candles.' It was not mere eccentricity that made Æschylus proudly record in his epitaph that he had fought at Marathon, without adding one word of the hundred dramas he had left posterity. And if this is but conjecture, I cannot but remember how much more it has meant even to my own experience, to have seen the horrible sublimity of that real Inferno stretched under the darkness of the flame-shot sky from Mametz to Ovillers La Boisselle, than even to have read Dante. And anyway, who would not rather never have opened Shakespeare than never have been in love? It is no service to literature to talk, like Flaubert, as if a perfect sentence was the supreme crown of all the effort of mankind. It is not in libraries that the great books are written. It is better to be Launcelot than the lady of Shalott; there is a curse upon her, magic though her mirror be. But of course we need both; if it is fatal to sever literature from life, life would be a miserably poor thing without literature. None will ever forget it, who has once seen the jagged peaks of Pindus bitten as on steel against the western sky, while the dusk sweeps up from Pheræ across the

Thessalian Plain and the low lands that Achilles ruled; or watched the rising moonlight strike across the Vale of Lacedæmon on the long rampart of the snows of Taygetus; and yet how much less even that untold loveliness would have been without the memories of the poetry of Greece! The vividest poetry is that which sets itself like music, generation after generation, to the acts of life, as even Nero died with Homer on his lips, or Taillefer rode chanting the song of Roland up Senlac Hill, or Wolfe passed up the darkness of the St. Lawrence to his last battle, repeating the *Elegy* of Gray. It is true that most of our existence has to be spent on far other and more prosaic levels than this. That active, many-sided beauty of daily life which men have dreamed as existing in Periclean Athens or the Florence of the first Medici, or which makes the life of William Morris as fine and finished as a work of art among the depressing biographies of most of his contemporaries, has been the lucky gift of only a few in only a few ages of the world. Not many can hope for the opportunities of a Morris, still less for the genius which enabled him both to make his own life what it was, and to imagine the only Utopia in which poetry could live. But far better fail to attain that than cease to desire it. And I cannot believe that much lasting good is to be looked for from the sort of writer who sees nothing in the world to chronicle but small beer, or no way of facing it except an intoxication which refuses to reason.

If these are the besetting faults of the present, it is at least very understandable in the light of the past that it should be so. The state of modern poetry is certainly not satisfactory; it is limited to a rather dangerously small circle, so that it is common to find wide and cultivated readers who never look at a line of it. Yet its technical handling of the established forms is often extremely competent, and we have in fairness to remember how hard it is becoming to say anything both good and new. If our time cannot compare in poetry with the best periods of the last two centuries, it is certainly much better than the worst. What augurs least well for the future is the scarcity of younger writers of promise, and the difficulty of seeing in what new directions poetry can develop. If the nineteenth century with its succession of revivals of the mediæval and Elizabethan was our Alexandrian Age, what is to follow now? Only a series of slight and exquisitely finished short poems like the epigrams which the Greek decadence went on producing almost up to the fall of Constantinople? Clearly it is fatal for poetry to be perpetually reviving the past; and our writers can hardly go on and on, turning, like Hardy and Synge, to the older world of the peasant. It sounds plausible enough to say that poetry must keep pace with the growing complication of modern life. In practice it is not so simple. A hundred years ago Wordsworth looked forward to a new poetry of science; we are still waiting for it. The truth is, I think, partly, that though poetry can follow science and invention, it cannot keep up—it lags behind. Give time, and flowers will spring even on factory-wall and slag-heap; but only when a deep enough soil of human associations has formed itself there. These things will not be hurried. Railway and steamship can find a natural place in poetry to-day that would have been impossible a century ago. But it is not merely a question of time. Some things seem to remain prosaic to eternity, resisting the genius and audacity even of a Meredith or a Hardy; and it is depressing to think of how many of the ugly objects with ugly names that fill our mechanicalised world this seems to be true. It is somehow possible poetically to liken a mountain-peak to a horn, or call it *'la Dent du Midi'*; but not to compare it to a screw-driver or a toothpick, even though it be more like those than anything else. Associations refuse to be ignored, as the more imbecile poems of Wordsworth exist to remind us; and daring as some of our modernists may think themselves, they are unlikely to go further or fare better than Fracastoro with his poem entitled *Syphilis.*

The new constructions which the modern mind so self-consciously puts together do not easily acquire the beauty which we find in immemorial things that seem insensibly to have grown as natural as human nature itself. A factory chimney may on occasion seem beautiful, but it generally does not; a tree or a team ploughing or a smithy may sometimes not seem beautiful, but they generally do. The reasons of such differences are a tangle of æsthetics and associations; but it is at least intelligible that, as our view of the world has become ever less anthropomorphic and more inhuman, it should have become correspondingly less poetic. Proteus rising from the sea and a common seal, Iris the messenger of Heaven and the refractive power of drops of water, are conceptions that appeal to the imagination with extremely different intensity. Otherwise, how is it that European poetry after three thousand years still finds repeated inspiration, not in Newton or Einstein, but in the fancied forms with which a few prehistoric Greeks humanised the unknown universe? The whole march of science has been occupied with hunting down and exterminating everything anthropomorphic in our ideas of the world about us. The process has, indeed, been slow and desperately resisted by the human imagination; long after men had realised that there was no earthly reason for attributing to God a human beard, they continued, and continue, to think that there must be some reason for crediting Him with a human mind and human feelings. It is not simply because the glamour of the past lies over the world of Athene and Aphrodite, of Odin and Thor, of elf and fay, that it seems more poetical; it actually was more poetical, because more human and alive; and let us face that. Poetry has long been living on its capital; the raw material of which it is made is no longer added to as fast as it once was. And the poetry of science and modern life is more easily talked about than written.

Of putting into verse the complexity of modern emotions there seems to be much more hope. In that way the sonnet-sequence of Meredith and the poems of Hardy point out a road which still leads somewhere, and may, I think, be considered the most truly modern poetry of high rank that we possess. But there are two ways of treating such complex states of mind—as a welter of incomprehensible ideas and impulses; or as a battle of desires, incompatible indeed and inconsistent, but in themselves both rational and familiar. The first method leaves the reader in mystery, the second gives the pleasure of new and deepened understanding. There are readers, of course, who ask nothing better than mystification; that is a matter of temperament; one cannot argue with owls. But we are, I feel, more complex than Elizabethans, because we are conscious of more moods and more conflicting impulses at once, rather than because the fundamental impulses themselves are much altered. That is the real difference between the hero of *Modern Love* and Othello; and Meredith's sequence is great as a triumph of passionate intellectual analysis, where the heart never blurs the brain.

It is in fact towards more brain that poetry must probably continue to travel, as it has travelled since it began. There is no going back. If the reason has taken much, it has given other things; if it destroyed the ballad, it brought us Donne; we need more of it, not less. Arnold was being extreme, but not unsound, when after criticising Tennyson's lack of intellect, he added: 'No modern poet can make much of his business unless he is preëminently strong in this.' There has always been and, one hopes, always will be the poetry of pure beauty beside the poetry of ideas; if less has been said of it in this discussion, it is because the poets who write it either have or have not the needful gifts of eye and ear and tongue—and in either case there is no more to say. Very few poets, however, have in practice lived by the beauty of the senses alone; they have felt the need to express ideas, as even Keats came to feel it. And it is in pieces not more than a few pages in length, sometimes lyric, sometimes narrative, which express, glimpse-wise, the emotions of men sensitive, clear-headed, but not cold at heart, in answer to the bitter wit of nature, as Peer Gynt saw her, to the subtle ironies, the sudden flashes of passion and pity that make life so tragic and yet enthralling —it is in such work that I seem to see the most hopeful poetry of the present and future.

As for its form, I have not much faith in experiments which loosen metre into *vers libre*. Often it would be better to turn frankly to downright prose, through which indeed, with its greater freedom and adaptability, more and more of our poetic impulses may come to find expression. This too is only a continuance of a trend we have already traced. A prose novel or play can always soar into poetry at its supreme moments, whereas a verse narrative or drama is spoilt the moment it sinks to the prosaic; and the more critical we become of verse, and of bathos in it, the more this disadvantage tells. Accordingly the novel has long since replaced the epic, the prose history the verse-chronicle, while the simple cadences of Maeterlinck and Synge and D'Annunzio have produced a far more poetic type of play than would now be possible in metre. There is, in short, more poetry in Gibbon's work than if he had written an epic on the *Decline* in heroic couplets; there is more poetry in the close of Mr. Strachey's *Queen Victoria* than all the verse elegies on that sovereign put together can have contained. Apart from this, the infinite variety of the English stanza, with the new individuality it will always take in the hands of masters like Housman or Walter de la Mare, should for long yet provide music enough for all we are likely to find to say. There is no question of legislating for genius; genius can generally look after itself in any epoch; it is the good writer, not of genius, who is often made or marred by the fashions and tendencies of his age. And thence the importance of clearer writing and thinking, of a clearer sense of some standards or other alike in life and literature, if our progressive poetry is to progress into anything but speedy oblivion.

But though we may grow impatient at times with the flood of little poetry-books written in the old fashion or the new that pours upon us, it is only justice to remember that these writers are at all events contributing to keep the practice of their art, if hardly their own memories, alive. After all, the first singers were content to be forgotten when they had left their great verse to a little clan; and perhaps some of our present irritable individualism about literary property and literary immortality may drop away, and leave us none the poorer. That the race of poets, however, is in such danger of dying, as some have suggested, I cannot easily believe. We cannot indeed foresee what effect changes in the external world may have on poetry. It is possible, to take a single instance, that when broadcasting has ceased to be a toy, it might be the means of bringing the poet's living voice once more, as in the childhood of poetry, direct to the ears of men. It is possible that another social upheaval might liberate a new flood of hopes and energies like the French Revolution, or another war bring a new Dark Age and eventually the beginning of the whole long cycle over again. Or a new basis of society might transform men's literature together with their lives. Most Utopias indeed might well be the end of poetry, if they ever came to be established; only, if they ever came to be established, one trusts that human nature would even more speedily be the end of the Utopias. Anatole France has pictured a future world where with the human passions poetry itself has passed away and only music remains. It is not altogether a new idea; the old-fashioned Heaven was much the same. But in fact, though the founders of cloud-cities almost always forget it, they can never really barricade their shadowy streets against the eternal forces of human unhappiness, love and jealousy and grief and separation, all the sorrows to which man delivered himself and his posterity, when he ceased to live like the beasts that are glad or grieve for the moment only, and laid bare his soul to the past that torments him and the future that dismays. Humanity could only be made perfectly happy by being so changed as to be no longer human, a new race of beings. And towards man's destiny of pain there remain two attitudes which can give at least some consolation, the best that there is to be had—the religious and the poetic. Some take one, some the other, some both. But while men have eyes for transient beauty, while they suffer and pity suffering, while they fear, and cherish courage, while they love and lose and remember, we may believe that the last poet will not find his grave.

οὔπω μῆνας ἄγων ἔκαμ' οὐρανὸς οὐδ' ἐνιαυτούς·
πολλοὶ κινήσουσιν ἔτι τροχὸν ἅρματος ἵπποι.

Leisure without books is death, and the burial of a man alive.

SENECA—*Ep.* 82.

THE CULT OF UNINTELLIGIBILITY[1]

By Max Eastman

Two tendencies are confused in the literary movement called modernist which ought to be distinguished. They are clearly distinguished for me, because I like one of them and the other I regard as an affliction. But many people see only one tendency here and are puzzled to define it. The tendency that I like might be called the cultivation of pure poetry. The tendency that I do not like I call the cult of unintelligibility.

If you pick up a book by Hart Crane, E. E. Cummings, James Joyce, Gertrude Stein, Edith Sitwell, or any of the "modernists," and read a page innocently, I think the first feeling you will have is that the author isn't telling you anything. It may seem that he isn't telling you anything because he doesn't know anything. Or it may seem that he knows something, but he won't tell. In any case he is uncommunicative. He is unfriendly. He seems to be playing by himself, and offering you somewhat incidentally the opportunity to look on.

All poetry, according to Mr. I. A. Richards, is an act of communication. It is that, whether the poet thinks so or not, because words are in their very nature communications. All literature, indeed, Mr. Richards describes as a verbal communication of values. I defer to him because he is a psychologist who teaches literature. I accept his assertion that all literature is *in some degree* a communicative act, and I say that modernist literature is characterized by an increasing stinginess in the performance of this act.

[1] Reprinted by the kind permission of the author.

A dominant tendency of the advancing schools of poetry for the last twenty years has been to decrease the range, the volume, and the definiteness of communication. To my mind that statement, which has a verifiable meaning, might take the place of about one-half of the misty literarious talk of the poets and the poet-critics of the modernist movement. They are not "abandoning romanticism," "returning to the eighteenth-century tradition," "inaugurating a new-classical era"—it is the height of romanticism to imagine that they are. They are not "overcoming the distinction between subject-matter and form," "revolting against tyranny of the general reader," being "primitive," being "intellectual," being "aesthetic," instituting an "artificial barbarism," or clinging to the "hard matter-of-fact skeleton of poetic logic." There is no such skeleton and no such logic. What they are doing is withdrawing into themselves. They are communicating to fewer people, they are communicating less, and what they communicate is less definitely determined. And this is true of the whole movement, all the way from free verse to free association.

Free verse decreases the definiteness of communication by introducing into the transcription of poetry a gross mark of punctuation which has no significance commonly agreed upon. Suppose that instead of this arbitrary line-division I made up a new character, a semicolon composed of two commas with the tails going opposite ways. And suppose I announced that as a poet I was going to use that comma-colon wherever and whenever I wanted to, like the joker in the pack, without any agreement as to its value, either rhythmical or grammatical. It would be obvious, would it not, that the freedom I had acquired was not a freedom to communicate more to my readers, but a freedom from the terms of communication—a freedom to play by myself? This is the principal thing accomplished by the line-division in free verse, except in a few poems where it is employed, as Blake and Whitman usually employed it, to divide the actual phrases of a chant.

From free verse it was a short step to free punctuation. I mean the habit of turning loose a handful of punctuation marks like a flock of bacteria to browse all over the page, and even eat their way into the insides of apparently healthy words. Let us see an example of this from the poetry of E. E. Cummings. We have to *see* his poetry because it is composed so largely of punctuation that it cannot be heard. In fact we shall soon have to exhibit Cummings in a projection-room; for undoubtedly the next step in modernism will be to show these punctuation marks in the actual process of entering a word, and show how the nucleus of the word, its meaning divides, and the new and more delicate meanings are formed by a process of endogastric proliferation. For the present we must content ourselves with examining the poem first in its normal condition, and then seeing how it looks when infected or impregnated with punctuation marks.

Among these red pieces of day—against which, and quite silently, hills made of blue and green paper, scorch-bending themselves, upcurve into anguish, climbing spiral, and disappear—satanic and blasé, a black goat lookingly wanders. There is nothing left of the world, but into this nothing "il treno per Roma signori?" jerkily rushes.

That is the poem, and it might be an excellent one, if the poet would come down and tell us where he is and what he is talking about. Here is the way it looks after an attack of punctuation, and as it appears in published form:

Among
    these
        red pieces of
day (against which and
quite silently hills
made of blueandgreen paper

scorchbend ingthem
-selves-U
pcurv E, into:
                    anguish(clim
b)ing
s-p-i-r-a-
l
and,disappear)
                    Satanic and blasé
a black goat lookingly wanders

There is nothing left of the world but
into this noth
ing il treno* per
Roma si-gnori?
jerk.
ilyr, ushes

You can see from this that punctuation is a serious disease. Moreover, it is quite possible that if you put poetry under the microscope you would find that the commas and parentheses themselves have been attacked by still more minute grammatical organisms, and that the whole thing is simply honeycombed with punctuation.

To show the length to which a sane man will go when he sets out to be literary, let me quote the comment of Paul Rosenfeld on Cummings's use of punctuation marks:

> The typographical display exists upon his pages never in the intention of picture-writing, and always for the purpose of marking the acceleration and hesitation of the rapid, capricious, and melodic line.

What would a man who was trying to be scientific say about this same question? Or rather what would he do

*I venture to correct Mr. Cummings's spelling of this word, hoping that "trene" was a typographical mistake and not a part of his lyrical inspiration.

about it—for science has a way of answering questions by doing something. He would take two of the most enthusiastic admirers of this poetry—Paul Rosenfeld might be one, and E. E. Cummings another—lead them into seperate soundproof chambers and permit them to read this poem in the august presence of a sphygmograph, a machine designed to record in a white line on a black roller the actual pulsations of the "rapid, capricious, and melodic line" as it is "marked" by these signs of punctuation. Is there any reason to believe that, punctuation being what it is and human nature being what it is, the two of them would produce curves showing the same "accelerations and hesitations" at the points where these punctuation marks appear? Of course they would not. It is only necessary to mention the experiment. The critic, therefore, is not talking sense. He is talking literarious nonsense.

Science is nothing but a persistent and organized effort to talk sense. And science would tell us that these punctuation marks on the rampage do not promote accuracy of communication, but destroy it. They may have a very subtle, fine, and real value within the poet's mind. It is a mere conspiracy of folly to pretend that they have an identic value in the mind of any reader.

From free punctuation it is an easy step to free grammar—or rather, freedom from grammar. I use this inexact expression to characterize the kind of freedom attained, in its ultimate purity, by Gertrude Stein. Let us examine a passage of Gertrudian prose:

The Hartford pigpen never supported, never confirmed food, therefore are not supported and this building will pay for that and food which confirmed it. White immortal eternal receipt for food. The war planet Mars. I have the white immortal eternal receipt. . . .

I was looking at you, the sweet boy that does want sweet soap. Neatness of feet does not win feet, but feet win the neatness of men. Run does not run west but west runs east. I like west strawberries best.

One can hardly deny a beauty of ingenuity to these lines. They have a fluency upon the tongue, a logical intricacy that is intriguing. But any deeper value they may have, value for the mind or the passions of a reader, will be composed of elements not objectively implied but accidentally suggested by them. No doubt anyone who dwells with idle energy upon their plausible music will find thoughts and impulses from his own life rising to employ them as symbol or pattern for a moment of thought or imaginative realization. But the impulses that rise to these lines from the reader's life will never by any chance be the same that dictated them in the life of the author. Communication is here reduced to a minimum. The values are private as the emotional life of the insane. In fact the passage quoted was not from Gertrude Stein, but from the ravings of a manic-depressive cited by Kraepelin in his *Clinical Psychiatry*. Here is a passage from Gertrude Stein:

> Any space is not quiet it is so likely to be shiny. Darkness is sectional. There is a way to see in onion and surely very surely rhubarb and a tomato, surely very surely there is that seeding.

It is essentially the same thing, except that Gertrude Stein perpetrates it voluntarily, and—to judge by the external appearance—not quite so well. It is private literature. It is intracerebral art.

Edith Sitwell says, in her *Poetry and Criticism*, that Gertrude Stein is "bringing back life to our language by what appears at first to be an anarchic process. First she breaks down the predestined groups of words, their sleepy family habits; then she rebrightens them, examines their texture, and builds them into new and vital shapes." If this engaging statement means anything except what every good and vivid writer does, it means that Miss Stein is emptying words of the social element. Words are vessels of communion; she is treating them as empty vessels, polishing them and setting them in a row.

James Joyce not only polishes the words that he sets in a row, but molds them and fires them in his own oven. From free grammar he has taken a farther step to free etymology. All boisterous writers have made up words, but they have made them in such a way or placed them in such a context that their meaning or value was conveyed to the reader. Joyce, in his recent writing, makes up words to suit the whim-chances of a process going on only in his own brain.

For if the lingo gasped between kicksheets were to be preached from the mouths of wickerchurchwardens and metaphysicians in the row and advokaatoes, allvoyous, demivoyelles, longuoaths, lesbiels, dentelles, gutterhowls and furtz, where would their practice be or where the human race itself were the Pythagorean sesquipedalia of the panepistemion, grunted and gromwelled, ichabod, habakuk, opanoff, uggamyg, hapaxle, gomenon, ppppfff, over country stiles, behind slated dwellinghouses, down blind lanes, or, when all fruit fails, under some sacking left on a coarse cart?

This literary form also finds its involuntary parallel in the madhouse. There too the inevitable step is taken from free grammar to free etymology. That automatic "flight of ideas," the result of some pathological drying upward of the deeper associational roots of words, naturally passes over into a mere flight of syllables. Indeed anyone can imitate both these symptoms by compelling himself to talk faster than he can think or feel. But he cannot imitate them with the rare and various genius of James Joyce. Joyce is equipped for creative etymology as few men ever were. He has a curious and wide learning in languages and their ways; he has a prodigiously fine ear. You feel that he lives in a world of spoken sounds, through which he goes hearing as acutely as a dog goes smelling, that all the riches of his mind are but an ingenious complication of the neural paths from ear to tongue. The goal toward which he seems to be traveling with all this equipment of genius is the creation of a language of his own—a language which might be superior poetically, as Esperanto is practically, to any of the known tongues. It might be immortal—as immortal as the steel shelves of the libraries in which it would rest. But how little it would communicate, and to how few. When it is not a humorous emotion—as praise God it often is—that we enjoy with Joyce in his extreme etymological adventures, what is there that we experience in common with him? A kind of elementary tongue dance, a feeling of the willingness to perform it. This may be enriched a little among the devoted by prolonged hard work with a pile of dictionaries, but in the main the richer values—except the mere value of devotion—will be supplied by the reader's own mind and imagination. They will be accidental and his own.

For better or worse, it results from the indefiniteness of the matter communicated in these extreme kinds of freedom that only one genius can distinguish himself in each kind. Gertrude Stein discovered the flight of ideas as a literary form some twenty years ago, and she has been hammering away at it, lonely and immortal, ever since. No one else can distinguish himself in this form, because there are no definite distinctions in it. A similar thing is true of Joyce in so far as he speaks a private language, and of Cummings as the discoverer of intraverbal punctuation. They cannot be rivalled; they can only be imitated. Their glory is secure.

Young modernists ought not be discouraged by the fact, however, for there are other freedoms still to be won. There is alphabetical freedom, for instance. Why should letters within a word be permitted to congregate forever in the same dull, old, conventional and sleepy groups? Why not a little spontaneity of arrangement here, and the occasional eruption of an Arabic or Chinese or Russian letter that happens to linger in the memory and chime with the whims of the poet? The Russians have a great, fat, double-squatting letter that looks like a toad sitting on his grandmother waving his arms. One poet might enrich the alphabet with borrowings like this. Another might abandon the alphabet altogether and make a new one more congenial to his inner life.

Moreover, with all respect to the typographical genius of E. E. Cummings, he is a mere infant in the free art of punctuation. Why content oneself with meagerly redistributing a handful of tame signs, dried up, stale, dead and familiar to all Western European civilization for upwards of three thousand years? Can you wake a man up with an exclamation point that was known to his father and his grandfather and his great-grandfathers before him? Can you stop the modern breath with a colon that was a bore to Cleopatra? Let us have a little real creative activity in these fields. A little cross-breeding between plus signs and semicolons would be a good beginning. By crossing the minus sign with the colon we got the sign of division; a cross between a plus sign and a semicolon might give us something even more remarkable. That has never been tried. And why not introduce a few foreign strains here, too? Spanish question marks behave in very queer ways, too, standing on their heads in front of a question as well as jumping up and making faces behind it. All these things would help to jazz up the rapid, capricious, and melodic line. Each of them would give one more incommunicative poet a place of distinction.

And then there is free type-setting still to be adequately exploited in English, although known long ago to the futurist poets of Italy. And there is free photo-engraving still to be imported from Russia. I have a volume given me by the Russian poet, Maiakovsky, in which a large part of the total effect is produced by a series of scrapbook designs made out of reproduced photographs and magazine half-tones. The cover design is a picture of the poet's wife, a charming girl in real life, apparently entering the first stages of an epileptic fit. On another page she appears, more tranquilly, as an insert in a menagerie. Another page shows Maiakovsky himself being shampooed by a dinosaur while engaging in a long-distance telephone conversation through an automobile horn with his cook who seems to be standing on the poop-deck of an astronomical observatory getting ready to do the family wash. If Paul Rosenfeld thinks that E. E. Cummings's typography is not picture writing, it may be so, although the question is subtle. But here is a far more powerful poet than E. E. Cummings—the most gifted Slavic poet of his generation—and several volumes of his rhapsodical mixtures of poetry with picture writing of the most childlike type have been published by the State Printing House and sold by the tens of thousands in Soviet Russia.

Maiakovsky's crazy-quilt photo-designs are actual illustrations of the themes of his poems. Both the themes and the illustrations are infected with unintelligibility, and I find the designs distasteful because they are inexpressive and old-fashioned. Even in progressive kindergartens the scrapbook has been replaced by picture writing of a more active and original kind. Nevertheless, in so far as these typographical experiments *are* picture writing, and overtly so, they are not so much a part of the cult of unintelligibility as an effort to escape from it. The marks in the book, having lost their clear character as signs suggesting imaginary experience to the reader, begin to be cultivated as an offering of actual experience to him. Following this road, the modernist poets might become exquisite painters of letters as the poets of ancient China were. They might give their creative attention to the mixing of inks, the selecting or inventing of textures and tints of paper, and the binding of books. They might even anoint their verses, as once the Persian poets did, with an appropriate odor—not always as in those days, you may be sure, a pleasant one. And in this manner they could revive, if they had money enough, on a small cultural island in the midst of our machine civilization, some of the charms of a past age of the world. But in so far as they are really modern, and not wealthier than is usual with poets, I do not see how they can go very far in this direction, except to abandon poetry altogether and become either painters, on the one hand, or on the other, printers and manufacturers of ink and paper. And that is, perhaps, the logical outcome of the tendency I am describing—a tendency to ignore the terms of the act of verbal communication.

I have described only the cruder manifestations of this tendency. It appears, however, in poetry that is quite sociable in the matter of verse-form and grammar and punctuation and etymology. A freedom to make unlimited use of all the foreign languages that happen to be known to the author is one of its manifestations. A freedom to make unexplicit allusions to some book or manuscript he happens to have been reading—accessible perhaps only in the Bibliothèque Nationale or the British Museum—is another. Mr. Graves and Miss Riding in their *Survey of Modernist Poetry* speak with great enthusiasm of this kind of freedom.

In a single volume of Ezra Pound's *Lustra,* they tell us, "occur literary references to Greek, Latin, Spanish, Italian, Provençale, and Chinese literature—some of these incorrectly given. Mr. Eliot, who is a more serious scholar, has references in *The Waste Land* to Greek, Latin, Spanish, Italian, French, German, and Sanskrit. The English classics quoted or referred to are not the stock-classics to which Victorian and post-Victorian poets paid tribute, not Chaucer, Spenser, Shakespeare, Milton, Burns, but others known only to the cognoscenti—Peele, Kyd, Lyly, the less familiar Shakespeare, Webster, Marvel, Dryden, Swift, Darley, Beddoes; making the succession of English poetry wear a more varied look. The same enlargement is made with the Greek, Latin, Italian, and French poets."

The authors call this a method of "civilizing and enlarging poetry." Its actual effect is to narrow the circle of communication to a small group of specialists in a particular type of learning—by no means the most important type—and to communicate even to the members of this circle only a part of the content of the poem. Most of the "cognoscenti," as I know them, will be so tickled by the poet's assuming they know everything he is alluding to, that they will get along better than others without the more specific pleasure of finding out what he is alluding to. Even those who do find out, will have enjoyed a cerebral exercise rather than the emotional experience of the poem.

I use the word *cerebral*, because it is the firm conviction of the modernist poets and their admirers that they are extremely intellectual, and it is my firm conviction that they are not. They have a great deal going on inside their heads in proportion to what goes on in their organs of vital emotion, but so has a bridge player or a tired business man devoting his idle moments to cross-word puzzles. In my opinion, the admirers of modernist poetry as a distinctively *intellectual* phenomenon, may be divided into two classes. First, those who think they understand what is unintelligible because they do not know what it is to understand. They are the same people who listen in a theatre to a foreign actor speaking an unknown tongue, and come home and tell us his acting was so wonderful that they understood the whole play. Second, those who do know what it is to understand, but find so little in real life to exercise their understandings upon that they develop a devout passion for conundrums, riddles, rebuses, anagrams, charades, logogriphs, and games of dumb-crambo and twenty questions. My own playful tastes lie very strongly in the opposite direction. Life itself as I try to live it is puzzle enough, and there is no dearth of riddles even when the talk is clear. Therefore, when the modernist critics object to Mr. Cummings's poems that they are too lucid—"they do not present the eternal difficulties that make poems immortal"—I can only bow and retire. I do not live in that world. When they object to the established punctuation of Shakespeare because it "restricts his meaning to special interpretations of special words," and say that "if we must choose one meaning, then we owe it to Shakespeare to choose one embracing as many meanings as possible, that is, the most difficult meaning," I feel that they have never touched the mind of Shakespeare. And when they describe one of the great sonnets, punctuated in a manner that they consider, on very flimsy evidence, to be Shakespeare's own, as "a furiously dynamic cross-word puzzle which can be read in many directions at once," I feel that I am confronted with beings of a different species. It seems to be a species in which the cerebral cortex is severed from the midbrain and the rest of the vital system, and seeks the experience of life in speeding up all by itself like a racing motor.

T. S. Eliot had discovered another kind of freedom that deserves comment. It is to be found in a series of explanatory notes which he appends at the end of his poems. A similar device was adopted by Dante in his *Vita Nuova.* But Mr. Eliot's notes differ from Dante's, and from all other explanatory notes, in being almost entirely free from explanation.

Another friendly custom of the older poets has been abandoned by the modernists—the custom of giving the poem a title which tells us what it is about. The modernist titles tell us what the poem is not about, and they usually tell us that in a foreign language. Here, for example, is a poem by Edith Sitwell. Edith Sitwell is, in my opinion, the most gifted of the modernist poets—the one who is most unaffectedly expressing a genuine and inevitable poetic character—but she is also one of the most wilfully unfriendly to me, her admiring reader. She has entitled this poem "Aubade," and if you do not happen to know what "Aubade" means, that is your good luck. You will have less difficulty in finding out what her poem is about.

Jane, Jane,
Tall as a crane,
The morning light creaks down again.
Comb your cockscomb-ragged hair,
Jane, Jane, come down the stair.

Each dull, blunt wooden stalactite
Of rain creaks, hardened by the light,

Sounding like an overtone
From some lonely world unknown.

But the creaking, empty light
Will never harden into sight,

Will never penetrate your brain
With overtones like the blunt rain.

The light would show, if it could harden,
Eternities of kitchen garden,

Cockscomb flowers that none will pluck,
And wooden flowers that 'gin to cluck.

In the kitchen you must light
Flames as staring red and white

As carrots or as turnips—shining
Where the cold dawn light lies whining.

Cockscomb hair on the cold wind
Hangs limp, turns the milk's weak mind.

Jane, Jane,
Tall as a crane,
The morning light creaks down again.

Perhaps you can guess what Jane is—or who she is—or whether she is, indeed, a who or a what. But will you ever feel sure that your guess is right? If not, you do not belong to the "cognoscenti," the very intellectually élite, to whom Edith Sitwell addresses her poems. Fortunately for you, however, she has condescended to explain this particular poem to the vulgar and uncultivated.

The modernist poet's brain (she tells us) is becoming a central sense, interpreting and controlling the other five senses. . . . His senses have become broadened and cosmopolitanized; they are no longer little islands, speaking only their own narrow language, living their own sleepy life alone. When the speech of one sense is insufficient to convey his entire meaning, he uses the language of another.

After that much by way of general explanation—if you are "intellectual" enough to accept this rather confused psychology as explanation—Miss Sitwell takes up the difficulties of her poem, phrase by phrase:

"The morning light creaks down again."

The author said "creaks," because in a very early dawn, after rain, the light has a curious uncertain quality, as though it does not run quite smoothly. Also, it falls in hard cubes, squares, and triangles, which, again, give one the impression of a creaking sound, because of the association with wood. *"Each dull, blunt wooden stalactite of rain creaks, hardened by the light."* In the early dawn, long raindrops are transformed by the light, until they have the light's own quality of hardness; also they have the dull and blunt and tasteless quality of wood; as they move in the wind, they seem to creak. *"Sounding like an overtone from some lonely world unknown."* Though it seems to us as though we heard them sensorily, yet the sound is unheard in reality; it has the quality of an overtone from some unknown and mysterious world. . . .

So far we are still in the dark—are we not? We have found out that the author is rather hypnotized by the idea that sights can be compared to sounds, sounds to things touched, and so forth. We knew this long ago, have observed it in poetry as far back as the Rig-Veda—"the fire cries with the light"—and read about it also in the text-books of psychology, where its extreme manifestations are described as "synaesthesia." But we have never seen it piled on quite so thick before. We have never seen a poem in which these comparisons were coldly and deliberately and, therefore, unconvincingly perpetrated throughout twelve or fourteen stanzas by a poet seeking to exemplify what she imagines to be a new psychological discovery. So far, then, her explanation has made us aware of her capabilities in bad taste, but we are still unaware of the subject of her poem. But now she suddenly, and quite recklessly it seems to me, condescends to tell us what she is talking about:

> The poem is about a country servant, a girl on a farm, plain and neglected and unhappy, and with a sad bucolic stupidity, coming down in the dawn to light the fire.

Is not that a wonderful relief? And how beautifully it is expressed! We must say one thing for the modernist poets—they all write excellent prose. When they do want to tell us something, they tell it with lucid and luminous precision.

As poets they do not want to tell us. They do not want to sacrifice, in order to tell us, any least value that their poems may have untold. The act of communication is irksome to them. It is irksome at times to us all. It is inadequate. How much *can* we communicate, indeed, by this elementary device of tongue-wagging or by making these tiny inkwiggles on a sheet of paper? Little enough. Everyone who has composed poems knows how often he has to sacrifice a value that is both clear and dear to him, in order to communicate his poem to others. Abandon that motive, the limitation it imposes, and you will find yourself writing modernist poetry. I know this because I have tried it.

The modernist tendency may be defined, then—this first element of it—as a tendency toward privacy combined with a naïve sincerity in employing as material the instruments of social communication. In a later paper—a happier one—I am going to define the other element of modernism, the tendency toward pure poetry, and show why it is confused with this one and why it ought not to be.

> Books should to one of these four ends conduce,
> For wisdom, piety, delight, or use.
>
> SIR J. DENHAM—*Prudence.*

A NOTE ON CRITICISM[1]

By George Jean Nathan

The useless always has an irresistible appeal for me; that is why I devote myself to dramatic criticism, perhaps the most useless thing in the world. I have an unconquerable fondness for the purposeless luxuries of life, the things that are not practical, the little circuses of the soul and heart and taste and fancy that make for the merriment and pleasure of the race if not for its improvement and salvation. Years ago, in my nonage, I said to myself: "what is the pleasantest and most useless thing to which you may devote your life?" After considerable deliberation I concluded and replied to myself, "Dramatic criticism"; and I have since followed, and profitably, my own advice. For centuries men have written criticism of the drama in an effort to improve it, and with it the public taste. What has been the result? The "Frogs" of Aristophanes, written 405 years before Christ, has never been bettered in any way for dramatic satire; and the "Iphegenia" of Euripides, written 425 years before Christ, in any way for profoundly moving drama; or the "Oedipus Rex" of Sophocles, written 440 years before Christ, in any way for stirring melodrama. The imperishable romantic drama of Shakespeare fingers its nose at all the dramatic criticism written before its time, or since. And in the matter of improved public taste the most widely successful play in the civilized world in this Year of Our Lord 1923 is a crook mystery play by Avery Hopwood and Mary Roberts Rinehart called "The Bat."

[1] Reprinted from *The World in Falseface* by George Jean Nathan by and with permission of and special arrangement with Alfred A. Knopf, Inc., authorized publishers.

THE BIOGRAPHICAL PLAY

By George Jean Nathan

Of all plays, the so-called biographical one is undoubtedly the easiest to write. Consider, in example, the following scene from a famous play:

Enter Jean Jacques Rousseau

Rousseau—I am deeply grieved, Madame—(*he recognizes Thérèse Le Vasseur with a start*). Mon Dieu! You, Thérèse—here!

Thérèse—Ah, Jean Jacques, I could not die until I had your forgiveness. Do not turn away from me—bear with me one small moment—only say that you will forgive me, and I can rest in peace.

Rousseau—Why did you come here?

Thérèse—I could not stay away from you and my children. The longing for the sight of them was killing me. I knew no moment's peace after the mad act I was guilty of—in leaving you. Not an hour had I departed ere repentance set in. Even then I would have come back, but I did not know how. My sin was great, and my punishment has been greater; it has been one long, long mental agony.

Rousseau—Why did you go away?

Thérèse—Did you not know why?

Rousseau—No, it was ever a mystery to me.

Thérèse—I went out of love for you. Ah, do not look at me in that reproachful way! I loved you dearly, and I grew to doubt you. I thought you false and deceitful to me; that your love was given to another, and in my sore jealousy, I listened to the temptings of the man who whispered of revenge. But it was not so—tell me it was not so, Jean!

Rousseau—Can you ask me that, knowing me as you did then, and as you must have known me since? I was not false to you in word, in thought, or in deed, Thérèse.

Thérèse—I know it now, mon cher, but I was mad. I could not have committed the act save in madness. Say, mon Jean Jacques, that you will forget all and forgive me!

Rousseau—I cannot forget—I have forgiven already.

You will recognize it immediately, if a bit vaguely. One of the greatest successes the theatre has ever known. But you cannot recall its title? I supply it: "East Lynne." I have quoted the old lulu word for word and have merely renamed Archibald Carlyle, Jean Jacques Rousseau and Lady Isabel, Thérèse Le Vasseur. The dialogue fits the lives of Rousseau and his mistress-wife quite as snugly and accurately as is the general case in biographical plays. And the same thing may be done just as simply, effectively and no doubt as profitably, with "The Lady of Lyons" by calling Claude Melnotte, Verlaine, with "Camille" by calling Marguerite Gautier, Madame Rachel and renaming Armand after one of her more persistent lovers, and with "Up in Mabel's Room" by naming the central male character King Edward VII, late Prince of Wales.

THE SMILE VERSUS THE LAUGH

By George Jean Nathan

Charles Frohman insisted throughout his producing career that there was no money in what he called "a smile play," that is, a play that provoked merely smiles and not laughter. Charles Frohman for thirty years produced his plays upon this principle. And Charles Frohman died a poor man. . . . Laugh and the world laughs with you; smile and you smile alone. This, the doctrine that lost Charles Frohman so much of his money. And the irony of it that the doctrine is true.

An American theatrical audience does not want to smile; it wants to undo its top trouser button and let go. It will spend three hundred thousand dollars to laugh at "Fair and Warmer" but it will not spend a cent to smile at "The Steamship Tenacity." Frohman went nigh bankrupt because, though his credo was sound, his talent for differentiating between the smile and laugh was not. He often produced serious plays so comically and comic plays so seriously that he confused his customers. They found themselves smiling when they should have laughed, and laughing when they should have smiled. After a few years of this sort of thing they became so embarrassed that they gave up Frohman, and moved bag and baggage across the street to A. H. Woods. But although there is more theatrical money to be made out of laughter than out of smiles, this does not prove that laughter is superior to the smile any more than the fact that there is more money to be made out of "Don't Kiss Me on the Nose, Dearie: My Dog Has Spanish Blood" than out of "Sardanapale" proves that Berlin is superior to Berlioz. The smile is the true aristocrat of dramatic literature; the laugh is the peasant. The smile is a child of the intelligence; the laugh is a child of the belly. "Gentlemen smile; their valets laugh," wrote Lord Chesterfield. Christ smiled, but did not laugh. We know from the records that Caesar and Napoleon smiled, but there is no record of their laughter. George Washington, it appears, smiled: Warren Gamaliel Harding, we know, laughed. . . . .

What America needs is more smilers and less laughers, There is too much laughter in the country. Go into a railway smoking car and a dozen Elks are hard at it. Go into a restaurant and two dozen drummers and manicure girls are neighing like jackasses. Go to Washington and you find the entire coloured population laughing itself half to death over the Administration. Go to the theatre and a houseful of emotional Dadaists is bellowing at the spectacle of a fat comedian trying to hide himself in a phonograph box. There is gargantuan laughter for the "Cruise of the Kawa" but there are too few smiles for "Jurgen." There is a roar for Frank Tinney, but there are not enough smiles for Maurice Baring. The cocktail may have followed the flag once upon a time, but taste in America never followed laughter. Taste and perception follow the smile. One laughs at Topsy, "Charley's Aunt" and Woodrow Wilson, much as one laughs at a man who sits upon a tack; but one smiles at Tartuffe, "The Last Night of Don Juan" and Arthur Balfour, much as one ever smiles at something wistful in its superiority. They smile in Downing Street: they laugh in Bloomingdale.

The American laughter at "The Demi-Virgin" has a million times the voltage of the American smiles at "Anatol." The laughter over "Billy Baxter's Letters" has a million times the voltage of the smiles over "The Revolt of the Angels." Taste coughs its way to a phthisical death, and the mourners have to bite their tongues to still their loud chuckles. Consider the theatre. What is the quality of the plays that provoke the loudest and the most commercially profitable laughter? I give a few recent examples: "Getting Gertie's Garter," "Six-Cylinder Love," "Bluebeard's Eighth

Wife," "Thank You," "Captain Applejack," "Lilies of the Field," and "Kiki." Again, what is the quality of the plays that provoke smiles, but alas unprofitably? I give a few more recent examples: Gribble's "March Hares," Bataille's "Don Juan," Lennox Robinson's "The White-Headed Boy," de Caillavet's and de Flers' "The Fan," Brieux's "Madame Pierre," and Courteline's "Boubouroche," the aforementioned Vildrac's "S. S. Tenacity." . . .

The easiest thing in the world is to make a theatre-goer laugh. He will laugh when a blackface comedian turns around for the thousandth time and discloses two large white pearl buttons sewed upon the seat of his pants. He will laugh when the same comedian trips over an imaginary object and, regaining his balance, purses his mouth in an effeminate manner and says "Oh sassafras!" He will laugh when anyone alludes to a Ford automobile or Carter's Liver Pills, to an onion, a prune or a Congressman, to wood alcohol or William Jennings Bryan, to holes in doughnuts, socks and Swiss cheese, to hell or Yonkers, to Gatti-Casazza, frankfurter sausages, spaghetti, Trotski, apple sauce, cabbage (if only it be pronounced cab-bah-ge), the Erie railroad, the New York, New Haven and Hartford or the B. and O., to Altoona, Pa., or a dill pickle, to September Morn or the Albany Night boat, to anyone named Oswald, Rudolph, Clarence, or Percy, to Philadelphia, the police force or Limburger cheese, to the telephone service, Meyerbeer, the *Ladies' Home Journal*, lobsters, ear muffs, insufficient bathing, the "Götterdämmerung," rhubarb, alfalfa, Pittsburgh or to several thousands of other such phenomena. But the matter of making him smile is reserved for artists—that is, if a smile is not beyond his learning. Yet beyond his talent such smiles apparently are—and what he misses! The rare smiles of Bahr's "Master," of Molnar's "Phantom Rival," of Galsworthy's "Pigeon," of Barrie's "Legend of Leonora," of a score of delightful things—all rapidly sent into the theatrical discard by our herd of humourless laughers.

SOME PLATITUDES CONCERNING DRAMA [1]

By John Galsworthy

A drama must be shaped so as to have a spire of meaning. Every grouping of life and character has its inherent moral; and the business of the dramatist is so to pose the group as to bring that moral poignantly to the light of day. Such is the moral that exhales from plays like *Lear, Hamlet,* and *Macbeth.* But such is not the moral to be found in the great bulk of contemporary Drama. The moral of the average play is now, and probably has always been, the triumph at all costs of a supposed immediate ethical good over a supposed immediate ethical evil.

The vice of drawing these distorted morals has permeated the Drama to its spine; discolored its art, humanity, and significance; infected its creators, actors, audience, critics; too often turned it from a picture into a caricature. A Drama which lives under the shadow of the distorted moral forgets how to be free, fair, and fine—forgets so completely that it often prides itself on having forgotten.

Now, in writing plays, there are, in this matter of the moral, three courses open to the serious dramatist. The first is: To definitely set before the public that which it wishes to have set before it, the views and codes of life by which the public lives and in which it believes. This way is the most common, successful, and popular. It makes the dramatist's position sure, and not too obviously authoritative.

The second course is: To definitely set before the public those views and codes of life by which the dramatist himself lives, those theories in which he himself believes, the more

[1] From *The Inn of Tranquillity;* copyright, 1912, by Charles Scribner's Sons. By permission of the publishers.

effectively if they are the opposite of what the public wishes to have placed before it, presenting them so that the audience may swallow them like powder in a spoonful of jam.

There is a third course: To set before the public no cut-and-dried codes, but the phenomena of life and character, selected and combined, *but not distorted*, by the dramatist's outlook, set down without fear, favor, or prejudice, leaving the public to draw such poor moral as nature may afford. This third method requires a certain detachment; it requires a sympathy with, a love of, and a curiosity as to, things for their own sake; it requires a far view, together with patient industry, for no immediately practical result.

It was once said of Shakespeare that he had never done any good to any one, and never would. This, unfortunately, could not, in the sense in which the word "good" was then meant, be said of most modern dramatists. In truth, the good that Shakespeare did to humanity was of a remote, and, shall we say, eternal nature; something of the good that men get from having the sky and sea to look at. And this partly because he was, in his greater plays at all events, free from the habit of drawing a distorted moral. Now, the playwright who supplies to the public the facts of life distorted by the moral which it expects, does so that he may do the public what he considers an immediate good, by fortifying its prejudices; and the dramatist who supplies to the public facts distorted by his own advanced morality, does so becauses he considers that he will at once benefit the public by substituting for its worn-out ethics, his own. In both cases the advantage the dramatist hopes to confer on the public is immediate and practical.

But matters change, and morals change; men remain—and to set men, and the facts about them, down faithfully, so that they draw for us the moral of their natural actions, may also possibly be of benefit to the community. It is, at all events, harder than to set men and facts down, as they ought, or ought not to be. This, however, is not to say that a dramatist should, or indeed can, keep himself and his temperamental philosophy out of his work. As a man lives and thinks, so will he write. But it is certain, that to the making of good drama, as to the practice of every other art, there must be brought an almost passionate love of discipline, a white-heat of self-respect, a desire to make the truest, fairest, best thing in one's power; and that to these must be added an eye that does not flinch. Such qualities alone will bring to a drama the selfless character which soaks it with inevitability.

The word "pessimist" is frequently applied to the few dramatists who have been content to work in this way. It has been applied, among others, to Euripides, to Shakespeare, to Ibsen; it will be applied to many in the future. Nothing, however, is more dubious than the way in which these two words "pessimist" and "optimist" are used; for the optimist appears to be he who cannot bear the world as it is, and is forced by his nature to picture it as it ought to be, and the pessimist one who can not only bear the world as it is, but loves it well enough to draw it faithfully. The true lover of the human race is surely he who can put up with it in all its forms, in vice as well as in virtue, in defeat no less than in victory; the true seer he who sees not only joy but sorrow, the true painter of human life one who blinks nothing. It may be that he is also, incidentally, its true benefactor.

In the whole range of the social fabric there are only two impartial persons, the scientist and the artist, and under the latter heading such dramatists as desire to write not only for to-day, but for to-morrow, must strive to come.

But dramatists being as they are made—past remedy—it is perhaps more profitable to examine the various points at which their qualities and defects are shown.

The plot! A good plot is that sure edifice which slowly rises out of the interplay of circumstance on temperament, and temperament on circumstance, within the enclosing atmosphere of an idea. A human being is the best plot there is; it may be impossible to see why he is a good plot, because the idea within which he was brought forth cannot be fully grasped; but it is plain that *he is a good plot.* He is organic. And so it must be with a good play. Reason alone produces no good plots; they come by original sin, sure conception, and instinctive after-power of selecting what benefits the germ. A bad plot, on the other hand, is simply a row of stakes, with a character impaled on each—characters who would have liked to live, but came to untimely grief; who started bravely, but fell on these stakes, placed beforehand in a row, and were transfixed one by one, while their ghosts stride on, squeaking and gibbering, through the play. Whether these stakes are made of facts or of ideas, according to the nature of the dramatist who planted them, their effect on the unfortunate characters is the same; the creatures were begotten to be staked, and staked they are! The demand for a good plot, not unfrequently heard, commonly signifies: "Tickle my sensations by stuffing the play with arbitrary adventures, so that I need not be troubled to take the characters seriously. Set the persons of the play to action, regardless of time, sequence, atmosphere, and probability!"

Now, true dramatic action is what characters do, at once contrary, as it were, to expectation, and yet because they have already done other things. No dramatist should let his audience know what is coming; but neither should be suffer his characters to act without making his audience feel that those actions are in harmony with temperament, and arise from previous known actions, together with the temperaments and previous known actions of the other characters in the play. The dramatist who hangs his characters to his plot, instead of hanging his plot to his characters, is guilty of cardinal sin.

The dialogue! Good dialogue again is character, marshalled so as continually to stimulate interest or excitement. The reason good dialogue is seldom found in plays is merely that it is hard to write, for it requires not only a knowledge of what interests or excites, but such a feeling for character as brings misery to the dramatist's heart when his creations speak as they should not speak—ashes to his mouth when they say things for the sake of saying them—disgust when they are "smart."

The art of writing true dramatic dialogue is an austere art, denying itself all license, grudging every sentence devoted to the mere machinery of the play, suppressing all jokes and epigrams severed from character, relying for fun and pathos on the fun and tears of life. From start to finish good dialogue is hand-made, like good lace; clear, of fine texture, furthering with each thread the harmony and strength of a design to which all must be subordinated.

But good dialogue is also spiritual action. In so far as the dramatist divorces his dialogue from spiritual action—that is to say, from progress of events, or toward events which are significant of character—he is stultifying τὸ δϱάμα the thing done; he may make pleasing disquisitions, he is not making drama. And in so far as he twists character to suit his moral or his plot, he is neglecting a first principle, that truth to Nature which alone invests art with hand-made quality.

The dramatist's license, in fact, ends with his design. In conception alone he is free. He may take what character or group of characters he chooses, see them with what eyes, knit them with what idea, within the limits of his temperament; but once taken, seen, and knitted, he is bound to treat them like a gentleman, with the tenderest consideration of their mainsprings. Take care of character; action and dialogue will take care of themselves! The true dramatist gives full rein to his temperament in the scope and nature of his subject; having once selected subject and characters, he is just, gentle, restrained, neither gratifying his lust for praise at the expense of his offspring, nor using them as puppets to flout his audience. Being himself the nature that brought them forth, he guides them in the course predestined at their conception. So only have they a chance of defying Time, which is always lying in wait to destroy the false, topical, or fashionable, all—

in a word—that is not based on the permanent elements of human nature. The perfect dramatist rounds up his characters and facts within the ring-fence of a dominant idea which fulfills the craving of his spirit; having got them there, he suffers them to live their own lives.

Plot, action, character, dialogue! But there is yet another subject for a platitude. Flavor! An impalpable quality, less easily captured than the scent of a flower, the peculiar and most essential attribute of any work of art! It is the thin, poignant spirit which hovers up out of a play, and is as much its differentiating essence as is caffeine of coffee. Flavor, in fine, is the spirit of the dramatist projected into his work in a state of volatility, so that no one can exactly lay hands on it, here, there, or anywhere. This distinctive essence of a play, marking its brand, is the one thing at which the dramatist cannot work, for it is outside his consciousness. A man may have many moods, he has but one spirit; and this spirit he communicates in some subtle, unconscious way to all his work. It waxes and wanes with the currents of his vitality, but no more alters than a chestnut changes into an oak.

For, in truth, dramas are very like unto trees, springing from seedlings, shaping themselves inevitably in accordance with the laws fast hidden within themselves, drinking sustenance from the earth and air, and in conflict with the natural forces round them. So they slowly come to full growth, until warped, stunted, or risen to fair and gracious height, they stand open to all the winds. And the trees that spring from each dramatist are of different race; he is the spirit of his own sacred grove, into which no stray tree can by any chance enter.

One more platitude. It is not unfashionable to pit one form of drama against another—holding up the naturalistic to the disadvantage of the epic; the epic to the belittlement of the fantastic; the fantastic to the detriment of the naturalistic. Little purpose is thus served. The essential meaning, truth, beauty, and irony of things may be revealed under all these forms. Vision over life and human nature can be as keen and just, the revelation as true, inspiring, delight-giving, and thought-provoking, whatever fashion be employed—it is simply a question of doing it well enough to uncover the kernel of the nut. Whether the violet come from Russia, from Parma, or from England, matters little. Close by the Greek temples at Paestum there are violets that seem redder, and sweeter, than any ever seen—as though they have sprung up out of the footprints of some old pagan goddess; but under the April sun, in a Devonshire lane, the little blue scentless violets capture every bit as much of the spring. And so it is with drama—no matter what its form—it need only be the "real thing," need only have caught some of the precious fluids, revelation or delight, and imprisoned them within a chalice to which we may put our lips and continually drink.

And yet, starting from this last platitude, one may perhaps be suffered to speculate as to the particular forms that our renascent drama is likely to assume. For our drama is renascent, and nothing will stop its growth. It is not renascent because this or that man is writing, but because of a new spirit. A spirit that is no doubt in part the gradual outcome of the impact on our home-grown art, of Russian, French, and Scandinavian influences, but which in the main rises from an awakened humanity in the conscience of our time.

What, then, are to be the main channels down which the renascent English drama will float in the coming years? It is more than possible that these main channels will come to be two in number and situated far apart.

The one will be the broad and clear-cut channel of naturalism, down which will course a drama poignantly shaped, and inspired with high intention, but faithful to the seething and multiple life around us, drama such as some are inclined to term photographic, deceived by a seeming simplicity into forgetfulness of the old proverb, "Ars est celare artem," and oblivious of the fact that, to be vital, to grip, such drama is in every respect as dependent on imagination, construction, selection, and elimination—the main laws of artistry—as ever was the romantic or rhapsodic play. The question of naturalistic technique will bear, indeed, much more study than has yet been given to it. The aim of the dramatist employing it is obviously to create such an illusion of actual life passing on the stage as to compel the spectator to pass through an experience of his own, to think, and talk, and move with the people he sees thinking, talking, and moving in front of him. A false phrase, a single word out of tune or time, will destroy that illusion and spoil the surface as surely as a stone heaved into a still pool shatters the image seen there. But this is only the beginning of the reason why the naturalistic is the most exacting and difficult of all techniques. It is easy enough to *reproduce* the exact conversation and movements of persons in a room; it is desperately hard to *produce* the perfectly natural conversation and movements of those persons, when each natural phrase spoken and each natural movement made has not only to contribute toward the growth and perfection of a drama's soul, but also to be a revelation, phrase by phrase, movement by movement, of essential traits of character. To put it another way, naturalistic art, when alive, indeed to be alive at all, is simply the art of manipulating a procession of most delicate symbols. Its service is the swaying and focussing of men's feelings and thoughts in the various departments of human life. It will be like a steady lamp, held up from time to time, in whose light things will be seen for a space clearly and in due proportion, freed from the mists of prejudice and partisanship.

And the other of these two main channels will, I think, be a twisting and delicious stream, which will bear on its breast new barques of poetry, shaped, it may be, like prose, but a prose incarnating through its fantasy and symbolism all the deeper aspirations, yearning, doubts, and mysterious stirrings of the human spirit; a poetic prose-drama, emotionalizing us by its diversity and purity of form and invention, and whose province will be to disclose the elemental soul of man and the forces of Nature, not perhaps as the old tragedies disclosed them, not necessarily in the epic mood, but always with beauty and in the spirit of discovery.

Such will, I think, be the two vital forms of our drama in the coming generation. And between these two forms there must be no crude unions; they are too far apart, the cross is too violent. For, where there is a seeming blend of lyricism and naturalism, it will on examination be found, I think, to exist only in plays whose subjects or settings—as in Synge's "Playboy of the Western World," or in Mr. Masefield's "Nan"—are so removed from our ken that we cannot really tell, and therefore do not care, whether an absolute illusion is maintained. The poetry which may and should exist in naturalistic drama, can only be that of perfect rightness of proportion, rhythm, shape—the poetry, in fact, that lies in all vital things. It is the ill-mating of forms that has killed a thousand plays. We want no more bastard drama; no more attempts to dress out the simple dignity of everyday life in the peacock's feathers of false lyricism; no more straw-stuffed heroes or heroines; no more rabbits and goldfish from the conjurer's pockets, nor any limelight. Let us have starlight, moonlight, sunlight, and the light of our own self-respects.

My library
Was dukedom large enough.
SHAKESPEARE—*Tempest Act 1, 2.*

BOCCACCIO, THAT HARBINGER OF THE RENAISSANCE [1]

By HERBERT L. MATTHEWS

IF THE modern style of biography is less a strain on the writer, it is no less so on the reader. It is no longer necessary to provide new material, or a radically new interpretation, as a *raison d'être* for the book to be produced: it is enough if the existing work of scholars is adequately digested and a readable synthesis, breathing life and color into the protagonist, is offered. From such a standpoint this latest biography of Boccaccio is eminently successful and was well worth writing. It will take its place, undoubtedly, as the best account of the author of the "Decameron" available to present-day readers. In content, and as an interpretation, to be sure, it adds little, if anything, to Edward Hutton's study, written some twenty years ago, but nobody reads Hutton's book any more, and here is a more entertaining work, sound in its scholarship, sincerely and freshly written.

The best excuse for the new biographies is that they animate figures that would otherwise be simply names, and enrich our appreciation of the products of genius. Few characters in literature are more lovable, more human or more interesting to study than this personality who stood at the turning point in history, where the forces that were to bring about the Renaissance had gathered enough strength to make themselves manifest here and there, in great figures such as himself and his friend Petrarch. He was a perplexing, paradoxical creature, who least of all understood himself, and

[1] Reprinted by permission of the author and the *New York Times*. A review of THE LIFE OF GIOVANNI BOCCACCIO. By Thomas Caldecott Chubb.

who offers the biographer a baffling problem in character analysis.

Mr. Chubb attacks his problem valiantly, and brings enough knowledge, sympathy and love to succeed at least as well as, if not better than, those who preceded him. One can quarrel with his bias in Boccaccio's favor, and his unwillingness to accept the essentially bourgeois temperament of his subject, his personal pettishness, his vile temper, his self-importance, the frequent ignobility of his actions, but all of us do as much in reading his works, just as we all overlook the faults of those we love.

Although the library of Boccacciana is immense, there is not any too much verified material on which to construct a life. After all, it was still the days before the printing of books, and Boccaccio, though famous, was not nearly so highly regarded then as later. In fact, the "Decameron," on which his reputation now rests almost exclusively, was enjoyed only as a series of amusing trifles to while away one's leisure hours. What literary fame he had in the fourteenth century was far more confined to his Latin works and poetry.

The biographer, therefore, is faced with the necessity of confessing ignorance of most details, or supplying them cautiously, either from the imagination, or in accepting probability as fact. Mr. Chubb, like all others of the modern school, has done the latter, but so carefully and diffidently that there can be little quarrel with his conclusions. After all, they are based on the best available information, and they may be right. The framework of fact on which the biography is reconstructed is as follows:

Boccaccio was born in 1313, the son (illegitimate in all likelihood) of a Certaldese banker and an unknown Parisienne. His childhood is veiled in obscurity, but we know that the woman his father later married made it rather unhappy for him, and his father did, too, for that matter, by his insistence on Giovanni becoming a banker, like himself. Youth—the happiest period of his life, and the one in which was developed the experience and turn of mind which was to make the "Decameron" possible—was spent in Naples, at the court of Robert of Anjou.

There he fell in love with the "Fiammetta" he was to make so famous in all his writings. She was Maria d'Aquino, "a fairly hard-boiled and fairly worldly young lady," as Mr. Chubb aptly states. Like Hutton, and numerous other biographers before him, the present historian gives a touching and highly circumstantial account of how Boccaccio's desire for the young lady was satisfied. However, it is one of those instances based on probability, rather than fact.

When Boccaccio was about 25 years old his father lost his money, and, except for very brief intervals, the rest of his life was spent in poverty, for the most part in Florence, but with frequent excursions to other parts of Italy. Florence at that time was in a ruinous state, ruled, as Boccaccio bitterly wrote, "by gluttons, innkeepers, whore-mongers and other similar filth," though on the whole they treated Boccaccio well enough. When the great plague of 1346-50 came—probably the most calamitous "act of God" that has ever visited the human race—Boccaccio seems to have been in Naples. At any rate, he escaped unscathed.

It was in 1350 that his friendship with Petrarch matured—a relationship of such importance to Italian culture that it probably merits the designation by Mr. Chubb of being "virtually the most distinguished literary friendship in the whole course of history." Petrarch it was whose wise counsel saved Boccaccio from the possible consequences of his amazing "conversion" to religiosity. In that event, more than anywhere, lies the key to the mystery of Boccaccio's character. There was the very essence of the man, and one could only wish that Mr. Chubb had given more space to developing a study of the frame of mind which made it possible.

Then followed years of public service, in the intervals of which numerous ponderous and scurrilous works were produced. On Dec. 21, 1375, a year after his friend Petrarch, he died.

Each of the many writings comes in for its due share of acute analysis in the present book. Nowadays few but scholars read anything but the "Decameron." A recent translation of the "Filostrato" offers an excellent version of that fine poem to the English-reading public, and most of the other works have been translated. For the most part, however, to read the poetry in translation is largely to miss its virtues, and the long Latin works in any language are an unmitigated bore. It will always be the incomparable "Decameron" by which Boccaccio will be known to posterity. Mr. Chubb's treatment of it and the other works is admirable for its balance and soundness, and no one can read his book without getting a due appreciation of the great part the Italian played in the history of literature.

In one instance only does the biographer's enthusiasm run away with his critical acumen, and that is in the value he places on Boccaccio's critical and biographical studies of Dante. In this, too, Mr. Chubb agrees with Hutton, but both have an opinion at variance with that of nearly all Dante scholars. What Mr. Chubb strangely fails to bring out (perhaps because he would disagree) is Boccaccio's utter incapacity really to appreciate the genius of Dante. The two were worlds apart in character and in their outlook on life—as far apart as the Middle Ages and the Renaissance.

One cannot but wish that Mr. Chubb had made a more determined effort to delineate Boccaccio's many-sided character and fuse it into an interpretive whole which would explain the man to us. But that, perhaps, is asking too much. He does put his finger on a vital spot when, speaking of Dioneo, one of the story-tellers of the "Decameron," he says:

That gay gentleman, who insists on telling his tale last and on being exempted from conforming to the subject assigned so that he can end each day on the note of some riotous and full-blooded comedy, that irrepressible and self-confident funmaker, who, when called on to give in his turn the sentimental song with which each day is concluded, offers instead the first lines of half a dozen taproom jingles which are so outspoken that even the ladies of this tolerant group will not permit him to go on with them, is the one character in the troupe of story-tellers that stands out with anything like reality. If he does not represent Boccaccio as he actually was, he represents him as he wished to be, or as he imagined he was.

Mr. Chubb introduces a number of his own good verse translations of Boccaccio's poems, and the publishers have provided an attractive format. The proofreading was unfortunately careless in spots, resulting, even, in two misspelled names in the bibliography.

Taking it all in all, this is a highly interesting and sound piece of work which deserves a reading by all who love their "Decameron."

> The value of many men and books rests solely on their faculty for compelling all to speak out the most hidden and intimate things.
>
> FRIEDRICH WILHELM NIETZSCHE—*Maxims.*

COUNT LEO TOLSTOI[1]

By Matthew Arnold

In reviewing at the time of its first publication, thirty years ago, Flaubert's remarkable novel of *Madame Bovary*, Sainte-Beuve observed that in Flaubert we come to another manner, another kind of inspiration, from those which had prevailed hitherto; we find ourselves dealing, he said, with a man of a new and different generation from novelists like George Sand. The ideal has ceased, the lyric vein is dried up; the new men are cured of lyricism and the ideal; 'a severe and pitiless truth has made its entry, as the last word of experience, even into art itself.' The characters of the new literature of fiction are 'science, a spirit of observation, maturity, force, a touch of hardness.' *L'idéal a cessé, le lyrique a tari.*

The spirit of observation and the touch of hardness (let us retain these mild and inoffensive terms) have since been carried in the French novel very far. So far have they been carried, indeed, that in spite of the advantage which the French language, familiar to the cultivated classes everywhere, confers on the French novel, this novel has lost much of its attraction for those classes; it no longer commands their attention as it did formerly. The famous English novelists have passed away, and have left no successors of like fame. It is not the English novel, therefore, which has inherited the vogue lost by the French novel. It is the novel of a country new to literature, or at any rate unregarded, till lately, by the general public of readers: it is the novel of Russia. The Russian novel has now the vogue, and deserves to have it. If fresh literary productions maintain this vogue and enhance it, we shall all be learning Russian.

[1] Published in the *Fortnightly Review*, December 1887.

The Slav nature, or at any rate the Russian nature, the Russian nature as it shows itself in the Russian novels, seems marked by an extreme sensitiveness, a consciousness most quick and acute both for what the man's self is experiencing, and also for what others in contact with him are thinking and feeling. In a nation full of life, but young, and newly in contact with an old and powerful civilisation, this sensitiveness and self-consciousness are prompt to appear. In the Americans, as well as in the Russians, we see them active in a high degree. They are somewhat agitating and disquieting agents to their possessor, but they have, if they get fair play, great powers for evoking and enriching a literature. But the Americans, as we know, are apt to set them at rest in the manner of my friend Colonel Higginson of Boston. 'As I take it, Nature said, some years since: "Thus far the English is my best race; but we have had Englishmen enough; we need something with a little more buoyancy than the Englishman; let us lighten the structure, even at some peril in the process. Put in one drop more of nervous fluid, and make the American." With that drop, a new range of promise opened on the human race, and a lighter, finer, more highly organised type of mankind was born.' People who by this sort of thing give rest to their sensitive and busy self-consciousness may very well, perhaps, be on their way to great material prosperity, to great political power; but they are scarcely on the right way to a great literature, a serious art.

The Russian does not assuage his sensitiveness in this fashion. The Russian man of letters does not make Nature say: 'The Russian is my best race.' He finds relief to his sensitiveness in letting his perceptions have perfectly free play, and in recording their reports with perfect fidelity. The sincereness with which the reports are given has even something childlike and touching. In the novel of which I am going to speak there is not a line, not a trait, brought in for the glorification of Russia, or to feed vanity; things and characters go as nature takes them, and the author is absorbed in seeing how nature takes them and in relating it. But we have here a condition of things which is highly favourable to the production of good literature, of good art. We have great sensitiveness, subtlety, and finesse, addressing themselves with entire disinterestedness and simplicity to the representation of human life. The Russian novelist is thus master of a spell to which the secrets of human nature—both what is external and what is internal, gesture and manner no less than thought and feeling—willingly make themselves known. The crown of literature is poetry, and the Russians have not yet had a great poet. But in that form of imaginative literature which in our day is the most popular and the most possible, the Russians at the present moment seem to me to hold, as Mr. Gladstone would say, the field. They have great novelists, and of one of their great novelists I wish now to speak.

Count Leo Tolstoi is about sixty years old, and tells us that he shall write novels no more. He is now occupied with religion and with the Christian life. His writings concerning these great matters are not allowed, I believe, to obtain publication in Russia, but instalments of them in French and English reach us from time to time. I find them very interesting, but I find his novel of *Anna Karénine* more interesting still. I believe that many readers prefer to *Anna Karénine* Count Tolstoi's other great novel, *La Guerre et la Paix*. But in the novel one prefers, I think, to have the novelist dealing with the life which he knows from having lived it, rather than with the life which he knows from books or hearsay. If one has to choose a representative work of Thackeray, it is *Vanity Fair* which one would take rather than *The Virginians*. In like manner I take *Anna Karénine* as the novel best representing Count Tolstoi. I use the French translation; in general, as I long ago said, work of this kind is better done in France than in England, and *Anna Karénine* is perhaps also a novel which goes better into French than into English, just as Frederika Bremer's *Home* goes into English better than into French. After I have done with *Anna*

Karénine I must say something of Count Tolstoi's religious writings. Of these too I use the French translation, so far as it is available. The English translation, however, which came into my hands late, seems to be in general clear and good. Let me say in passing that it has neither the same arrangement, nor the same titles, nor altogether the same contents, with the French translation.

There are many characters in *Anna Karénine*—too many if we look in it for a work of art in which the action shall be vigorously one, and to that one action everything shall converge. There are even two main actions extending throughout the book, and we keep passing from one of them to the other—from the affairs of Anna and Wronsky to the affairs of Kitty and Levine. People appear in connection with these two main actions whose appearance and proceedings do not in the least contribute to develop them; incidents are multiplied which we expect are to lead to something important, but which do not. What, for instance, does the episode of Kitty's friend Warinka and Levine's brother Serge Ivanitch, their inclination for one another and its failure to come to anything, contribute to the development of either the character or the fortunes of Kitty and Levine? What does the incident of Levine's long delay in getting to church to be married, a delay which as we read of it seems to have significance, really import? It turns out to import absolutely nothing, and to be introduced solely to give the author the pleasure of telling us that all Levine's shirts had been packed up.

But the truth is we are not to take *Anna Karénine* as a work of art; we are to take it as a piece of life. A piece of life it is. The author has not invented and combined it, he has seen it; it has all happened before his inward eye, and it was in this wise that it happened. Levine's shirts were packed up, and he was late for his wedding in consequence; Warinka and Serge Ivanitch met at Levine's country-house and went out walking together; Serge was very near proposing, but did not. The author saw it all happening so—saw it, and therefore relates it; and what his novel in this way loses in art it gains in reality.

For this is the result which, by his extraordinary fineness of perception, and by his sincere fidelity to it, the author achieves; he works in us a sense of the absolute reality of his personages and their doings. Anna's shoulders, and masses of hair, and half-shut eyes; Alexis Karénine's up-drawn eyebrows, and tired smile, and cracking finger-joints; Stiva's eyes suffused with facile moisture—these are as real to us as any of those outward peculiarities which in our own circle of acquaintance we are noticing daily, while the inner man of our own circle of acquaintance, happily or unhappily, lies a great deal less clearly revealed to us than that of Count Tolstoi's creations.

I must speak of only a few of these creations, the chief personages and no more. The book opens with 'Stiva,' and who that has once made Stiva's acquaintance will ever forget him? We are living, in Count Tolstoi's novel, among the great people of Moscow and St. Petersburg, the nobles and the high functionaries, the governing class of Russia. Stépane Arcadiévitch—'Stiva'—is Prince Oblonsky, and descended from Rurik, although to think of him as anything except 'Stiva' is difficult. His *air souriant*, his good looks, his satisfaction; his 'ray,' which made the Tartar waiter at the club joyful in contemplating it; his pleasure in oysters and champagne, his pleasure in making people happy and in rendering services; his need of money, his attachment to the French governess, his distress at his wife's distress, his affection for her and the children; his emotion and suffused eyes, while he quite dismisses the care of providing funds for household expenses and education; and the French attachment, contritely given up to-day only to be succeeded by some other attachment to-morrow—no never, certainly, shall we come to forget Stiva. Anna, the heroine, is Stiva's sister. His wife Dolly (these English diminutives are common among Count

Tolstoi's ladies) is daughter of the Prince and Princess Cherbatzky, grandees who show us Russian high life by its most respectable side; the Prince, in particular, is excellent —simple, sensible, right-feeling; a man of dignity and honour. His daughters, Dolly and Kitty, are charming. Dolly, Stiva's wife, is sorely tried by her husband, full of anxieties for the children, with no money to spend on them or herself, poorly dressed, worn and aged before her time. She has moments of despairing doubt whether the gay people may not be after all in the right, whether virtue and principle answer; whether happiness does not dwell with adventuresses and profligates, brilliant and perfectly dressed adventuresses and profligates, in a land flowing with roubles and champagne. But in a quarter of an hour she comes right again and is herself—a nature straight, honest, faithful, loving, sound to the core; such she is and such she remains; she can be no other. Her sister Kitty is at bottom of the same temper, but she has her experience to get, while Dolly, when the book begins, has already acquired hers. Kitty is adored by Levine, in whom we are told that many traits are to be found of the character and history of Count Tolstoi himself. Levine belongs to the world of great people by his birth and property, but he is not at all a man of the world. He has been a reader and thinker, he has a conscience, he has public spirit and would ameliorate the condition of the people, he lives on his estate in the country, and occupies himself zealously with local business, schools, and agriculture. But he is shy, apt to suspect and to take offence, somewhat impracticable, out of his element in the gay world of Moscow. Kitty likes him, but her fancy has been taken by a brilliant guardsman, Count Wronsky, who has paid her attentions. Wronsky is described to us by Stiva; he is 'one of the finest specimens of the *jeunesse dorée* of St. Petersburg; immensely rich, handsome, aide-de-camp to the emperor, great interest at his back, and a good fellow notwithstanding; more than a good fellow, intelligent besides and well read—a man who has a splendid career before him.'

Let us complete the picture by adding that Wronsky is a powerful man, over thirty, bald at the top of his head, with irreproachable manners, cool and calm, but a little haughty. A hero, one murmurs to oneself, too much of the Guy Livingstone type, though without the bravado and exaggeration. And such is, justly enough perhaps, the first impression, an impression which continues all through the first volume; but Wronsky, as we shall see, improves towards the end.

Kitty discourages Levine, who retires in misery and confusion. But Wronsky is attracted by Anna Karénine, and ceases his attentions to Kitty. The impression made on her heart by Wronsky was not deep; but she is so keenly mortified with herself, so ashamed, and so upset, that she falls ill, and is sent with her family to winter abroad. There she regains health and mental composure, and discovers at the same time that her liking for Levine was deeper than she knew, that it was a genuine feeling, a strong and lasting one. On her return they meet, their hearts come together, they are married; and in spite of Levine's waywardness, irritability, and unsettlement of mind, of which I shall have more to say presently, they are profoundly happy. Well, and who could help being happy with Kitty? So I find myself adding impatiently. Count Tolstoi's heroines are really so living and charming that one takes them, fiction though they are, too seriously.

But the interest of the book centres in Anna Karénine. She is Stiva's sister, married to a high official at St. Petersburg, Alexis Karénine. She has been married to him nine years, and has one child, a boy named Serge. The marriage had not brought happiness to her, she had found in it no satisfaction to her heart and soul, she had a sense of want and isolation; but she is devoted to her boy, occupied, calm. The charm of her personality is felt even before she appears, from the moment when we hear of her being sent for as the good angel to reconcile Dolly with Stiva. Then she arrives at the Moscow station from St. Petersburg, and we see the gray eyes with their long eye-lashes, the graceful carriage, the gentle and caressing smile on the fresh lips, the vivacity restrained but waiting to break through, the fulness of life, the softness and strength joined, the harmony, the bloom, the charm. She goes to Dolly, and achieves, with infinite tact and tenderness, the task of reconciliation. At a ball a few days later, we add to our first impression of Anna's beauty, dark hair, a quantity of little curls over her temples and at the back of her neck, sculptural shoulders, firm throat, and beautiful arms. She is in a plain dress of black velvet with a pearl necklace, a bunch of forget-me-nots in the front of her dress, another in her hair. This is Anna Karénine.

She had travelled from St. Petersburg with Wronsky's mother; had seen him at the Moscow station, where he came to meet his mother, had been struck with his looks and manner, and touched by his behaviour in an accident which happened while they were in the station to a poor workman crushed by a train. At the ball she meets him again; she is fascinated by him and he by her. She had been told of Kitty's fancy, and had gone to the ball meaning to help Kitty; but Kitty is forgotten, or at any rate neglected; the spell which draws Wronsky and Anna is irresistible. Kitty finds herself opposite to them in a quadrille together:—

> 'She seemed to remark in Anna the symptoms of an over-excitement which she herself knew from experience—that of success. Anna appeared to her as if intoxicated with it. Kitty knew to what to attribute that brilliant and animated look, that happy and triumphant smile, those half-parted lips, those movements full of grace and harmony.'

Anna returns to St. Petersburg, and Wronsky returns there at the same time; they meet on the journey, they keep meeting in society, and Anna begins to find her husband, who before had not been sympathetic, intolerable. Alexis Karénine is much older than herself, a bureaucrat, a formalist, a poor creature; he has conscience, there is a root of goodness in him, but on the surface and until deeply stirred he is tiresome, pedantic, vain, exasperating. The change in Anna is not in the slightest degree comprehended by him; he sees nothing which an intelligent man might in such a case see, and does nothing which an intelligent man would do. Anna abandons herself to her passion for Wronsky.

I remember M. Nisard saying to me many years ago at the École Normale in Paris, that he respected the English because they are *une nation qui sait se gêner*—people who can put constraint on themselves and go through what is disagreeable. Perhaps in the Slav nature this valuable faculty is somewhat wanting; a very strong impulse is too much regarded as irresistible, too little as what can be resisted and ought to be resisted, however difficult and disagreeable the resistance may be. In our high society with its pleasure and dissipation, laxer notions may to some extent prevail; but in general an English mind will be startled by Anna's suffering herself to be so overwhelmed and irretrievably carried away by her passion, by her almost at once regarding it, apparently, as something which it was hopeless to fight against. And this I say irrespectively of the worth of her lover. Wronsky's gifts and graces hardly qualify him, one might think, to be the object of so instantaneous and mighty a passion on the part of a woman like Anna. But that is not the question. Let us allow that these passions are incalculable; let us allow that one of the male sex scarcely does justice, perhaps, to the powerful and handsome guardsman and his attractions. But if Wronsky had been even such a lover as Alcibiades or the Master of Ravenswood, still that Anna, being what she is and her circumstances being what they are, should show not a hope, hardly a thought, of conquering her passion, of escaping from its fatal power, is to our notions strange and a little bewildering.

I state the objection; let me add that it is the triumph of Anna's charm that it remains paramount for us nevertheless;

that throughout her course, with its failures, errors, and miseries, still the impression of her large, fresh, rich, generous, delightful nature, never leaves us—keeps our sympathy, keeps even, I had almost said, our respect.

To return to the story. Soon enough poor Anna begins to experience the truth of what the Wise Man told us long ago, that 'the way of transgressors is hard.' Her agitation at a steeplechase where Wronsky is in danger attracts her husband's notice and provokes his remonstrance. He is bitter and contemptuous. In a transport of passion Anna declares to him that she is his wife no longer; that she loves Wronsky, belongs to Wronsky. Hard at first, formal, cruel, thinking only of himself, Karénine, who, as I have said, has a conscience, is touched by grace at the moment when Anna's troubles reach their height. He returns to her to find her with a child just born to her and Wronsky, the lover in the house and Anna apparently dying. Karénine has words of kindness and forgiveness only. The noble and victorious effort transfigures him, and all that her husband gains in the eyes of Anna, her lover Wronsky loses. Wronsky comes to Anna's bedside, and standing there by Karénine, buries his face in his hands. Anna says to him, in the hurried voice of fever:—

' "Uncover your face; look at that man; he is a saint. Yes, uncover your face; uncover it," she repeated with an angry air. "Alexis, uncover his face; I want to see him."

'Alexis took the hands of Wronsky and uncovered his face, disfigured by suffering and humiliation.

' "Give him your hand; pardon him."

'Alexis stretched out his hand without even seeking to restrain his tears.

' "Thank God, thank God!" she said; "all is ready now. How ugly those flowers are," she went on, pointing to the wall-paper; "they are not a bit like violets. My God, my God! when will all this end? Give me morphine, doctor—I want morphine. Oh, my God, my God!" '

She seems dying, and Wronsky rushes out and shoots himself. And so, in a common novel, the story would end. Anna would die, Wronsky would commit suicide, Karénine would survive, in possession of our admiration and sympathy. But the story does not always end so in life: neither does it end so in Count Tolstoi's novel. Anna recovers from her fever, Wronsky from his wound. Anna's passion for Wronsky reawakens, her estrangement from Karénine returns. Nor does Karénine remain at the height at which in the forgiveness scene we saw him. He is formal, pedantic, irritating. Alas! even if he were not all these, perhaps even his *pince-nez*, and his rising eyebrows, and his cracking finger-joints, would have been provocation enough. Anna and Wronsky depart together. They stay for a time in Italy, then return to Russia. But her position is false, her disquietude incessant, and happiness is impossible for her. She takes opium every night, only to find that 'not poppy nor mandragora shall ever medicine her to that sweet sleep which she owed yesterday.' Jealousy and irritability grow upon her; she tortures Wronsky, she tortures herself. Under these trials Wronsky, it must be said, comes out well, and rises in our esteem. His love for Anna endures; he behaves, as our English phrase is, 'like a gentleman'; his patience is in general exemplary. But then Anna, let us remember, is to the last, through all the fret and misery, still Anna; always with something which charms; nay, with something, even, something in her nature, which consoles and does good. Her life, however, was becoming impossible under its existing conditions. A trifling misunderstanding brought the inevitable end. After a quarrel with Anna, Wronsky had gone one morning into the country to see his mother; Anna summons him by telegraph to return at once, and receives an answer from him that he cannot return before ten at night. She follows him to his mother's place in the country, and at the station hears what leads her to believe that he is not coming back. Maddened with jealousy and misery, she descends the platform and throws herself under the wheels of a goods train passing through the station. It is over—the graceful head is untouched, but all the rest is a crushed, formless heap. Poor Anna!

We have been in a world which misconducts itself nearly as much as the world of a French novel all palpitating with 'modernity.' But there are two things in which the Russian novel—Count Tolstoi's novel at any rate—is very advantageously distinguished from the type of novel now so much in request in France. In the first place, there is no fine sentiment, at once tiresome and false. We are not told to believe, for example, that Anna is wonderfully exalted and ennobled by her passion for Wronsky. The English reader is thus saved from many a groan of impatience. The other thing is yet more important. Our Russian novelist deals abundantly with criminal passion and with adultery, but he does not seem to feel himself owing any service to the goddess Lubricity, or bound to put in touches at this goddess's dictation. Much in *Anna Karénine* is painful, much is unpleasant, but nothing is of a nature to trouble the senses, or to please those who wish their senses troubled. This taint is wholly absent. In the French novels where it is so abundantly present its baneful effects do not end with itself. Burns long ago remarked with deep truth that it *petrifies feeling*. Let us revert for a moment to the powerful novel of which I spoke at the outset, *Madame Bovary*. Undoubtedly the taint in question is present in *Madame Bovary*, although to a much less degree than in more recent French novels which will be in every one's mind. But *Madame Bovary*, with this taint, is a work of *petrified feeling;* over it hangs an atmosphere of bitterness, irony, impotence; not a personage in the book to rejoice or console us; the springs of freshness and feeling are not there to create such personages. Emma Bovary follows a course in some respects like that of Anna, but where, in Emma Bovary, is Anna's charm? The treasures of compassion, tenderness insight, which alone, amid such guilt and misery, can enable charm to subsist and to emerge, are wanting to Flaubert. He is cruel, with the cruelty of petrified feeling, to his poor heroine; he pursues her without pity or pause, as with malignity; he is harder upon her himself than any reader even, I think, will be inclined to be.

A good book is the precious life-blood of a master-spirit, embalmed and treasured up on purpose to a life beyond life.

JOHN MILTON—*Areopagitica.*

FOOTNOTE ON CRITICISM[1]

By H. L. Mencken

Nearly all the discussions of criticism that I am acquainted with start off with a false assumption, to wit, that the primary motive of the critic, the impulse which makes a critic of him instead of, say, a politician, or a stockbroker, is pedagogical—that he writes because he is possessed by a passion to advance the enlightenment, to put down error and wrong, to disseminate some specific doctrine: psychological, epistemological, historical, or æsthetic. This is true, it seems to me, only of bad critics, and its degree of truth increases in direct ratio to their badness. The motive of the critic who is really worth reading—the only critic of whom, indeed, it may be said truthfully that it is at all possible to read him, save as an act of mental discipline—is something quite different. That motive is not the motive of the pedagogue, but the motive of the artist. It is no more and no less than the simple desire to function freely and beautifully, to give outward and objective form to ideas that bubble inwardly and have a fascinating lure in them, to get rid of them dramatically and make an articulate noise in the world. It was for this reason that Plato wrote the "Republic," and for this reason that Beethoven wrote the Ninth Symphony, and it is for this reason, to drop a million miles, that I am writing the present essay. Everything else is afterthought, mock-modesty, messianic delusion—in brief, affectation and folly. Is the contrary conception of criticism widely cherished? Is it almost universally held that the thing is a brother to jurisprudence, advertising, laparotomy, chautauqua lecturing and the art of

[1] Reprinted from *Prejudices,* Third Series, by H. L. Mencken, by and with permission of and special arrangement with Alfred A. Knopf, Inc., authorized publishers.

the schoolmarm? Then certainly the fact that it is so held should be sufficient to set up an overwhelming probability of its lack of truth and sense. If I speak with some heat, it is as one who has suffered. When, years ago, I devoted myself diligently to critical pieces upon the writings of Theodore Dreiser, I found that practically every one who took any notice of my proceedings at all fell into either one of two assumptions about my underlying purpose: (*a*) that I had a fanatical devotion for Mr. Dreiser's ideas and desired to propagate them, or (*b*) that I was an ardent patriot, and yearned to lift up American literature. Both assumptions were false. I had then, and I have now, very little interest in many of Mr. Dreiser's main ideas; when we meet, in fact, we usually quarrel about them. And I am wholly devoid of public spirit, and haven't the least lust to improve American literature; if it ever came to what I regard as perfection my job would be gone. What, then, was my motive in writing about Mr. Dreiser so copiously? My motive, well known to Mr. Dreiser himself and to every one else who knew me as intimately as he did, was simply and solely to sort out and give coherence to the ideas of Mr. Mencken, and to put them into suave and ingratiating terms, and to discharge them with a flourish, and maybe with a phrase of pretty song, into the dense fog that blanketed the Republic.

The critic's choice of criticism rather than of what is called creative writing is chiefly a matter of temperament—perhaps, more accurately of hormones—with accidents of education and environment to help. The feelings that happen to be dominant in him at the moment the scribbling frenzy seizes him are feelings inspired, not directly by life itself, but by books, pictures, music, sculpture, architecture, religion, philosophy—in brief, by some other man's feelings about life. They are thus, in a sense, secondhand, and it is no wonder that creative artists so easily fall into the theory that they are also second-rate. Perhaps they usually are. If, indeed, the critic continues on this plane—if he lacks the intellectual agility and enterprise needed to make the leap from the work of art to the vast and mysterious complex of phenomena behind it—then they *always* are, and he remains no more than a fugelman or policeman to his betters. But if a genuine artist is concealed within him—if his feelings are in any sense profound and original, and his capacity for self-expression is above the average of educated men—then he moves inevitably from the work of art to life itself, and begins to take on a dignity that he formerly lacked. It is impossible to think of a man of any actual force and originality, universally recognized as having those qualities, who spent his whole life appraising and describing the work of other men. Did Goethe, or Carlyle, or Matthew Arnold, or Sainte-Beuve, or Macaulay, or even, to come down a few pegs, Lewes, or Lowell, or Hazlitt? Certainly not. The thing that becomes most obvious about the writings of all such men, once they are examined carefully, is that the critic is always being swallowed up by the creative artist—that what starts out as the review of a book, or a play, or other work of art, usually develops very quickly into an independent essay upon the theme of that work of art, or upon some theme that it suggests—in a word, that it becomes a fresh work of art, and only indirectly related to the one that suggested it. This fact, indeed, is so plain that it scarcely needs statement. What the pedagogues always object to in, for example, the *Quarterly* reviewers is that they forgot the books they were supposed to review, and wrote long papers—often, in fact, small books—expounding ideas suggested (or not suggested) by the books under review. Every critic who is worth reading falls inevitably into the same habit. He cannot stick to his task: what is before him is always infinitely less interesting to him than what is within him. If he is genuinely first-rate—if what is within him stands the test of type, and wins an audience, and produces the reactions that every artist craves—then he usually ends by abandoning the criticism of specific works of art altogether, and setting up shop as a general merchant in general ideas, *i. e.,* as an artist working in the materials of life itself.

Mere reviewing, however conscientiously and competently it is done, is plainly a much inferior business. Like writing poetry, it is chiefly a function of intellectual immaturity. The young literatus just out of the university, having as yet no capacity for grappling with the fundamental mysteries of existence, is put to writing reviews of books, or plays, or music, or painting. Very often he does it extremely well; it is, in fact, not hard to do well, for even decayed pedagogues often do it, as such graves of the intellect as the *New York Times* bear witness. But if he continues to do it, whether well or ill, it is a sign to all the world that his growth ceased when they made him *Artium Baccalaureus*. Gradually he becomes, whether in or out of the academic grove, a professor, which is to say, a man devoted to diluting and retailing the ideas of his superiors—not an artist, not even a bad artist, but almost the antithesis of an artist. He is learned, he is sober, he is painstaking and accurate—but he is as hollow as a jug. Nothing is in him save the ghostly echoes of other men's thoughts and feelings. If he were a genuine artist he would have thoughts and feelings of his own, and the impulse to give them objective form would be irresistible. An artist can no more withstand that impulse than a politician can withstand the temptations of a job. There are no mute, inglorious Miltons, save in the hallucinations of poets. The one sound test of a Milton is that he functions as a Milton. His difference from other men lies precisely in the superior vigor of his impulse to self-expression, not in the superior beauty and loftiness of his ideas. Other men, in point of fact, often have the same ideas, or perhaps even loftier ones, but they are able to suppress them, usually on grounds of decorum, and so they escape being artists, and are respected by right-thinking persons, and die with money in the bank, and are forgotten in two weeks.

Obviously, the critic whose performance we are commonly

called upon to investigate is a man standing somewhere along the path leading from the beginning that I have described to the goal. He has got beyond being a mere cataloguer and valuer of other men's ideas, but he has not yet become an autonomous artist—he is not yet ready to challenge attention with his own ideas alone. But it is plain that his motion, in so far as he is moving at all, must be in the direction of that autonomy—that is, unless one imagines him sliding backward into senile infantilism: a spectacle not unknown to literary pathology, but too pathetic to be discussed here. Bear this motion in mind, and the true nature of his aims and purposes becomes clear; more, the incurable falsity of the aims and purposes usually credited to him becomes equally clear. He is not actually trying to perform an impossible act of arctic justice upon the artist whose work gives him a text. He is not trying with mathematical passion to find out exactly what was in that artist's mind at the moment of creation, and to display it precisely and in an ecstasy of appreciation. He is not trying to bring the work discussed into accord with some transient theory of æsthetics, or ethics, or truth, or to determine its degree of departure from that theory. He is not trying to lift up the fine arts, or to defend democracy against sense, or to promote happiness at the domestic hearth, or to convert sophomores into right-thinkers, or to serve God. He is not trying to fit a group of novel phenomena into the orderly process of history. He is not even trying to discharge the catalytic office that I myself, in a romantic moment, once sought to force upon him. He is, first and last, simply trying to express himself. He is trying to arrest and challenge a sufficient body of readers, to make them pay attention to him, to impress them with the charm and novelty of his ideas, to provoke them into an agreeable (or shocked) awareness of him, and he is trying to achieve thereby for his own inner ego the grateful feeling of a function performed, a tension relieved, a *katharsis* attained which Wagner achieved when he wrote "Die Walküre," and a hen achieves every time she lays an egg.

Joseph Conrad is moved by that necessity to write romances; Bach was moved to write music; poets are moved to write poetry; critics are moved to write criticism. The form is nothing; the only important thing is the motive power, and it is the same in all cases. It is the pressing yearning of every man who has ideas in him to empty them upon the world, to hammer them into plausible and ingratiating shapes, to compel the attention and respect of his equals, to lord it over his inferiors. So seen, the critic becomes a far more transparent and agreeable fellow than ever he was in the discourses of the psychologists who sought to make him a mere appraiser in an intellectual customs house, a gauger in a distillery of the spirit, a just and infallible judge upon the cosmic bench. Such offices, in point of fact, never fit him. He always bulges over their confines. So labelled and estimated, it inevitably turns out that the specific critic under examination is a very bad one, or no critic at all. But when he is thought of, not as pedagogue, but as artist, then he begins to take on reality, and, what is more, dignity. Carlyle was surely no just and infallible judge; on the contrary, he was full of prejudices, biles, naïvetés, humors. Yet he is read, consulted, attended to. Macaulay was unfair, inaccurate, fanciful, lyrical—yet his essays live. Arnold had his faults too, and so did Sainte-Beuve, and so did Goethe, and so did many another of that line—and yet they are remembered to-day, and all the learned and conscientious critics of their time, laboriously concerned with the precise intent of the artists under review, and passionately determined to set it forth with god-like care and to relate it exactly to this or that great stream of ideas—all these pedants are forgotten. What saved Carlyle, Macaulay and company is as plain as day. They were first-rate artists. They could make the thing charming, and that is always a million times more important than making it true.

Truth, indeed, is something that is believed in completely only by persons who have never tried personally to pursue it to its fastnesses and grab it by the tail. It is the adoration of second-rate men—men who always receive it at second-hand. Pedagogues believe in immutable truths and spend their lives trying to determine them and propagate them; the intellectual progress of man consists largely of a concerted effort to block and destroy their enterprise. Nine times out of ten, in the arts as in life, there is actually no truth to be discovered; there is only error to be exposed. In whole departments of human inquiry it seems to me quite unlikely that the truth ever *will* be discovered. Nevertheless, the rubber-stamp thinking of the world always makes the assumption that the exposure of an error is identical with the discovery of the truth—that error and truth are simple opposites. They are nothing of the sort. What the world turns to, when it has been cured of one error, is usually simply another error, and maybe one worse than the first one. This is the whole history of the intellect in brief. The average man of to-day does not believe in precisely the same imbecilities that the Greek of the fourth century before Christ believed in, but the things that he *does* believe in are often quite as idiotic. Perhaps this statement is a bit too sweeping. There is, year by year, a gradual accumulation of what may be called, provisionally, truths—there is a slow accretion of ideas that somehow manage to meet all practicable human tests, and so survive. But even so, it is risky to call them absolute truths. All that one may safely say of them is that no one, as yet, has demonstrated that they are errors. Soon or late, if experience teaches us anything, they are likely to succumb too. The profoundest truths of the Middle Ages are now laughed at by schoolboys. The profoundest truths of democracy will be laughed at, a few centuries hence, even by school-teachers.

In the department of æsthetics, wherein critics mainly disport themselves, it is almost impossible to think of a so-called truth that shows any sign of being permanently true.

The most profound of principles begins to fade and quiver almost as soon as it is stated. But the work of art, as opposed to the theory behind it, has a longer life, particularly if that theory be obscure and questionable, and so cannot be determined accurately. "Hamlet," the Mona Lisa, "Faust," "Dixie," "Parsifal," "Mother Goose," "Annabel Lee," "Huckleberry Finn"—these things, so baffling to pedagogy, so contumacious to the categories, so mysterious in purpose and utility—these things live. And why? Because there is in them the flavor of salient, novel and attractive personality, because the quality that shines from them is not that of correct demeanor but that of creative passion, because they pulse and breathe and speak, because they are genuine works of art. So with criticism. Let us forget all the heavy effort to make a science of it; it is a fine art, or nothing. If the critic, retiring to his cell to concoct his treatise upon a book or play or what-not, produces a piece of writing that shows sound structure, and brilliant color, and the flash of new and persuasive ideas, and civilized manners, and the charm of an uncommon personality in free function, then he has given something to the world that is worth having, and sufficiently justified his existence. Is Carlyle's "Frederick" true? Who cares? As well ask if the Parthenon is true, or the C Minor Symphony, or "Wiener Blut." Let the critic who is an artist leave such necropsies to professors of æsthetics, who can no more determine the truth than he can, and will infallibly make it unpleasant and a bore.

It is, of course, not easy to practice this abstention. Two forces, one within and one without, tend to bring even a Hazlitt or a Huneker under the campus pump. One is the almost universal human susceptibility to messianic delusions—the irresistible tendency of pratically every man, once he finds a crowd in front of him, to strut and roll his eyes. The other is the public demand, born of such long familiarity with pedagogical criticism that no other kind is readily conceivable, that the critic teach something as well as say something—in the popular phrase, that he be constructive. Both operate powerfully against his free functioning, and especially the former. He finds it hard to resist the flattery of his customers, however little he may actually esteem it. If he knows anything at all, he knows that his following, like that of every other artist in ideas, is chiefly made up of the congenitally subaltern type of man and woman—natural converts, lodge joiners, me-toos, stragglers after circus parades. It is precious seldom that he ever gets a positive idea out of them; what he usually gets is mere unintelligent ratification. But this troop, despite its obvious failings, corrupts him in various ways. For one thing, it enormously reënforces his belief in his own ideas, and so tends to make him stiff and dogmatic —in brief, precisely everything that he ought not to be. And for another thing, it tends to make him (by a curious contradiction) a bit pliant and politic: he begins to estimate new ideas, not in proportion as they are amusing or beautiful, but in proportion as they are likely to please. So beset, front and rear, he sometimes sinks supinely to the level of a professor, and his subsequent proceedings are interesting no more. The true aim of a critic is certainly not to make converts. He must know that very few of the persons who are susceptible to conversion are worth converting. Their minds are intrinsically flabby and parasitical, and it is certainly not sound sport to agitate minds of that sort. Moreover, the critic must always harbor a grave doubt about most of the ideas that they lap up so greedily—it must occur to him not infrequently, in the silent watches of the night, that much that he writes is sheer buncombe. As I have said, I can't imagine any idea—that is, in the domain of æsthetics—that is palpably and incontrovertibly sound. All that I am familiar with, and in particular all that I announce most vociferously, seem to me to contain a core of quite obvious nonsense. I thus try to avoid cherishing them too lovingly, and it always gives me a shiver to see any one else gobble them at one gulp. Criticism, at bottom, is indistinguishable from skepticism. Both launch themselves, the one by æsthetic presentations and the other by logical presentations, at the common human tendency to accept whatever is approved, to take in ideas ready-made, to be responsive to mere rhetoric and gesticulation. A critic who believes in anything absolutely is bound to that something quite as helplessly as a Christian is bound to the Freudian garbage in the Book of Revelation. To that extent, at all events, he is unfree and unintelligent, and hence a bad critic.

The demand for "constructive" criticism is based upon the same false assumption that immutable truths exist in the arts, and that the artist will be improved by being made aware of them. This notion, whatever the form it takes, is always absurd—as much so, indeed, as its brother delusion that the critic, to be competent, must be a practitioner of the specific art he ventures to deal with, *i. e.,* that a doctor, to cure a belly-ache, must have a belly-ache. As practically encountered, it is disingenuous as well as absurd, for it comes chiefly from bad artists who tire of serving as performing monkeys, and crave the greater ease and safety of sophomores in class. They demand to be taught in order to avoid being knocked about. In their demand is the theory that instruction, if they could get it, would profit them—that they are capable of doing better work than they do. As a practical matter, I doubt that this is ever true. Bad poets never actually grow any better; they invariably grow worse and worse. In all history there has never been, to my knowledge, a single practitioner of any art who, as a result of "constructive" criticism, improved his work. The curse of all the arts, indeed, is the fact that they are constantly invaded by persons who are not artists at all—persons whose yearning to express their ideas and feelings is unaccompanied by the slightest capacity for charming expression—in brief, persons with absolutely nothing to say. This is particularly true of the art of letters, which interposes very few technical obstacles to the vanity and garrulity of such invaders. Any effort to teach them to write better is an effort wasted, as every editor discovers for himself; they are as incapable of it as they are of jumping over the moon. The only sort of criticism that can deal with them to any profit is the sort that employs them frankly as laboratory animals. It cannot cure them, but it can at least make an amusing and perhaps edifying show of them. It is idle to argue that the good in them is thus destroyed with the bad. The simple answer is that there *is* no good in them. Suppose Poe had wasted his time trying to dredge good work out of Rufus Dawes, author of "Geraldine." He would have failed miserably—and spoiled a capital essay, still diverting after three-quarters of a century. Suppose Beethoven, dealing with Gottfried Weber, had tried laboriously to make an intelligent music critic of him. How much more apt, useful and durable the simple note: "Arch-ass! Double-barrelled ass!" Here was absolutely sound criticism. Here was a judgment wholly beyond challenge. Moreover, here was a small but perfect work of art.

Upon the low practical value of so-called constructive criticism I can offer testimony out of my own experience. My books are commonly reviewed at great length, and many critics devote themselves to pointing out what they conceive to be my errors, both of fact and of taste. Well, I cannot recall a case in which any suggestion offered by a constructive critic has helped me in the slightest, or even actively interested me. Every such wet-nurse of letters has sought fatuously to make me write in a way differing from that in which the Lord God Almighty, in His infinite wisdom, impels me to write—that is, to make me write stuff which, coming from me, would be as false as an appearance of decency in a Congressman. All the benefits I have ever got from the critics of my work have come from the destructive variety. A hearty slating always does me good, particularly if it be well written. It begins by enlisting my professional respect; it ends by making me examine my ideas coldly in the privacy of my chamber. Not, of course, that I usually revise them, but I at least examine them. If I decide to hold fast to them, they are all the dearer to me thereafter, and I expound them with a new passion and plausibility. If, on the contrary, I discern holes in them, I shelve them in a *pianissimo* manner, and set about hatching new ones to take their place. But constructive criticism irritates me. I do not object to being denounced, but I can't abide being schoolmastered, especially by men I regard as imbeciles.

I find, as a practicing critic, that very few men who write books are even as tolerant as I am—that most of them, soon or late, show signs of extreme discomfort under criticism, however polite its terms. Perhaps this is why enduring friendships between authors and critics are so rare. All artists, of course, dislike one another more or less, but that dislike seldom rises to implacable enmity, save between opera singer and opera singer, and creative author and critic. Even when the latter two keep up an outward show of good-will, there is always bitter antagonism under the surface. Part of it, I daresay, arises out of the impossible demands of the critic, particularly if he be tinged with the constructive madness. Having favored an author with his good opinion, he expects the poor fellow to live up to that good opinion without the slightest compromise or faltering, and this is commonly beyond human power. He feels that any let-down compromises *him*—that his hero is stabbing him in the back, and making him ridiculous—and this feeling rasps his vanity. The most bitter of all literary quarrels are those between critics and creative artists, and most of them arise in just this way. As for the creative artist, he on his part naturally resents the critic's air of pedagogical superiority and he resents it especially when he has an uneasy feeling that he has fallen short of his best work, and that the discontent of the critic is thus justified. Injustice is relatively easy to bear; what stings is justice. Under it all, of course, lurks the fact that I began with:

the fact that the critic is himself an artist, and that his creative impulse, soon or late, is bound to make him neglect the punctilio. When he sits down to compose his criticism, his artist ceases to be a friend, and becomes mere raw material for his work of art. It is my experience that artists invariably resent this cavalier use of them. They are pleased so long as the critic confines himself to the modest business of interpreting them—preferably in terms of their own estimate of themselves—but the moment he proceeds to adorn their theme with variations of his own, the moment he brings new ideas to the enterprise and begins contrasting them with their ideas, that moment they grow restive. It is precisely at this point, of course, that criticism becomes genuine criticism; before that it was mere reviewing. When a critic passes it he loses his friends. By becoming an artist, he becomes the foe of all other artists.

But the transformation, I believe, has good effects upon him: it makes him a better critic. Too much *Gemütlichkeit* is as fatal to criticism as it would be to surgery or politics. When it rages unimpeded it leads inevitably either to a dull professorial sticking on of meaningless labels or to log-rolling, and often it leads to both. One of the most hopeful symptoms of the new *Aufklärung* in the Republic is the revival of acrimony in criticism—the renaissance of the doctrine that æsthetic matters are important, and that it is worth the while of a healthy male to take them seriously, as he takes business, sport and amour. In the days when American literature was showing its first vigorous growth, the native criticism was extraordinarily violent and even vicious; in the days when American literature swooned upon the tomb of the Puritan *Kultur* it became flaccid and childish. The typical critic of the first era was Poe, as the typical critic of the second was Howells. Poe carried on his critical jehads with such ferocity that he often got into lawsuits, and sometimes ran no little risk of having his head cracked. He regarded literary questions as exigent and momentous. The lofty aloofness of the don was simply not in him. When he encountered a book that seemed to him to be bad, he attacked it almost as sharply as a Chamber of Commerce would attack a fanatic preaching free speech, or the corporation of Trinity Church would attack Christ. His opponents replied in the same Berserker manner. Much of Poe's surviving ill-fame, as a drunkard and dead-beat, is due to their inordinate denunciations of him. They were not content to refute him; they constantly tried to dispose of him altogether. The very ferocity of that ancient row shows that the native literature, in those days, was in a healthy state. Books of genuine value were produced. Literature always thrives best, in fact, in an atmosphere of hearty strife. Poe, surrounded by admiring professors, never challenged, never aroused to the emotions of revolt, would probably have written poetry indistinguishable from the hollow stuff of, say, Prof. Dr. George E. Woodberry. It took the persistent (and often grossly unfair and dishonorable) opposition of Griswold *et al* to stimulate him to his highest endeavors. He needed friends, true enough, but he also needed enemies.

To-day, for the first time in years, there is strife in American criticism, and the Paul Elmer Mores and Hamilton Wright Mabies are no longer able to purr in peace. The instant they fall into stiff professorial attitudes they are challenged, and often with anything but urbanity. The *ex cathedra* manner thus passes out, and free discussion comes in. Heretics lay on boldly, and the professors are forced to make some defence. Often, going further, they attempt counter-attacks. Ears are bitten off. Noses are bloodied. There are wallops both above and below the belt. I am, I need not say, no believer in any magical merit in debate, no matter how free it may be. It certainly does not necessarily establish the truth; both sides, in fact, may be wrong, and they often are. But it at least accomplishes two important effects. On the one hand, it exposes all the cruder fallacies to hostile examination, and so disposes of many of them. And on the other hand, it melodramatizes the business of the critic, and so convinces thousands of bystanders, otherwise quite inert, that criticism is an amusing and instructive art, and that the problems it deals with are important. What men will fight for seems to be worth looking into.

> Sir Henry Wotton used to say that critics were like brushers of noblemen's clothes.
>
> FRANCIS BACON—*Apothegms.*

MR. MENCKEN, THE JEUNE FILLE, AND THE NEW SPIRIT IN LETTERS[1]

By Stuart P. Sherman

A woman whose husband has made money in the war likes to have her portrait painted and her friends coming in to admire it. So a new public, grown conscious of itself, demands a new literature and a new literature demands a new criticism. Fine gentlemen with a touch of frost above the temples, sitting at ease in quiet old clubs under golden-brown portraits of their ancestors, and turning the pages of the *Athenaeum* or Mr. More's *Nation,* have seen with disdainful yet apprehensive glance through plate-glass windows the arrival of all three: the formation of a reading public of which they are not a part, the appearance of a literature which they do not care to read, the development of a criticism in which their views are not represented. Since a critic is of no importance except with reference to what he criticizes, you will please bear with me while I bring in the new literature and the new readers. When the stage is properly set, Mr. Mencken will appear.

How shall one indicate the color and spirit of it?—this new public now swarming up the avenues of democratic opportunity; becoming prosperous, self-conscious, voluble; sunning itself in the great cities; reaching out greedily to realize its "legitimate aspirations." This latest generation of Americans, so vulgar and selfish and good-humored and sensual and impudent, shows little trace of the once dominant Puritan stock and nothing of the Puritan temper. It is curiously and richly composed of the children of parents who dedicated themselves to accumulation, and toiling inarticulately in

[1] Reprinted by permission of Chas. Scribner's Sons.

shop and field, in forest and mine, never fully mastered the English definite article or the personal pronoun. It is composed of children whose parents or grandparents brought their copper kettles from Russia, tilled the soil of Hungary, taught the Mosaic law in Poland, cut Irish turf, ground optical glass in Germany, dispensed Bavarian beer, or fished for mackerel around the Skagerrak. The young people laugh at the oddities of their forbears, discard the old kettles, the Mosaic law, the provincial dialect, the Lutheran pastor. Into the new society breaking without cultural inheritance, they derive all their interests and standards from their immediate environment, and gravitate towards refinement through more and more expensive gratifications of the senses.

The prettiest type of this swift civilization—and I must have something pretty to enliven a discourse on current criticism—the prettiest type is the *jeune fille,* who, to modernize the phrase of an old poet, aspires to a soul in silken hosiery and doeskin boots. She springs, this young creature with ankles sheathed and shod like a Virginia deer—ankles whose trimness is, æsthetically speaking, quite the finest thing her family has produced in America—she springs from a grandmother who clumped out in wooden shoes to milk a solitary cow in Sweden. She has no soul, the young thing, but she trusts that the tailor, the milliner, the bootmaker, the manicurist, the hairdresser, and the masseuse can give her the equivalent. Wherever art can work on her surfaces, she is finished. When the car is at the door in the morning "a distinctive body on a distinguished *chassis*"—and she runs down the steps with somewhat more than a flash of her silken perfections, she is exquisite, what though the voice is a bit hard and shrill with which she calls out, "H'lo, kiddo! Le's go't Bretana's."

She is indeed coming—the new reader! She will bring home an armful of magazines, smelling deliciously of the press, books with exciting yellow jackets, plays newly translated and imported, the latest stories, the most recent ideas, all set forth in the current fashion, and all, as it will seem to her, about herself, her sort of people, her sort of world, and about the effort which her fair young ego is making to emerge from the indiscriminated mass and to acquire the physical form and line congruous with that "distinctive body mounted on a distinguished chassis," which bears her with such smooth speed up Riverside Drive. She will have no American literature of the "classical period" in her library; for the New England worthies who produced it wrote before the public of which she is a part began to read or to be noticed in books. The *jeune fille,* though a votary of physical form, feels within herself an exhilarating chaos, a fluent welter, which Lowell and Longfellow and James and Howells do not, but which her writers must, express.

Therefore, she revels in the English paradoxers and mountebanks, the Scandinavian misanthropes, the German ego-maniacs, and, above all, in the later Russian novelists, crazy with war, taxes, hunger, anarchy, vodka, and German philosophy. She does enjoy, however, the posthumous pessimism of Mark Twain—it is "so strong and virile"; and she relishes his pilot oaths—they are "so sincere and unconventional." She savors Mr. Masters' hard little naturalistic sketches of "passion" on Michigan Boulevard; they remind her of her brother. Sherwood Anderson has a place on her shelves; for by the note of revolt in *Winesburg, Ohio* she recognizes one of her own spirit's deserted villages. Lured by a primitive instinct to the sound of animals roving, she ventures a curious foot into the fringes of the Dreiserian wilderness vast and drear; and barbaric impulses in her blood "answer the wail of the forest." She is not much "intrigued" by the frosty fragilities of imagist verse; but at Sandburg's viking salute to the Hog-Butcher of the World she claps her hands and cries: "Oh, boy, isn't it gorgeous!" This welter of her "culture" she plays, now and then, at organizing on some strictly modern principle, such as her father applies to his business, such as her brother applies to his pleasures—a principle of egotistical combat, a principle of self-indulgence, cynical and luxurious. She is not quite happy with the result. Sometimes, I imagine, she wishes that her personal attendants, those handmen and maidens who have wrought so wonderfully with her surfaces, could be set at work upon her interior, so that her internal furnishing and decoration could be brought into measurable concord with the grace and truth of her contours, the rhythm of her hair.

Imagine a thousand *jeunes filles* thus wistful, and you have the conditions ready for the advent of a new critic. At this point enters at a hard gallop, spattered with mud, H. L. Mencken high in oath—thus justifying the Goethean maxim: *Aller Anfang ist schwer.* He leaps from the saddle with sabre flashing, stables his horse in the church, shoots the priest, hangs the professors, exiles the Academy, burns the library and the university, and, amid the smoking ashes, erects a new school of criticism on modern German principles, which he traces through Spingarn to Goethe, but which I should be inclined to trace rather to Eckermann.

Of my own inability to interpret modern Germany, however, I have recently been painfully reminded by an 86-page pamphlet sent to me from Hamburg, with blue-pencil marks kindly inserted by the author, one Hansen—apparently a German-Schleswigian-American who has studied rhetoric in Mr. Mencken's school—inquiring what the masses can possibly know of the real Germany, "so long as the Shermans squat like toads in the portals of the schools and the Northcliffes send their Niagaras of slime through the souls of the English-speaking peoples." I was amused, of course, to find a great lord of the press so quaintly bracketed with an obscure teacher of literature in a Middle Western university as an effective obstacle between the sunlight and Germany. All the same, my conscience was touched; and I remembered with satisfaction that, on the appearance of Mr. Mencken's *Prefaces,* I made a conscientious effort to tell my countrymen where they should go, namely, to Mr. Mencken, if they desired a really sympathetic presentation of the modern Teutonic point of view with reference to politics, religion, morals, women, beer, and *belles-lettres*.

On the appearance of Mr. Mencken's new volume, *Prejudices*—continuing my humble service as guide to what I am not thoroughly qualified to appreciate—I can only say that here I find again the Nietzschean "aristocrat" of yesteryear, essentially unchanged. He is a little sadder, perhaps, since democracy has unhorsed the autocrats; but his skepticism of democracy is unshaken. He is a shade more cynical since the extension of women's suffrage; but he is as clear as ever that he knows what girls were made for. He is a little more sober since the passage of the national prohibition act, and a bit less lyrical about the Pilsener-motive in the writings of Mr. Huneker; but, come rain come shine, he still points with pride to a digestion ruined by alcohol. In other respects, former patrons of his school for beautifying American letters will find his familiar manners and customs essentially unaltered.

If we are to have a Menckian academy, Mr. Mencken shows the way to set it up—with vigor and rigor, with fist and foot, with club and axe. The crash of smashing things, the knocking of heads together, the objurgations which accompany his entrance have a high advertising value, fascinating to all the gamins of the press and attractive to our *jeune fille,* who will pay for a copy of *Prejudices* and form her taste upon it. And far be it from me to deny that she may learn something from her heavy-handed disciplinarian. Mr. Mencken, like most men, has his merits, of which it is a pleasure to speak. He is alive; this is a merit in a good man and hardly a defect even in a bad critic. He has a rough, prodding wit, blunted by thrusting at objects which it cannot pierce, but yet a wit. He is passionately addicted to scoffing; and if by chance a sham that is obnoxious to him comes in his way, he will scoff at a sham. He has no inclination to the softer forms of "slush" or to the more diaphanous varieties of "pishposh." He has a style becoming a retired military man —hard, pointed, forcible, cocksure. He likes a sentence stripped of baggage, and groups of sentences that march briskly off at the word of command, wheel, continue to march, and, at word of command, with equal precision, halt. He has the merits of an efficient rhetorical drill-sergeant. By his services in pointing out to our fair barbarian that she need not, after all, read Mr. Veblen, she should acknowledge that he has earned the royalty on her copy of *Prejudices*. He has given her, in short, what she might expect to get from a stiff freshman course in rhetoric.

When he has told her who fits sentences together well and who ill, he has ended the instruction that was helpful to her. He can give her lessons in derision, lessons in cynicism, lessons in contempt; but she was mistress of all these when she entered school. He can offer to free her from attachment to English and American literary traditions; but she was never attached to these traditions. He will undertake to make her believe that Baptists and Methodists, professors and academicians, prohibition societies and marriage covenants are ridiculous; but she always thought them ridiculous. He is ready to impregnate her mind with the wisdom of "old Friedrich," Stirmer, Strindberg, and the rest of the crew; but her mind is already impregnated with that sort of wisdom. "When one has turned away from the false and the soft and the silly," this is the question she is asking, "where does one go to find true and beautiful things?" She has heard somewhere by chance, poor girl, that one who pursues truth and beauty is delivered from the grosser tyrannies of the senses, escapes a little out of the inner welter, and discovers serenity widening like a fair dawn in the mind, with a certain blitheness and amenity. This is æsthetic liberation.

For one seeking æsthetic liberation there is a canon of things to be thought on which the worldiest of sound critics, Sainte-Beuve, pronounced as clearly and insistently as Saint Paul. The Germans, as the great Goethe explained to the saucer-eyed Eckermann, are "weak on the æsthetic side." Æsthetic appreciation is superficially an affair of the palate, and at bottom an affair of the heart, embracing with elation whatsoever things are lovely. Mr. Mencken has no heart; and if he ever had a palate he has lost it in protracted orgies of literary "strong drink." He turns with anguish from the pure and simple flavors that please children as the first gifts of nature, and that delight critics as the last achievements of art. His appetite craves a fierce stimulation of sauces, a flamboyance and glitter of cheeses, the sophisticated and appalling ripeness of wild duck nine days old.

He devotes, for example, two pages to leading the *jeune fille* away from Emerson as a writer of no influence. He spends more in showing her that Howells has nothing to say. He warns her that Mr. Garland's *Son of the Middle Border* is amateurish, flat, banal, and repellent. He gives a condescending *coup de pied* to the solider works of Arnold Bennett and singles out for intense admiration a scarlet-lattice scene or so in his pot-boilers. As the author of a work on the American language, over-ambitiously designed as a wedge to split asunder the two great English-speaking peoples, and as an advocate of an "intellectual artistocracy," it has suddenly occurred to him that we have been shamefully neglecting the works of George Ade; accordingly, he strongly commends to our younger generation the works of Mr. George Ade. But the high light and white flame of his appreciation falls upon three objects as follows: the squalid story of an atrocious German bar-maid by Sudermann; an anonymous autobiographical novel, discovered by Mr. Mencken himself, which exhibits "an eternal blue-nose with every wart and pimple glittering," and is "as devoid of literary sophistication as an operation for gallstones"; and third and last, the works of Mr. Mencken's partner, Mr. George Jean Nathan, with his divine knack at making phrases "to flabbergast a dolt."

I imagine my bewildered seeker for æsthetic liberation asking her mentor if studying these things will help her to form "the diviner mind." "Don't bother me now," exclaims Mr. Mencken; "don't bother me now. I am just striking out a great phrase. Æsthetic effort tones up the mind with a kind of high excitement. I shall say in the next number of the *Smart Set* that James Harlan was the *damnedest ass* that America ever produced. If you don't know him, look him up. In the second edition of my book on the American language I shall add a new verb—to *Menckenize*—and perhaps a new noun, *Menckenism*. The definition of these words will clear up matters for you, and summarize my contribution to the national *belles-lettres*. It is beginning to take—the spirit is beginning to spread."

While Mr. Mencken and the *jeune fille* are engaged in this chat on the nature of beauty, I fancy the horn of a "high-powered" automobile is heard from the street before the Menckenian school. And in bursts Mr. Francis Hackett, looking like a man who has just performed a long and difficult operation under the body of his car, though, as a matter of fact, he has only just completed a splashing, shirt-sleeve review for *The New Republic*. "Let's wash up," cries Mr. Hackett, stripping off his blouse of blue jeans, "and go out to luncheon."

"Where shall we *fressen?*" says Mr. Mencken.

"At the Loyal Independent Order of United Hiberno-German-Anti-English-Americans," says Mr. Hackett. "All the New Critics will be there. Colum, Lewisohn, Wright, and the rest. I tried to get Philip Littell to come along. He's too gol darn refined. But I've got a chap in the car, from the West, that will please you. Used to run a column in the World's Greatest. Calls Thomas Arnold of Rugby 'that thrice-damned boor and noodle'."

"Good!" Mr. Mencken exclaims. "A Menckenism! A Menckenism! A likely chap!" And out they both bolt.

The *jeune fille,* with a thoughtful backward glance at Mr. Hackett's blouse, goes slowly down into the street, and, strolling up the walk in the crisp early winter air, overtakes

Mr. Littell, who is strolling even more slowly. He is reading a book, on which the first snowflake of the year has fallen, and, as it falls, he looks up with such fine delight in his eye that she asks him what has pleased him.

"A thought," he replies gently, "phrased by a subtle writer and set in a charming essay by a famous critic. Listen: *"Où il n'y a point de délicatesse, il n'y a point de littérature."* [1]

"That's a new one on me," says the *jeune fille.*

[1] Translated: "When one begins to Menckenize, the spirit of good literature flees in consternation."

Critics must excuse me, if I compare them to certain animals called asses; who, by gnawing vines, originally taught the great advantage of pruning them.

WILLIAM SHENSTONE.

THE "NEW" HUMANISTS FORMULATE THEIR FOURTEEN POINTS[1]

By JOHN CHAMBERLAIN

THIS summing up of a group credo, the credo of the band of critics in America who are most determined upon preempting the title of "humanist" for themselves, comes at a very opportune moment, for the winds of doctrine in criticism have been chasing themselves wildly over the cultural landscape for more than a year now, and it is time for a little clarity; one must know where one stands in relation to one's fellows. The symposium should be of great use, both to its friends and its enemies. For those who seek a middle ground between the so-called "naturalistic" thinkers who stick to the nineteenth century theories of mechanical determinism and those who exhibit a desire to fall back on the old traditions and authority that have so thoroughly crumbled before Walter Lippmann's "acids of modernity," it should act as a spur to formulate a third credo, a credo that already exists in embryo in the writings of a number of thinkers, including Lippmann, Lewis Mumford, Irwin Edman and James Truslow Adams.

The publication of "Humanism and America" is important also because it is evidence of an inner need. It is symptomatic. About a year ago a rash of articles broke out in the magazines discussing the pros and cons of humanism. At the time the phrase was loosely employed; it was used to designate the beliefs of thinkers as far apart as Walter Lippmann and Irving Babbitt, Harry Emerson Fosdick and Paul Elmer More, Bishop Potter and Norman Foerster. Those whose interest in the movement was undogmatic were ready to concede that

[1] Reprinted by permission of the author and the *New York Times*. A review of HUMANISM AND AMERICA—Essays on the Outlook of Modern Civilization. Edited by Norman Foerster.

Mumford was an "unacademic" humanist. In any case, the recrudescence of the term indicated a healthy dissatisfaction with a satire that in Sinclair Lewis had degenerated from "Babbitt" to "Elmer Gantry," a dissatisfaction with Dreiser for hanging on, tooth and nail, to a scientific theory of novel writing that was no longer scientifically respectable, a dissatisfaction with a Sherwood Anderson who had gone from poetry to what Gorham Munson, one of the contributors to "Humanism and America," has called "simplism."

Although the movement away from "naturalism" was, at first, largely inchoate, it soon became evident that there were two schools of the dissatisfied. The older humanists, followers of Irving Babbitt and Paul Elmer More, were not, judging from their expression, particularly willing to admit Lippmann, Van Wyck Brooks, Randolph Bourne, Mumford and Edman as undogmatic allies, brothers in so far as they all had repudiated theories of impressionism in criticism of literature, and in so far as they all desired to put back the "light of grandeur" into the universe from whence Joseph Wood Krutch, author of "The Modern Temper," had banished it. "Humanism and America" is the book of the dogmatic wing of those who have revolted from pure impressionism in criticism, and from the mood so perfectly expressed by the characters of Aldous Huxley, the post-war mood of disillusion whose roots, in reality, go back of the war.

The tenets of the contributors to this book may be summed up briefly. To begin with, belief in the moral responsibility of the individual is assumed, not as something scientifically proved, but merely as something arrived at through the study of mankind as man. This responsibility rests on the assumption of the freedom of the will, which, in the words of Professor Babbitt, takes the form of a will to "refrain," or to "discriminate," to set an "inner check" working upon the natural desires of the expansive man to get all that is coming to him. Science is regarded as something *hors concours;* it teaches much about quantity, or "how much," but nothing about quality, or "how good," and hence is something to be used, not something to be worshipped in itself. In literature the humanists lean heavily on Aristotle and his ideas concerning fit heroes for tragedy, heroes who are neither wholly good nor wholly bad, but who are endowed with a power of choice between good and evil, the conflict of the choosing making the drama. (This, of course, rules out Dreiser's gallery of Cowperwoods, Sister Carries, Eugene Witlas and Clyde Griffithses.) In education, the humanists take their stand with Professor Babbitt, who has criticized President Eliot's formulas of education for "power and service," and who has opposed to these formulas a belief in the efficacy of the classics in giving undergraduates a fit image of the cultured man.

Specifically, in this book, a number of the "new" humanists —so called to distinguish them from a more liberal breed of the Renaissance—make frontal assaults on what they regard as prime fallacies. Louis Trenchard More, for example, attempts to undermine "the pretensions of science." Irving Babbitt makes an essay at definition of humanism. The idea of God promulgated by Professor Whitehead is attacked by Paul Elmer More, who leans on divine revelation for his support. T. S. Eliot, who has already endeavored to show, in a magazine article, that humanism cannot get along without the support of religion, takes another line of attack and aims to establish as fact that religion needs the sword arm of humanism. Our fine arts are seen as in a "plight" by Frank Jewett Mather, Jr., who calls for "a few thousand humanists" to rescue them. Three men, Alan Reynolds Thompson, Robert Shafer and Harry Hayden Clark, write on the dearth in America of humanistic fiction, Mr. Thompson focusing his searchlight on the death of classical tragedy in a world that no longer believes in the "moral choice" of the individual, Mr. Shafer concentrating an attack on Theodore Dreiser, and Mr. Clark conceiving most American literature as the contents of a "Pandora's box." Gorham B. Munson investigates "Our Critical Spokesman," and comes to the conclusion that they are all failures—excepting, of course, the new humanists and perhaps a number of younger critics who are not brought into the discussion. Other papers speak of "Dionysus in Dismay," "The Well of Discipline" and "Courage and Education."

So far, so good. One can sympathize fully with many of the beliefs of the new humanists, especially their belief in the freedom of the individual to exercise choice between good and evil. But their discriminations ought properly to be predicated upon a study of modern society, a study which the humanists have so far largely ignored. Louis More's objections to Watsonian psychology are very intelligent. But the suspicion occurs that Watson's behaviorism may be worth something as method, if worth little as philosophy. And will the "dualism" of the world of "thing" and the world of "man," a dualism that sets man off from the quantitative order of nature, stand scrutiny? Isn't it the nature of man as man to seek a monistic explanation of the universe, an explanation that will reconcile all diversity, all dualism, into a synthetic philosophy that accounts for everything? And why should Louis More write of the "pretensions of science" just after Whitehead, Edington, Millikan, and any number of scientists, have entered disclaimers to pretension? Furthermore, Louis More's willingness to ignore the later theories of physics (which reduce matter and force to different manifestations of something ultimately mysterious, and which lead, in a philosophy of process, to the rehabilitation of relative freedom of the will as a working hypothesis, the most fruitful of two admittedly unproved working hypotheses)—the willingness to ignore something that really plays into his hands and might convince some one is, in reality, a denial of interest in will, whether it be a will to "refrain" or a will to create.

Whitehead is not only attacked by Louis More, but by Paul Elmer More. The latter's objections will be unconvincing to those who cannot believe in the actuality of any historic divine revelation; it will be unconvincing because Whitehead and More each start from different postulates, and the argument, in consequence, ends where it began, with one man telling the other he is wrong because his basic assumptions are different.

The new humanists do not look for guidance from "inexact" sciences any more than they look for it from the physical sciences. Bernard Brandler and others have a cold eye for psychology and sociology. Here, we think, they miss something, and it is because of this oversight that much of the new humanistic literary criticism sounds shallow. For art, as Mary Colum (a cool and level critic of Babbitt) has pointed out, is the result of significant mind working on significant material; and our knowledge of both significant mind and significant material can be enhanced by a study of both psychology and sociology, inexact though they may be.

The really worthwhile essays in the symposium are those of Frank Jewett Mather, Jr., and Harry Hayden Clark. The latter, it is true, misses the import which the late Stuart Sherman found in Willa Cather, but his essay on American fiction is skillful as objective diagnosis. And every one will admit, with Mr. Mather, that our arts have declined. Few, however, will be ready to say that Mr. Mather is wholly correct in his prescriptions. "A few thousand genuine humanists in America would make our society humanistic," writes Mr. Mather. "A hundred humanist painters, sculptors, architects, musicians and men of letters would make our art solidly humanistic." But how to get his number of humanists? Assuming that Mr. Mather isn't particularly set on the narrow academic brand of humanism, the brand that puts its emphasis, unfortunately, on decorum at the expense of vitality, the way to get it is by a vigorous social criticism. For art is symptomatic of inner forces and to change the sort of art that is prevalent we must change the forces. It is a matter for education and education proceeds by positive criticism. (Can any one who has followed the success of H. L. Mencken doubt the effect of social criticism?) We have had much of this positive criticism for the past fifteen years—the social criticism of Van Wyck Brooks, of James Truslow Adams, of Waldo Frank, of Mumford, Lippmann, the late Sherman, Dr. Canby, Irwin Edman, all of whom have attacked what Mr. Adams has happily called the "philosophy of the counting house," and the maintenance of a civilization on the "sole basic idea of profit." Indeed, if the new humanists are having a hearing at present, it is the work of these men that has gained the hearing for them.

It is the ignoring by Mr. Mather and others of the symposium of the positively beneficial work already done by American criticism that makes "Humanism and America" sound like the product of men who have been unhealthily cloistered. Mr. Munson alone among them has shown any interest in the nurture of art in America. It is not the new humanists, by and large, who have sought to assess American literature at its growing points. It is not the humanists who have discovered, in the field of the novel, Elizabeth Madox Roberts, Thornton Wilder, Glenway Wescott or Ernest Hemingway, all of whom are the logical answers to Dreiser, Anderson and Lewis. And if the ground has been prepared for these writers, it is not because of the interest of the new humanists, but because of the work of Brooks and others who bore the brunt fifteen years ago and carried the battle against the desiccated "genteel" tradition away from the purely negative protest offered by Cabell and Dreiser to the more positive protests of those who have begun to grow in the 'twenties.

ANGRY PROFESSORS[1]

By Malcolm Cowley

I

The opposition lately encountered by the disciples of More and Babbitt can be explained in part, though only in part, by a fundamental confusion in the minds of the American Humanists themselves, a confusion between humanism with a small "h" and their own sort of capitalized Humanism.

Humanism with a small "h" is a general attitude which is difficult or impossible to define. Partly it is an emphasis on the qualities it considers to be essentially human. Partly it is a defense of human dignity, of human possibilities; partly it is an opposition to all the forces that threaten them, whether these forces be religious, social, governmental, economic, or those of an anti-human philosophy. This attitude received its name during the Renaissance, when it was revived by the study of Greek and Roman antiquity. The Chinese sages were humanists in their time, and so, it might be added, are vast numbers of thinking men today.

The Humanism we spell with a capital letter is a body of doctrine assembled by Professors Irving Babbitt, of Harvard, and Paul Elmer More, of Princeton. These two men are among the foremost American critics of their generation, and this in itself surrounds their philosophy with a certain prestige. Their system appeals, moreover, to the critics who wish to apply fixed standards to literature; and it is not uncongenial to the somewhat conservative temper of the younger generation. Thus, in the midst of enemies, this doctrinal Humanism

[1] Reprinted with the kind permission of the author and of the *New Republic*.

has grown in power. Today there are Humanist magazines, Humanist publishers, Humanist professors in all the larger universities; there are Humanist critics, scientists and political thinkers (if not Humanist artists); and the movement has even enlisted the editorial support of the *New York Times,* which doesn't quite know what it is all about, but which feels, somehow, that Humanism is safe and reactionary. Yet in spite of all these activities, American Humanism is only one school of thought among many: it is a movement that may be compared in scope with Ethical Culture, or at the most with Christian Science.

Now, the Humanists themselves have unconsciously confused their specific cult with the general attitude. When Babbitt, for example, speaks of founding a Humanist university or of banding his followers together into a Humanist "communion" from which most of us will be excluded for doctrinal reasons, he is evidently referring to the contemporary cult. When, on the other hand, he speaks of humanism as something comparable in importance to religion in general—when he says that "a more definite feeling of limitation . . . lies at the base of both humanism and religion," or that "the question remains whether the more crying need just now is for positive and critical humanism or for positive and critical religion," or again that "the solution of this problem as to the relation between humanism and religion . . . lies in looking upon them both as only different stages in the same path" —in all these instances he is obviously referring to humanism as a general attitude, and one which is shared not only by Socrates and Confucius, but also by many contemporary writers whom Babbitt himself disowns. His followers profit vastly by this confusion. It enables them to claim all the humanist past for their modern doctrine; it enables them to speak of "Homer, Phidias, Plato, Aristotle, Confucius, Buddha, Jesus, Paul, Virgil, Horace, Dante, Shakespeare, Milton, Goethe . . . Matthew Arnold in England and Emerson and Lowell in America" as their own collaborators; and it subjects them to a great deal of justified ridicule which they might have avoided by a little Socratic thinking.

Their philosophy should be considered in itself. And so, in the present essay, I intend to deal chiefly with capitalized Humanism, though I shall sometimes contrast it with other forms of the general attitude which impress me as being more valid. I shall deal with the doctrines of More and Babbitt, first as theories, then as practised in their own writings and those of their disciples; and lastly I shall try to criticize these doctrines from the standpoint of imaginative writers in general.

II

American Humanism begins with the assumption that life can be divided into three planes: the natural, the human and the religious. It holds that we should cultivate the second of these planes, not in opposition to religion, but rather to the natural plane, which is represented today by the scientific descendants of Francis Bacon and the romantic descendants of Jean-Jacques Rousseau. Thus, says Robert Shafer writing in The Bookman:

> Against romanticism, humanitarian sympathy, mechanistic or vitalistic determinism, the doctrine of progress and the like, has been opposed a skeptical criticism of life and letters which rests ultimately on the proposition that man differs not alone in complexity of organization, but in kind, from the animal, and that his happiness depends upon his recognition and cultivation of that element in his being which is distinctive of him. This is held to be possible; man is held to be, within limits, capable of responsible choice. . . . To choose is to discriminate, and, for this, habituation to self-restraint is essential; it is, indeed, the foundation on which the whole structure of distinctively human life rests.

Everything is reduced, in the end, to the morality of the individual. By practising self-restraint, by applying the *law of measure,* by the *imitation* of great models chosen from the antiquity of all nations, he can arrive at the Humanistic virtues of *poise, proportionateness, decorum,* and finally attain "the end of ends"—which, Babbitt says, is individual happiness.

These are the general doctrines of Humanism, and it seems to me that they can be accepted, so far as they go, by many opponents of More and Babbitt. They can also be criticized, but chiefly for what they omit. They can be criticized in theory, first, for their incompleteness as a system of ethics, and second, for their total disregard of social and economic realities.

The ethic of Humanism consists of a single precept: namely, that we should exercise self-restraint (or the will to refrain, or the Inner Check, Veto Power, *frein vital, Entsagung* or whatever else it may be called at the moment). We are offered no other guide. But why—we ask like children repeating a Shorter Catechism—why should we exercise self-restraint?

A. In order to achieve decorum.

Q. And why should we achieve decorum?

A. The end of ends is happiness. (Be good and you will be happy. If you can't be good, be careful. With all their paraded learning, all their analysis of texts, all their quotations from the French, German, Latin, Greek, Sanskrit and Chinese, can the Humanists tell us nothing more than this?)

In theory, they can tell us nothing more. In practice, we find them basing their moral judgments on a set of conventions which have nothing to do with their logic. In practice, at this critical point in their philosophy, they renounce a "positive and critical" humanism for tradition and theology. Yet this silent renunciation, which damages their own position without benefiting the church, was quite unnecessary. Without ceasing to be strictly humanist, they could have developed a complete system of ethics, but only by considering man in relation to society. This they have failed to do: in this increasingly corporate world of ours, they have confined their attention to the individual.

Economically, socially, their doctrine is based on nothing

and answers no questions. Out of what society does Humanism spring, and toward what society does it lead? Has it any validity for the mill hands of New Bedford and Gastonia, for the beet-toppers of Colorado, for the men who tighten a single screw in the automobiles that march along Mr. Ford's assembly belt? Should it be confined to the families who draw dividends from these cotton mills, beet fields, factories, and to the professors who teach in universities endowed by them? Can one be Humanist between chukkers of a polo match, or can the steel workers be Humanists, too —once every three weeks, on their Sunday off? Has Babbitt any social program?

In his "Democracy and Leadership," which gingerly touches on some of these problems, he rejects the whole conception of social justice as a dangerous fallacy. He asserts that the economic problem, including the relations between capital and labor, runs into the political problem, which runs into the philosophical problem, which in turn is almost indissolubly bound up with the religious problem. The root of the whole matter is in the psychology of the individual. For unemployment, low wages, long hours, intolerable working conditions, for all the realities of the present system, he has one solution, perhaps the most unreal that could be offered. "The remedy," he says, "for the evils of competition is found in the moderation and magnanimity of the strong and successful, and not in any sickly sentimentalizing over the lot of the underdog."

Yet it would be incorrect to say that Babbitt offers no social program. For all his hatred of terms like humanitarianism and social justice, he does suggest a mild path toward a Humanist utopia. "The first stage," he says, "would . . . be that of Socratic definition; the second stage would be the coming together of a group of persons on the basis of this definition . . . the third stage would almost inevitably be the attempt to make this convention effective through education." Babbitt seems to contemplate the salvation of society through a private-school system culminating in a Humanist university. For one of his collaborators, Frank Jewett Mather, Jr., of Princeton, the salvation of the country seems even simpler. He says, in a recent group-statement of the Humanist faith:

> We contributors to this symposium have actually seen a few humanists made, have helped a little to make them perhaps; and we are dealing with spiritual values which transcend ordinary statistics. A few thousand genuine humanists in America would make our society humanistic; a hundred humanist painters, sculptors, architects, musicians and men of letters would make our art solidly humanistic.

A few thousand Humanists in business and the professions, a hundred Humanists in the arts. . . . I submit that these rash professors, in their aversion for utopian visions, have produced the lamest utopia ever imagined. The vast economic machine that is America would continue to function aimlessly; great fortunes would continue to grow on the ruins of smaller fortunes; several million factory workers would continue to perform operations so subdivided and standardized as to be purely automatic; two million former workers, the "normal" army of the unemployed, would seek vainly for the privilege of performing the same dehumanizing tasks; the Chicago beer barons would continue to seek their fortunes and slaughter their rivals, revealing once more a deplorable ignorance of the Inner Check; the students in the new Humanist university, after the two-o'clock lecture on Plato, would spend an hour at the talkies with the It Girl—and meanwhile, because of a few thousand Humanists, our society, our government, our arts would be genuinely and ideally Humanistic.

III

When a philosophy like that of More and Babbitt presents itself as a way of life, it is dangerous for that philosophy to omit important aspects of life. These gaps in thought do not remain empty. They are filled unconsciously, irresistibly, by the conventions that prevail in the world surrounding the philosopher. If these conventions are blind and narrow, the philosophy will be blind and narrow in practice, however enlightened it may seem in theory.

Such has been the misfortune of American Humanism. At birth, the world that surrounded it was the American university of the 1890's, and from this world the Humanists have borrowed their underlying convictions. Economic problems at Harvard or Princeton before 1900 were less urgent than they became after the War: the young instructor was sure of being fed and clothed; he was comfortably lodged; and his salary was fixed by an individual arrangement with the university. The moral problem, however—or at least the problem of self-restraint—was of primary importance. Any sort of enthusiasm was suspicious. Any failure to restrain one's impulses toward frankness of judgment, freedom of thought, sympathy with the dispossessed, and love most of all—love for one's neighbor or his wife—might lead to immediate dismissal. And what was Babbitt's reaction? "The wiser the man," he says, "the less likely he will be to indulge in a violent and theatrical rupture with his age. He will like Socrates remember the counsel of the Delphian oracle to follow 'the usage of the city.'" Even Socrates himself, as Babbitt adds in another passage, "was perhaps needlessly unconventional and also unduly inclined to paradox."

The American Humanists, less paradoxical than Socrates and more faithful to the usage of the city, have adopted the older conventions of the universities where most of them teach. One of these conventions is a snobbery both intellectual and social—a snobbery which does not seem out of place in a professor's drawing room, but which becomes grotesque when applied to literature and art. Paul Elmer More, for example, damns a whole school of American fiction, partly for literary reasons, but partly because its leading members are men of no social standing, men "almost without exception from small towns sprinkled along the Mid-Western states from Ohio to Kansas . . . self-made men with no inherited background of culture." One of More's disciples, Seward Collins, couples this accusation with another: namely, that some prominent American writers are Jews, "the sons of recent arrivals in this country!" It is as if Parnassus were a faculty club, at the doors of which More and Collins stood armed with blackballs. It is as if the world of letters were a university—one which applied the quota system to Irishmen and Jews, and which demanded a signed photograph with every request for admission.

Sometimes the snobbery of the humanists is carried from the sphere of esthetics into that of government, and here it leads them into a dangerous alliance with the forces of reaction. Babbitt, for example, is not unwilling to have his Inner Check on conduct reinforced by the outer check of civil authority: he speaks with approval of the policeman who arrested Raymond Duncan for wearing a Greek costume in the streets. Paul Elmer More, in the same fashion, feels that the cause of Humanism was somehow strengthened by the Princeton officials who "rusticated" a student for his "aspiration towards free morals in literature." Seward Collins vehemently defends the Watch and Ward Society; his only regret is that there are not two such societies in Boston. And this alliance between Humanism and reaction was emphasized some years ago at the Scopes trial, when Bryan took a book on evolution by Louis Trenchard More—brother of Paul Elmer More and author of the leading essay in the Humanist symposium—along with him to Dayton, Tennessee, in order to confute the ungodly biologists and establish the Bible as the one American text book of natural science.

And so these angry professors, in following the usage of the city, have come to defend the social and intellectual prejudices of the universities where they teach and the churches where some of them worship. To themselves, they seem to play a more distinguished rôle. Gorham B. Munson claims for his Humanist colleagues the virtue of swimming against the current; but so, apparently, do straws caught in an eddy. Norman Foerster absolves himself and his condisciples from "the professorial vices of pedantry, indolence, timidity and . . . sluggish tolerance"; he commends their boldness in attack. Boldness of a sort they have, but it is not the courage of lonely men treading their own paths: it is the boldness of reactionary professors in the classroom, lecturing to students most of whom agree with their ideas and none of whom will rise in rebuttal.

IV

Partly from the moral atmosphere of our eastern universities in the 1890's, the Humanists imbibed another quality, one which their enemies describe as Puritanism. The word is dangerously vague: it connotes or denotes a number of characteristics, good or bad, sentimental or realistic. The single quality to which I refer is clear, definite, unmistakable: it consists in a profound belief in chastity, a belief which forms no part of their official theories, which is revealed only in their practice of criticism, and yet which is so fundamental that it distorts the moral, the social and especially the literary judgments of the American Humanists.

Babbitt, for example, in the course of his long attack on Rousseau, happens to discuss the question of wages. "If a working girl falls from chastity," he ironically says, "do not blame her, blame her employer. She would have remained a model of purity if he had only added a dollar or two to her wage." I expect this remark to be utilized—perhaps it has already been utilized—by those of Babbitt's pupils who are now employing girls in the cotton mills of Fall River and New Bedford. If chastity is all-important, if chastity is unaffected by wages, why should they ever raise wages? . . . One might answer from the standpoint of a humanism just as valid as Babbitt's, that a working girl may be chaste or unchaste and still remain human, but that it is almost impossible to be either human or Humanist on ten or twelve dollars a week.

Elsewhere, in speaking of Goethe, he adopts the same tone as with the working girl. "Anyone," Babbitt says, "who thinks of the series of Goethe's love affairs prolonged into the seventies, is scarcely likely to maintain that his *Entsagung* was of a very austere character even for the man of the world, not to speak of the saint." By what right does Babbitt summon him to the Dean's office?—a little jestingly, it is true, but still with profound disapproval, as if Goethe were a Harvard or Princeton sophomore with aspiration toward free morals in literature. And by what right does the professor deliver this lecture? Is he speaking in behalf of humanistic standards, to be deduced from the conduct of a hundred generations of sages, including Socrates, Dante and Goethe himself—or is he applying the religious standards of the Reformation? And is he willing to assure us that his opinion of Goethe's books, as books, is not affected by this smoking-room gossip about Goethe's life?

He believes, not without jurisdiction, that morality and esthetics cannot be separated, but he destroys the value of his esthetic judgments by confusing morality in general with the one virtue of chastity. "Restoration Comedy," he says with a professorial smile, "is a world not of pure but of impure imagination." "A greater spiritual elevation . . . is found in Wordsworth's communings with nature than in those of Rousseau and Chateaubriand." The reason, he explains, is because in Wordsworth "the erotic element is absent." At other times he delivers lectures on the sex-life that could not be surpassed by the professor of Mental Hygiene in a fresh-water college. Yet Babbitt, after all, never quite reaches the heights of chaste absurdity that are attained by Paul Elmer More.

Consider More's "Note on Poe's Method," an essay that mingles some keen literary judgments (and others less keen) with an inexcusable ignorance of the poet's life. At the end, after deciding that "Poe remains chiefly the poet of unripe boys and unsound men," More goes on to say:

> Yet it is to the honor of Poe that in all his works you will come upon no single spot where the abnormal sinks to the unclean, or where there is an effort to intensify the effect of what is morbid emotionally by an appeal to what is morbid morally. The soul of this man was never tainted. (That is, Poe lied, flattered, slandered, drank to excess, took opium; his characters indulged in strange forms of necrophilia; but neither they nor their author committed fornication.) . . . If you wish to understand the perils he escaped, read after "The Sleeper" one of the poems in which Baudelaire, Poe's avowed imitator and sponsor to Europe, gropes with filthy hands among the mysteries of death. (That is, in which he writes of physical unchastity.)

On the next page, after delivering this judgment which reeks of Rufus Wilmot Griswold, S. Parkes Cadman, and all the psychological and literary ingenuousness that could very well be packed into a single paragraph, More turns to a new subject, "My Debt to Trollope." . . . As a "professed Trollopian," he praises the ethical atmosphere of Trollope's novels, regretting only that Trollope the moralist should yield so much to Trollope the entertainer; he exults over the fashion in which the good little Trollopes are rewarded and the bad Trollopes punished by the great Trollope their creator; and meanwhile he pauses to comment on the one class of modern writers who have followed Trollope's virtuous example:

> The only form of literature today wherein you may be sure that the author will not play tricks with the Ten Commandments is the detective story; the astonishing growth of which brand of fiction can be traced in no small measure, I suspect, to the fact that there alone murder is still simply murder, adultery simply adultery, theft simply theft, and no more about it.

In other chapters of the same volume, More writes about

Joyce, Dos Passos and the Super-realists, but he seems not to have read them very carefully. They seem to him unchaste as do most of the serious contemporary authors. Like his Humanist colleagues in general, he has no taste for such authors. He reads detective stories.

V

Outside the room where I am writing, a flooded New England river bends over the dam of an abandoned paper mill, sometimes falling in one smooth sweep, sometimes rising in spray under the March wind. The sky is gray, with floating, clear blue islands; there are flurries of snow in the intermittent sunlight. And, in this place of winds and waters, it seems futile to attack the Humanists—just as futile as it would be to rage against the branches circling in an eddy beneath the dam.

The opinions they express—I think, looking out the window—the old attitudes to which they cling, have as much right to survival as these New England houses rising squarely from the ground. They remind us of the past; and this is, I feel, the special value in the controversy over Humanism. It distracts our attention as readers and critics from the masterpieces of the moment—from "the greatest poem since 'John Brown's Body,'" from "the last word in American fiction"—and directs it toward questions of permanence, toward a judgment based on centuries. The Humanists, moreover, have performed another service to American letters: they have reaffirmed the connection between ethics and esthetics, thereby helping to rescue art from the sort of moral vacuum to which it had been condemned by another school of critics. But—I think as the first lights flash out in the village—they have made art the servant of morality. And what have these Humanists ever said about the humanizing function which art in itself performs?

All good art—at least all good literary art—has a thesis. Its thesis is that life is larger than life—that life as portrayed by the creative imagination is more intense, more varied, more purposeful or purposeless, more tragic or more comic, more crowded with moral decisions, than is the life we have been leading day by day. Sometimes we are discouraged by the contrast; sometimes we merely escape into the world of art. Sometimes, however, we try to reinterpret our lives in the light of the artist's vision. The new values we derive from his work, when projected into our own experience, make it seem more poetic, dramatic or novelistic, more significant, more sharply distinguished from the world of nature—in a word more human.

But art has another humanizing function perhaps no less important: it is the humanization of nature itself. The world about us was alien in the beginning; vast portions of it are alien to us today. Before man can feel at ease in any milieu, whether that of forest, plain or city, he must transform the natural shapes about him by infusing them with myth. Perhaps I am choosing a too pretentious word; perhaps I should merely say that certain streets in New York are rendered habitable for me by snatches of old ragtime, that I never *saw* a telephone until I saw it in one of Charles Sheeler's drawings, that my memory of Hawthorne transforms and humanizes a New England village like this. I might say that this creation of myth, by whatever name we call it, has continued since the earliest times; that it is, indeed, a necessity of the human mind. It is a sort of digestive process, one that transforms the inanimate world about us into food without which the imagination would starve.

Now, this double humanizing function of literature (and to a lesser degree of the other arts) cannot wholly be performed by the masterpieces of the past. The values of Sophocles still hold good today, but to interpret them in terms of our own life requires more knowledge of Greek civilization than most of us possess—more even than is possessed by Babbitt himself, whose picture of Sophocles is that of a rate-paying Victorian professor. The myths of Homer still people the shores of the Ionian Sea, but they are alien to the prairies, the sky-presuming city, and even to this New England village of old men. Our own myths, our values, must be renewed from generation to generation. They will so be renewed as long as artists live; they will be renewed in spite of the critics who cling to exiled legends and values long since dead.

One of the real tasks for American critics today is to assess our contemporary literature on the basis of this double humanizing function. They will find that some values and myths have been created or renewed. They will find that E. E. Cummings, John Dos Passos, Hart Crane, Yvor Winters, Glenway Wescott, William Carlos Williams, Elizabeth Madox Roberts—to mention a few names at random—have each succeeded in humanizing some district, landscape, year or city. They will also find, I fear, that our mechanical civilization has outmarched its artists. Once more, as in Shelley's day, "We want the creative faculty to imagine that which we know; we want the generous impulse to act that which we imagine; we want the poetry of life: our calculations have outrun conception; we have eaten more than we can digest." . . . But what has this got to do with American Humanism? And what, in turn, has Humanism to do with the scene outside my window: with the jobless men who saunter in the dusk, or the dying village, or the paper mill abandoned across the river—this mill whose owners have gone South where labor is cheap?

'Tis the good reader that makes the good book.

EMERSON—*Success.*

CENSORING THE CENSOR[1]

By Heywood Broun

Mice and canaries were sometimes employed in France to detect the presence of gas. When these little things began to die in their cages the soldiers knew that the air had become dangerous. Some such system should be devised for censorship to make it practical. Even with the weight of authority behind him no bland person, with virtue obviously unruffled, is altogether convincing when he announces that the book he has just read or the moving picture he has seen is so hideously immoral that it constitutes a danger to the community. For my part I always feel that if he can stand it so can I. To the best of my knowledge and belief, Mr. Sumner was not swayed from his usual course of life by so much as a single peccadillo for all of *Jurgen*. His indignation was altogether altruistic. He feared for the fate of weaker men and women.

Every theatrical manager, every motion picture producer, and every publisher knows, to his sorrow, that the business of estimating the effect of any piece of imaginative work upon others is precarious and uncertain. Genius would be required to predict accurately the reaction of the general public to any set piece which seems immoral to the censor. For instance, why was Mr. Sumner so certain that *Jurgen*, which inspired him with horror and loathing, would prove a persuasive temptation to all the rest of the world? Censorship is a serious and drastic business; it should never rest merely upon guesswork and more particularly not upon the guesses of men so staunch in morals that they are obviously of distant kin to the rest of humanity.

The censor should be a person of a type capable of being

[1] Reprinted by permission of the author and Doubleday, Doran & Co., Inc.

blasted for the sins of the people. His job can be elevated to dignity only when the world realizes that he runs horrid risks. If we should choose our censors from fallible folk we might have proof instead of opinions. Suppose the censor of *Jurgen* had been someone other than Mr. Sumner, someone so unlike the head of the vice society that after reading Mr. Cabell's book he had come out of his room, not quivering with rage, but leering and wearing vine leaves. In such case the rest would be easy. It would merely be necessary to shadow the censor until he met the first dryad. His wink would be sufficient evidence and might serve as a cue for the rescuers to rush forward and save him. Of course there would then be no necessity for legal proceedings in regard to the book. Expert testimony as to its possible effects would be irrelevant. We would know and we could all join cheerfully in the bonfire.

To my mind there are three possible positions which may logically be taken concerning censorship. It might be entrusted to the wisest man in the world, to a series of average men,—or be abolished. Unfortunately it has been our experience that there is a distinct affinity between fools and censorship. It seems to be one of those treading grounds where they rush in. To be sure, we ought to admit a prejudice at the outset and acknowledge that we were a reporter in France during the war at a time when censors seemed a little more ridiculous than usual. We still remember the young American lieutenant who held up a story of a boxing match in Saint-Nazaire because the reporter wrote, "In the fourth round MacBeth landed a nice right on the Irishman's nose and the claret began to flow." "I'm sorry," said the censor, "but we have strict orders from Major Palmer that no mention of wine or liquor is to be allowed in any story about the American army."

Nor have we forgotten the story of General Petain's mustache. "Why," asked Junius Wood of the *Globe* "have you held up my story? All the rest have gone."

"Unfortunately," answered the courteous Frenchman, "you have twice used the expression General Petain's 'white Mustache.' I might stretch a point and let you say 'gray mustache,' but I should much prefer to have you say 'blond mustache.' "

"Oh, make it green with purple spots," said Junius.

The use of average men in censorship would necessitate sacrifices to the persuasive seduction of immorality, as I have suggested, and moreover there are very few average men. Accordingly, I am prepared to abandon that plan of censorship. The wisest man in the world is too old and too busy with his plays and has announced that he will never come to America. Accordingly we venture to suggest that in time of peace we try to get along without any censorship of plays or books or moving pictures. I have no desire, of course, to leave Mr. Sumner unemployed; it would perhaps be only fair to allow him to slosh around among the picture post cards.

Once official censorship had been officially abolished, a strong and able censorship would immediately arise consisting of the playgoing and reading public. It is a rather offensive error to assume that the vast majority of folk in America are rarin' to get to dirty books and dirty plays. It is the experience of New York managers that the run of the merely salacious play is generally short. The success which a few nasty books have had has been largely because of the fact that they came close to the line of things which are forbidden. Without the prohibition there would be little popularity.

To save myself from the charge of hypocrisy I should add that personally I believe there ought to be a certain amount of what we now know as immoral writing. It would do no harm in a community brought up to take it or let it alone. It is well enough for the reading public and the critic to use terms such as moral or immoral, but they hardly belong in the vocabulary of an artist. I have heard it said that before Lucifer left Heaven there were no such things as virtues and vices. The world was equipped with a certain number of traits which were qualities without distinction or shame. But when Lucifer and the heavenly hosts drifted into their eternal warfare it was agreed that each side should recruit an equal number of these human, and at that time unclassified, qualities. A coin was tossed and, whether by fair chance or sharp miracle, Heaven won.

"I choose Blessedness," said the Captain of the Angels. It should be explained that the selection was made without previous medical examination, and Blessedness seemed at that time a much more robust recruit than he has since turned out to be. A tendency to flat foot is always hard to detect.

"Give me Beauty," said Lucifer, and from that day to this the artists of the world have been divided into two camps—those who wished to achieve beauty and those who wished to achieve blessedness, those who wanted to make the world better and those who were indifferent to its salvation if they could only succeed in making it a little more personable.

However, the conflict is not quite so simple as that. Late in the afternoon when the Captain of the Angels had picked Unselfishness and Moderation and Faith and Hope and Abstinence, and Lucifer had called to his side Pride and Gluttony and Anger and Lust and Tactlessness, there remained only two more qualities to be apportioned to the contending sides. One of them was Sloth, who was obviously overweight, and the other was a furtive little fellow with his cap down over his eyes.

"What's your name?" said the Captain of the Angels.

"Truth," stammered the little fellow.

"Speak up," said the Captain of the Angels so sharply that Lucifer remonstrated, saying, "Hold on there; Anger's on my side."

"Truth," said the little fellow again but with the same somewhat indistinct utterance which has always been so puzzling to the world.

"I don't understand you," said the Captain of the Angels,

"but if it's between you and Sloth I'll take a chance with you. Stop at the locker room and get your harp and halo."

Now to-day even Lucifer will admit, if you get him in a corner, that Truth is the mightiest warrior of them all. The only trouble is his truancy. Sometimes he can't be found for centuries. Then he will bob up unexpectedly, break a few heads, and skip away. Nothing can stand against him. Lucifer's best ally, Beauty, is no match for him. Truth holds every decision. But the trouble is that he still keeps his cap down over his eyes, and he still mumbles his words, and nobody knows him until he is at least fifty years away and moving fast. At that distance he seems to grow bigger, and he invariably reaches into his back pocket and puts on his halo so that people can recognize him. Still, when he comes along the next time and is face to face with any man of this world, the mortal is pretty sure to say, "Your face is familiar but I can't seem to place you."

There is no denying that he isn't a good mixer. But for that he would be an excellent censor.

> A borrowed book is but a cheap pleasure, an unappreciated and unsatisfactory tool. To know the true value of books . . . you must first feel the sweet delight of buying them.
>
> J. M. Baldwin.

GREATNESS AND POPULARITY IN LITERATURE[1]

By Carl Van Doren

The greatness and the popularity of a book have no indissoluble connection. A book may be genuinely great without being in the least popular, or may be immensely popular without having any important element of greatness. This distinction has not been often enough observed.

The failure to observe it, or the refusal to admit it when it is suggested, has led to much sighing among critics. They find that this or that great book steals into the world without a din of welcome and survives, as it is indeed likely to do, upon the nourishment of praise from only a few sagacious judges in each of its generations. They find that this or that popular book arouses a din altogether disproportioned to its intrinsic merits, though it does not, as a rule, have quite as good luck with posterity as one of its greater rivals. What follows such discoveries is generally not explanation but accusation. The public is accused of trivial estimates, natural bad taste, or even of instinctive aversion to excellence. The hurt experts assail the vulgar mob with, at best, condescension, write tearful elegies over the great books which have not been popular, and by confusing the issue widen the gulf. The confusion is particularly painful in democratic societies, where decent critics, innocent of coxcombry or of scorn, may begin with wondering why it is that so many good books have to go without recognition from the voice of the people and why so much recognition is given to bad books, and may end with either a broad damnation of democratic opinion or else a weak conclusion that the voice of the people is the voice of taste.

[1] Reprinted from *The Forum*, copyright, March, 1927.

Critics need not sigh or sneer if only they have the courage to perceive the distinction between greatness and popularity and to acknowledge it. They must not, however, slip into the error of thinking that because there is a distinction there is consequently an opposition between these qualities. The distinction is so marked that no opposition exists. A book may be great without being popular or popular without being great; but it may also be at once great and popular. What makes it great does not necessarily keep it from being popular. What makes it popular does not necessarily keep it from being great. In fact, the elements of greatness and of popularity have been confused for the reason, most of all, that they are very frequently seen together. Association has illogically been regarded as relation, as with religion and morals. To distinguish between the associated elements, analysis has to go behind their ordinary appearances and to insist, with what may seem wire-drawn precision, upon their essences.

Still, the distinction is not especially hard to make or to express. A book is great when it speaks to the best minds. It is popular when it speaks to the most minds. While this statement does raise the further, and the endless, question which are the best minds, it is at least simple enough to serve as a point of departure into argument and illustration.

Illustration comes properly before argument, if there is to be as little as possible of reasoning in a vacuum. Such a book as Doughty's *Arabia Deserta* furnishes a plain example of greatness without popularity. It has chosen an entire civilization to be its province and has represented, interpreted, and distilled its civilization. The hills, wastes, oases, plants, and animals of that ancient country stand as clear in these pages as in the light which falls upon them. Here, too, are the ruins which mark the long past of the land, the roads by which men travel over it, the resting-places of caravans, the villages, and, along the borders of the desert, the old and the new cities. Moreover, this desert is far from uninhabited. It is peopled with its own tribes, seen moving about their customary occupations, studied by the traveler not only in their outward costume and gesture, but in their folkways, mental processes, and language. What they do is traced naturally back to what their ancestors have done, and that explained as the outgrowth of immemorial conditions, of soil, climate, religion, social organization. Furthermore, the book is not a treatise merely. It is a poem, conceived on an ample scale, developed with abundant power, written in an idiom which had to be created for the purpose, an idiom at once rich, noble, stately, flexible, and exact. Every paragraph bears some mark of greatness in the writer. As only a great will could have survived these adventures, so only a great mind could have held all the materials of the book, and only a great character could have carried out the scheme without ever seriously flagging in passion, wisdom, or craftsmanship. Even to read it calls for a kind of athletic sympathy with greatness on the part of the reader.

Yet *Arabia Deserta* has hardly a single element of popularity. Few of those who have listened to excited rumor concerning it and have bought it, seem able to prove that they have read beyond a few harmonious pages. Arabia is so far away from England and America that not many imaginations have the curiosity to venture among the Bedouins. And the Arabia of Doughty is too Arabian for casual visitors. The mere details of topography and history and manners which he includes are enough to make amateur heads swim. What is worse for amateur sightseers, such as give books of travel their popularity, he takes it for granted that the Arabs have somehow a right to be Arabs, without apology. He does not forever confirm his readers in their own prejudices by knowing airs of superiority. He is no Briton shocked at the improprieties of nomadic life. He is no American contemptuous of a people ignorant of labor-saving devices. And he makes the least effort to catch the restless attention and hold it. He does not repeat, he does not emphasize, he does not sum up in easy conclusions, he does not indicate his course with convenient milestones. His language is a language of eternity, not a quick, lucid language of the sort which does all its work the moment it appears upon a page.

These distinctions can be made clearer by a second example. Such a book as *The Americanization of Edward Bok* has almost all the elements of popularity and almost none of the elements of greatness. The scene, instead of lying in a strange distant region, among tribes of men incredible to readers who live upon the two sides of the Atlantic, lies close at hand. The closeness is by no means a mere matter of geography. If the scene lies close to the average American or European experience, the action lies even closer. It tells one of the two stories—how a man wins a fortune, how a man wins a wife, —which surpass all other stories whatever in their appeal to the interest of mankind. Edward Bok in this narrative rises in the world as dramatically as the orphaned prince of a fairy tale. But he does not rise by the arts of magic, and so remain only an agreeable figure of romance. He makes his way by qualities no stranger,—to common doctrine if not to common practice,—than industry, sobriety, perseverance. His account of his march to wealth and reputation might serve as a conduct-book to any youth ambitious for a similar career. All is familiar ground. The hero is torn by no philosophic doubts, diverted by no wayward impulses, stayed in his course by no wild beauty, urged by no quirk in his constitution to do anything ecstatic or extravagant. At every triumph the ordinary reader is once again persuaded that the familiar principles of behavior are sound. Honesty is the best policy, and here is a man who is incorrigibly honest. The rotten apple spoils its companions, and here is a man who avoids all dubious associates. Money makes the mare go, and here is a man who drives his golden horses to the sun without a tumble. The average man who has followed this hero to his last page has had a romantic adventure which he can imagine without an effort; he closes the book comfortably assured that his average manner of life is both more interesting and more advantageous than any other. Finally, the language of the book is as satisfactory as its moral. It is brisk, perspicuous, adequate.

These are the qualities which make a book popular. The *Americanization* has a few to make it great. Its scene and action both belong in a small world. That world, of course, is more busy and more populous than the dry wilderness of *Arabia Deserta*, but greatness is not to be measured by quantity. To be great, a book must somehow exhibit or suggest a spacious world, with implications at least here or there of magnificent horizons. The boundaries of Edward Bok's universe are snug and tidy. And the deeds of the hero are too unimpassioned to hold the rigorous attention of profound or elevated mind. They seem, rather, like exercises in ingenuity. He who does them is not face to face with merciless nature or with dreadful doubt or with strong, subtle emotions. Rather, he is working out a puzzle, fitting not very mysterious parts together into a not very difficult pattern. With ingenuity a profound or elevated mind is seldom much concerned. Ingenuity belongs in games, of which the rules have already been laid down by other players. It is an old story, neatly told again. Edward Bok might have told an old story with such glints of irony or with such depths of poetry that the bones could get up and walk, fully clothed. But in his *Americanization* he is naïve and prosaic. His story has not been told in any of the languages of eternity, able to make him remembered as the hero of a book long after his physical existence is forgotten. This is the language of journalism, which reports but does not perpetuate.

It is difficult to speak of greatness or popularity in literature without sounding partisan, because the terms of criticism have been so long employed on one side of the apparent conflict or the other that they can hardly be trusted to convey just meanings, no matter how justly they may be intended. Perhaps the argument that the two qualities are distinct may be more impartially advanced by a third example, that of a book which is equally great and popular. *Gulliver's Travels* is great enough to arouse continual wonder in the most penetrating and detached minds. It is popular enough to have become a classic of the nursery. A little study of the book, however, will show that it is, in a sense, two books in one.

One of these books is purely a romantic narrative. Gulliver, voyaging into strange lands, comes first among a race of pigmies, then among a race of giants, then, after a topsy-turvy interlude, among a race of horses who have man-like creatures for their slaves. The story seems to move under its own power. Each step is from wonder to wonder, but from a known wonder by easy graduation to an unknown wonder. The element of ingenuity is displayed in the calculation of relative sizes. The element of familiarity is no less strikingly displayed, for, though the pigmies and giants and horses live at the ends of the earth, they concern themselves in these records with nothing more unusual than food, clothing, domestic habits, trade, sport, politics, and war. The most average reader, even a child, observing their behavior, may marvel, but he marvels without real effort. At the outset surprised into these singular universes, he thereafter gets no shock. The story is delusively simple, as is also the language in which it is told, as easy to read as water to swallow or as air to breathe.

The other of these books towers like an ominous shadow behind the easy, original substance of the first. The complete text does, indeed, go forward almost as rapidly as the abridgments. There is always the tremendous original conception to drive the narrative. But by a thousand hints Swift makes clear that to him the shadow is more than the substance. Would he waste the strength of his pen upon a seaman's yarn about a country of insectile pigmies? Only if thus he could bring home his belief that the race of man, reduced to its smallest dimensions, would still have room for all its ugliest follies and vices. Would he then turn to giants merely to reverse his picture and repeat himself in other dimensions? Only to show that large, generous, beneficent creatures may be hopelessly dull. Would he work out the details of his absurd Laputa only to satirize the Royal Society? This gave him an excuse to have his say about mankind in general when it plays at topsyturvy. And as to his horses, he wrote of them not to celebrate those useful, beautiful beasts, but to indicate by comparison how mean and filthy are the human beings who elsewhere are first in the animal kingdom. With these intentions of his, Swift could never have expected to win the sympathy of the most minds. To them he lavishly, it may be contemptuously, flung a beguiling tale. But he invited the best minds to stand off with him at a distance which they alone could reach and there scrutinize the race, including themselves, and to weep or laugh or rage as the mood might take them. Nor did he stop there. Though he doubted that the race deserved even to be allowed to live, much less to occupy the thoughts of a man who could perceive its vanity and nastiness, he did not spare himself, but bent all his art to the task of making his story worthy of its theme. That look of power which he conveys by being able to stand so far away from his world is increased by his willingness to stoop to it and shape it in his satiric hands.

To hate or despise the world is not, it must be quickly added, a surer evidence of greatness than to love and enjoy it, in the manner of Fielding or Wordsworth. The greatness of a writer consists in his ability to stand a little without and above the materials of a book, and thus to command them, whether in hate or in love. The merely popular writer, on the other hand, may be sunk in his materials without notable disadvantage to his popularity. In fact, this may be the secret of his success. If he is to please the most minds, he must draw near them. His stories must not burden their imaginations. His sentiments must not give offense to their prejudices. His characters must be of promptly recognizable types. His language must as far as possible be that of his readers, though it may be either some undistinguished idiom or the slang or dialect of the hour. These are the only elements he needs, and when he possesses them in sufficient measure he may dispense with the elements which make an author great: living stories, original sentiments, unforgettable characters, individual language.

It is scarcely carrying a biological analogy too far to say that there are various universes into which books are born and in which they perish or survive. Nor is it wholly unscientific to reduce the number of these universes, for the convenience of discussion, to two. In the universe populated by the best minds, the condition of survival is a commanding originality. In the universe populated by the most minds, the condition of survival is an ingratiating familiarity. To complain, therefore, that great books are not always popular or popular books necessarily great, is like complaining because flamingoes do not fly about the Pole or walrusses climb the Andes. Survival depends upon special adaptability, not upon general endowment. The creations of man, like the creatures of the earth, survive by their craft and not by their virtues.

Any persons who care to do so may raise the argument that there is compensation in either case. But compensations are the affair of moralists, who like to dig in that field.

Whether the distinction thus drawn between greatness and popularity has what is called a practical bearing suggests unanswerable questions. Can a writer choose to please with either a commanding originality or an ingratiating familiarity? The believers in free-will may say that he has the same liberty of choice in this concern as he has in the selection of his hat or of his house. The believers in determinism may say that he has no more choice than a woman has in the sex or the complexion of her child. Fortunately, a decision on this point can wait till free-will and determination are at peace. Meanwhile, the majority of writers are neither great nor popular, a few are popular without being great, fewer still are great without being popular, and the fewest and greatest of all are both at once. The different universes of greatness and popularity, now barely overlapping, may hardly be expected to coincide, however, till that millennial era when there are no writers but the very greatest.

> A man ought to read just as inclination leads him; for what he reads as a task will do him little good.
>
> BOSWELL—*Life of Johnson.*

THE PROFESSOR AND THE DETECTIVE[1]

By Marjorie Nicolson

The deadly after-dinner pause had arrived. During the hour of the banquet itself, conversation had been general, if desultory; but in the drawing-room an awkward hush descended. The hostess surveyed with some alarm her tame lions, the most distinguished delegates to an international convocation of scholars. Nervously she threw into the arena for dissection the latest sensations in the world of books, the "most provocative" of all provocatives, the "most startling" of all exposés of human weakness. With weary courtesy the lions oped their mastic jaws; but it was only too obvious that the animals were lethargic. Desperately, she turned to the distinguished scholar at her right—a man whose name is known even to thousands who have never read his contributions.

"Tell me," she begged, "what do you think is the most significant book of recent years?"

"There you have me," the great man declared with candor. "I never can make up my mind between *The Bellamy Trial* and *The Murder of Roger Ackroyd*. Of course, I know there *are* people who would say that *Greene Murder Case*, but . . ."

His hostess gasped. But in another moment her horror had turned to amazement. Her lions forgot their tameness; the bodies thrown into the arena were no longer the lay figures by which they had been fooled so long. The odor of blood was in their nostrils. For an hour the struggle raged; and when at last the lions, gorged with prey, had departed to their cages, they left behind them a hostess who realized that her

[1] Reprinted by the kind permission of the author and of *The Atlantic Monthly*.

dinner had been a complete triumph, who had learned the most valuable of all lessons for her future entertainment of the academic guest: when all else fails, start your professors upon the detective story—if they have not already started themselves!

Throughout England and America to-day, you will find the same thing to be true. Lending libraries in college towns are hard put to it to keep up the supply; university librarians are forced to lay in a private stock "for faculty only." Let but two or three academics gather together, and the inevitable conversation ensues. At the meetings of learned societies this year, it will not be of the new physics or the new astronomy, of the new morality or the new psychology, that your specialists in these fields will be debating, but of footprints and thumb marks, of the possibility of poisoning by means of candles, of the chances of opening a locked door with a pair of tweezers and a piece of string! More heated the arguments, more violent the discussions, than ever were the contentions of mediæval schoolmen. And in time to come, when we shall have been gathered to our ancestors, you will find us, not in Paradise, but, like that little group of Milton's fallen angels in Hell, "in discourse more sweet" than were ever hymns of rejoicing, sitting apart on some "retir'd" hill, unaware of Pandemonium, unaware of Hades, while around us giants and demons tear up mountains and cast them into the sea, "reasoning high" of clues and openings, of poisons and daggers, of tricks for disposing of unwanted bodies, of Dr. Thorndyke and of Colonel Gore.

I

That glib expositor of all mysteries, the pseudo-psychologist, has an explanation, of course. To the academic mind, he avers, detective stories constitute the "literature of escape." He goes even further: our lives, we hear, are barren and narrow; our college walls (not even modern American architecture can shake this metaphor) hem in a little unreal world, in which wander lost spirits, ghosts and shades as melancholy as any who ever haunted the tenebrous Styx, wailing—not, like those spirits, for a life they had lost—but for a life we have never had. Inhibited by our unnatural existence, we find "release" in books of blood and thunder. Through tales of abduction and poisoning, shooting and stabbing, we are able to wallow for a moment in adventures we cannot share, to lose ourselves for an evening in a world of excitement, and return next day to our dry-as-dust lectures, refreshed by vicarious violence. Unworldly, unnatural academics, who would deny us our brief moment's respite! So, having explained us to his own satisfaction, having neatly docketed us in his capacious catalogue, the pseudo-psychologist passes on to fresher woods. Like an earlier gentleman, somewhat hasty in generalization, he does not stay for an answer.

Nor, I must confess, would we bother to give it to him, did he stay. For how can we explain to such as he that escape, in the sense in which he means it, is the last thing in the world the academic mind either requires or wishes? How can he know that, as a group, we are more free from "suppressed desires," "inhibitions," and "complexes" than any other group in the world to-day? It is not from the life of the mind that we seek release, nor is it that we may flee from the bondage of academic walls that we revel in the literature of escape.

Yet, in a sense which he does not understand, the academic reader is turning to the detective story to-day seeking release. Consciously in eighty per cent of the cases, unconsciously in the other two tenths, he has reached the limit of his endurance of characteristically "contemporary" literature. Contrary to the usual belief, the college professor to-day does keep up with recent literature. Gone is the bearded visionary who was a child in the affairs of the world, the pedant who boasted that he had read nothing published since 1660. There are few professors in the colleges of the arts who are not familiar with the "latest" in drama, in fiction, in poetry. If the family budget will not cover the new books, there are the local book clubs; and, when all else fails, there are always the community bookshops, whose tables are surrounded by poverty-stricken academics, grimly reading the newest arrivals, standing now on one foot, now on the other, peering determinedly between uncut pages. Probably no other group except the professional book reviewers has, during the last ten years, waded through so many thousands of pages of psychological analysis. And now we are reaping the whirlwind.

Yes, the detective story does constitute escape; but it is escape not from life, but from literature. We grant willingly that we find in it release. Our "revolt"—so mysteriously explained by the psychologists—is simple enough: we have revolted from an excessive subjectivity to welcome objectivity; from long-drawn-out dissections of emotion to straightforward appeal to intellect; from reiterated emphasis upon men and women as victims either of circumstances or of their glands to a suggestion that men and women may consciously plot and consciously plan; from the "stream of consciousness" which threatens to engulf us in its Lethean monotony to analyses of purpose, controlled and directed by a thinking mind; from formlessness to form; from the sophomoric to the mature; most of all, from a smart and easy pessimism which interprets men and the universe in terms of unmoral purposelessness to a rebelief in a universe governed by cause and effect. All this we find in the detective story.

We are not alone in our revolt against the "psychological novel," but perhaps our cry for release is more passionate than that of any other group. As the new book lists appear in spring and autumn, as the brilliant new covers in violent hues bedeck the windows of the bookshops, as the publishers' blurbs grow necessarily more and more superlative, you may hear rising and swelling in protest the litany of the professors: "From the *most profound and searching dissection of human emotions;* from the *poignant cry of a human soul;* from the *daring analysis of the springs of human action;* from the *wings of pain and ecstasy;* from the *brutal frankness of the seeker after truth;* from the *lyric passion of a youthful heart;* from the *biting and mordant wit of a satirist swifter than Swift;* from the provocative demolishment of a *fusty Victorianism;* from the *ruthless exposure of the shams and hypocrisies of the age*—Good Lord, deliver us!"

The chant is not ours alone; but assuredly our groans are deeper, our revolt more violent. For, to all whose daily contact is with college students, but most to those who profess to teach "English," the characteristic contemporary novel seems but the student theme, swelled to Gargantuan proportions. We wade yearly through pounds of paper liberally sprinkled with the pronoun "I"; we have long ceased to expect complete sentences—and never even hope for complete thoughts; dots and dashes we accept as the only possible marks of punctuation. We read with a jaundiced eye dissections of human nature which their authors at least believe to be *profound* and *searching*. We listen to *lyric cries* and *passionate outbursts* until our ears are weary. We follow the *brutal destruction* and the *searching for truth* of young authors, automatically correcting their spelling as we do so. We suggest as delicately as possible—remembering always the sacred "individuality" of these young people with which we must not interfere—that imitation of Mr. Mencken is not always the sincerest form of flattery. We labor all day with a generation which has always *reacted*—never been forced to *think* or *consider* or *judge*. Is it any wonder that, when the last paper has been corrected, the last reaction tabulated, we reach out a weary hand for books which will be as different as possible? Having labored all day with minds that are—and should be—those of sophomores, is there any reason why we should wish to spend our nights with literature that is sophomoric?

We revolt truly enough against subjectivity, because we are

too used to promising young authors, who interpret their individual growing pains in terms of cosmic convulsions. We are clearly aware that adolescence will always emphasize the "I"; will always find dissection of emotion more thrilling than analysis of intellect; will always fall victim to easy philosophies of pessimism and skepticism; will always prefer the formless, the vague, to the ordered, the defined; will always believe that it is facing the facts with candor and fearlessness—though, in reality, facts are so much less spectacular and so much less interesting than youth believes. But all this is the inevitable and natural feeling of adolescence. We whose business it is to teach the young accept it with tolerance, with sympathy—more frequently than the world believes, with humor. It is not strange, however, that we do not turn to-day for release to those children of a larger growth, the contemporary novelists, the "bad boys" and "smart girls" of literature. It is not mere chance that this decade is seeing a recrudescence of interest, on the part of thoughtful readers, in that most mature age of writing, the eighteenth century; that to-day Boswell and Johnson, Swift and Voltaire, are being read by constantly increasing numbers. These were men, not boys; their wit was intellectual, their method analytical; their appeal is constantly to the mind, never to the emotions.

It is likewise not mere coincidence that scholars, philosophers, economists, are creating a demand for detective stories unparalleled in the past; that the art which might otherwise have been expended upon literature is transforming the once-despised "thriller" into what may easily become a new classic; that Oxford and Cambridge dons, a distinguished economist, a supposedly distinguished æsthetician (we have only his pseudonymous word for his identity), an historian, and a scientist should have set themselves to this new and entrancing craft. More than one well-known author, weary unto death of introspective and psychological literature, has turned with relief to this sole department of fiction in which it is still possible to tell a story. Gilbert Chesterton and Hilaire Belloc were pioneers; Lord Charnwood, A. A. Milne, and J. B. Priestley follow gladly after. It is, we granted earlier, escape; but the more one ponders, the more the question insistently thrusts itself forward: Is it not also return?

II

Certainly it is a return to the novel of plot and incident—that genre despised these many years by *littérateurs*. The appeal of the detective story lies in its action, its episodes. Gone are the pluperfect tenses of the psychical novel, the conditional modes; the present, the progressive, the definite past—these are the tenses of the novel of action. Character—so worshiped by the psychological novelists—troubles us little, though characters we have in abundance. Characters addicted to dependence upon the subconscious or upon the glands need not apply; men and women need all their conscious wits about them in the detective yarn. One brooding moment, one pluperfect tense, one conditional mode, may be fatal. We grant that our characters are largely puppets, and we are delighted once more to see the marionettes dance while a strong and adept hand pulls the strings cleverly. Our real interest is not in the puppets, but in the brain which designed them. Yet characters have emerged from the new detective form, in spite of their authors. The modern detective is as individual as Sherlock Holmes—though less and less often is he patterned after that famous sleuth. Our detective is made in our image and in that of the author; like ourselves, he can make mistakes; he is no longer omniscient or ubiquitous. We are passing away from the strong silent man who, after days of secret working, produces a villain whom we could never have suspected. Sometimes, indeed, the detective is wrong until the last chapter; sometimes, again, both he and we suspect the villain long before we can prove his guilt, and our interest, like the detective's, is less in the discovery than in the establishment of guilt. The nameless inspector of Scotland Yard has become, for instance, Inspector French, who more than once is puzzled and confused by false trails.

Often the detective is not a professional at all, or at least not one connected with one of the central bureaus here or abroad. There is Poirot, who is conveniently found upon the Blue Train at the needed moment, who even was known to settle down in England for a time, growing cabbages, while he waited for murder to be committed. There is Dr. Thorndyke, the medico-legal wizard, from whom we simple academics have learned most of the natural science we know. There is the amateur Colonel Gore, who began his career by a chance application for a golf secretaryship, and has now opened his own private inquiry office—a movement which his admirers greet with pleasure, as promising an indefinite number of cases for the future. There is our friend the expert in poisons, who lives in his house around the corner from the British Museum, whence he is summoned at dead of night by the butler to a noble family and precipitated into a mystery he does not choose to solve. There is even the psychological detective, keeping us up with the times. Yet, though we welcome the technique of his creator, and call him master, many of the weary academics are inclined to resent that upstart Philo Vance, whose manners—like his footnotes—smack too much of the "smart" young novelists and students from whom we are escaping. With all these characters, however, familiar though they are to us, the interest of the reader lies never in what they are, but in what they do. If they emerge as individuals, they emerge still from the novel of action.

We have revolted also against contemporary realism, and in these novels we return to an earlier manner. As every connoisseur knows, the charm of the pure detective story lies in its utter unreality. This is a point the untrained reader does not comprehend. He wonders at our callousness, at our evident lack of sensitiveness; he cannot understand how we can wade eagerly through streams of blood, how we can pursue our man even to the gallows with the detachment of Dr.

Thorndyke himself. He is tortured by visions of bloodstained rugs; he shudders at the smoking revolver, the knife still sticking in the wound. "I dreamed all night of people lying in pools of blood," declared my unsympathetic friend at breakfast this morning. "How *can* you read those things and go to sleep at all?" And she will never believe me quite a human being again because I assured her that after five murders I can put out the light and sleep like a child until morning, the reason being that where she has seen, with horrible distinctness, an old man lying in a pool of his own blood, I had seen—a diagram. She brings to the thriller a mind accustomed to realism. But the essence of this new detective story lies in its complete unreality.

Hence, though we may read them also, we connoisseurs tend to disparage those novels of the Poe school, whose authors attempt to work upon the emotions; interesting they may be, but never in the purest style. No one of us ever believes that the murder actually occurred; no one of our best authors attempts to persuade us that it ever could occur. We come to the detective story with a sigh of relief—the one form of novel to-day which does not insist that we must lose ourselves to find ourselves; the one form of contemporary literature in which our cool impersonality need never fail. That, of course, is the great difference between detective literature and contemporary journalistic accounts of murders, in which we have no interest. Not for a moment can you fool us, either, with collections of *True Detective Stories,* or confessions of actual criminals. We seek our chamber of horrors with no adolescent or morbid desire to be shocked, startled, horrified. We handle the instruments of the crime with scientific detachment. It is for us an enthralling game, which must be played with skill and science, in which the pieces possess no more real personality than do the knights and bishops and pawns of chess, the kings and queens of bridge. Mediæval writers, to be sure, delighted in allegories of chess, in which the pieces took on moral or spiritual significance; but those who seek to read character and emotion into our pieces and our cards miss the essence of this most entrancing game.

Here perhaps we approach the real centre of the whole matter, which explains both our revolt and our return, and suggests the peculiar characteristic of this new style of writing. Your chess player will sit by the hour in frowning contemplation before a board set with pieces. Your true bridge player finds his real life when the cards are dealt and the contest of wits begins. Your crossword-puzzle expert, dictionary on knee, spends evening after evening in solitary occupation. In each case the expert, though kind enough in other relations of life, despises the amateur. So too the connoisseur of detective stories. We restrain ourselves with difficulty when the occasional reader seeks to dispute with us, to enter into conversations and debates sacred to the initiate. It is as if a body of specialists,—physicists, astronomers, and mathematicians,—met to discuss the Einstein theory, were to be forced, for politeness' sake, to talk about the concept of relativity with a bright youngster who labored under the popular delusion that Mr. Einstein has somehow reformed—or destroyed—the moral standard. We who are connoisseurs are profound and constant students of the new science, as regular in our practice of the art as the most passionate bridge or chess player. We "keep up" as assiduously with the output as the physician, the scientist, the scholar, with learned journals. From ten to one at night is our favorite period for reading; the bedside table holds a varied assortment, drawn from rental collections or from the libraries of our wealthier colleagues.

Like the crossword puzzle, ours is a game which must be played alone; yet on the other hand, as in chess, the antagonists are really two, for the detective story is a battle royal between the author and the reader, and the great glory of the contemporary form is that we both accept it as such. How their eyes must twinkle—those creators of heroes and villains—as they set out their pieces before the game begins. They are the only authors, we must believe, who to-day find fun in writing. As in all other games, much depends upon the opening move, the significance of which each expert fully understands. We have our favorite openings, to be sure, though we recognize all the traditional ones. The familiar scene in the oak-paneled library, the white-haired man sprawling upon his desk, two glasses beside him, the electric light still burning—it is for us photographically real, though never realistic. We know it as a type opening in our game of chess. No detective quicker than we to be on the watch for clues: the torn letter, the soiled blotter, the burned paper on the hearth, the screen moved askew, particularly the book out of place on the shelves—if our author is an expert, each of these has had its meaning to him, and must to us. Or there is that other familiar opening move—the body discovered in a place far from all human haunts (this year tending to be fished up in a basket or packing case from the depths of the sea). There is no limitation to the number of places in which murder may be committed; the very spot a real criminal would most surely avoid becomes for us a glorious experiment. We have had more than one murder on a golf links; no less than three of the season's favorites occur on a train—a device more customary in the English carriages than in American cars, though we still remember loyally *The Man in Lower Ten.*

As the game proceeds, there are countless other signals which we know and watch for. The move of your opponent and his discard are as important here as ever in bridge or chess. We learn new moves and tricks at every game. We can distinguish with deadly precision among tobaccos we have never seen; let but a character casually be caught smoking an exotic cigarette in a yellowish paper, and we have our eye upon him till the end. You cannot fool us with the obvious tricks of a decade ago—and what scorn we heap upon an amateur who attempts to write for us, knowing far less of technique than we know ourselves. We are aware that finger prints may be forged; we can tell you more accurately than many a scientist what will happen to your footprints if you try to walk backward, if you are wearing borrowed shoes, or if you insist on carrying through the garden the corpse of the gentleman you have recently killed. We can tell you the exact angle at which your body will hang if you commit suicide with your silk stockings. We can detect with unerring precision whether the body found by the railroad tracks is that of a man killed by accident or murdered before the train passed. We can distinguish with more deadly accuracy than your hairdresser whether your hair is dyed, whether its wave is permanent or real.

Modern inventions are daily making our task more difficult. We have long been familiar with the dictaphone as a device for securing an alibi. We are not fooled by photographic evidence, which we know may have been faked. But the radio and the wireless, and particularly the airplane, give us pause. We used to know, as well as Bradshaw, the exact time of departure of every train in the British Isles, and the length of every journey in the United States. We know the location of every public airport in three countries; but the growing tendency toward private ownership of aircraft occasionally causes us trouble in our computations.

On the whole, we incline to deprecate the use of utopian devices on the part of our authors—the death ray, the drug which produces indefinite hypnosis, the fourth dimension. We dislike as a group the unfair use of amnesia and aphasia, just as we dislike the subconscious. Being the fairest-minded of all readers, we demand that our characters be given every chance, and we feel it is not "cricket" if they are forced to work against undue psychological influence. We demand of our authors fair play; and for the most part we get it in full measure. Gone are the days of the identical twin, the long-lost brother from Australia. Gone for the most part is the trick ending—though over the last pages of *Roger Ackroyd* we divide into two passionate camps. My own party insists that that is not a trick ending in which every single thread has been put into our hands, every device has been a familiar one. Regretfully we acknowledge that, once used, that ending can never be employed again; nevertheless, the novel remains to us a classic, one of the few that ever completely fooled us.

And as we grow in knowledge and experience, it is becoming increasingly hard to fool us. It is seldom, indeed, that we do not know the identity of the murderer long before he is taken into custody. But if you think that such foreknowledge spoils the interest, you do not understand the new science. In that grimly contested battle of wits, it is inevitable that we should guess, unless the author is far more skilled than we. But once the decision is fairly certain in our minds, we have the added pleasure of watching the author's technique, of checking those passages in which he is trying to send us off the track. Just as he tries his best (and less than his best we will not have) to deceive us, so we do our best to catch him out. In this new game, both scrupulously observe the rules, but both of us know the rules so well that we take delight in reading each other's signals. The burden which the connoisseur is laying upon the writers of detective fiction to-day is a heavy one; but gallantly the best of them are accepting the challenge. This very interaction of specialized authors and readers in a new and international game is producing some of the cleverest technique in fiction to-day, and is developing in that fiction some remarkably interesting characteristics.

It is forcing upon the author a complete objectivity and impersonality in the handling of his material, which in the past has been peculiar to the highest art. I have suggested that this lack of subjectivity constitutes the chief appeal of the detective novel to its academic readers to-day. From the self-consciousness of youthful writers, who, having psychoanalyzed themselves, would seek to persuade us also of the astounding discovery that we are much like other men, we turn to breathe the purer air serene of complete impassivity, forced upon authors by the exigencies of the situation. One false step, and the enemy is ours. Let the author for a moment suggest a personal reaction, a sentimental affection for his character, and we have him on the hip. There is no group of readers so quick to catch a false cadence in an author's voice. And this requirement is having another effect upon technique. The author must weigh and balance all his characters; he cannot have a single unnecessary one; he cannot introduce a servant whom we will not scan sharply. The simplest action, the slightest gesture, is pregnant with meaning. He knows it, and so do we.

Very different, this insistence upon selection, from the all-inclusiveness of a *Ulysses*. The author is forced every moment to be alert, on guard; nothing can be left to chance, no unnecessary comments introduced. In this form of contemporary literature alone, ungoverned emotional reactions are fatal. Hence the pure detective story to-day is never—and what a relief!—a love story. If the love element is introduced at all, —the connoisseur prefers that it be omitted,—it must be distinctly subordinated, for to make your hero and your heroine sympathetic enough to permit their love story is at once to free them from the list of possible suspects. And in the pure detective story, as in that grimmest of legal theories, every man and woman is guilty until he has proved himself innocent. Our detective story has thus returned to-day to a welcome insistence that love between the sexes is not the only possible motif for fiction: jealousy, hatred, greed, anger, loyalty, friendship, parental affection—all these are our themes. No longer is the wellspring of man's conduct to be found only in the instinct of sex.

And, indeed, this change of emphasis is producing a curious effect upon the treatment of women in the detective novel. Men characters are always in the majority; the detective story, indeed, is primarily a man's novel. Many women dislike it heartily, or at best accept it as a device to while away hours on the train. And while we do all honor to the three or four women who have written surpassingly good detective stories of the purest type, we must grant candidly that the great bulk of our detective stories to-day are being written by men—again, perhaps, because of their escape from a school of fiction which is becoming too largely feminized. It is noticeable also that the women characters in these contemporary stories are no longer inevitably sympathetic. More than once the victim is a woman; and even here, where our authors might become sentimental, we notice their impassivity. For in the great majority of cases the victim in a murder story is one who richly deserved to die. One or two authors have experimented with the woman detective, but for the most part with little success. Apart from minor characters, the two important rôles in the detective story for women are, alliteratively enough, victim and villainess. With the changing standards of sentimentality, there is no longer any assurance that a woman character is not the murderer. Time was when we could dismiss women with a wave of the hand; but all of us think of at least four contemporary heroines, three of them young and beautiful, who in the end turn out to be cold and calculating murderers. Inevitably, too, we recall the more subtle ending of *The Bellamy Trial*. Whatever may be the sentimental reaction of modern judges and juries in our courts of law, in the high tribunal of the detective story women are no longer sacred.

A high tribunal it is. Earlier, I suggested that our revolt was from a smart and easy pessimism, which interprets the universe in terms of relativity and purposelessness, our return to an older and more primitive conception of the cosmic order. Here lies, I believe, the really unique contribution of the detective story to contemporary ethics. With the engaging paradox of the old lady in *Punch*, who sought through shelves of psychological literature for "a nice love story—without any sex," we weary academics seek refreshment in a highly moral murder. Perhaps we are protesting against a conception of the universe as governed—if governed at all—by chance, by haphazard circumstance; against a theory which interprets the way of life as like the river in the "Vision of Mirza," the bridge of San Luis Rey; against a conception of men and women as purposeless, aimless, impotent; against a theory of the world as wandering, devoid of purpose and meaning, in unlimited space. In our detective stories we find with relief a return to an older ethics and metaphysics: an Hebraic insistence upon justice as the measure of all things—an eye for an eye, and a tooth for a tooth; a Greek feeling of inevitability, for man as the victim of circumstances and fate, to be sure, but a fate brought upon him by his own carelessness, his own ignorance, or his own choice; a Calvinistic insistence, if you will, upon destiny, but a Calvinistic belief also in the need for tense and constant activity on the part of man; last of all, a scientific insistence upon the inevitable operation of cause and effect. For never, in the just world of the detective story, does the murderer go undetected; never does justice fail in the end. No matter how charming, how lovable, the murderer, or how justifiable the killing, there is no escaping the implacable avenging Nemesis of our modern detective, Fury and Fate in one.

To be sure, we will not condemn our charming murderer to the gallows, for we are artists as well as moralists. We will allow the debonair, the charming rogue one final gallant moment—the sudden spurt of the match's flame as, for the last time, he lights his cigarette with that nonchalance we know so well. Do we not realize as well as he that that last cigarette is the one all well-trained murderers carry constantly for this purpose? We allow the murderess the reward of her cleverness—the last swift motion as the cyanide reaches her lips or the knife her heart. Yet the life must be spent for the life. Like the Greek dramatist, we excuse neither ignorance nor carelessness. No matter how great the personality, how masterful the mind, by one single slip he is hoist with his own petard. By fate or predestination,—what you will,—the murderer is from the beginning condemned to his end; his election is sealed. Not for a moment does our neo-Calvinistic justice permit him to go down to punishment without an intense struggle to escape the consequence of his act. But our science and our theology, our ethics and our metaphysics, are based upon a belief in implacable justice, in the orderly operation of cause and effect, in a universe governed by order, founded on eternal and immutable law.

III

Perhaps it is for this reason that the most persistent readers of detective literature to-day are the philosophers and the scientists who were bred under an older system of belief. It may be that their revolt from a changing universe, without standard and without order, is a return to a simpler causality under which they are more at home. They alone can tell. One thing more, however, I may add to our apologia. What effect this addiction to detective literature is having without the college world I cannot pretend to say; another must speak for its influence upon the life of the capitalist, the physician, the president-elect. But I dare challenge the academic critics to say that in the field of scholarship it is not making for a new vitality. After all, what essential difference is there between the technique of the detective tracking his quarry through Europe and that of the historian tracking his fact, the philosopher his idea, down the ages? Watch the behavior of your professor for but an hour, and you know him for what he is. Do his eyes sparkle, his cheeks flush, as he pursues his idea, forgetting his class, forgetting his audience, as he leaps from historical thumb mark to ethical footprint, from cigarette stub to empty glass? If so, he's the man for your money. In the long conversation which follows, though you begin with the quantum theory or the influence of Plato, you will end with Dr. Thorndyke or Hercules Poirot.

And if you come to compare the methods by which the scientist or the philosopher has reached his conclusions, you will find that they are merely those of his favorite detective.

Only two methods are open to him, as to them. He may work by the Baconian method of Scotland Yard: he may laboriously and carefully accumulate all possible clues, passing over nothing as too insignificant, filling his little boxes and envelopes with all that comes his way, making no hypothesis, anticipating no conclusion, believing the man innocent until he can prove him guilty. Here he finds a single thread, there a grain of rice dropped in a drawing-room; here he measures a footprint, there he photographs a thumb mark. His loot finally collected, he of Scotland Yard will select the "dominant clue," and that he will follow with grim persistence until the end. Weary but victorious, he stands at last outside the prison to which he has condemned his idea, and listens to the passing bell. That is one method. But if he is of the opposite nature, he will follow the method of "intuition," upon which the detective bureaus of the country of Descartes have based their work. To him the torn cigarette and the discarded blotter are of little importance; he leaves such things for his indefatigable rivals of Scotland Yard. Tucked away behind the rose bushes in the garden maze, he devotes himself to thought. Having, like his great predecessor, thought away all else in the universe, nothing remains but the culprit. By strength of logic alone, he has reconstituted the universe, and in his proper place has set the villain of the piece.

Yes, those are the only two methods, both in scholarship and in the pursuit of criminals. For, after all, scholars are, in the end, only the detectives of thoughts. The canvas is vaster, the search more extensive; the "case" takes, not a few weeks, but a lifetime. Yet, in the end, method and conclusion are the same. Evening after evening, throughout the length and breadth of the country, lights burn longer and longer in academic studies, and philosophers, scientists, historians, settle down with sighs of content to the latest and most lurid murder tale. Yet the professorial reader, pursuing with eager interest the exploits of Dr. Thorndyke or of Colonel Gore, is not, in the last analysis, escaping from his repressions; is not even consciously returning from the present to the past; but is merely carrying over to another medium the fun of the chase, the ardor of the pursuit, which makes his life a long and eager and active quest, from which he would not willingly accept release.

> Whatever an author puts between two covers of his book is public property; whatever of himself he does not put there is his private property, as much as if he had never written a word.
>
> MARY ABIGAIL DODGE—*Country Living and Country Thinking.*

DETECTIVES IN FICTION[1]

ANONYMOUS

It is, we are assured by the observant, to the complexity of modern life that we owe the increasing vogue of the detective story. The exponents of the particular form of science which deals with the subject claim that the minds of most people never really grow up, but remain at the happy age of twelve or fourteen. The adult mind, wearied with the cares of business, and the immature mind still eager for tales of adventure, between them provide a vast public for the writer of detective stories; and, as a rule, he seasons his wares to the taste of one or the other. The mature brain will reject the slapdash productions of the writer who relies too much for effect upon the *outré,* upon wholesale violence, or too obvious conclusion-jumping on the part of his hero. It has a palate for a fine bouquet of reasoning and deduction; its taste for mental relaxation is not so jaded as to require constant murder to excite and hold its curiosity. It can be content with vegetarian fare, and will relish a well-written salad of forgery, impersonation, insurance fraud, blackmail, or theft.

The mental Peter Pan, on the other hand, is inclined to be more carnivorous in his tastes. For him the corpse of loathly and splenetic millionaire, venerated nobleman, or beauteous damsel should decorate the carpet in the first chapter, with horrifying adjuncts of hot lead, cold steel, or colder poison, regardless of the fine sport which its owner might have made while still in health if in the charge of a writer of the Vegetarian, as opposed to the Carnivorous, School. It must not be denied, however, that a salad-monger who has won his spurs as such and collected a band of admirers by his skill in charming them with stories of handing over rogues to nothing

[1] Reprinted with the permission of the London *Times.*

worse than penal servitude can, if he suddenly turns man-eater, give them a very much finer thrill by unexpectedly hunting a man to the gallows than if he had already familiarized them with an unvarying diet of corpses at either end of his mysteries. It is to be regretted, therefore, that comparatively few authors practise this system of contrasting alternation, and that so many, yielding doubtless to the solicitations of publishers, create millionaires merely to massacre them, and follow up that process by providing their detectives and policemen with strange implements described as "toothcombs" with which to separate the unwanted just from the wanted unjust.

But just as not all writers are carnivorous, so are not all publishers reprobate; and, indeed, it is to their enterprise and judgment that the present generation owes a debt of gratitude for reissuing in cheap editions the finer achievements of the Old Masters of this form of craft. In this way we can readily compare the technique of those who thrill us now with that of the men who kept our sires and grandsires awake till dawn with the prowess of heroes who landed each criminal fish in turn without the assistance of finger-prints or chemical reagents, telegraphic warnings over the official tape-machine to all police stations, wireless messages to shipmasters upon the high seas, photography, the telephone, or any means of locomotion more rapid than a hansom cab. It is, indeed, remarkable what those giants of old were able to accomplish with their almost unaided brains and eyes. The last of them was, perhaps, that charming Canadian creation, who as November Joe, the Detective of the Woods, brought an unrivaled mastery of venery and woodcraft to the assistance of the police of North America in clearing up the mystery surrounding crimes committed in the open air. Doubtless he perished in the war; and few there are among modern detectives who are at their best under the sky. Probably this is inevitable. In this town-bred age the average reader is better able to appreciate urban tracking amid the countless bolt holes and the myriad unobservant eyes of a metropolis than to follow the finesse of a man able to read a cold trail through a wood or across a moor. There are so many books on town work that with a little application and some personal practice and experience a writer can produce a reasonably convincing urban chase; but it needs much longer preparation to produce an effective essay in cross-country work which will satisfy the experts.

Mr. Austin Freeman, a Carnivorous writer who occasionally enjoys pleasant excursions into the investigation of Vegetarian crime, has, in Dr. Thorndyke, a detective who can track just as efficiently under the sky as under a ceiling. He is just as able as the most scientific American characters to make use of modern resources, but, unlike so many of them, he is neither overburdened by his equipment nor helpless without it. Sherlock Holmes, now in a well-earned retirement, used almost to boast that he had no use for knowledge other than that which would assist him in his profession. Mr. H. C. Bailey's Mr. Fortune, on the other hand, shares with Dr. Thorndyke the conviction that a successful modern detective, while he knows he can never be omniscient, should be as nearly so as it is possible to be. That, in itself, is a proof of the progress made in the profession since Holmes first put up his plate in Baker Street—even if he did so only metaphorically—nearly forty years ago and admitted Dr. Watson to a certain, rather limited, degree of confidence.

Since then great men have helped to make the career of a detective what it is to-day. Like that of journalist, it has risen wonderfully in self-confidence, and in the eyes both of the public and of the police. Holmes and Arthur Morrison's Martin Hewitt were tolerated, but no more, by the uniformed professionals; their successors have frequently been quite politely treated; and now Dr. Thorndyke is frequently retained for the Crown,—for he, unlike so many of his predecessors, can appear in court in wig and gown,—and Mr. Fortune is at least a semi-official, and probably has a room, laboratory, and secretary of his own at Scotland Yard.

It is chiefly in America nowadays that we find in fiction that antagonism which it was once fashionable to assume in England between the private practitioner and the police. That probably arises from the fact that fiction almost always presents a policeman in the United States as overbearing, incompetent, needlessly suspicious, generally a torturer, and in most things quite careless of law, often dishonest, and not seldom a criminal himself. Naturally the atmosphere of bellowing and bullying, of flagrant illegality and corruption, with which so many writers in the United States surround the police in their fiction is unfavorable for the careful and conscientious detective work played according to our rules of cricket and hunting as adapted to crime; and a decent detective naturally keeps the police at arm's length, just as the unhappy relatives of the American corpse, or witnesses in the case, wish that the murderer had chosen them for his victims instead of leaving them exposed to the tender mercies of the arm of the law. It is probably because of her unwillingness to expose her creature, even a very little, to so uncongenial an atmosphere that Carolyn Wells usually introduces Fleming Stone at such a late stage in her stories, and makes him in consequence work at such high pressure to rescue the innocent from the verbal and physical buffetings of the official detectives.

In this country, under more favorable conditions due to that coöperation with the authorities on the part of the public which is characteristic of our authors and of the public for whom they write, there are several rising private practitioners, and it is even possible plausibly to present a police hero in a detective story. The creator of Inspector French undoubtedly made a mistake in first introducing him in his 'greatest case,' as any subsequent appearance can hardly fail to have a suggestion of anticlimax about it—a fate which the author of *Trent's Last Case* has escaped by making his man, as it were, *a hapax legomenon*. Mr. Wallace, on the other hand, repeatedly introduces a brilliant and attractive young detective who stands high in the confidence of his superiors at Scotland Yard, but it is always under a different name. In this way the author is able to flavor his record of crime and detection with a love interest and to marry off his hero and heroine in nearly every volume. But it is rather like making an otherwise acceptable character commit bigamy, two or three times a year, under an alias—a proceeding reprehensible in the eyes of the public, and possibly dangerous even for an important official. Mr. Reeder, on the other hand, another of Mr. Wallace's creations, about whose first appearance there is some uncertainty,—owing to a careful confusion of names for the purpose of deceiving some rogues,—is rather a misogynist, who confines himself to his very efficient work and leaves philandering to the uniformed constabulary.

Among the unofficial practitioners who are making names for themselves are Mr. Lynn Brock's Colonel Gore, who has a pretty flair for outdoor tracking, and Mr. Landon's 'Grey Phantom,' who, like Arsène Lupin years ago, turns against the world of rogues in which he used to have his lawless being and has to work hard to clear himself of a carefully concocted accusation of murder, a crime which he very properly abhors. Mr. Strong, in recently presenting Professor Criddle to his readers, reverts to the eccentric type which was popular some years ago, when an exaggeration of the well-known mannerisms of Holmes was considered appropriate to a private investigator of crime. Somewhat of the same type was Mr. Herbert Jenkins's Malcolm Sage, a man who found it impossible to work with incompetent superiors but figured very efficiently in a number of remarkable adventures. Dr. Hailey, fortunately, still has his feet on the ladder of fame up which Mr. Antony Wynne is conducting him, in spite of a well-concealed tendency to obesity, which in no way militates against the nimbleness of his wits or his activity in the prosecution of his cases. The fact that Dr. Hailey is a physician shows that Mr. Wynne shares the opinion, now increasingly prevalent, that the modern detective should be provided with a medical training; for the murderers in stories of the Carnivorous School are usually exceedingly subtle in their methods, and are able to throw dust into the eyes of the laymen, no matter how observant he may be in general. It is indeed largely due to this modern requirement that the two men who are at the head of the profession are both physicians—Mr. Fortune and Dr. Thorndyke.

Of these two, Fortune is gifted with the ability to sense evil, and is frequently aided in his work by the intuition that such and such a state of affairs "is all wrong" or that some character is 'not really a nice person'; but for all that, he is as careful over his evidence as anyone could wish, although he often comes to his conclusions a little ahead of it, so far as the reader is concerned, and produces it in a subsequent retrospect of the case. Thorndyke, on the other hand, is disinclined to rely on intuition, and, although happy in the possession of a rich vein of dry humor, and in no way eccentric, cannot compete in charm of conversation with Fortune, who is the wittiest detective who has yet appeared in fiction. Thorndyke, a grave and sober medico-legal practitioner and counsel, conforms with the early practice which demands that a detective, like a priest of old, be celibate; but Fortune gayly marries early in his career, and is nowise hampered by the possession of a wife, although it is possible that some enemy may in the future strike at him through her.

That other shining light of the Intuitionist school, Mr. Chesterton's Father Brown, who is even more capable than Fortune of, as it were, 'smelling out' sin, is as a priest, naturally unmarried. Thorndyke, however, by no means steers his course through loveless pages, as Mr. Freeman has devised a most ingenious scheme of harnessing a love interest to his plot without affecting the equanimity of his hero. By the same device he also overcomes another difficulty. Sherlock Holmes as a type caught the fancy of the public to such an extent that Sir Arthur Conan Doyle set a fashion in the presentation of detective stories through the medium of a companion to the hero whose intelligence and powers of observation were so nicely calculated as to give the reader a pleasing sense of slightly contemptuous superiority. The Watson who was the *fidus sed hebes Achates* of Holmes was supported in his task of setting a precedent in this usage by the rather more intelligent Brett who chronicled the achievements of Martin Hewitt; and the fashion became prevalent. It has its advantages. By allowing his reader to follow the working of his hero through the senses of a third party an author is able to give him something for his mind to chew upon. He thus keeps the reader more interested in the mechanism of detection than if he were to tell the story direct and run the risk of serving up a diet of predigested facts. Mr. Bailey is able to chronicle the achievements of Fortune directly, and is never insipid; but Fortune is not quite so interesting to follow while at work as Thorndyke. With the former the reader is like the man who waits outside the covert until the hounds come out in full cry. In the case of Thorndyke he is more in the position of the Master or hunt-servant who is able to watch and appreciate the nicety of his work through the covert as well.

Mr. Freeman, therefore, having decided to adopt the Watson system, improves on it. The original Watson fell a prey to matrimony in "The Sign of Four," and was ever after quite as useless as Holmes himself as a partner in a love interest. Mr. Freeman, realizing the limitations thus imposed upon a single Watson, escapes from them with a masterly simplicity by putting his Watson into commission. His commissioners, like their chief, are physicians, or barristers, or both; and with an almost unfailing regularity one or another of them is sacrificed to Cupid, while Thorndyke moves through each successive book heart-whole and unharmed. In this way Mr. Freeman cleverly enables Thorndyke to stand well both with those who hold that a detective should be celibate and with those who enjoy an additional thrill in a detective story by finding an appeal to the heart interwoven with that to the head.

In this matter of matrimony for detectives there is a difference of opinion; but, in deference to the older and, as many think, sounder tradition of celibacy, a detective benedick, although he may use up a whole book in catching her, seldom obtrudes his wife in any following volume. Mr. Bailey, who makes precedents, portrays Mr. Fortune as quite a ladies' man as well as a husband; and Mr. Bennet Copplestone provided his truculent, efficient, but hardly lovable Dawson with a wife who must have been sorely distressed by her lord's disguises and by some of the things which he considered it to be his duty to do while professionally engaged. Often, however, marriage is like retirement from business for a detective; and an enterprising young New Yorker of the name of Jones, who plainly had a great future before him half a generation ago, has never been heard of again since his wedding day—a fate predicted for him at the time by an interested reviewer.

If some authors clutter up their detectives with a love affair of their own when they ought to be busy elsewhere, more spoil their man's chances by saddling him with an impossible weight of irritating or clumsy dialogue which makes the poor fellow appear to be a prig, a vulgarian, or a propagandist. Mr. Chesterton at times provides the characters who associate with or impinge on Father Brown with such unusual opinions and philosophies that the reader is left with nothing but the certain faith that the little priest will make it all right in the end after behaving, en route, rather like those clever cartoonists who appear to draw a landscape or a face and then by turning it upside down or sideways show it to be a battleship or the representation of a Guildhall banquet. If some writers hamper their man by the ungainliness of their style, or by exciting his heart, others tend to cramp his style by serving up his adventures in so compressed a form as to give the reader but little opportunity to get the flavor of the case before he finds that it is finished. Mr. Foster is rather like this in his treatment of Ravenhill, a reporter-detective, who at least deserves as much space from his creator as that which his editor cannot fail to allow him. Given elbow room, Ravenhill may yet go far.

The detective story is a thing of comparatively recent growth, possibly because it is a matter of only a few generations since readers could be persuaded to allow their sentiment to support law and order and those who labored to uphold them, instead of as a matter of course taking the side of the picturesque and outlawed under-dog fighting against odds. In old times a detector was on a par with a delator and shared the obloquy reserved by schoolboys for sneaks, by the lower classes for "narks" and "noses," and by others for spies, informers, and blackmailers. "Detective," as an adjective in the quasi-respectable society of the not yet popular New Police, dates back only fourscore years, and as a substantive has not yet reigned as long as Queen Victoria. The thief-taker of old, or his more efficient successor the Bow Street runner, is seldom the hero of a story; and the public, unless directly aggrieved, does not appear to have done much to help them against rogues. Consequently the detective story as we know it is a modern development and its technique is still in the making. That is fortunate, as for the best part of a generation there was a tendency to stereotype it on fixed and rather narrow lines.

Of late, however, there has been a move to introduce novel features, particularly in the direction of a break away from conventions which tended to hamper an author's freedom of action. Mr. Freeman, for example, will often give his readers an exciting prologue, a full story in itself, of how and why the crime is committed before unleashing Thorndyke to build it up again from its remains, like an archaeologist engaged in reconstructing a forgotten civilization from the contents of a tomb or the foundations of a ruin. Or he will allow Thorndyke to make play with things like finger-prints or bloodhounds, which long enjoyed an almost sacrosanct prestige in the eyes of the public after Mark Twain's Puddenhead Wilson rescued a man from a lifetime of slavery on the strength of his thumb-marks recorded while in his cradle. Thorndyke shows how bloodhounds can be used to mislead the police, and how the ends of justice can be almost hopelessly defeated by the interested manipulation of finger-prints. Mr. Freeman does not disdain to allow Thorndyke to busy himself in exposing the harmless machinations of a jester in the case of Angelina Frood, and makes a very good story of it, capped as it is with one of those dramatic instances of an opponent's case being shattered in the moment of its triumph with a thunderbolt of evidence forged by Thorndyke with the assistance of the constant and invaluable Polton and the Watson-commissioner for the time being.

Further, Mr. Freeman and Mr. Bailey alike find it unsporting to keep their man in safety while he is engaged in pitting his wits against a hunted and presumably harassed criminal. It is all very well for a commander-in-chief to conduct his campaign from the reasonable security of a sheltered G. H. Q.; but a duelist should take equal risks with his opponent, and the wearing of secret armor is forbidden by the code of honor. A private detective is not exactly either the one or the other, but is more like a hunter of big game, who may be assisted by beaters or even ride upon an elephant in tolerable comfort, yet is likely at any moment to be called upon to provide for his own safety.

Thus there is a pleasing sense of hazard attaching to the careers of both Thorndyke and Fortune, as determined and well-planned attempts are made upon their lives and reputations. In such hands as those of Mr. Freeman and Mr. Bailey, whose delicacy of touch is rivaled only by the prowess of Thorndyke and Fortune, the English detective story has grown of late years into a very fine flower from the stock planted by Poe and grafted and watered so cunningly by Sir Arthur Conan Doyle and Mr. Morrison.

THE LEGISLATORS VIEW LITERATURE

RECORD OF CONGRESSIONAL DEBATE ON CENSORSHIP OF IMMORAL BOOKS[1]

(IN PART)

MR. CUTTING. I started to quote from the Senator from Utah. I am sure he will not object to this quotation, because he has allowed it to go into the RECORD:

If a customs inspector—

Said the Senator yesterday afternoon—

at the port of New York, with his knowledge of the world, regards on his own initiative a book as obscene it is about the nearest approach to a jury trial that can be had.

Mr. President, I lived in New York a good many years. The "Knowledge of the world" which is requisite to enable a man to hold the office of customs inspector at the port is exactly the knowledge which it takes to get from your home on the Bowery to the pier on the Hudson river, and then to open travelers' trunks, remove the contents from the trunks, and, after thoroughly confusing it, to replace it in such order as may be possible under the circumstances.

That is the "knowledge of the world" which is prevalent among the customs inspectors at the port of New York; and that is the "knowledge of the world" which presumably entitles them to judge the literature of the ages.

I deplore—

The Senator went on—

the contemptuous references to the personnel of the Customs Service which ran through the debate in the Committee of the Whole. Many of the members of this personnel are veterans of the service, tried and true. I know from personal contact

[1] From the Congressional Record, Vol. 72, No. 79.

that many are men of education, legal training, and broad information.

Now let us see about this deputy customs collector in Baltimore. According to the *Baltimore Sun*—

George W. Hill, deputy customs collector and mail examiner, came into the limelight at a trial in the Customs Court here in December, 1928, when he testified he did not make a practice of reading much, and was unable to answer questions as to whether Chaucer, Fielding, Beaumont, Fletcher, or any of the Elizabethan writers were still living.

This is the gentleman under whose decision the works of Francois Rabelais were recently seized.

Mr. Smoot. Mr. President—

The Presiding Officer (Mr. Fess in the chair). Does the Senator from New Mexico yield to the Senator from Utah?

Mr. Cutting. I do.

Mr. Smoot. Before ever those books are finally prevented from coming in, they are always sent to the office here in Washington. They are finally passed on here in Washington; not by the man who takes the book out of the package or out of the hands of the person coming in.

Mr. Cutting. Oh, yes, I understand that, Mr. President; I am going to deal with that in a little while.

The books which were seized, according to the *Baltimore Sun*, were the property of Mr. Douglas H. Gordon, 1009 North Charles Street, an attorney, and a graduate of the Harvard Law School. Mr. Gordon took the books to Paris with him to have them rebound. He had purchased them in this country. The Senators will understand that it was when they were returned with the new binding on them that they were taken, under the provisions of the tariff act of 1922. I read from the *Baltimore Sun:*

It is the first seizure in this country of the French edition of these works, Mr. Gordon said, which are found in every important library in the world. The French edition is not published in this country, he said.

In addition to the 14 French editions of the work, the Library of Congress has 7 in English, Mr. Gordon said. The Harvard University library has 56 editions in French, the oldest (recently acquired) of 1558 and the latest a 1920 edition. Princeton University has a special collection of Rabelais. The Enoch Pratt Free Library has 13 of Rabelais's work on index.

I am sure the Senator from Maryland will have no objection to my quoting from a letter written to him by the gentleman in question.

Mr. Tydings. Not at all.

Mr. Cutting. He makes the same statements, on the whole, that are found in the *Baltimore Sun*. He writes:

The Harvard Library has 56 editions of Rabelais in French, the earliest printed in 1558 and the latest printed in 1920; this count is of separate editions and does not reckon duplicate copies; there are also 11 editions in English, printed from 1694 to 1921.

The Andover Theological Seminary has two editions, one in French (1835) and one in English (1849).

The Library of Congress has 14 complete works of Rabelais in French and 7 in English; and has 15 single works in French and 8 in English.

The Johns Hopkins Library has 7 editions of the works of Rabelais in French and 4 in English.

The Princeton Library has a special collection of the works of Rabelais.

The Enoch Pratt Free Library, of Baltimore, contains 13 author entries from Rabelais, some of them, however, being merely excerpts from his works.

It would be possible to continue this list indefinitely, as no library of any importance is lacking in copies of this great classic. In each library there are also many critical and scholarly works dealing with Rabelais's life and writings.

I shall quote only one accessible criticism of Rabelais's position in the history of literature. This is the critical estimate appearing in the article on French Literature in the Encyclopedia Britannica, eleventh edition, at page 124—which is reprinted in the recent fourteenth edition—written by George Saintsbury, the leading English critic of French literature. Professor Saintsbury says:

"Among these—novelists and romantic writers of the sixteenth century—there can be no doubt of the precedence, in every sense of the word, of Francois Rabelais (c. 1490-1530), the one French writer (or with Molière, one of the two), whom critics the least inclined to appreciate the characteristics of French literature have agreed to place among the few greatest of the world. With an immense erudition representing almost the whole of the knowledge of his time, with an untiring faculty of invention, with the judgment of a philosopher, and the common sense of a man of the world, with an observation that let no characteristic of the time pass unobserved, and with a tenfold portion of the special Gallic gift of good-humored satire, Rabelais united a height of speculation and depth of insight and a vein of poetical imagination rarely found in any writer."

Mr. President, the Senator from Utah has said—and, of course, he is absolutely correct—that after the deputy collectors at the different ports have passed on the literature, the books are then sent up to Washington for the deputy commissioner to pass on. The deputy commissioner who passes on those works, according to an article obviously inspired by the Bureau of Customs which appeared in the press recently, is Mr. J. D. Nevius. His assistant, Mr. Corridon, and himself go over the works together.

If there is any doubt as to the correctness of the decision of the local man at the port, the matter is taken up with the Commissioner of Customs, and later, in exceptional cases, with Mr. Seymour Lowman, the assistant Secretary of the Treasury.

While all those officials are undoubtedly very estimable gentlemen, I do not believe there is a Member of the Senate who knows them who would ask for the opinion of any one of them on a work of literature or who would allow any of them, or all of them put together, to dictate the contents of his library or the quality of the books which he should be allowed to read. The proof of that is in the black list which I commented on to the Senate in October. There are on that list 739 books, many of them books of the most innocent description. I admit that among the 739 probably those authorities have stumbled here and there on books which actually are improper and indecent and which no doubt ought to be excluded.

I am not going to comment any further on that particular phase of the matter. One of the greatest living critics has declared Rabelais's book the most extraordinary book ever written by anyone. It is a book which has been read for 400 years by people of all classes and ages and conditions. So far as I know it has never corrupted a single human being.

Moreover, Mr. President, the works of Rabelais are published in this country. They can be purchased at any book store. One does not have to depend on the European editions, as Mr. Gordon unfortunately did; at least, he depended on a European binding, and lost his books in consequence. There are plenty of editions published all over this country. So there are of Boccaccio, another author who has been read considerably by the youth of this country, as well as all other countries in the world. There may be people whose downfall and degeneration in life have been due to reading Boccaccio, but I confess I do not know who they are.

Mr. President, let me quote again from the Senator from Utah. He said:

So far as the customs is concerned, standard textbooks of medicine and surgery for the profession have not been banned.

If that is true, I am rather at a loss to understand this article from the *Baltimore Sun* of Sunday morning, March 16, which is fairly illustrative of the complicated methods and processes which are necessary to solve these great problems at the ports. I should like to read a part of this article.

Baltimore customs agents, it was revealed yesterday, are a resourceful crew.

I hope the Senator from Maryland will realize that I am not reflecting on his State in any way. So many of the cases happen to come from his State because they are well reported by the *Baltimore Sun*, and because Baltimore is close to Washington, and we get the facts about them.

MR. TYDINGS. Mr. President, will the Senator yield?

MR. CUTTING. I yield.

MR. TYDINGS. Part of it is because of the desire on behalf of a great many Maryland people to get these books. That is the reason why so many of them come to Baltimore.

MR. CUTTING. I appreciate that. The article reads:

Baltimore customs agents, it was revealed yesterday, are a resourceful crew.

Having seized a medical book and having had it pronounced obscene in the proper manner by authorities at Washington, having notified its owner and promised to return it for him to publisher in London, the question of how to get it out of the country arose.

The postal authorities will not accept for postage any book pronounced obscene by customs officials. An express company was suggested, but, it was said, some difficulty having been experienced by the company in a previous handling of barred published matter, it refused to accept it.

PHYSICIAN NOTIFIED

The book, ordered by a professor in a Baltimore medical school, deals with medical matters. As soon as it was seized the physician was notified. He was acquainted by the customs officials of the various laws and rules of censorship covering the handling of such obscene matter as the book was alleged to contain.

Finally, to get the book out of the country in a legal manner, arrangements and the necessary papers were made out to have the volume shipped from Baltimore as parcel freight aboard a vessel bound direct from Baltimore to London.

NO RECORD OF RETURN

The captain could carry the tome as parcel freight, but the professor to whom the book was consigned said yesterday latest information from London disclosed that there is no record that the book has ever reached London.

It cost the importer a good portion of three days' time and $8.25, besides the cost of the book, to have it returned. It was purchased, he said, after advertisements sent out with scientific publications had been received here by him.

So much for the liberty of the medical profession.

A prominent professor told me the other day that his specialty in life is the study of the Restoration Dramatists. He is writing a final and authoritative book on the subject of the Restoration Dramatists.

There is one of the most celebrated dramatists whose works he has not yet been able to procure. They are not published in this country in full, though many of the more unseemly extracts have been published many times. The works, as a whole, were published only a few years ago, and he has been unable to import them from England. They are the works of Rochester, one of the most famous politicians, statesmen, writers, and dramatists of the restoration period.

The professor is hampered in his scientific investigations because he is unable to get the works of Rochester into this country. Yet Senators will remember that the original black list of the Customs Service made a distinction between the classics published in English and the books in another language, which, according to them, were improper for circulation in this country.

Not long ago I received a letter from a bookshop in New York which said:

For the first time in our experience we have been notified

that the New York customs bureau is holding a book addressed to us because it is obscene, and we would like to know if there is no redress from this ridiculous idea of some customs official.

The books in question were by Daniel Defoe, entitled "Moll Flanders" and "Roxanna." Both of these works, as Senators undoubtedly know, have been published in a great many American editions. They are not unusual books. They are books which are read in school in the discussion of English literature of that time. Yet the foreign editions can not be imported into this country on account of the decision, first, of one of these inspectors at the port, whose "knowledge of the world" tells him that the book should be kept out, and again by the final decision of these gentlemen in the Customs Bureau here in Washington.

Mr. President, I am devoting too much time to the question of these books alleged to be indecent. As I have said before, that is not the really serious part of the legislation which is being proposed now. Those indecent books which we saw last night, which we see no more to-day, and on which perhaps our eyes will never fall again are a red herring drawn across the trail of this discussion. Yet before I conclude that phase of the matter I would like to remind the Senate that a great many Senators last night agreed that "these books" were bad, that "these books" could be compared with the importation of opium or some deadly poison.

I ask in all candor, before dropping this part of the subject, when the Senator says "these books," which books does he mean? There was a motley collection last night on the desk of the Senator from Indiana. Many of them, I agree with the Senator from Utah, were thoroughly indecent and improper books. If I were a censor and if the Senator from Utah were a censor we should agree in keeping a good many of them out. I may add that neither the Senator from Utah nor myself is a censor; that the Senate of the United States as a whole is not a censor; that the agents of the Treasury

Department ought not to be censors in the way in which they have interpreted their duties in the past.

But in addition to the books which the Senator from Utah and I would agree are improper literature, there were a number of other books on the desk of the Senator from Indiana which I should consider unfit for general circulation, but which are entirely proper to be read by scientists, specialists, authors, editors, and people of generally well-matured minds.

There was another lot of books on the Senator's desk which are perfectly proper to be read by anyone and which have been read continuously by school children for 400 or 500 years without any damage to their morals or to the morals of the communities in which they live. That is why I do not think we can talk about "these" books. It depends on the individual book about which we are talking.

Mr. President, we have denounced foreign books for a long time. I do not think the foreign countries have very much on us in the way of indecent literature. From a railway book stall in Chicago, before taking the Capital Limited to come here the other day, I purchased these important works, which I now exhibit to the Senate:

Joy Stories, published in New York City, I think, though it does not give the name of the publisher.

Paris Nights, published in Philadelphia, Pa.

Hot Dog, published in Cleveland, Ohio.

Hot Lines for Flaming Youth, Detroit, Michigan.

Jim Jam Gems, from St. Paul, Minn.

Whiz Bang, from Robbinsdale, Minn.

Unlike the Senator from Indiana (Mr. Watson) I am not going to circulate these books among the Members of the Senate. I think that the standards of the Senate ought to be maintained. I do not think any risk should be run of corruption of the morals of the Members of this honorable body. I think their morals are quite as important as the morals of those who sit in the galleries and are listening to my remarks, because, after all, if we corrupt the legislative body of the country, that corruption, it seems to me, will, sooner or later, seep out all over the country in channels of contamination. If any Senator wants to see any of this literature, he can communicate with me, and, upon giving a certificate of good moral character, I shall consider showing it to him. (Laughter.) I want to state further that these are the January numbers and I am sure Senators can obtain them, if they insist on it, at the railway book stalls, and, if they do so, it is at their own risk and not mine. No doubt by now the February and March numbers of these magazines are also available. I have looked through them casually and I consider them far more indecent in every way than any of the literature accumulated last night on the desk of the Senator from Indiana.

Here (exhibiting) is a book which is contained in the Congressional Library. It was published in 1888 by Vizetelly, who was the publisher of Zola's works, which the British Government attempted to ban on the ground of obscenity. Vizetelly's attorney published this book to show that if Zola's works should be excluded, the works of all the English classics should be excluded. This is a book consisting of extracts from all the leading English authors, beginning with Shakespeare. It does not include the indecencies of Chaucer and Skelton and the pre-Shakespearian authors, but, starting with Shakespeare, it goes through the list. It is the condensed indecency of the English authors.

This book has been in the Congressional Library so long, it has been fingered so often by so many people, that the original copy is going to pieces, and one is not allowed now to read it in its original form, but any citizen of the United States who wished to have it can get a photostatic copy by paying for it. Here (exhibiting) is one, and I now assure the Senator from Utah that there is a great deal of matter in it of exactly the same kind as the matter which was submitted last night. Also, it is just in extracts. The whole of the works are not included. It is just little bits here and there from the English classics.

Mr. Smoot. Mr. President, will the Senator yield?

The Presiding Officer. Does the Senator from New Mexico yield to the Senator from Utah?

Mr. Cutting. I yield.

Mr. Smoot. The statement made by the Senator now does not conform with the statement made by officials of the Congressional Library. I took that matter up with them. All of these rotten books are kept in one place, and no one sees them unless there is some special action taken by the officials of the Congressional Library. That is what I am told.

Mr. Cutting. My information was different in that respect.

Mr. Smoot. I have not tried to get any of them, but I want to say to the Senator that that is what they tell me, that that is the practice of the Congressional Library.

Mr. Cutting. Will the Senator tell me with whom he consulted in the library in that respect?

Mr. Smoot. The Senator can consult with anybody he wants to there.

Mr. Cutting. Will the Senator tell me from whom he got his information?

Mr. Smoot. I got it from officials of the Library. That is sufficient.

Mr. Cutting. I do not mind stating that my information came from Doctor Putnam, the Director of the Library, who said in the first place that the Library prided itself on having the most complete collection of indecent English literature in the world, that all adults are admitted to the place where the books are kept, but that there was someone sitting there to see that they did not make any improper use of the books while they were there. (Laughter.)

Mr. Smoot. That place is not in the reading room.

Mr. Cutting. No; but no one has ever been excluded who is apparently a normal adult. There is nothing indecent about this book which I have displayed except what indecency there may be in the actual classics which are on every one's bookshelves and which have been read for generations and centuries. For a legal purpose these matters were concentrated in this volume, but the book can be obtained. I know a good many citizens who have gone over to the Congressional Library and obtained copies of it.

Mr. Smoot. I suppose it is along the same line as the books displayed in the Chamber yesterday, is it? Is it as rotten as the words used in Lady Chatterley's Lover?

Mr. Cutting. The same words are used, and the same words are used, of course, in Shakespeare that are used in these books.

Mr. Smoot. Not at all.

Mr. Cutting. I think I can prove to the contrary.

Mr. Smoot. The Senator has never read the book that he wanted to be permitted to come in here if he makes that statement now. There can not be viler language, there can not be words put together so vile and rotten as in those books.

Mr. Cutting. The subject can not be discussed in detail here; but, if the Senator will come to see me at any time, I think I can show him in Shakespeare all of the matters which were contained in the extracts which had been pointed out in the books on the desk of the Senator from Indiana.

Mr. Smoot. I have read Shakespeare, and there is no more comparison between what is in Shakespeare and what is in the books for which the Senator is speaking now than there is between heaven and hell.

Mr. Cutting. I am not making the comparison. I am speaking only of words.

Mr. Couzens. Mr. President, will the Senator from New Mexico yield?

The Presiding Officer. Does the Senator from New Mexico yield to the Senator from Michigan?

Mr. Cutting. I yield.

Mr. Couzens. I would be much interested to have the Senator tell me the difference between hell and heaven. I have not been able to get any definition of it.

Mr. Smoot. This is not the proper place; but I should be glad to give the Senator the first lesson to-morrow at his office.

Is a book bad? Nothing can plead for it. Is it good? All the kings cannot crush it. They suppress it at Rome, and in London they admire it; the Pope proscribes it, and all Europe wants to read it.

Voltaire—*to the King of Denmark.*

SCIENCE AND LITERATURE

ON SCIENCE vs. LORE, AND THE CURRENT HOSTILITY TO A SCIENTIFIC ATTITUDE OF MIND[1]

By James Harvey Robinson

Science, we ought always to recollect, is nothing more or less than the most accurate and best authenticated information that exists, subject to constant rectification and amplification, of man and his world. It is by no means confined to stars, chemicals, physical forces, rocks, plants and animals, as is often assumed. There is a scientific way of looking at ourselves—our thoughts, feelings, habits and customs; at their origin and interworkings. *Science, in short, includes all the careful and critical knowledge we have about anything of which we can come to know something.*

Perhaps the easiest way of getting a notion of the unity and comprehensiveness of science is to set it off against *lore*[2] of various kinds—traditional beliefs which recommend themselves in virtue of their familiarity, antiquity, sanctity, nobility, goodness or general acceptance by respectable people. These beliefs seem to many firm and lasting compared with the ever shifting and tentative conclusions reached through scientific research and re-examination. A great part of mankind is taught to believe that ancient prophets and seers were wiser than we can hope to be, and that divine truth was vouchsafed them which can never be transcended, and should never be questioned by the scientifically disposed. Those who oppose Faith to Reason do not think of Faith as blind, but as divinely keen-eyed and secure, as well as sweet and comforting. All mystics are at one in this. Scien-

[1] Reprinted from the *Humanizing of Knowledge* by permission of Doubleday, Doran and Co., Inc.

[2] This is one of Veblen's ironical words. See his admirable *Place of Science in Modern Civilization*, essays I and II.

tific investigation, they would concede, has its own sphere, but it is limited by God's word, as they have been taught to interpret it, and by the narrow compass of the human understanding.

We are all familiar with this attitude toward revealed and mystic truth, and it has long been a subject of bitter controversy whether the Bible should be read and studied and criticized like any other collection of ancient writings, and its contents interpreted in the light of the beliefs and the ignorances prevailing at the time its various parts were written or revealed. Comparatively few persons even yet have any scientific knowledge of the Bible, such as is easily available in such delightful books as Solomon Reinach's *Orpheus,* George F. Moore's *Literature of the Old Testament*, Morris Jastrow's *Gentle Cynic;* Conybeare's *Myth, Magic and Morals.* Accordingly one of the great obstacles to a spread of scientific thought is still the old conception of the Bible.

Our childhood impressions are likely to be permanent unless circumstances are very favorable for their later modification. We would tend to become scientifically minded the moment we began to suspect that the people with whom we associated in childhood were in all probability hardly abreast of the times, as the saying is. We might conjecture that much had probably been found out about both evolution and the Bible during the last half century which had escaped us. And our suspicions, could they be aroused, would probably be amply justified.

The same confidence in *lore* as contrasted with science may be noted not merely in religious beliefs but in traditional ideas of morality, patriotism, private property, the state, the family, war, etc. To cite a single example: One who pronounces birth control sinful, opposed to religion and sound morality and who contends that the dissemination of knowledge in regard to contraceptual methods is "obscene," takes a stand and uses a vocaburaly approved by moral tradition.

On the other hand one might see in the issue a curious and essential problem. Without being driven to prompt and final condemnation he might feel free to think the matter over in the light of such knowledge as he might gain. He would first remedy his ignorance of human embryology and of the way in which each of us comes about. He would ponder on the hallowed methods of reducing births through monastic institutions and the enforced celibacy of the clergy, or by economic pressure. He might then turn to the larger questions of the relation of birth control to disease, mental deficiency, poverty and the question of over population. Then, and then only, might he be ready from a scientific standpoint to form some opinion on the probable expediency of repealing our present laws relating to this matter. No one would question the propriety of such an approach were it not assumed that there is something essentially improper in submitting the case to the verdict of intelligence.

Havelock Ellis wisely says: "It may seem that in setting forth the nature of the sexual impulse in the light of modern biology and psychology, I have said but little of purity and less of morality. Yet that is as it should be. We must first be content to see how the machine works and watch the wheels go round. We must understand before we can control."[1] And to understand requires pains and care. It will not do simply to shut our eyes and be sure that we are right. Of all human ambitions an open mind eagerly expectant of new discoveries and ready to remould convictions in the light of added knowledge and dispelled ignorances and misapprehensions, is the noblest, the rarest, and the most difficult to achieve.

What is true of the general attitude toward religion and sex is true also of our prevailing notions of politics, business, international relations and education. There is much defensive and offensive discussion but no great play of intelligence. Even those who attack existing institutions, ideas and habits often do so in a semi-religious spirit. The good and the bad, right and wrong, just and unjust are apt to be the *starting point* rather than the *outcome* of the inquiry. And yet, if we but stop to think, all these seemingly so solid and reliable

[1] *Little Essays of Love and Virtue* (Doran) p. 55.

things have varied tremendously in different times and places. We have to find out what things are good and right and just, before we can appropriate them. They are not labelled, ready to our hand.

And yet they are tacitly assumed to be settled, at least in their larger aspects. It is not supposed to be well or safe to invite the young or the "masses" to think of important matters with a critically open mind. The traditional lore must first be instilled and then only, if at all, may some thoughtfulness be permitted. But it is usually agreed that this should be controlled and directed by those wise and prudent persons who are keenly alive to the dangers of doubt and skepticism and who are sure to come out just where they went in. I take it this is the attitude of the overwhelming majority of good and respectable people, who in the last analysis control our education and represent the taste to which newspapers, magazines and lecturers must appeal. There is, in short, some confidence in the value of scientific discussion within certain limits, but so far as man and his doings are concerned it is as yet far from sanctioned by public opinion.

No one can be more poignantly conscious of the groping nature of intelligence than I. The misgivings of the mystics as to our ability to reach ultimate truth are shared by every scientifically-minded person. If we could be assured that there exist better, more secure and more profound sources of knowledge than human intelligence we ought, of course, to accept them. But as yet the human mind can hardly be said to have had a show, and I, for one, have faith that if we gave it a show, mere human intelligence, based upon our ever increasing knowledge, would tend to remedy or greatly alleviate many forms of human discontent and misery. This is a matter of faith, I admit. But holding this faith, the chief end of education seems to me to be the encouragement of a scientific attitude of mind and a full and vivid appreciation of the inherent obstacles that oppose themselves to its successful cultivation in the human species.

Fifty years ago Matthew Arnold described the aim of education as "The getting to know on all matters which concern us the best which has been thought and said in the world; and through this knowledge turning a stream of fresh and free thought upon our stock notions and habits." He also said that we do not change our minds as the result of logic and refutation; but as we learn more the ground gently shifts beneath us, and we no longer look at things as we formerly did. This is so very true and so very important! I am sure that attempts directly to cultivate the judgment through teaching logic or the various branches of science have failed and are destined always to fail. At bottom they are an unconscious avoidance of the responsibility which would be involved in really turning a stream of fresh and free thought upon our stock notions and habits. *We are not yet in a position so to revise our education that a new type of mind will be cultivated appropriate to our present knowledge and circumstances.*

For education is controlled to a large extent by those who still adhere to many ancient conceptions which appear to them to be based on the best wisdom of the past, to be tested by time and substantiated by a consensus of human experience. These they do not wish to see disturbed. No two persons might agree as to exactly what these approved findings are, but so long as a notion is familiar it is assumed that it will not do any particular harm.

Now, new knowledge, if taken seriously, is very likely to prove an indictment of those very ideas which are dearest to the ill-informed. So in order to avoid inconvenient discussion the doctrine has become popular that so-called "controversial" matters should be carefully excluded from both the schools and colleges.

This means, when stated in a bald form, that instruction which might stir religious distrust, no matter how unintelligent, business, political or racial prejudice, or violate the proprieties, must be avoided. College presidents, school superintendents, text-book writers and their publishers are at present almost helpless in this situation. Teaching must be made as little disturbing as possible, when its chief function should be to stimulate thought and furnish new and reconstructive ideas.

The plight of the directors of education is indeed pitiable. College presidents have to sit up late at night reconciling the noble doctrine of freedom of teaching with the practical necessity of dodging controversial questions—for at all costs nothing must happen to arouse the resentment of timid parents and donors. The college head can not endure the humiliating imputation that his teachers are under "the wardship of an overweening fist," as Milton puts it; and yet he is constantly haunted by the nightmare of the fist which will refuse to write any more checks to the order of the institution if an instructor is carelessly charged by some ill-informed onlooker with "Bolshevism," "radicalism," or "socialistic leanings."

For what is perhaps still worse, the religious, moral or patriotic critics rarely take the trouble to find out what an instructor or text-book writer whom they attack really has said or believes. This scandalous state of affairs is too little understood. Those best informed about it are for various reasons disinclined to tell all they know. Those who plan out courses of study and write books for the schools are not free, but must often make very humiliating terms with unintelligence.

Matthew Arnold's ideal would be accepted in theory by most educators, but how very far are we from realizing it in practice. Teachers and text-book writers can not proceed directly toward this goal as they conceive it. They must hedge and suppress, compromise and extenuate, lest the authentic facts which it concerns boys and girls to learn should unluckily start them thinking. For this might rouse the apprehension of some defender of the social and moral order, some professional patriot or some adherent of the Mosaic authorship of the Pentateuch. The politicians in the Kentucky and other legislatures think themselves competent to decide whether the state should grant funds to any institution in which man's animal extraction is taught; the politicians in the New York legislature provided that no one should teach in the schools of the state who was known at any time to have expressed any distrust of our institutions.[1]

Now nothing could be more diametrically opposed to the cultivation of a scientific frame of mind. Education ought to be largely devoted to the issues upon which the young as they grow up should be in a position to form an intelligent opinion. They should understand that scientific advance has greatly altered, and promises still further to alter, our environment and our notions of ourselves and possibly the expediency of existing moral, social and industrial standards. We should have a dynamic education to fit a dynamic world. The world should not be presented to students as happily standardized but as urgently demanding readjustment. How are they to be more intelligent than their predecessors if they are trained to an utterly unscientific confidence in ancient notions, let us say of religion, race, heredity and sex, now being so fundamentally revised.[2]

[1] In reviewing my *Mind in the Making* Professor Harry N. Gardiner of Smith College says: The book is full, as it seems to him, of "crudities and exaggerations." "When for example, it is asserted (p. 11) that no publisher would accept a historical text-book based on an explicit statement of our present knowledge of man's animal ancestry, it is hard to believe that we are dealing with a statement of fact and not rather an opinion expressing a prejudiced animus" (*American Historical Review,* Vol. xxvi, p. 768, July, 1922). I fear that one of the difficulties in the way of educational reform is that of convincing such worthy persons as Professor Gardiner that what I am saying here is not merely the delusions of one afflicted with a persecution complex. Having been writing and editing historical text-books for a quarter of a century I can only invite Professor Gardiner to consult the text-book publishers as to the truth of the facts given above.

[2] One who wishes to study this matter is referred to Veblen, *The Higher Learning in America,* a profound analysis of the deep-lying deficiencies of our system, full of somewhat esoteric humor: Upton Sinclair, *The Goose-step,* in which a wealth of material is collected which will startle and perhaps vex those who have never considered the half-unconscious coalescence of forces directed against the full modernization of our education. Some statements and some inferences in this book appear to me hazardous, and I wonder if Mr. Sinclair does not occasionally discover subtle demons of economic greed where there are only panicky and ignorant college presidents and trustees. See also Ludwig Lewisohn, *Up Stream* and Samuel Butler's marvellous satire on higher education in *Erewhon*, chaps. xxi-xxii. For the larger setting see Chaffee, *Freedom of Speech* and Lippmann, *Public Opinion.*

LITERATURE AND SCIENCE[1]

By J. Middleton Murry

A friend of mine wrote to me the other day that "the sceptre has passed from literature to science." He is, of course, a man of science himself. And it seemed rather strange that he should use such a very literary phrase to express his triumph. It would have been more appropriate if he had sent me an equation. I should not have known what the equation meant. Perhaps that was the reason why he sent me a metaphor instead.

While I pondered his phrase it began to look to me like a barefaced contradiction in terms, and I wondered what kind of an equation would adequately express his satisfaction that literature had at last to play second fiddle to science. Even if an equation could be discovered with the proper nuance of "I told you so", what would be the pleasure for him if I did not appreciate it? No enemy is stronger than one who does not know he is beaten. And, to compare large things with small, would not the effect upon literature of the victory of science be precisely the same as the effect upon me of my defeat by an equation I could not understand? Literature may be shorn of its sceptre and its purple, but if there is no little boy to call out the Emperor is naked, who will be the wiser? If nobody knows, who will care?

Nevertheless, since my friend is a brilliant man, I have done my utmost to extract a meaning from his phrase. I am sure that he means something more than to make my flesh creep. My flesh refuses to creep, but I want to know what he means. I suspect that his metaphor was badly chosen, and that he would have done better with two sceptres instead of one.

[1] Reprinted from *Pencillings* by courtesy of Albert and Charles Boni, Inc.

Probably he meant that literature and science each had a sceptre, but the sceptre of science had of late become heavier and more imposing than the sceptre of literature. Literature now rules a little kingdom, while science rules a big one. But the kingdom of literature has certainly not been incorporated into the kingdom of science, nor is it likely to be. You might as well try to marry Boyle's Law to a bookcase.

But even if we take my friend to mean that science is now become a more important activity of the human mind than literature, is he saying more than that Boyle's Law is more valuable than a bookcase? And is not that judgment without import, as the logicians say? Is he not like the man who insists on comparing the value of logarithms and love? And if we suppose he means only that at the present time abler minds are engaged in scientific discovery than in literary creation—a question exceedingly difficult to judge—the issue is not affected. Quite possibly our bridges are better built than our poems nowadays. As Socrates would have said, our bridges have more of the goodness of bridges than our poems have of the goodness of poems. But that does not mean that a bridge is more than a bridge.

I suspect that what my friend has in his head is that the Einstein theory is a discovery of supreme philosophical importance; that for the first time the metaphysical doctrine of subjective idealism has been backed by a scientific proof; and that this will have a determining influence upon the future evolution of literature. The last of these propositions is the most doubtful. It is quite true that scientific theory does have an influence upon literary creation. But it has to be translated into emotional terms. In order to affect literature it has to affect our attitude of life. The theory of Natural Selection, emotionally interpreted as handing man over to the play of blind and uncontrollable forces, certainly gave a pessimistic tinge to the literature of the nineteenth century. The Copernican Revolution no doubt contributed to that emphatic isolation of the individual which is the beginning of modern romanticism. But we cannot say that the literature of the nineteenth century is either more or less important than Darwinism or the Copernican Revolution. There is no means of comparing them. What we can say is that the literature may wear better. When those two scientific theories have been exploded, as we are told they are being exploded now, the great books created by minds coloured by them will remain as fresh and valuable as ever.

For the truth of the matter surely is that there are very few emotional attitudes towards life which a man can truly and instinctively hold. He may believe life is painful and pitiful; he may believe it is glorious and splendid: he may confidently hope, he may continually despair, he may alternate between hope and despair. What his attitude will be is determined by many things: his heredity, his personal destiny, and to some degree by the scientific theories that obtain in his lifetime. A scientific theory which directly affects his hope of long life or immortality or better things to come, colours his mind and gives a twist to his sensibility. He becomes, if he is a writer, differently interested in life. In so far as either the Einstein theory or modern biology opens up new vistas of the significance or duration of human life, they will determine a change of tone in literature. Possibly the pessimism which still hangs about us like a cloud will be dissipated for a season. But it will return, simply because it is an eternal mode of the human spirit. And it may be dispelled without the cleansing wind of science, because optimism also is a natural mode of the human spirit.

Literature changes tone in obedience to these modes. But its substance is unchanged, for that is based on a delighted interest in human life and destinies. Science has no power over that interest, which is a gift of the gods like the genius of communicating it. When the man of science has power to determine or to change the structure of our minds, then literature may begin to fear him. By that time ordinary men will fear him also, and there will be a massacre of biologists. But till that day science can do no more to literature than to help to decide whether its vision of life shall be tinged with pity or happiness, resignation or confidence.

This may equally be decided by the indifference of the writer's mistress or his happiness in love. Science is only one of the things which colour the glass through which the writer looks at life; at present it can neither give nor take away the gift of seeing clearly through the glass; neither can it increase nor diminish the pleasure of those who take delight in what the writer can show them. The sceptre of science may be the more majestic. Beside its massy steel the rod of literature may appear slight and slender. We do not expect a magician's wand to look otherwise.

> Books must follow sciences, and not sciences books.
>
> FRANCIS BACON—*Proposition Touching Amendment of Laws.*

PREFACE TO FOLK-LORE IN THE OLD TESTAMENT [1]

By Sir James G. Frazer

Modern researches into the early history of man, conducted on different lines, have converged with almost irresistible force on the conclusion, that all civilized races have at some period or other emerged from a state of savagery resembling more or less closely the state in which many backward races have continued to the present time; and that, long after the majority of men in a community have ceased to think and act like savages, not a few traces of the old ruder modes of life and thought survive in the habits and institutions of the people. Such survivals are included under the head of folk-lore, which, in the broadest sense of the word, may be said to embrace the whole body of a people's traditionary beliefs and customs, so far as these appear to be due to the collective action of the multitude and cannot be traced to the individual influence of great men. Despite the high moral and religious development of the ancient Hebrews, there is no reason to suppose that they formed an exception to this general law. They, too, had probably passed through a stage of barbarism and even of savagery; and this probability, based on the analogy of other races, is confirmed by an examination of their literature, which contains many references to beliefs and practices that can hardly be explained except on the supposition that they are rudimentary survivals from a far lower level of culture. It is to the illustration and explanation of a few such relics of ruder times, as they are preserved like fossils in the Old Testament, that I have addressed myself in the

[1] Reprinted from Frazer, *Folk-Lore in the Old Testament,* by permission of the Macmillan Company, publishers.

present work. Elsewhere I have had occasion to notice other similar survivals of savagery in the Old Testament, such as the sacrifice of the first-born, the law of the uncleanness of women, and the custom of the scapegoat; but as I am unwilling to repeat what I have said on these topics, I content myself with referring readers, who may be interested in them, to my other writings.

The instrument for the detection of savagery under civilization is the comparative method, which, applied to the human mind, enables us to trace man's intellectual and moral evolution, just as, applied to the human body, it enables us to trace his physical evolution from lower forms of animal life. There is, in short, a Comparative Anatomy of the mind as well as of the body, and it promises to be no less fruitful of far-reaching consequences, not merely speculative but practical, for the future of humanity. The application of the comparative method to the study of Hebrew antiquities is not novel. In the seventeenth century the method was successfully employed for this purpose in France by the learned French pastor Samuel Bochart, and in England by the learned divine John Spencer, Master of Corpus Christi College, Cambridge, whose book on the ritual laws of the ancient Hebrews is said to have laid the foundations of the science of Comparative Religion. In our own age, after a lapse of two centuries, the work initiated by these eminent scholars and divines was resumed in Cambridge by my revered master and friend William Robertson Smith, and the progress which the study made during his lifetime and since his too early death is due in a large measure to the powerful impulse it received from his extraordinary genius and learning. It has been my ambition to tread in the footsteps of these my illustrious predecessors in this department of learning, and to carry on what I may be allowed to call the Cambridge tradition of Comparative Religion.

It is a familiar truth that the full solution of any one problem involves the solution of many more; nay, that nothing short of omniscience could suffice to answer all the questions implicitly raised by the seemingly simplest inquiry. Hence the investigation of a point of folk-lore, especially in the present inchoate condition of the study, naturally opens up lines of inquiry which branch out in many directions; and in following them we are insensibly drawn on into wider and wider fields of inquiry, until the point from which we started has almost disappeared in the distance, or, to speak more correctly, is seen in its proper perspective as only one in a multitude of similar phenomena. So it befell me when, many years ago, I undertook to investigate a point in the folk-lore of ancient Italy; so it has befallen me now, when I have set myself to discuss certain points in the folk-lore of the ancient Hebrews. The examination of a particular legend, custom, or law has in some cases gradually broadened out into a disquisition and almost into a treatise. But I hope that, apart from their immediate bearing on the traditions and usages of Israel, these disquisitions may be accepted as contributions to the study of folk-lore in general. That study is still in its infancy, and our theories on the subjects with which it deals must probably for a long time to come be tentative and provisional, mere pigeon-holes in which temporarily to sort the multitude of facts, not iron moulds in which to cast them for ever. Under these circumstances a candid inquirer in the realm of folk-lore at the present time will state his inferences with a degree of diffidence and reserve corresponding to the difficulty and uncertainty of the matter in hand. This I have always endeavoured to do. If anywhere I have forgotten the caution which I recommend to others, and have expressed myself with an appearance of dogmatism which the evidence does not warrant, I would request the reader to correct all such particular statements by this general and sincere profession of scepticism.

Throughout the present inquiry I have sought to take account of the conclusions reached by the best modern critics with regard to the composition and dates of the various books of the Old Testament; for I believe that only in the light of these conclusions do many apparent discrepancies in the sacred volume admit of a logical and historical explanation. Quotations are generally made in the words of the Revised English Version, and as I have occasionally ventured to dissent from it and to prefer a different rendering or even, in a very few places, a different reading, I wish to say that, having read the whole of the Old Testament in Hebrew attentively, with the English Version constantly beside me, I am deeply impressed by the wonderful felicity with which Translators and Revisers alike have done their work, combining in an extraordinary degree fidelity to the letter with justice to the spirit of the original. In its union of scrupulous accuracy with dignity and beauty of language the English Revised Version of the Old Testament is, as a translation, doubtless unsurpassed and probably unequalled in literature.

The scope of my work has obliged me to dwell chiefly on the lower side of ancient Hebrew life revealed in the Old Testament, on the traces of savagery and superstition which are to be found in its pages. But to do so is not to ignore, far less to disparage, that higher side of the Hebrew genius which has manifested itself in a spiritual religion and a pure morality, and of which the Old Testament is the imperishable monument. On the contrary, the revelation of the baser elements which underlay the civilization of ancient Israel, as they underlie the civilization of modern Europe, serves rather as a foil to enhance by contrast the glory of a people which, from such dark depths of ignorance and cruelty, could rise to such bright heights of wisdom and virtue, as sunbeams appear to shine with a greater effulgence of beauty when they break through the murky clouds of a winter evening than when they flood the earth from the serene splendour of a summer moon. The annals of savagery and superstition unhappily compose a large part of human literature; but in what other volume shall we find, side by side with that melancholy record, psalmists who poured forth their sweet and solemn strains of meditative piety in the solitude of the hills or in green pastures and beside still waters; prophets who lit up their beatific visions of a blissful future with the glow of an impassioned imagination; historians who bequeathed to distant ages the scenes of a remote past embalmed for ever in the amber of a pellucid style? These are the true glories of the Old Testament and of Israel; these, we trust and believe, will live to delight and inspire mankind, when the crudities recorded alike in sacred and profane literature shall have been purged away in a nobler humanity of the future.

'Twer well with most if books that would engage
Their childhood, pleased them at a riper age.

COWPER—*Tirocinium.*

MEDICAL AND PSYCHOLOGICAL VIEWS OF LITERATURE

HENRY FIELDING[1]

By C. MacLaurin

In the gloomy procession of drink, gluttony, and syphilis which makes up so large a part of history—always excepting for a moment Joan of Arc, that "one white angel of war" whom the English and French burned because she did not and could not ever become mature, as I have shown in *Post Mortems*—there is at least one very great man whom one can only pity, if my ideas about him are correct, without the faintest trace of censure—the author of that "foul, coarse and abominable" book, *Tom Jones*, which has been such a nightmare to the prude and yet shows human nature better than most of the books which are welcomed in country parsonages.

On January 1st, 1753, a young servant girl named Betty Canning, disappeared from a house in Aldermanbury, London, where she had been employed as a servant; she reappeared on the 29th of the month at her mother's home, starving, half-clad, and with a fine story of abduction and imprisonment. She identified an old gipsy-woman as her assailant, who, being a gipsy, old and ugly, was promptly seized and sentenced to be hanged after the light-hearted manner of the eighteenth century. Though London was divided into two camps, for and against Betty Canning, there seems to have been no talk of a vigilance committee, probably because the great heart of the people was not stirred by evening newspapers about the woes of a little servant. One of Betty's witnesses was a little servant girl named Virtue Hall, whose delightful name alone should have induced credence; and Virtue appeared before Fielding, who was then a magis-

[1] From *Post Mortems of Mere Mortals* by C. MacLaurin, copyright 1925, 1930, by Doubleday, Doran and Company, Inc.

trate looking into the mystery of Betty Canning, to support Betty's claims for vengeance. If the gipsy had been a man no doubt she would have been hanged promptly; but, as she was a woman, the psychology of those days could not imagine why Betty should have accused her of abduction and a certain amount of trouble was taken to test the truth of Betty's accusations. As a result the gipsy was by a miracle let off, and Betty got seven years for perjury. Nowadays it seems quite an ordinary sort of case, where a hysterical girl will perjure her immortal soul in order to attract attention to herself, whatever may be the results to others; but the real interest to us lies in the light that it casts on the sick mind of Fielding himself; for he actually believed Virtue and published a pamphlet in support of her evidence.

This done, Fielding's health began to warn him that he must take care of himself, and he set about curing the chronic gout which had long crippled him. He took an ancient remedy of Galen's, called "the Duke of Portland's remedy"—Fielding was always fond of experimenting upon himself with quack medicines—and was advised to try the waters of Bath. Meantime he had busied himself with dogging the footsteps of no less than five gangs of street-robbers; and in the midst of the turmoil there came a peremptory message from the Duke of Newcastle to attend at Newcastle House and discuss the depredations of yet more cut-throats. For months he worked hard at the pursuit, with splendid results for the peace of London, but disastrous results upon his own health, for he had become deeply jaundiced and "fallen away to a shadow." No more was to be seen that handsome Harry Fielding who had worked so hard for literature and civic peace; whose generosity and goodness to the poor, outcast, and oppressed has become proverbial; but a wasted, dropsical man of pinched face, who could hardly leave his chair, so crippled was he with the gout, and so heavy with the dropsy. The time had long gone by for Bath, if indeed it had ever existed. The winter of 1753-4 was terribly severe and his doctors told him that he must seek a warmer climate. Even Bishop Berkeley's tar-water had failed, so things must have looked black indeed for Fielding as he was carried laboriously on board the ship *Queen of Portugal* for the long voyage to Lisbon. His wife, the successor of that beloved woman whom he has immortalised in Sophia Western and Amelia Booth, accompanied him to nurse him, though I am afraid the poor lady was not much use as a nurse to a sick man whose every movement caused him pain; the very winds fought against him, and it was weeks before the ship could get away from the Isle of Wight into the blue water.

It must have been a miserable voyage for Fielding; he was confined to the cabin because he could not mount the companion ladder owing to his weakness and pain. Twice he had to be tapped for his dropsy; the food was bad, his wife confined to her bed with a terrible toothache that could not be relieved because the tooth seems to have had a peculiar root that defied all attempts at removal; but he himself, sitting propped up in the stuffy cabin, wrote the most delightful and uncomplaining journal imaginable, which is quite as brilliant as, and even more moving than, any of his novels. It is written in Fielding's own half-jocular, half-satirical and wholly sympathetic style, but is entirely free from that occasional coarseness that has shocked even a generation that seems to revel in the sex-neurotic and introspective psycho-analytical novel. Better to use an occasional naughty word than to give the impression of being constantly possessed by unclean thoughts of sex, which seems to be the unhappy fate of some modern novelists.

Although he has given us an excellent description of his symptoms it is difficult to reduce it to terms of modern pathology and to name his actual sickness. I thought at first that he must have had cirrhosis of the liver, because it is well known to cause severe dropsy, wasting, haggard face, and despair. But after carefully reconsidering the symptoms I came to the conclusion that such an idea was untenable, for cirrhosis is not noted for its jaundice, and moreover it is caused by long and continuous drinking, whereas Fielding is known to have been a reasonably abstemious drinker. But there is an even more terrible disease which would even better than cirrhosis exactly suit the conditions of our problem, cancer. If we imagine Fielding to have suffered from a certain form of internal malignant tumour spreading to the peritoneum, all his symptoms would be at once explained, deep jaundice, dropsy, wasting and frightful appearance. I am assuming that Fielding's form of "dropsy" was what we now call "ascites," that is to say, an outpouring of serous fluid into the peritoneum. His so-called asthma may possibly have been due to heart trouble owing to the strain on his heart caused by oppression from the dropsy, and his "gout" to septic disease of his teeth, which would account for the toothless condition which so disfigured him toward the end of his life and prevented him from eating the ship's food.

Unlike some writers who, being possessed by their own unconscious minds, are led into filth, Fielding, though occasionally coarse, is never dirty. I remember during some months, when all the cats, dogs and roosters in the neighbourhood combined in an assault upon sleep, and an occasional kookooburra joined in the noise, I read through the whole of *Amelia* and thought it one of the most delightful books in the world; and a rereading of it tends to confirm me in that belief. Amelia, for all her scarred nose, is one of the most charming women in fiction, though she had a great deal to put up with in her husband, Captain Booth, and though she *would* call him "Billy."

Fielding himself was what the Americans would call a "he-man." He was not one of the miserable, whining, introspective heroes of post-war fiction; and in Tom Jones and Captain Booth he has drawn a man as he thought a man should be, and as good men probably are if we would stop our ears to the howls of the old women. And these heroes of his were probably drawn from himself. That terrible ironic creature, Jonathan Wild, of course represents his knowledge of Old Bailey; it is a grim book, and far too ironical for most people, though it has not the sardonic and shuddering laughter of Dean Swift and his Struldbrugs.

But if he had cancer when he started on his last voyage he must have had it coming on when he believed Virtue's tarradiddle, and possibly it was because of his poor health that he believed her. No man with a cancer beginning to gnaw at his vitals could possibly take the trouble to cross-examine a brazen hussy who was determined to deceive him, and we can even understand that chapter in Amelia when he stops the narrative to deliver a violent attack upon the medical profession, possibly because when he was writing *Amelia* he must occasionally have felt the slight twinge and noticed the slight jaundice that would be the first symptom that all was not well.

But he was a very kind man, even as a magistrate. He knew too much about human nature to be harsh with anybody, and possibly Virtue, in telling untruths, had touched a soft spot in his generous heart; in other words, Virtue and Betty must have "vamped" him.

> Reading maketh a full man, conference a ready man, and writing an exact man.
>
> FRANCIS BACON—*Of Studies.*

THE KALEIDOSCOPE[1]

By Charles A. Bennett

There was a time when novels used to begin like this: About ten o'clock of a wild December night in the year 18— a solitary horseman might have been seen ascending the hill that led. . . . The rest of the chapter would fulfil this early promise. You would have a straight-forward narrative of events. Chapter two gave you as much information about the local scenery and about the ancestry, past history, and present character and prospects of the chief persons as it was necessary for you to know. With chapter three the author got into his stride. From that point on it was "story" or "plot." But those days are gone. No one with any serious literary pretensions would write a book like that now. For the moderns have discovered the "inner life of the mind." To write a book with a plot were naïve. To deal with the events of the visible tangible world would be to lapse into a grossness unworthy of people of the finer shades. The vicissitudes of the stream of consciousness are the only events vouchsafed to us. The inner world is alone important.

This change in the centre of interest has naturally brought with it a change of literary convention. The omniscient, omnipresent author who pervaded the old-fashioned story without intruding himself upon the reader's notice, who told everything in a direct impersonal way, has disappeared. Nowadays nothing may be reported unless it has first been filtered through the mind of one of the characters. If it is necessary to relate the events that precede the opening of the story, then someone must fall into a convenient reverie—a reverie that may last for ten pages. If coarse material things

[1] Reprinted by permission of *The Saturday Review of Literature.*

like weather or scenery are to be mentioned, it must be by means of someone's emotions or impressions about them. The narrative is punctuated with "she thought," "she asked herself," "he reflected," "she remembered," "he mused," "he knew."

> The hill seemed very long. How long was it now since he had started? he asked himself. Three hours? Four? Impossible to tell! One lost count of time when one was slogging along like this in the dark. . . . The dark! One hated the dark, ever since the time when as a little boy one had had to pass that landing on the way up to bed. Emma used to say there was a bogey man there. Good old Emma! One remembered the queer feel of her gnarled bony hands . . . Come up there, you brute!

There you have your solitary horseman, modern style. Observe that the general situation has to be guessed at from the disjointed mutterings of a maundering mind. As for Emma—"and who the deuce may *she* be?"—Emma probably does not appear in the story again except as a symbol of some infantile neurosis, skotophobia, perhaps. And the horse, poor beast, never gets beyond the status of a subtle inference. But we are not to worry about such trifles. It is the horseman's stream of consciousness that matters.

An extreme example of the thing I have in mind is Tomlinson's recent book, "Gallions Reach." True, it contains a story; the murder, the flight, the shipwreck, adventures in a tropical jungle, the return of the murderer. But these are not the things of primary interest. The real story, from the author's point of view, is the drama of the murderer's emotions and reflections. Above all, of his reflections! No incident is so trivial that it cannot release a flood of philosophical meditation. Never was criminal so sensitive and self-conscious. "Gallions Reach," for all its apparatus of external adventure, is nothing but the prolonged soliloquy of a murderer for whom every quiver of the nerves is translated into a thought.

Some psychologists maintain that when children at play

"pretend" they do not deceive themselves. They simply use the things of the external world as temporary supports for that world of imagination in which they spend so much of their time. Here is a walking stick. No, it's a gun! "Look, Mother, I'm a soldier, I'm a soldier!" "Gallions Reach" is like that. The only function of the visible tangible world is to supply so many *points d'appui*, so many places of rest and renewed flight, for that tenuous inner life of the hero.

Now I have no objection to any writer's choosing the inner life as his subject. If we have indeed discovered a new world—the hidden, mysterious, subconscious region of the mind—, then that world offers a fair field for exploration. Neither dogmatist nor censor has the right to forbid entry. My complaint is directed against the methods now in vogue for revealing that world and its influence upon explicit thought and conduct. The technique seems to me crude. Thus when I am told that at a certain point the hero fell into a prolonged reverie over the past which just happens to recall the necessary information, I detect at once the manipulating hand of the author. I know that the hero did not fall into a reverie, or if he did, it was into a chaotic and irrelevant daydream. The writer says he did. But I don't believe him. It is just a dodge, and a feeble one. When the bang of a door starts the hero off, as it so often does in modern novels, on a philosophical meditation upon noise, noise in general, noisiness of modern civilization, decay of leisure, lack of opportunity for tranquillity in modern life, Oriental Calm against Western Feverishness, Buddhism, Nirvana, and so on for pages, I feel inclined to cry out to the author, "Away with these desperate expedients of banging doors and musing minds! Tell me straight what your hero's philosophy of noise was. That is all you really want to do, so why go in for being modern and clever and psychological?" That is bad art which does not conceal art, and what I have called the old-fashioned convention really did not obtrude the author and his technique upon the reader's notice nearly so much as do the new-fangled tricks.

* * *

If I should be asked for examples of less inadequate methods, I should give two. The first is from "Alice-for-Short." Charles Heath, it may be remembered, has brought Alice, that forlorn little waif, to his mother's house for shelter. He has been afraid to tell his mother. Mrs. Heath is, in her own estimation, a much abused but long-suffering person. Partridge is the Perfect Servant. Mrs. Heath learns about Alice's coming from Partridge.

"I am not attaching any blame to you, Partridge, in any sense—but I feel that I *ought* to have been told."

Whereupon Partridge coughs expressively and sympathetically. She endeavors to make this cough say,

I feel that your son and daughter do not recognize to the full your position in the house, nor the weight of cares and responsibilities that beset you, nor the administrative skill of your domestic economy; but I perceive that they are guileless, owing to the purity of their extraction, and while willingly admitting that you ought to have been told, venture to hope that a *modus vivendi* may be discoverable, and above all that I may be recognized as blameless, and remain always your obedient humble servant.

Perhaps she hardly succeeds in making the cough say all that, but she feels it was a good and useful cough, as far as it went.

There you have the old-fashioned, omniscient author giving you a straightforward account of Partridge's subconscious. And though De Morgan makes no solemn claim to psychological profundity, indeed seems to be smiling at himself, is he not just as discerning and profound as any exponent of the current mode?

For my second example practically any one of the short

stories of Katherine Mansfield would serve. She is one of the few "psychological" writers who does not, if I may so put it, take the "sub" out of the subconscious. She does not drag the subconscious into the light where it loses all its iridescence, like some of those deep sea fish when brought to the surface. Her method is indirect. She hints; she suggests. If you ask me to be more precise and tell you how it is done I can only reply, after many vain attempts to discover the secret, that I do not know. But let anyone who is interested read "Bliss"; let him read it carefully, several times, and let him study the part played by the pear tree in that story, and although at the end he will probably know no more than I do how it is done, I think he will agree with me in saying, "That is the way it ought to be done."

In trying to explain the failure of the modern method I find two causes for its ineffectiveness. The first concerns literary craftsmanship, the second involves a point of theoretical psychology.

Those writers who devote themselves to a description of the stream of consciousness proceed, I suppose, upon the theory that the life of the mind taken in its totality is not luminous, definite, and orderly, but chaotic, vague, and obscure. It is really like a river, running now muddy, now clear, here tumbling into rapids, there flowing in quiet reaches, a thing of deep pools, of shallows and eddies and stagnant backwaters, a stream that moves from a hidden source to an unknown destination. Let us grant that this is true. The problem then arises how this truth is to be conveyed in literature. The solution reached by novelists to-day seems to have been determined by the following assumption: If the mind is a stream, then the language you use to describe it must be in flux: if the consciousness is an affair of broken lights then our language must be shattered; if consciousness is confused then our prose must be incoherent. To call this sheer dogma, as I believe it to be, is not a sufficient criticism. The final test, after all, must be practical. We must ask: Does the structureless prose that is now fashionable really convey the thing that our novelists wish to convey? For myself I must answer that it does not feel at all like this to be a mind. These truncated sentences, these verbs without subjects and these subjects without verbs, these rows and rows of exasperating dots, evoke no sense of mental life whatever. They suggest nothing so much as a prolonged convulsion of hiccoughs. I have no doubt that my mind and your mind are dark disorderly affairs, but I simply do not recognize myself or you in this version. And I conclude that the reason the artist has failed to convince me is that he has too rashly assumed that if you are to depict chaos the only way it can be done is by adopting a chaotic style that combines the worst mannerisms of Alfred Jingle Esq. and Miss Bates.

In stating the second cause I shall have to begin by being dogmatic myself. There is no such thing as a mere state of mind. A state of mind has no independent existence of its own. It always refers to something beyond itself and cannot be defined apart from that reference. An idea is an idea *of* something, an emotion is an emotion *about* something, an attitude is an attitude *towards* something. The temptation of the professional psychologist is to suppose that you can separate the state of mind from that to which it refers, regard it as an event in the natural history of the mind, establish its connections with other similar events, and so formulate "laws of mental process." To this temptation many writers to-day have succumbed, and there, I think, lies the root of the trouble. They have set out to describe mental life directly, whereas, if I am right, it is best described, for purposes of literary evocation, not directly, but indirectly, by means of that *to* which the mind refers. An illustration may help to make this clear.

A friend of mine tells me that the most successful representation of fear he ever saw was a picture of a man looking over his shoulder and running away as hard as he could from something—something that lay outside the frame of the picture. What happens, I suppose, in such a case is that the observer projects himself imaginatively into the place of the figure in the picture and sends his mind out towards that unknown shape of terror. Fear is not described so much as evoked, by giving the observer something to be afraid *of*.

In actual life intense emotions have a way of seizing upon some apparently trivial circumstance—"a fancy from a flower bell"—which becomes as it were emotionally charged and afterwards serves in recollection as a symbol potent to call up the original emotion. Poets know that the most effective way of conveying such an emotion is not to attempt a direct psychological description of it but to focus attention upon its symbol. Half the art of poetry consists in finding words and images that have the power of arousing vast tracts of "subconscious" meaning.

My objection therefore to the psychological school of writers comes to this, that instead of learning from the poets and giving us art they are sitting at the feet of the psychologists and giving us—well, what they are giving us! One can hardly call it psychology. The business of the psychologist, I take it, is to constitute himself observer of the mind of the other person and report what he, as observer sees there. The business of the artist, as far as our present discussion is concerned, is not to observe and describe mind, but to evoke, by indirection, the sense of what it feels like to be a mind. Suppose the mind is a self-moving kaleidoscope. The psychologist, "one who is outside looking in," records and tries to discover law in the changing patterns. But if the mind is a kaleidoscope the function of the artist is to tell what it feels like to be a kaleidoscope, and you will never accomplish that by piling up descriptions of patterns, however ingenious and exact they may be.

If someone would write a book to be called "The Kaleidoscope Looks at its World!"

> The world may be divided into people that read, people that write, people that think, and fox-hunters.
>
> WILLIAM SHENSTONE.

THE HUMORIST
PARODIES
LITERATURE

MAVRONE*

By Arthur Guiterman

(ONE OF THOSE SAD IRISH POEMS, WITH NOTES)

From Arranmore the weary miles I've come;
  An' all the way I've heard
A Shrawn [1] that's kep' me silent, speechless, dumb,
  Not saying any word.
An' was it then the Shrawn of Eire,[2] you'll say,
  For him that died the death on Carrisbool?
It was not that; nor was it, by the way,
  The Sons of Garnim [3] blitherin' their drool;
Nor was it any Crowdie of the Shee, [4]
  Or Itt, or Himm, nor wail of Barryhoo [5]

* Reprinted from *The Laughing Muse* by Arthur Guiterman, published by Harper and Brothers.

[1] A Shrawn is a pure Gaelic noise, something like a groan, more like a shriek, and most like a sigh of longing.

[2] Eire was daughter of Carne, King of Connaught. Her lover, Murdh of the Open Hand, was captured by Greatcoat Mackintosh, King of Ulster, on the plain of Carrisbool, and made into soup. Eire's grief on this sad occasion has become proverbial.

[3] Garnim was second cousin to Manannan MacLir. His sons were always sad about something. There were twenty-two of them, and they were all unfortunate in love at the same time, just like a chorus at the opera. "Blitherin' their drool" is about the same as "dreeing their weird."

[4] The Shee (or "Sidhe," as I should properly spell it if you were not so ignorant) were, as everybody knows, the regular, stand-pat, organization fairies of Erin. The Crowdie was their annual convention, at which they made melancholy sounds. The Itt and Himm were the irregular, or insurgent, fairies. They *never* got any offices or patronage. See MacAlester, *Polity of the Sidhe of West Meath*, page 985.

[5] The Barryhoo is an ancient Celtic bird about the size of a Mavis, with lavender eyes and a black-crape tail. It continually mourns its mate (Barry-which, feminine form), which has an hereditary predisposition to an early and tragic demise and invariably dies first.

For Barrywhich that stilled the tongue of me.
'Twas but my own heart cryin' out for you,
Magraw! [6] Bulleen, Shinnanigan, Boru,
Aroon, Machree, Aboo! [7]

[6] Magraw, a Gaelic term of endearment, often heard on the baseball fields of Donnybrook.

[7] These last six words are all that tradition has preserved of the original incantation by means of which Irish rats were rhymed to death. Thereby hangs a tale, which I should be glad to tell you in this note; but the publishers say that being prosed to death is as bad as being rhymed to death, and that the readers won't stand for any more.

Some books are to be tasted, others to be swallowed, and some few to be chewed and digested.

Francis Bacon—*Of Studies.*

IMPUDENT INTERVIEWS

By Arthur Guiterman

GEORGE BERNARD SHAW

A cheerful, well-appointed study at Number 10, Adelphi Terrace, London, W. C., the blaze of a crackling fire, within, rendered doubly alluring by the bluster of the March night, without. Substantial furniture, neatly arranged bookcases filled with orderly volumes, notably the works of Nietzsche, Schopenhauer, Karl Marx and Plato, with dramatists old and new, suggest that the inmate is a methodical person possessed of philosophic and literary tastes. This diagnosis is borne out by the appearance of the victim himself as he stands with his back to the glow, his tall, thin, alert, Satanic figure sharply outlined against the yellow flames. How old is he? His somewhat scanty hair and beard, once red, but now almost colorless, indicate that he has emerged from the larval stage of youthful cynicism and despondency and is now in the full enjoyment of that radiant benevolence and optimism granted only to those who have known the triumphs and accomplished promises of half a century and more. His brown suit, red tie, and soft flannel shirt, as well as the broad-brimmed Alpine hat which he has thrown upon the table, reveal the Socialist; his excessive pallor betrays confirmed vegetarianism; while his steel blue eyes of soldierly directness give assurance that here is one who would sooner quarrel than eat a bushel of turnips. Upon the bookcase facing him stands a bronze portrait-bust, clearly of himself (for it is by the hand of no less a sculptor than Rodin), upon which his eyes fall quizzically, yet, on the whole, with great respect. To the right and left of this masterpiece are other works of art—an effigy of Ibsen upon which our Protagonist, as he speaks, confers a glance of condescending approbation; a bas-relief of Wagner, which he notices with a slight nod that seems to say, "Very well, old man; but it's lucky for you that I devoted myself to Drama instead of Opera"; and an engraving of the Stratford bust of Shakespeare which must, perforce, be content with a commiserating smile that may be interpreted as signifying, "Poor chap! You meant well, but you didn't know!"

My birth? I beg you, let us call
  That mystery unsolved.
In fact, I was not born at all,
  But, so to speak, evolved.

My Education? Books are naught;
  At schools I've always spurned;
So just put down, "The man was taught";
  Or, better still, "He learned."

You seek to know my aim in life?—
  To write as best I can,
To stir a little wholesome strife
  And hunt the Superman.

Myself, the First of Supermen,
  I levitate above
Your wabbling world, and now and then
  I give the thing a shove.

In motley clad ("the only wear!")
  I watch with fiendish grin
Your childish bubbles float in air
  And prick them with a pin.

My creed, though big and broad, insists
  On ten perfervid hells,

Say one for anti-Socialists
  And nine for H. G. Wells.

Ah, yes; I've written loads of stuff
  From changing points of view,
And all of it is bright enough,
  And much, I fear, is true.

My works? Behold them, bound in calf
  Upon the middle shelf.
They're great; yet, somehow, more than half
  I don't believe myself.

For what is Truth? How well I know
  A jest confutes the wise!
But this, at least, I'm sure is so—
  It pays to advertise!

The author who speaks about his own books is almost as bad as a mother who talks about her own children.

BENJAMIN DISRAELI, *Speech, Nov. 19, 1870*

SONG BY ROGERO

By GEORGE CANNING AND GEORGE ELLIS

(GERMAN TRAGEDY)

WHENE'ER with haggard eyes I view
  This dungeon that I'm rotting in,
I think of those companions true
Who studied with me at the U-
    -niversity of Gottingen—
    -niversity of Gottingen.

[*Weeps, and pulls out a blue 'kerchief, with which he wipes his eyes; gazing tenderly at it, he proceeds.*]

Sweet 'kerchief, check'd with heavenly blue,
  Which once my love sat knotting in,
Alas, Matilda *then* was true,
At least I thought so at the U-
    -niversity of Gottingen—
    -niversity of Gottingen.

[*At the repetition of this line* ROGERO *clanks his chains in cadence.*]

Barbs! barbs! alas! how swift you flew,
  Her neat post-wagon trotting in!
Ye bore Matilda from my view;
Forlorn I languish'd at the U-
    -niversity of Gottingen—
    -niversity of Gottingen.

This faded form! this pallid hue!
  This blood my veins is clotting in!
My years are many—They were few

When first I enter'd at the U-
    -niversity of Gottingen—
    -niversity of Gottingen.

There first for thee my passion grew,
  Sweet! sweet Matilda Pottingen!
Thou wast the daughter of my tu-
-tor, Law Professor at the U-
    -niversity of Gottingen—
    -niversity of Gottingen.

Sun, moon, and thou vain world, adieu,
  That kings and priests are plotting in;
Here doom'd to starve on water gru-
-el never shall I see the U-
    -niversity of Gottingen!—
    -niversity of Gottingen!

[*During the last stanza* ROGERO *dashes his head repeatedly against the walls of his prison, and, finally, so hard as to produce a visible contusion. He then throws himself on the floor in an agony. The curtain drops—the music still continuing to play, till it is wholly fallen.*]

THE COCK AND THE BULL [1]

By Charles Stuart Calverley

(BROWNING)

You see this pebble-stone? It's a thing I bought
Of a bit of a chit of a boy i' the mid o' the day—
I like to dock the smaller parts-o'-speech,
As we curtail the already cur-tail'd cur
(You catch the paronomasia, play 'po' words?),
Did, rather, i' the pre-Landseerian days.
Well, to my muttons. I purchased the concern
And clapt it i' my poke, having given for same
By way o' chop, swop, barter or exchange—
'Chop' was my snickering dandiprat's own term—
One shilling and fourpence, current coin o' the realm.
O-n-e one and f-o-u-r four
Pence, one and fourpence—you are with me, sir?—
What hour it skills not: ten or eleven o' the clock,
One day (and what a roaring day it was
Go shop or sight-see—bar a spit o' rain!)
In February, eighteen sixty nine,
Alexandrina Victoria, Fidei
Hm—hm—how runs the jargon? being on throne.

Such, sir, are all the facts, succinctly put,
The basis or substratum—what you will—
Of the impending eighty thousand lines.
'Not much in 'em either,' quoth perhaps simple Hodge.
But there's a superstructure. Wait a bit.
Mark first the rationale of the thing:
Hear logic rivel and levigate the deed.
That shilling—and for matter o' that, the pence—

[1] Reprinted with the permission of G. Bell & Sons Ltd.

I had o' course upo' me—wi' me say—
(*Mecum's* the Latin, make a note o' that)
When I popp'd pen i' stand, scratch'd ear, wip'd snout,
(Let everybody wipe his own himself)
Sniff'd—tch!—at snuffbox; tumbled up, he-heed,
Haw-haw'd (not hee-haw'd that's another guess thing:)
Then fumbled at, and stumbled out of, door,
I shoved the timber ope wi' my omoplat;
And *in vestibulo,* i' the lobby to-wit,
(Iacobi Facciolati's rendering, sir,)
Donn'd galligaskins, antigropeloes,
And so forth; and, complete with hat and gloves,
One on and one a-dangle i' my hand,
And ombrifuge (Lord love you!), case o' rain,
I flopp'd forth, 'sbuddikins! on my own ten toes,
(I do assure you there be ten of them,)
And went clump-clumping up hill and down dale
To find myself o' the sudden i' front o' the boy.
Put case I hadn't 'em on me, could I ha' bought
This sort-o'-kind-o'-what-you-might-call toy,
This pebble-thing, o' the boy-thing? Q.E.D.
That's proven without aid from mumping Pope,
Sleek porporate or bloated Cardinal.
(Isn't it, old Fatchaps? You're in Euclid now.)
So, having the shilling—having i' fact a lot—
And pence and halfpence, ever so many o' them,
I purchased, as I think I said before,
The pebble (*lapis, lapidis, -di, -dem, -de*—
What nouns 'crease short i' the genitive, Fatchaps, eh?)
O' the boy, a bare-legg'd beggarly son of a gun,
For one-and-fourpence. Here we are again.

Now Law steps in, bigwigg'd, voluminous-jaw'd;
Investigates and re-investigates.
Was the transaction illegal? Law shakes head.
Perpend, sir, all the bearings of the case.

At first the coin was mine, the chattel his.
But now (by virtue of the said exchange
And barter) *vice versa* all the coin,
Per juris operationem, vests
I' the boy and his assigns till ding o' doom;
(*In sæcula sæculo-o-o-orum;*
I think I hear the Abate mouth out that.)
To have and hold the same to him and them. . . .
Confer some idiot on Conveyancing.
Whereas the pebble and every part thereof,
And all that appertaineth thereunto,
Quodcunque pertinet ad eam rem,
(I fancy, sir, my Latin's rather pat)
Or shall, will, may, might, can, could, would or should,
(*Subaudi cætera*—clap we to the close—
For what's the good of law in a case o' the kind)
Is mine to all intents and purposes.
This settled, I resume the thread o' the tale.

Now for a touch o' the vendor's quality.
He says a gen'lman bought a pebble of him,
(This pebble i' sooth, sir, which I hold i' my hand)—
And paid for 't, *like* a gen'lman, on the nail.
'Did I o'ercharge him a ha'penny? Devil a bit.
Fiddlepin's end! Get out, you blazing ass!
Gabble o' the goose. Don't bugaboo-baby *me!*
Go double or quits? Yah! tittup! what's the odds?'
—There's the transaction view'd i' the vendor's light.

Next ask that dumpled hag, stood snuffling by,
With her three frowsy blowsy brats o' babes,
The scum o' the kennel, cream o' the filth-heap Faugh!
Aie, aie aie, aie! ὀτοτοτοτοτοτοῖ,
(Stead which we blurt out Hoighty toighty now)—
And the baker and candlestickmaker, and Jack and Gill,

Blear'd Goody this an queasy Gaffer that.
Ask the schoolmaster. Take schoolmaster first.

He saw a gentleman purchase of a lad
A stone, and pay for it *rite,* on the square,
And carry it off *per saltum,* jauntily,
Propria quæ maribus, gentleman's property now
(Agreeably to the law explain'd above),
In proprium usum, for his private ends.
The boy he chuck'd a brown i' the air, and bit
I' the face the shilling: heaved a thumping stone
At a lean hen that ran cluck clucking by,
(And hit her, dead as nail i' post o' door,)
Then *abiit*—what's the Ciceronian phrase?—
Excessit, evasit, erupit—off slogs boy;
Off like bird, *avi similis*—(you observed
The dative? Pretty i' the Mantuan!)—Anglice,
Off in three flea skips. *Hactenus,* so far,
So good, *tam bene. Bene, satis, male*—,
Where was I with my trope 'bout one in a quag?
I did once hitch the syntax into verse:
Verbum personale, a verb personal,
Concordat—ay, 'agrees,' old Fatchaps—*cum*
Nominativo, with its nominative,
Genere, i' point o' gender, *numero,*
O' number, *et persona,* and person. *Ut,*
Instance: *Sol ruit,* down flops sun, *et* and,
Montes umbrantur, out flounce mountains. Pah!
Excuse me, sir, I think I'm going mad.
You see the trick on 't though, and can yourself
Continue the discourse *ad libitum.*
It takes up about eighty thousand lines,
A thing imagination boggles at;
And might, odds-bobs, sir! in judicious hands,
Extend from here to Mesopotamy.

IF POPE HAD WRITTEN "BREAK, BREAK, BREAK"[1]

By J. C. Squire

Fly, Muse, thy wonted themes, nor longer seek
The consolations of a powder'd cheek;
Forsake the busy purlieu's of the Court
For calmer meads where finny tribes resort.
So may th' Almighty's natural antidote
Abate the worldly tenor of thy note,
The various beauties of the liquid main
Refine thy reed and elevate thy strain.

See how the labour of the urgent oar
Propels the barks and draws them to the shore.
Hark! from the margin of the azure bay
The joyful cries of infants at their play.
(The offspring of a piscatorial swain,
His home the sands, his pasturage the main.)
Yet none of these may soothe his mourning heart,
Nor fond alleviation's sweets impart;
Nor may the pow'rs of infants that rejoice
Restore the accents of a former voice,
Nor the bright smiles of ocean's nymphs command
The pleasing contact of a vanished hand.
So let me still in meditation move,
Muse in the vale and ponder in the grove,
And scan the skies where sinking Phoebus glows
With hues more rubicund than Cibber's nose. . . .

(*After which the poet gets into his proper stride*)

[1] Reprinted with the kind permission of the author.

IF GRAY HAD HAD TO WRITE HIS ELEGY IN THE CEMETERY OF SPOON RIVER INSTEAD OF IN THAT OF STOKE POGES[1]

By J. C. Squire

The curfew tolls the knell of parting day,
  The whippoorwill salutes the rising morn,
And wanly glimmer in her gentle ray,
  The sinuous windings of the turbid Spoon.

Here where the flattering and mendacious swarm
  Of lying epitaphs their secrets keep,
At last incapable of further harm
  The lewd forefathers of the village sleep.

The earliest drug of half-awakened morn,
  Cocaine or hashish, strychnine, poppy-seeds
Or fiery produce of fermented corn
  No more shall start them on their day's misdeeds.

For them no more the whetstone's cheerful noise,
  No more the sun upon his daily course
Shall watch them savouring the genial joys,
  Of murder, bigamy, arson and divorce.

Here they all lie; and, as the hour is late,
  O stranger, o'er their tombstones cease to stoop,
But bow thine ear to me and contemplate
  The unexpurgated annals of the group.

There are two hundred only: yet of these
  Some thirty died of drowning in the river,
Sixteen went mad, ten others had D. T's.
  And twenty-eight cirrhosis of the liver.

[1] Reprinted with the kind permission of the author.

Several by absent-minded friends were shot,
  Still more blew out their own exhausted brains,
One died of a mysterious inward rot,
  Three fell off roofs, and five were hit by trains,

One was harpooned, one gored by a bull-moose,
  Four on the Fourth fell victims of lock-jaw,
Ten in electric chair or hempen noose
  Suffered the last exaction of the law.

Stranger, you quail, and seem inclined to run;
  But, timid stranger, do not be unnerved;
I can assure you that there was not one
  Who got a tithe of what he had deserved.

Full many a vice is born to thrive unseen,
  Full many a crime the world does not discuss,
Full many a pervert lives to reach a green
  Replete old age, and so it was with us.

Here lies a parson who would often make
  Clandestine rendezvous with Claflin's Moll,
And 'neath the druggist's counter creep to take
  A sip of surreptitious alcohol.

And here a doctor, who had seven wives,
  And, fearing this ménage might seem grotesque,
Persuaded six of them to spend their lives
  Locked in a drawer of his private desk.

And others here there sleep who, given scope,
  Had writ their names large on the Scrolls of Crime,
Men who, with half a chance, might haply cope
  With the first miscreants of recorded time.

Doubtless in this neglected spot is laid
  Some village Nero who has missed his due,

Some Bluebeard who dissected many a maid,
  And all for naught, since no one ever knew.

Some poor bucolic Borgia here may rest
  Whose poisons sent whole families to their doom,
Some hayseed Herod who, within his breast,
  Concealed the sites of many an infant's tomb.

Types that the Muse of Masefield might have stirred,
  Or waked to ecstasy Gorboriau,
Each in his narrow cell at last interred,
  All, all are sleeping peacefully below.

. . . .

Enough! enough! But stranger, ere we part,
  Glancing farewell to each nefarious bier,
This warning I would beg you take to heart,
  "There is an end to even the worst career!"

Was there ever yet anything written long that was wished longer by its readers?—except *Don Quixote, Robinson Crusoe,* and the *Pilgrim's Progress!*

Dr. Samuel Johnson—*Remark as recorded by Mrs. Piozzi.*

IF HENRY JAMES HAD WRITTEN THE CHURCH CATECHISM[1]

By J. C. Squire

Q. What is your name?

A. I may possibly be conceived as standing in a relation of contiguity to a certain—shall we say?—somewhat complicatedly retilinear design—to put it colloquially, a symbol—employed by such of the races of mankind as follow the Roman usage to denote a sort of suppressed explosion, or rather, a confused hum "produced" when the upper and the nether lip are brought with some firmness—or even, as one might phrase it, "snap"—together, and a continuous sound is compelled for egress to flow through a less harmonious though undeniably more prominent organ. Or, on the other hand, its relation to that so interesting figure may be something even closer than one of mere contiguity, however proximate, something in the nature of coincidence, of body and soul identity even: in a word, it may be, or, more exactly, may be represented by, that symbol itself.

Q. Who gave you this name?

A. Which?

Q. Oh, no, *not* the other one, the quite inevitably discursive family "label."

A. You mean my. . . .

Q. Well yes, not that all so shared, and as it were almost—if one may forgivably say it—may one?—"vulgarized"—your, as they call it, "surname."

A. Oh, *not* that one?

Q. No. . . .

A. The other?

Q. Yes—that other—that more exquisitely personal, the more

[1] Reprinted with the kind permission of the author.

(dare one?) *appropriated,* the one of which, I had thought, we touched, even grasped, the skirts when our interlocution, or to put it quite brutally, when we began our conversation.

A. You refer. . . .

Q. I am, dear lady, all ears.

A. To, in fact, my—since we are both to be so frank—Christian name?

Q. Oh, but you are great!

A. Not *great,* not, I mean, really, in the sense that you mean. . . .

Q. *I* mean?

A. The other sense, you know.

Q. Yes, I apprehend you, but it wasn't that one I meant.

A. Then what in the world was it?

Q. Take it from another point of view, wasn't frankness to be, always, our splendid object?

A. Explicitly.

Q. Wasn't it?

A. Oh no, I wouldn't doubt it; I wouldn't, really wouldn't, let you down.

Q. Not even gently?

A. The other way, I meant.

Q. Divine clarity! And who gave it you?

* * *

Etc.

> To say a person writes a good style, is originally as pedantic an expression, as to say he plays a good fiddle.
>
> WILLIAM SHENSTONE.

A CHRISTMAS GARLAND OF BOOKS[1]

By Robert Benchley

Among the little bundle of books especially selected for Christmas-Wistmas, perhaps the most pat is "Rubber Hand Stamps and the Manipulation of India Rubber" by T. O'Conor Sloane. Into it Mr. Sloane has put the spirit of Yuletide which all of us must feel, whether we are cynical enough to deny it or not.

Beginning with a short, and very dirty, history of the sources of India Rubber, the author takes us by the hand and leads us into the fairy-land of rubber manipulation. And it is well that he does, for without his guidance we should have made an awful mess of the next rubber-stamp we tried to make. As he says on page 35: "It will be evident from the description to come that it is not advisable for anyone without considerable apparatus to attempt to clean and wash ('to sheet'), to masticate, or to mix india rubber." Even if we had the apparatus, we would probably be content with simply "sheeting" and mixing the india rubber and leave the masticating for other less pernickety people to go through with. We may be an old maid about such things, but it is too late now for us to learn to like new things.

It seems that in the making of rubber stamps, a preparation known as "flong" is necessary. Mr. Sloane assures us that anyone who has watched the stereotyping of a large daily newspaper knows what "flong" is. Perhaps our ignorance is due to the fact that we were on the editorial end of a daily newspaper and went down into the composing-room only when it was necessary to rescue some mistake we had made from

[1] Reprinted from *Twenty Thousand Leagues Under the Sea, or David Copperfield,* by permission of Henry Holt and Company, publishers.

the forms. At any rate, we didn't know what "flong" was and we don't want to know. A man must keep certain reticences these days or he will just have no standards left at all.

It is not generally known how simple it is to make things out of rubber. "The writer has obtained excellent results from pieces of an old discarded bicycle tire. The great point is to apply a heavy pressure to the hot material. Many other articles can be thus produced extemporaneously." (Page 78) This should lend quite a bit of excitement to the manipulation of india rubber. Imagine working along quietly making, let us say, rubber type and finding that, extemporaneously, you had a rubber Negro doll or balloon on your hands! A man's whole life could be changed by such a fortuitous slip of the rubber.

Not the least of Mr. Sloane's contributions to popular knowledge is his sly insertion, under the very noses of the authorities, of what he calls the "Old Home Receipt" (ostensibly for "roller-composition," but we know better, eh, Mr. Sloane?) The "Old Home Receipt" specifies "Glue 2 lbs. soaked over night, to New Orleans molasses 1 gallon. Not durable, but excellent while it lasts." We feel sure that we have been served something made from this "Old Home Receipt," but would suggest to Mr. Sloane that he try putting in just a dash of absinthe. It makes it more durable.

We can recommend Laurence Vail Coleman's "Manual for Small Museums" to all those who have received or are about to give small museums for Christmas. Having a small museum on your hands with no manual for it is no joke. It sometimes seems as if a small museum were more bother than a large one, but that is only when one is tired and cross.

From Mr. Coleman's remarkably comprehensive study of small museums, we find that, as is so often the case, income is a very serious problem. In financing special projects for the museum, such as the purchase of bird groups (if it is a museum that *wants* bird groups), there is a great play for ingenuity, and Dr. Abbott of the San Diego Museum of Natural History, tells of how they, in San Diego, met the problem:

The little cases containing bird-groups were offered to tradespeople in the city for display in their windows, the understanding being that the store should pay $50 for the advertising value. Thus, a meadowlark group, representing the male in a very bright dress, the female, the nest and eggs, was paid for by a men's and women's clothing store and displayed in its window in the early spring with the slogan: "Take a pointer from the birds. Now is the time for your new spring clothes." A savings-bank took a woodpecker group, showing the storing away of acorns, and a California shrike group (Dr. Abbott ought to know) showing a rather sanguinary example of empaling surplus prey on the spines of a cactus, both displayed under the euphemistic caption "The Saving Instinct" and "Are You Providing for the Future by storing up your dollars (or cadavers) now?" A bush-tit's nest was taken by a real-estate firm and a mockingbird group by a music house. The local lodge of Elks gave $1200 for a case holding four elks (not members) and so, in time, the entire housing of the groups was accomplished and paid for. We are crazy to know what business houses paid for the rabbit and owl exhibits.

In the chapter on "Protection from Pests" we looked for a way of dealing with the man in an alpaca coat who grabs your stick away from you as you enter the museum and the young people who use museums for necking assignations, but they were not specified. A blanket formula is given, however, which ought to cover their cases. "The surest way to get rid of pests is to fumigate with hydrocyanic acid in an airtight compartment, but this is a dangerous procedure which has resulted in a loss of human life. (Why 'but'?) Another fumigant that is widely used is carbon bisulphide, but this is highly explosive and has caused serious accidents." This presents a new problem to museum-visitors and would seem to make the thing one of the major risks of modern civilization. If a person can't be safe from asphyxiation and mutilation while looking at bird-groups, where *is* one to be safe? It would almost be better to let the pests go for a while, at least until the museum got started.

A collection of verse entitled "Through the Years with Mother," compiled by Eva M. Young, makes a nice gift which might perhaps be given to Father. It contains most of the little poems which have been written about mothers and the general tone of the thing is favorable to motherhood. One, entitled "A Bit O' Joy," wears off a little into child-propaganda, but probably would rank as a mother-poem too, for it is presumably the mother who speaks:

> Just a Bit-a-Feller,
> Lips a bit o' rose,
> Puckered sort o' puzzled like,
> Wonder if he knows——

There is one more verse explaining what the Bit-a-Feller might possibly know, but we didn't go into that. Another one which we left for reading on the train was entitled: "Muvvers" and begins:

> One time, I wuz so very small,
> I prit' near wuzn't there at all—

We can not even tell you what the first two lines are of "Mama's Dirl."

The introduction to "Are Mediums Really Witches?" by John P. Touey begins by saying: "The sole purpose of this book, as its title suggests, is to prove the existence of a personal evil force and demon intervention in human affairs." This frightened us right at the start, for we are very susceptible to any argument which presupposes a tough break for ourselves. There must be *some* explanation for what happens to us every time we stick our head out doors—or in doors, for that matter.

Mr. Touey begins with witchcraft in ancient times and comes right straight down to the present day. Even though he quoted "no less an authority than Porphyrius" in his early chapter, it was not until we got into the examples of modern people having their bed-clothes pulled off and their hats thrown at them that we began to feel uneasy. The story of the terrible time had by the Fox Sisters in Hydesville, N. Y., seemed pretty conclusive to us at the time of reading (2:15 A.M. this morning) and, frankly, we stopped there. And, believe it or not, a couple of hours later, during our troubled sleep, *some*thing pulled the bed-clothes out from the foot of *our* bed, and we awoke with a nasty head-cold.

We will pay $100 to Mr. Touey or Sir Oliver Lodge or anyone else who can help us locate the personal demon who has been assigned to us. We would just like to talk to him for five minutes, the big bully!

* * *

For those who like to browse along lazily with British royalty, we can think of no less charming way than to accompany Helen, Countess-Dowager of Radnor through her 361-page book: "From a Great-Grandmother's Armchair." We had almost decided not to begin at all, until we read in the Countess-Dowager's preface: "At the present time I am resting 'on my oars' (or rather, in my Armchair) at my quiet country home, which, amongst those of the third generation, goes by the name of 'Grannie's Peace-pool.'" This gave us incentive to read further.

And what a treat! "Grannie" certainly has earned her "peace-pool" after the exciting life she has led. Every year of her long career is given here in detail and it must make fascinating reading for the Radnors if only as a record of where the Countess left her umbrella that time in Godalming and who played zither in her "Ladies' String Band and Chorus" in 1879.

Among other things that are cleared up in this volume is the question of what the Countess did during those first hectic weeks of July, 1901.

"A good many engagements were crowded into the first fortnight of July," she writes modestly, "before going back to Venice. Among other things I passed a very pleasant weekend at Wendover Lodge with Alfred and Lizzie Gatty."

But the book does not dwell entirely in the past. Right up to the present day we have disclosures of equal importance. In September, 1920, while visiting in Bath, the following incident occurred:

"One Sunday I started off in the car to go and lunch with Mrs. Knatchbull. When we had gone a few miles, however, the car broke down, a 'rubber-washer' having perished and let the water through! We telephoned for a 'Taxi' which took me back to Bath, and the car was towed back. Later in the afternoon Mrs. Knatchbull sent a car for me to go over to tea, and I flew over hill and dale and reached her place in Babington in half an hour."

So you see, the Countess really *had* intended to lunch with Mrs. Knatchbull!

We neglected to mention that the authoress is by birth a Chaplin; so she probably can get free seats whenever Mary's boy Charlie comes to town in a picture.

Every abridgement of a book is a stupid abridgement.

MONTAIGNE, *Bk.* 3.